M000219706

MIRRORLANDS

ED PULFORD

Mirrorlands

Russia, China, and Journeys in Between

HURST & COMPANY, LONDON

First published in the United Kingdom in 2019 by
C. Hurst & Co. (Publishers) Ltd.,
41 Great Russell Street, London, WC1B 3PL
© Ed Pulford, 2019
Maps © Ruth Joyce, 2019
All rights reserved.
Printed in India

The right of Ed Pulford to be identified as the author of
this publication is asserted by him in accordance with the
Copyright, Designs and Patents Act, 1988.

Distributed in the United States, Canada and Latin America by
Oxford University Press, 198 Madison Avenue, New York, NY 10016,
United States of America.

A Cataloguing-in-Publication data record for this book
is available from the British Library.

ISBN: 9781787381384

This book is printed using paper from registered sustainable
and managed sources.

www.hurstpublishers.com

CONTENTS

Map 1: Entire *Mirrorlands* route.

Map 2: China's north-eastern corner and neighbouring Russia.

LIST OF ILLUSTRATIONS

All photographs are the author's.

PREFACE

Many stories do not make it beyond the borders of the world's largest and most populous countries, and fantasy visions of Russia and China have long filled the gaps in the minds of those observing from outside. Popular perceptions of each place in Europe and America today suggest a hazy sense of similarity between the two, as co-spoilers of Western-backed interventions or sanctions, rivals to US power, cyber-threats, or black-box authoritarian empires each embodied by a menacing spirit animal. But as foreign publics mull over whether dragons or bears worry them more, the deeper similarities between the two countries, their borderland relationship and their centuries of common history, are less discussed. Not that this is entirely the fault of the uninformed: central authorities in both places have long promoted a monolithic image of their respective realms, and like a big animal—serpentine or ursine—guarding a cave of treasures, such projections can make it difficult to find a point of entry.

My first guide to Russia was the protagonist of a novel I read as a seventeen-year-old, an errant chauvinist who—I have since been troubled to realise—must have appealed to my teenaged male megalomania.[1] In St Petersburg a year later, some less morally problematic new American friends took me on a trip to China's edge by train. These early experiences left me fascinated by both countries. During my twenties, this in turn morphed into a near-obsession with the parallels and past and present interconnections between these vast land empires that became socialist states in the twentieth century before convulsing again in divergent but equally enrapturing ways into post-socialist behemoths in the twenty-first. That at least was how I explained my late-2000s decision to spend a year of my undergraduate Russian degree studying Chinese in Vladivostok. In Vladik, as it is known to its friends (not that its state of post-Soviet decay made it seem very friendly at the time), spells of self-doubt and young love were punctuated by trips to the ramshackle Chinese border towns where my local classmates went shopping. Here in the 'Russian Far East', a distinct region on the other side of 'Siberia' (though even Muscovites and Petersburgers rarely distinguish the two), China was a large if still-exoticised presence in local lives.

More direct exposure to China came as I moved after graduating to Wuhan, a huge, central, and little-known city that straddles the River Yangtze. Two years' Chinese study there, many bowls of hot dry noodles, and extensive exposure to a place whose dust and chaos reflected an upward trajectory more or less the inverse of Vladivostok's slump showed me a China very far from Russia. Around Wuhan the country's borders were internal, between town and village, among provinces or dialect groups: Wuhan Chinese is in the same large family as the national standard 'Mandarin' (to which I will often refer in what follows simply as 'Chinese', specifying when I mean other dialects), but nevertheless remains only partially intelligible to me. Yet while central China offered blearily enjoyable evenings in the company of an excitable Russian Kazakh dorm neighbour, and intriguing Muscovite classmates who kept a cool distance from their less urbane Vladivostok compatriots, I was still interested in points of direct geographical contact. So it was back to the borderlands, this time to China's remote north-western Xinjiang region where all my fellow-students were Russian-speaking citizens of former-Soviet republics, and where—tragically—local Uyghurs and Kazakhs increasingly face twenty-first-century forms of Sino-Stalinist terror and Soviet-esque attempts to forcefully reshape their humanity.

But amid these formative years of drinking with Russian lorry drivers in Manchuria, roaming Kazakh-speaking villages in Xinjiang populated by Chinese Russians, or marvelling at the routineness with which people from the Russian Far East visited a foreign state just to buy new slippers, I felt there was more to learn about the two countries' borderland relationship. Moreover, while my growing familiarity with each place had been guided as much by novels and noodles as by strategic choice, understanding more about how they interconnected in space and time was also coming to seem an increasingly important task. As a borderland war brewed in Ukraine from 2014, maritime expansion roiled the South China Sea, and hackers crossed boundaries deep into Western affairs, both places and their borders were open to widespread debate, even as they appeared as misunderstood as ever. And so, as I returned to university for an anthropology PhD focusing on a single location—a small town situated where China and Russia meet North Korea—I also set out to look more broadly across territory and history. A borderland journey would, I hoped, help me learn about the wider relationship between these two countries where I had already spent over half my adult life.

Two comparably slick London processing centres each gave me a multiple-entry visa, and I left for Moscow to embark on one of the least sensible possible routes to Beijing, at least if my main aim had been simply to get there. Beginning and ending in the capitals and crisscrossing the 2,600-mile-long Sino-Russian border on trains, mini-buses, shared taxis and boats (and only a tiny bit of plane near the start), this journey would thrust me into the midst of day-to-day inter-actions between the ordinary residents of these immense worlds. Chance encounters and deliberate meetings would spark conversations with traders at Siberian or Manchurian markets, 'Asian' Russians trying to belong in a country ignorant of their existence, ethnically 'Russian' citizens of China who speak no Russian, rebellious Chinese millennials backpacking around China's minority-inhabited edges, Russian museum guides avoiding sensitive territorial questions during tours, indigenous groups divided for decades by the border, and ethnic Koreans from China and Russia whose rock star heroes sang in the fall of socialism. There would also be encounters from times other than the present. Using the languages I had studied, I would peruse memoirs and scour local histories, coming into contact with Chinese soldiers hiding out in the Soviet Far East alongside Kim Il Sung and his young son, a nineteenth-century Chuvash Russian missionary monk living in Beijing, and the last emperor of the Celestial Kingdom, a thrice-crowned demigod who spent five years as a Soviet captive and later ended life as a gardener.

Though travelling solo in the present, I would follow tracks left behind by generations of earlier voyagers whose travelogues would prove rich sources of comparison and, often, comic relief. Many revealing Sino-Russian journeys occurred a century ago, when, either side of Lenin's October Revolution, Russia and China's relationship underwent transformations whose effects endure to this day. My predecessor companions would mostly be from around this time. There would be a duo of Chinese leftists and a mirror pair of Russian revolutionary internationalists, excited intellectuals at the dawn of a new age, a *fin de siècle* Russian doctor better known for his plays about seabirds and orchards than his Siberian wanderings, and an anti-Communist English aristocrat unwilling to let revolution impede a perilous adventure with piles of hatboxes in tow. The voices of these and other explorers, schemers and dreamers, some of whom were already with me when I left London, others whom I encountered en route in museums or placards on buildings, inhabit these pages as much as those of the living people I met along the way. Our routes would crisscross one another and at times move in different directions to different ends. But their reflections on Sino-Russian contact, personal tales easily forgotten when contemplating historical cataclysms that have rocked two continents, would both have a credence outweighing the observations of an interloping British millennial, and would convey a richer story than is usually told about relations between distant capital cities. And in Eurasia distant means distant.

One thing these predecessors would help me understand was how, given the enormous space between them, it had historically taken a long time for Moscow and Beijing to work out who, and where, the other was. The story of this process of mutual familiarisation would turn out to have an importance extending beyond my own personal curiosity. Russian and Chinese citizens and governments alike remain preoccupied by interlocking pasts whose consequences rear up, sometimes violently, in the present. Territorial questions are central to this, and the clearest recent example of each country's sense of historical injustice—Russia's 2014 annexation of Crimea and China's maritime island-building—may at first appear unconnected. Yet Beijing's grievances over territorial dispossession have their origins in mid-nineteenth-century events when Russia, itself smarting from loss in a war over Crimea, joined other European powers in seizing lands previously considered 'Chinese'. Like Britain, France and Germany, Russia became a keen exploiter of colonial 'treaty ports' in China: even in distant Wuhan, one of the grandest nineteenth-century buildings to survive the city's twenty-first-century bulldozers remains the vast former Russian consulate. But unlike the British in Hong Kong or the French in Shanghai, Russia has held on to most of the acquisitions made during that post-Crimean War vogue for land-grabs. There would be other ways in which appreciating past Sino-Russian interactions would be vital for understanding the current relationship between the two and the place of each in the wider world today.

Borderland life would also show me how, throughout their enmeshed histories, both China and Russia have had crucial aspects of their identities shaped by mutual encounters, often very localised ones, in which each has served as a reflection of the other. In fact, through experiences in the present, insights from time-traversing fellow-travellers, and reading of relevant histories, I would come to see the Sino-Russian dynamic as like that between two vast mirrors. However opaque or shifting, these have consistently done what mirrors do, offering an image of one to the other that appears at once inverted and yet also extremely similar. Some reflections emerge through Russia's and China's similar fates as states. As Eurasian land empires for most of the last millennium, the fortunes and territories of each waxed and waned as successive dynasties battled neighbours or persuaded them to offer tribute to Beijing or Moscow/St Petersburg. Around the turn of the twentieth century, internal and external attack saw imperial families toppled, printing presses seized by revolutionaries, civil wars waged, republics declared, and by 1950 both were flawed socialist giants. Even amid their contrasting fortunes since each abandoned doctrinaire socialism from the 1980s—China as a burgeoning superpower, Russia as a militarily equipped but economically enfeebled giant trying to retain influence—both permuted post-socialist states are still ruled by figures who, in Vladimir Putin and Xi Jinping, distinctly resemble the dynastic emperors of old. Shifts from 'Russian Empire' via 'Soviet Union' to 'Russian Federation', or 'Qing Empire' through 'Republic of China' to 'People's Republic of China' (PRC) have seen political and social worlds in both places turned on their heads countless times. Yet, curiously, similar cultural entities identifiable as 'Russia' and 'China' have endured.

PREFACE

Other Sino-Russian reflections are subtler, becoming visible around the shared border which, itself playing the mirror role, only exists at all thanks to processes of imperial expansion that brought populations face to face. At the moment of first regular contact, when, in the late seventeenth century, the lengthening tendrils of Russian influence extended eastward to meet the north-westwardly expanding reach of a growing Qing Chinese empire, each met in mirrored incomprehension. Mutual ignorance about who the other was resulted in friction over trade and territory and skirmishes that ended in a Chinese victory and 1689 border treaty, the first modern inter-state agreement of its kind. Since then, the frontier between them has been a zone of reflection between two sides grappling with inversions of the same questions over destiny and identity. Among the most telling of these has been how Russian and Chinese people have looked on the other as 'Asian' or 'European' respectively.

For its part, Russia acquired through its distension of territory a vast internal 'East' sweeping towards the Pacific. With Anatolia at one end and China at the other, Asia is a southern continent when seen from Siberia, even if it is still referred to by the Euro-centric term 'Eastern' or 'Oriental' (*vostochnyi*). But if this label betrays Russia's desire to remain tethered to the western continent and its notional refinement, a version of 'Easternness' has also long been thought to lurk deep inside Russians themselves. This has been linked both to a sense of distinct Slavic destiny in northern Eurasia, to the population changes that expansion inevitably brought, and to still earlier cataclysms that once yoked Russia and China together. The thirteenth- to fifteenth-century Mongol subjugation of both Chinese and Russian lands—a legacy that reportedly led Napoleon to quip 'scratch a Russian and you'll find a Tatar'—has underlain much introspective musing in recent centuries over whether Russia is essentially a sort of abstractly Asian place. These have ranged from the mysticism-infused Slavophilia of novelist Fyodor Dostoevsky to the revolution-inspired claim by poet Alexander Blok that Russians are 'leaves of the Asian tree',[2] and the contemporary rants of firebrand Eurasianist-fascist commentator Alexander Dugin, possible source of inspiration for Putin's Crimean gambit. In the borderlands, I would often be made aware that speculation over Russia's Asian destiny remains an important aspect of how Sino-Russian relations are understood by ordinary people on both sides.

PREFACE

China's Occidentalist confrontation with its northerly 'European' neighbour, and with Sinicised evidence of its historical impact deep within China, have paralleled Russia's Orientalist negotiations with the blurred boundaries between its own Asian realm and other Easts. Residents of Manchuria proudly tout the European architecture of their cities but are frustrated in business interactions with unintelligible Russians. Indigenous Siberians love the 'Asian cool' of Korean pop music but consider China inscrutable. In the 1860s and 1990s alike, inhabitants of eastern Russia only survived because of Chinese trade. Marx and Engels' Moscow-mediated influence on modern China has been so profound that the pair is often spoken of there as though they are no longer considered really European.

The 1950s, a decade of harmonised Sino-Soviet socialism, was perhaps when the border-mirror most accurately reflected the images meeting across it. Yet, conversely, this was also when the borderline became an impermeable glass threshold, admitting only a select few who could cross, Alice-like, between worlds. Many people I would meet, including Koreans, indigenous North East Asian fishing people, and descendants of a mixed Russo-Chinese goldmining community on the Mongolian steppe, had traversed old Sino-Russian boundaries in pre-revolutionary days and thus saw the portal close behind them. After socialism, however, the mirror has changed in opacity once again, and some of these communities long separated from their ethnic or linguistic confreres have resumed contact. Although it is now often too late to remember what was once shared among these divided cross-border groups, since the 1990s almost all inhabitants of the borderlands have existed in a kind of mirrored mutual dependency, relying on one another for trade, and more recently marketing one another's perceived Asianness or Europeanness to attract tourists. Much mutual ignorance persists despite this greater contact, but whether they know it or not, local populations share a trove of common experience.

Eastern Siberia and north-east China, where most of my travels would be taking place, have each been places of imperial exile under bejewelled emperors and epauletted commissars, and sites where capital cities have projected very similar imperial designs. Today they form a space where contrasts and parallels are equally important components of mirrored twenty-first-century Sino-Russian lives. As political centres of Rome-like stature, Moscow and Beijing too have sought to shape these empires, which, as well as being political and military powers, have laid claim to people's minds and souls. Far from their borderland edges, the capitals have broadcast religious, political, economic and cultural messages whose echoes have set Eurasia's mirrored surface aquiver, running through its airwaves, along its rivers and railways, eventually to be received—distance-distorted—by counterparts in the other capital. Some of the resulting changes in Russian and Chinese ideas about society, power, work, family and how to live a good life have resembled transformations underway worldwide in recent centuries of colonialism and other globalisations. But as I would come to understand, many have also had a character specific to life in these immense Eurasian realms. Whether under Mao Zedong, Joseph Stalin, Tsar Alexander II or Emperor Qianlong, ordinary people's experiences have been coloured by encounters with their imperial counterparts during movements across thousands of miles of steppe, plain and forest for work, adventure or punishment. Conversely, in both places, cataclysmic political changes unfolding on a continental scale have caused the deaths of tens of millions of people. On this near-boundless canvas countless biographies have acquired Odyssean proportions, heroic, tragic and yet also deeply personal epics written across imperial space.

These currents have all fed into a broader stream. Sino-Russian relations have been forged amid the intrigue of late nineteenth-century imperial competition, the incoherence of early twentieth-century revolution, the superficial harmony of short-lived socialist brotherhood, and the zero-sum suspicion of the 1960s–80s Sino-Soviet Split. These relationships have never been of less than paramount importance for the states themselves, and the wider world. Today is no exception, and while Putinist Moscow has remembered its Asian neighbours amid ongoing truculence in Ukraine-poisoned relations with the West, China's equally bristly desire for a global role under President Xi has seen the launch of initiatives—among them the 'Belt and Road' infrastructural and investment strategy—whose vectors run through the old Russian Empire. Whether motivated by friction with Western friends or demands for resources and influence, Sino-Russian ties are thus at a high point. Learning more about how these broad trends were lived in the everyday would, I hoped, reveal a human picture of their significance beyond high politics. Having only retrospectively realised the unpalatability of the fictional man who had first lured me into Russian culture, it also seemed wise to get a better understanding, however belated, of the places that had shaped me.

1

MOSCOW

ASIA'S THIRD ROME

It was a July day whose heat smothered the visitor as only a city of thirteen million can. Once dubbed a 'Third Rome' and only three and a half hours' flight from London, Moscow boasts fanciful building ensembles designed by Italian architects and a ring of boulevards that would not look out of place in Paris. But its summer fugginess and sheer scale know few parallels in Europe, the continent to which it nominally belongs. Like its Eurasian twin—and 'Second Rome'— Istanbul, it is often more of an Asian capital.

I had been here several times before, and there was much that was familiar in the giddy sense of summer abandon about the city: places that spend months locked in steely winter frigidity often open up proportionately when it thaws. Seasonal spectacles included the recently reimagined Gorky Park's fountains and rides, and the warm-weather version of Russia's inimitable blend of sinister and slapstick. Descending into the cavernous metro at Paveletsky railway station mere minutes after arriving, I was shoved aside by a pair of burly policemen pursuing two youthful skinheads in cut-off denim shorts down a broken escalator, while other law-enforcers studiously ignored a cluster of topless drunks stumbling down the platform swearing at passers-by. But for all the familiarity, I was also seeing Moscow anew.

Having spent periods living in Siberia, Central Asia and China since my last visit, I was now more conscious of the city's Asianness. Getting off the metro and passing through underpasses thick with the sickly pastry smells of *pirogi*, I felt more attuned to the long vowels and stops of conversation in Uzbek and Azeri, and the lower-pitched slides of Tajik around me.

This being my first return for a few years, I had decided to get immediately to the heart of things, and so on my first morning in town made my way to Red Square. On the subtly convex expanse of black cobbles, it was now clearer to me who the clusters of Kazakhs and Buryats were as they posed in front of Lenin's Mausoleum, stances bolt upright, T-shirts skin-tight and expressions solemn. But I was here in search of a quite different set of Asian arrivals, and as I rested on the square's eastern flank trying hungrily to remember the location of a once-loved local pie restaurant, I was suddenly aware of a crowd of precisely the people who interested me most for the journey I was about to undertake. Wilting wearily under a nearby tree, around twenty Chinese tourists had been caught as off-guard as I had by the heat. In many regards, their appearance was unremarkable: flustered yet stoical, they were dressed in the bright clothes, visors and pouch-bags that are the uniform of many organised mainland tour-groups. Such accoutrements are an increasingly common sight the world over, as Chinese tourist trips abroad increased more than twelvefold between 2000 and 2016 to over 122 million, and continue to rise.[1]

Through my hunger haze I also perceived a certain symbolism in where the group was standing. It wasn't the shade-dispensing tree, for there was little unusual about that, except perhaps that, unlike many Russian trees of my acquaintance, it wasn't mysteriously painted white up to a height of 3 feet. More significantly, we were all located—they fanning their brows with brochures, I racking my brains for clues about pies—on the side of Red Square dominated by the cream-yellow trading arches of GUM, the old Soviet state department store. Once a supplier of more austere products, GUM today houses an explosion of luxury boutiques, supplying post-Soviet Moscow's fabulously wealthy with Gucci bags and Cartier watches and, increasingly, offering the same to Chinese tourists. Some shops in the building's long gleaming arcade have even begun to advertise discounts in Chinese. This was what the group under the tree was here for, and as a few posed for photographs across the southern section of the square towards the shallot-topped spires of St Basil's Cathedral, more were eying the Burberry and Louis Vuitton displays in the nearby windows. Tellingly, no one was paying any attention to Lenin, whose lonely and increasingly waxy repose continues under the Kremlin walls across the cobbles. Were it not likely to lead to his final bodily disintegration, I thought, the first Soviet leader might turn in his stone mausoleum at the sight of the masses from a neighbouring socialist country showing such a fascination for luxury. On reflection, though, I then remembered, he never wanted to be interred like this anyway, and having died a rather dispirited former-idealist, he would perhaps not have been unduly surprised at the twenty-first-century Chinese preference for handbags, watches and dress shirts over revolution's ghosts.

Although over a quarter of Russia's foreign tourists come from China, the most numerous single group by origin,[2] the Moscow-based Burberry-buying activities of these visitors are not usually part of the global image projected by either country. But to paraphrase Alice Cooper, Moscow has certainly had its fair share of visitors over the years—welcome and unwelcome—and many of these have come from Asia. Founded like many European towns as an expanding series of fortifications, churches, markets and moats alongside the Moscow River, the city had grown important enough by the 1230s to earn the dubious honour of being burnt to the ground by Mongol invaders as they conquered territory all the way to Austria. Recovering from this and strengthening its defences, the city then drafted in architects and engineers from Milan to shape the capital's more iconic quarters, a kind of European defiance against the eastern threat. But it was not long before Moscow's outlook again became decidedly Asia-focused. First as a bulwark from which the Mongol occupiers were driven back, and subsequently as the centre of an empire that pushed ever eastward to China's borders, Moscow was and remains bound to the Asian worlds radiating out around it.

* * *

As I set out to understand more about these Asias, I had settled in a sloping, attractively tsarist district of the capital named Kitai-gorod, which literally, but not actually, means 'China-Town'. Its two components 'China' ('Kitai' is cognate with the English 'Cathay') and 'town' are in fact not linked as Russian grammar would normally dictate. So it is disappointingly obvious that the place has nothing to do with the 'Empire under Heaven' (*podnebesnaya*) as Russians, translating the Chinese word *tianxia*, grandly call their neighbour. I was far from the first, however, to appreciate the false gesture to China made by the toponym's 'Kitai' element. The first of my historical fellow-travellers had also played with this orthographic association.

Writer Boris Pilnyak was in fact a literal 'fellow-traveller', a staunch if mercurial revolutionary who, like other figures bearing the label, maintained an antagonistic relationship with the Bolsheviks. In his first major work, an impressionistic 1922 novella entitled *The Naked Year* that documents the tumult of the October Revolution seen from several mostly provincial Russian locations, the following eerie passage echoes twice in the voice of one of his narrators:

> By day Kitai-gorod behind the Chinese wall … wears a bowler hat, carries a portfolio of stocks, shares, cheques, exchange certificates, icons, knives, manufactured goods, raisins, gold, platinum, Martyanich vodka—perfectly European in its bowler hat. But at night … out of the town houses and from under the archways crawls China with no bowler hat on, the Celestial Empire which lies somewhere beyond the steppes to the east, beyond the Great Stone Wall, and looks at the world with eyes like the buttons on a Russian soldier's greatcoat …[3]

Fragmentary and bewitching, *The Naked Year* reflects in both form and content the upheaval and stark personal and national transfigurations that Pilnyak witnessed during the revolution. Emerging here were age-old Russian struggles over their own easternness and westernness, reinvigorated by events. Yet not only these eastern Slavs, with their history of Mongol conquest, were confronted by such identity questions; many Chinese people too—particularly those travelling to Russia at the time—were also interrogating their own sense of belonging amid the turmoil. Tellingly, *The Naked Year*, which set Pilnyak on the way to the popularity he enjoyed throughout the 1920s and 1930s, predated most of his actual contact with 'Asia'. In 1926, the author travelled by train to China, Japan and Mongolia, dispatched by the USSR's All-Union Society for Cultural Relations with Foreign

Countries. There, it was hoped, he would forge internationalist cultural links with Asian writers and other revolutionaries in the region, although he purportedly spent much of his time promoting himself, offending his hosts with his arrogance, and generally frustrating his Soviet paymasters.[4] But these experiences left a deep mark on the writer, informing many of his later works, including *Stories from the East*, *A Chinese Tale* and *Roots of the Japanese Sun*.

For me, time in Kitai-gorod also provided a window on to Russia's complex approaches to various Easts, key concerns for my approaching trip. The small hotel I had chosen lay on a steep cobbled street overlooking one of Moscow's vertiginous Stalinist 'seven sisters' buildings, and on arrival I found habitually haphazard travelling company. In various states of inebriation, a French Canadian student, a Turkish software engineer and a Russian trader from Nizhny Novgorod were lolling around in the static late-night heat of the lobby. The Turk had just aborted a trip to Propaganda, a local nightclub, and was bemoaning the lack of dancing he had found there. 'Everyone was just standing round looking at the DJ like they were worshipping him,' he complained, suggesting that despite recent discussion of Turkey's slide towards illiberalism he at least retained a Kemalist suspicion of anything too religious-seeming.

Nobody much responded, but after a while the burly Russian, Misha, pierced the silence: 'Is this guy alright?' he enquired in Russian, addressing a bespectacled hotel staff member who was himself sprawled on a sofa. He nodded emphatically towards the Turk. 'I mean, you've talked to him and he seems ok?' Misha was looking for a drinking companion and wanted to verify, in his own language, whether the engineer would make a suitable wingman.

'He's fine,' the youthful staff member replied, looking up blearily from his chunky laptop, 'but you know we've had three wars with them, right?' This was a fitting omen, for Russia's love–hate interactions with Turkey over the centuries have been critical to its relations with 'Eastern' or 'Asian' places more broadly.

Tired after my arrival and knowing there would be plenty more chances to drink with traders, I went to bed before Misha's invitation-dispensing eye of Sauron turned to me. I therefore never learnt whether he and his mooted Turkish companion had overcome centuries of great power jostling to have a riotous night out. But thoughts of Russia's eastern ties persisted the next morning as I plotted my China-themed route around Moscow on a bench outside Kitai-gorod metro station. As it happened, a memorial chapel to the 1877–8 Russo-Ottoman War stood nearby, even if traces of 'Kitai' were absent. In fact, the term here likely derives from an old word for a defensive wall or stake fence surrounding a local fortification, the 'Chinese wall' Pilnyak toyed with in *The Naked Year* and a feature of many medieval Russian towns. But the only serried ranks of anything I observed were a few portable toilets by the entrance to the metro. As I sat, a wan-faced teenager barged queasily into one cubicle, upsetting both a twig broom and the middle-aged attendant on his way in. Whatever Misha and the Turk's success, someone had evidently found a watering hole the previous evening.

As a first destination, Red Square offered no respite from the ety-mological torment. Like Kitai-gorod, the square's name is something of a false friend, for the word translated as 'red' (*krasnaya*) in fact origi-nally meant 'beautiful' here, and for much of history 'red' and 'beauti-ful' jostled for supremacy in English translations of the Russian name. But by the beginning of the twentieth century, and still more so after an October 1917 revolution daubed in crimson, 'red' gained the domi-nant position it retains today. My walk around the square from where the Chinese tourists were milling to Lenin's red-and-black mausoleum took me under the soaring towers and tooth-tipped fortifications of the Kremlin's outer walls. Designed by Italian architects invited to Moscow by Grand Prince Ivan III ('the Great') in the late fifteenth century, these defences also serve as the outsized headstone for the Soviet gran-dees buried beneath them. This red monument to red leaders from Joseph Stalin and Leonid Brezhnev to Red Army officer Georgy Zhukov and Cold War statesman Mikhail Suslov is now more tourist attraction than pilgrimage site, although the two exist on a spectrum.

After being perfunctorily ushered through the mausoleum contain-ing the pallid glowing Lenin, whose embalmers established a precedent whereby all subsequent Communist founders including Mao would become similar relics in similar boxes, I exited to the row of pine trees and graves at the foot of the cliff-like walls. Among a group of solemn German pensioners, Lihua, a solo Chinese backpacker, was also brows-ing the necropolis. I asked what she was doing here.

'Lenin!' she said. 'If you come to Moscow you have to see him! I mean, Communism is bad, but he was an important man. Plus it's in the top ten Moscow sites in my book.'

Were there any other Communist-themed sights on the list? I asked.

'Not really, no,' she replied. 'The rest is all churches and parks and shopping. That's fine by me, I'm not really here for "red tourism".'

Much that is linked to both Mao-era Communism and the Soviet past is colour-coded like this in Chinese, and so the popularity of Russia as a tourist destination has been seen as part of a 'red' sub-strand of PRC citizens' growing passion for travel. Twenty-six-year-old Lihua may have been nonplussed, but older visitors from China enjoy trips to sites that evoke nostalgia for the 1950s when the USSR represented a nurturing 'older brother' to post-revolutionary China. Most Chinese people in their sixties and above learnt Russian as their first foreign language in school. Locations from picturesque St Petersburg, birthplace of the revolution, to the more obscure Ulyanovsk, birthplace of Lenin, have seen substantial upticks in visitor numbers over the last decade. What is more, and in one of many curious parallels, the colour red, while not specifically meaning 'beautiful' as it does at Red Square, has longstanding associations with auspiciousness in Chinese culture. A match made in the Empire under Heaven.

Yet China's socialism-based interest in Russia has much deeper roots than the memories of today's middle-aged 'red tourists'. A century ago, the post-1917 USSR, not just a new country but a new kind of country, and its mission to forge a new 'Soviet person', were gleaming beacons of inspiration for an entire generation of Chinese intellectuals. To citizens of another collapsed empire, Moscow became the centre of an entirely novel civilisation, living up to the 'Third Rome' label that had been conferred on it for quite different, Orthodox Christian, reasons 400 years earlier. The 1911 crumbling of the Qing dynasty, and with it China's long imperial past, generated furious intellectual debate and a devastating civil war between Communists and Nationalists over how and by whom the country should now be run. On both sides, but particularly on the political left, Chinese thinkers looked to the Soviet Union's liberationist example for inspiration, and during the 1920s and '30s no small number travelled to the new country to see for themselves how things were unfolding.[5]

Among these was Qu Qiubai, who throughout my journey would be another key historical travel companion. Arriving into Moscow's Yaroslavsky railway station on a snow-splattered train from the east in late January 1921, Qu was a linguistically gifted graduate of Beijing's Russian Language Institute,[6] first translator of the *Internationale* into Chinese, and journalist on assignment from the Beijing-based newspaper *Chenbao* (Morning news). Before leaving China, he had attended Marxism-focused seminars in Beijing alongside a young Mao Zedong and years later would serve as politburo chairman of the newly formed Chinese Communist Party. Qu's memoir of his journey to Moscow, which he christens 'Red City' (*Chidu*), capital of 'Red Land' (*Chiguo*), is entitled *Journey to the Land of Hunger*, a pun on the homophones 餓 meaning 'hunger' and 俄 meaning 'Russia' and a reference to the poverty he witnessed en route. But his is a mostly reverential account of the radical and all-encompassing experiment in human transformation that he witnessed in this brave new world, and his astonishment at this emerges from the moment he arrives.

Rolling through Red City's suburbs just before arrival, Qu passed the spewing smokestacks of nearby factories and observed: 'The child of the east was gradually becoming aware of its inner strength; human nature's impetus to seek out a beacon of inspiration had been lit, and the Land of Hunger's "hunger" would not stand in the way of its mission.'[7]

Similar birth imagery and visions of an inspirational beacon burning at Eurasia's heart appear throughout Qu's travelogue and reflect not only the unprecedented events that were occurring in Moscow but also the author's sense that he was leaving behind a China beset on all sides by a mirrored version of Russia's epochal and unintelligible changes. Before his journey had even begun, he had written from Beijing: 'The first years of the twentieth century are a new dawn in Chinese history. China is being rocked and shaken and is gradually waking from the sweet and over-comfortable reverie in which society has been lost.'[8]

Yet as the country emerged blearily rubbing its eyes from the stupor of empire and domination by foreign powers, paradoxically including imperial Russia, the new responsibility foisted on the masses to forge a new society was sparking a crisis over Chinese values and identity, muddling Qu's very notion of his own selfhood: 'I am no longer solely a product of Chinese culture,' he reflected. East and west seemed as blurred as they were in Pilnyak's Kitai-gorod.

It was thus with a cautious hope of discovering a new path by which his own ancient country might be rejuvenated that Qu journeyed to Russia. China's many afflictions demanded that it be reborn and awoken. Perhaps the brand-new society emerging north of the Heilongjiang River held answers.

Qu was one of many young Chinese leftists spending time in Moscow during this era, and work by other such writer-revolutionaries picks up motifs similar to those present in his work. In China and abroad, these figures saw themselves as the vanguard of a movement responsible for transmitting the Soviet example back to their homeland. As Yin Fu, a Shanghai-based activist, poet and editor of literary journal *Leninist Youth* who was imprisoned several times for his agitation activities, wrote in a 1930 verse:

We are the young Bolsheviks,
We are made entirely from steel:
Our brains,
Our language,
Our discipline!
We live under the beacon fire of revolution
We live by the pulse of the struggle,
We are the sons of the age,
We are brothers to the masses,
From our very cradles
We are flying the banner of the October Revolution![9]

The improbable image of politically conscious flag-waving babies reflects the powerful appeal that Moscow exerted before the catastrophic and murderous excesses of Stalin and Mao. Having swept across the vast former tsarist realm, global revolutionary thinking spilled over readily into a neighbouring former-empire.

Red Square lay at the centre of the new order and was among the destinations visited by Hu Yuzhi, another leftist and scholar of the internationalist language Esperanto, who came to the USSR in 1933. As recorded in his memoir *Impressions of Moscow*, Hu engaged in an early form of Esperanto couch-surfing, lodging with fellow-learners of what in Chinese is called simply *Shijieyu*—'world language'. Attending lectures, strolling the city streets, visiting a worker's apartment, inspecting automotive and garment factories, and listening to his friends' explanations, in Esperanto naturally, Hu learnt of the radical social, economic and political transformations afoot at all levels of Soviet society. Only a few years after the revolution, citizens of the USSR—which he dubs 'Proletariat Land'—seemed well on the way to becoming new people. Yet visiting Red Square, the expansive stage on which a new Soviet civilisation performed its rites, Hu was also aware of some curious continuities. Standing as I now was beneath the Kremlin walls, he marvelled at the new mausoleum for Lenin, dead less than a decade, and could not help noting with humour the strange irony that a society without religion so venerated its ideological leader. Why did history play games like this?, he wondered; and was there really such a big difference in the transformation of the Kremlin's role from palace of emperors to the 'basecamp' of global revolution?[10]

Whatever their sensitivity to such quirks, however, Qu, Hu, Yin and others were energised by the infant USSR, a fact that leaps out of their writing all the more forcefully when compared to the less favourable observations of some contemporary Western visitors. H. G. Wells may have been left with a broadly positive impression of Lenin during his 1920 Kremlin interview with the leader, but the author of the *Time Machine* nevertheless had little time for Marxism.[11] Still more categorically opposed to the prevailing politics of the time was another transcontinental traveller, English aristocratic explorer, writer and mingler in elite circles Ethel Brilliana Alec-Tweedie. Arriving in Moscow in May 1925, Alec-Tweedie witnessed the same deprivation as Qu, but considered it less the growing pains of a new society than a sign of the 'huge game of bluff' being played by the Soviet government on its own population.[12] During her doubtless genteel promenades around the capital's more 'European' quarters, her local guide, on whose Esperanto skills she passes no comment, boasted of the new waste bins, trees and street lighting that the Moscow authorities had supplied for the citizenry. Yet in her enigmatically entitled memoir *An Adventurous Journey*, Alec-Tweedie can barely contain her Edwardian outrage on learning that locals themselves had been encouraged to help erect these facilities:

'Ye gods—this was freedom!'[13] she exclaims breathlessly, before decrying the suffering visited on her fellow-aristocrats by the collectivisation of property in the city. Apparently most disturbing of all was the omnipresence of the words 'World Revolution', which echoed in the author's ears for much of her subsequent trans-Eurasian voyage. They 'literally haunt one in Russia and Siberia. They are placarded up. They are on everyone's lips. They appear in every play. They are shrieked in vulgar songs at music halls,' she complains in astonishment.[14]

Visitors' impressions of what was going on in Moscow in the 1920s and '30s thus depended very much on personal, political and indeed musical sensibilities, as well as the relative state of one's own country. But whether remarkably inspiring or remarkably appalling, all seemed to agree that something remarkable was happening here in Red City.

* * *

Aside from his reporting duties, Qu Qiubai's paramount concerns on arrival in Moscow included assessing the welfare of the local overseas Chinese community. Most were living in desperate material deprivation caused by the social disintegration around them. In the aftermath of the October Revolution, their position was further imperilled because, with the post-Qing Chinese Republican government still having no formal diplomatic ties with the new Soviet Union, they were without official representation. Back in the present, my own next stop was a visit to this group's contemporary successors, a somewhat, if not entirely, more settled community.

Novocherkizovsky Trade Centre is much less storied or bourgeois a commercial hub than GUM. Clad in cream panelling and with lurid reflective marine blue windows, the angular seven-story building stands next to a tangle of elevated flyovers and potholed side-roads in Moscow's north-eastern Izmailovo district. The tight-fitting double-layered doors of the entranceway are designed to provide insulation during the capital's freezing winters but in summer merely create a kind of unnecessary airlock through which patrons must shuffle awkwardly, squeezing past one another on their way in and out. After spending a brief moment being crushed against a wall by a portly Russian man carrying a rolled-up blanket, I made my way inside, ascending to the sixth floor past 'no smoking' signs in printed Russian Cyrillic and handwritten Chinese characters.

This was the cocooned world of Chinese fur coat vendors, and I was immediately greeted by the sight of Mr Zhao sitting outside his shop with some companions. Although it was early afternoon on a very humid day, no time for winter garments, these international tradespeople, all from China's northern Hebei province, had little notion of conditions outside. Monotonously air-conditioned windowless boutiques, made snugger by their fur-lined walls and grotesquely ornate mahogany-lacquer desks, ran down both sides of the hall. Legs crossed, the men perched together on stainless steel stools, cracking sunflower seeds between their teeth, spitting the shells across the slick faux-marble floor, and muttering sporadic conversation as they whiled away the long working day in this hive of hide-clad cells. There were no customers to be seen.

Approaching the group, I introduced myself as a previous resident of China, and after exchanging pleasantries and assurances that I was not an agent of the immigration police, asked Mr Zhao why he had chosen to come to Russia. 'You can't sell fur coats in England!' he scoffed indignantly at my question. I agreed that perhaps you couldn't.

'Sit down,' offered another of the men in a tight-fitting polo neck as he got up to shuffle towards a drinks vendor at the end of the hall for a cup of tea. I joined the others and conversation quickly moved beyond the generalities of the European fur coat scene.

Mr Zhao, it turned out, had been in Moscow for fifteen years representing his family firm that made the garments he sold. He lived alone here, supporting a distant wife and child he rarely saw by sending regular remittances back to China. 'We live separate lives,' he told me philosophically, words that in fact seemed to apply as much to his isolation from his kin as to his relations with the inhabitants of his adopted city. 'I also have no Russian friends,' he added, 'we Chinese all live near the market, come to work early, eat in here and then go home late to sleep.'

Did he like Russia?

'It's fine,' he responded non-committally. 'The people are ok but Russian food is disgusting. I have to add Laoganma [a well-known Chinese brand of chili seeds in oil] to anything Russian I eat, although I try to do that as little as possible.' These complaints explained the pan-Asian presence in Novocherkizovsky's basement of a stall operated by a Pakistani man selling imported Korean instant noodles, shrink-wrapped pickled radish and Chinese spices.

'What about leisure time and social activities?' I asked, for the distinctive 'separateness' of overseas Chinese communities worldwide is often marked out by their maintenance of traditional festivals and community ties from the old country.

'Ha! Leisure time?' Mr Zhao scoffed with a directness often thought typical of northern Chinese people. Either he was a serial scoffer or I was suffering from a bout of exceptionally wrongheaded questions that day. 'We get two days off for the Spring Festival, but not much else. We have to work. Even on our Chinese holidays we just eat our own food here in the market.' I tried to picture the group of Hebei men tucking into a festival feast of dumplings, noodles or glutinous rice cakes here in this pelt-lined corridor. It was difficult to imagine.

On a different tack, and noting that all the men around us were from Hebei, the province wrapped around Beijing, I asked if everyone in the market was from the same place. Mr Zhao gestured languidly, 'No, there are some down there from Wuhan,' he said, alluding to one of the Chinese cities I had lived in.

How about retaining regional ties, then, I wondered. After all, Gerrard and Wardour Streets in London's Chinatown are thronged with Cantonese-speaking old Hong Kongers, New York has recently sprouted an enclave of emigrants from Fuzhou, and Bangkok's sprawling historic Chinese community is essentially a dislocated suburb of the southern city of Chaozhou.

'Bah, what's the difference?' Mr Zhao spat. 'We're all Chinese people here. We get along fine. Although to be honest most of us just mind our own business. We're in competition and sales have been down recently, so relationships are a bit strained.'

Many Novocherkizovsky vendors I spoke to attested to the absence of socialising or solidarity among Moscow-based Chinese residents today. This impression of daily monotony, lives of work and sleep far from the bustle and human warmth so valued back in China itself, was further accentuated as the lack of natural light and thick garments all around dampened our words like a kind of acoustic blanket.

More comfortable in its material surroundings, this is a very different Chinese Moscow from that encountered by Qu Qiubai in the early

1920s. Back then, and likely in part because of the hardships they faced, the city's Overseas Chinese Association displayed a strong corporate ethic, and in 1918 had even nominated their own ambassador, Liu Shouqing, to travel to Beijing to petition for assistance. The advice they received—'come back to China'—was blunt, but for many there were few alternatives, and so they embarked on the treacherous transcontinental journey home using semi-functional Russian infrastructure devastated and over-burdened by the ongoing post-1917 Civil War. Yet if Moscow's twenty-first-century Chinese residents do not have such cataclysmic global events to navigate, they have nevertheless faced their own challenges, which, like struggles in the days of revolution, have resulted from political pendulum swings. After sitting with the men from Hebei and sharing a snack and a cup of tea in a plastic disposable cup almost too hot to hold, I exited the building to look for traces of this difficult recent past.

'Novocherkizovsky' simply means 'New Cherkizovsky', and Mr Zhao and his compatriots owed much of their lacklustre lives of padded tedium to the demise of their previous workplace, the old Cherkizovsky Market. Across the road from the new building is the former market site, and squeezing through a poorly secured gate I entered this now-deserted expanse of concreted scrubland with its twists of rusted metal and 5-foot-high weeds. Cherkizon, as Muscovites half-affectionately, half-condescendingly called it, was once the largest market in Europe and had a bustling clamour now much-missed here amid the ramshackle incoherence of peripheral Moscow. A 2009 crackdown on illegal migrants and counterfeit goods led to the closure of Cherkizon; bulldozers moved in to flatten the stalls, and many foreign vendors were rounded up and summarily deported. Most of these were from China, Central Asia and the Caucasus, and in a hint of the complicated entanglement of Russia's relationship with China and that with nearer 'Easts', Georgian market traders were also among the main targets for expulsion. This was the aftermath of the 2008 war with that erstwhile Soviet republic, and as such events change political winds, Russian cities operate on a constant cycle between crackdowns and tolerance of illegal or semi-legal foreign workers. In a vast country with thousands of miles of difficult-to-defend borders, arrivals from elsewhere in Eurasia are nearly impossible to stop entirely. Moreover, while harsh measures such as those at Cherkizon may be publicly popular, they often have mixed results for ordinary Russians. With everything from catering to construction reliant on informal migrants, mass expulsions often resemble the act of 'freezing off your ears to spite your mother', as the Russian saying goes.

After a desolate wander around the broken plastic bag-strewn landscape left since Cherkizon's repurposed shipping containers and corrugated sheds were cleared, I stepped back on to the street. Witnessing my clumsily mysterious emergence through the fence, a middle-aged woman in a zebra print blouse addressed me quizzically, asking me what on earth I thought I was doing wandering around in there. I muttered something about the old market, and her face suddenly lit up as she drifted off into misty-eyed nostalgia. The heyday of Cherkizon was amazing, she told me, you could get every ware imaginable at this truly Asian bazaar on the fringes of a European capital.

'The quality was often terrible,' she admitted with a wry grin, 'but the price was right and at least there was none of the pretentiousness of the new place.' She gestured over the road to Novocherkizovsky. 'Stuff you buy in there will be just as fake and fall apart in your hands like it did before, but now it's twice as expensive. Also no one in there speaks Russian and the service is still awful even though they have that fancy building.'

It seemed I was not the only one subjected to the bluntness of Mr Zhao, who, he had told me, was one of few legal vendors to survive the Cherkizon purge. I asked the woman, whose name was Tatyana, what she thought about the Chinese. 'Aha, the Chinese,' she said thoughtfully. 'They do sell a lot of fake things, but they certainly work hard …'

Glad that Mr Zhao's existence was at least partially appreciated, I bade her farewell and left this two-part monument to the precarious position of Moscow's Asian migrants. Half a mile down the road was another trading site whose recent success has matched its neighbour's demise, thanks, in part, to a very different group of Chinese arrivals. Here things were more colourful.

The springy faux-medieval wooden walkways of Izmailovo Market (Image 1) offer an iconographic smorgasbord of Soviet knick-knacks, Slavic handicrafts and military memorabilia. Medals commemorating Moscow's 1997 850th anniversary rub against Soviet and tsarist roubles, toy bears and posters of a half-naked Vladimir Putin. Rustic table-ware fashioned out of blocks of wood compete with World War II grenades and fur hats for the attention of global visitors. A complex of tourist hotel towers built for the 1980 Moscow Olympic Games stands grimly nearby, and so the market gets plenty of passing international custom. Many stalls are staffed by arrivals from distant parts of Russia and the neighbouring Central Asian 'Stan countries. But this is intended to be an unequivocally Slavic space, for looming over the market's awnings and piles of nesting *matrioshka* dolls is the neighbouring Izmailovo Kremlin Wedding Palace, an imposing wooden fortress with battlemented white walls completed in the early 2000s. Mimicking the lesser Kremlins of provincial Russian towns (many of which also have their own 'Red/Beautiful' Squares as well as their own Kitai-gorods), this concatenation of gaudy multi-coloured roof tiles, thunderous forti-fied towers and slender pyramid-shaped spires might, in the context of Cherkizon's demise, be interpreted as a dazzling reassertion of Russianness over an area that once seemed threateningly Asian. Certainly, this location's resemblance to a literal bastion of Eastern Slavic traditionalism is part of its appeal to outsiders. As I entered, a group of Chinese visitors was browsing a range of cigarette holders and antique tobacco pouches.

'Russians like smoking cigarettes just like Stalin did,' noted one of the group sagely to the others, who nodded in agreement. Consistent with its associations with the militarised socialist past, a general air of all-smoking, all-drinking masculine toughness is central to Russia's image in the eyes of many Chinese visitors, something I would be see-ing plenty more of later in my journey. Vladimir Putin in particular has gained a reputation in China as the very strongest and manliest of manly strongmen, leading to a publishing boom in books offering advice on how to be as witty, manly and impressive as he is.

I followed the group around the market for a time, watching as they bought overpriced faux-fur hats decorated with hammers and sickles and spent cartridge casings stamped with the word 'Russia' in Cyrillic. The thick wedges of 1,000-rouble notes emerging from their pockets made me reflect on the contrast between these leisurely visitors freely consum-ing souvenir trinkets to indulge their vague visions of Russia, and the fate of harder-pressed economic migrants such as Mr Zhao. Amid their confrontations with grouchy customers, indigestible food and a capricious state with a track record of arbitrarily booting out Chinese migrants, the fur coat-vendors deal with a version of their host country a world away from casually imparted tales of Stalin's smoking habits. Together, then, the tourists and the traders, situated a mere few hundred yeards apart, embodied the compound effects of China's 'rise' to global prominence over the last three decades, both as an exporter of affordable goods and, more recently, as a source of tourists. Here in this north-eastern corner of Moscow were two Chinas, and a newly mobile middle class promenaded just down the road from those hoping that their geographically distant children might one day afford to do the same.

* * *

These dual Chinese presences in Moscow in some respects reprise the coexistence 100 years ago of struggling traders and those, like Qu Qiubai, visiting for more mind-broadening purposes. But compared to today's tourists swapping the fruits of China's boom for luxury brands or trinkets, early leftists brought little capital of any kind, cultural, political or financial. Treated as inferiors coming to pay tribute at the heart of the new socialist realm, and knowing well the parlous state of their own country, many were driven to deep introspection about the differences between the mirror empires.

Lodging in a hotel near the Kremlin, Qu was greeted soon after his arrival by an official named Vason from the new Soviet Foreign Ministry's Eastern Section. While courteous, Vason betrayed signs of scepticism about China's prospects as a revolutionary nation and said that in his view the Chinese were yet to break out of the old world the Soviet system was busy destroying. If this situation were to change, Vason speculated, then 'the understanding between the Chinese and Russian peoples could reach new levels'.[15] But as things stood, he seemed to hold out little hope.

Qu, however, was more positive, voicing a conviction that the futures of the Soviet and Chinese people were inseparably yoked together. 'We have the same dream, the same dream!' he wrote following his meeting with Vason, agitated in all senses of the word. 'Whether in Russia or China it makes no difference, Eastern and Western culture must break out of the same cycles.'[16] Central here were visions of a Europe and an Asia that would mirror one another.

Casting off the shackles of the past was a concern that also preoccupied Chinese revolutionary poet Guo Moruo during the 1920s, long before he served as first president of the PRC's Academy of Sciences or won the (1951) Stalin Peace Prize. In a 1920 poem entitled *Sky Dog*, Guo exclaimed:

Aha, I am a sky dog!
I have swallowed the moon,
I have swallowed the sun,
I have swallowed all the planets,
I have swallowed the entire universe,
I am I!

This was an era when no fantasy about airborne canine planet-ingestion seemed too far-fetched a metaphor for Chinese revolutionary spirit and the germination of trans-Eurasian socialism. Entire peoples, be they Soviet or Chinese, might now be uplifted as individuals liberated by this spirit, and find new international kinship.

Yet negative voices such as that of the dour Vason were common, and often predicated their doubts on beliefs about the irreconcilable differences between the 'West' and 'East' mentioned by Qu. Scepticism about the prospects for 'Asian' socialism was not unique to the Russian side, and even the robustly optimistic Hu Yuzhi was prone to baleful ruminations over China's opaque destiny.[17] For his part, Lenin himself remained cautiously optimistic about China, to which he dedicated copious musings.[18] But questions over the viability and legitimacy of a Chinese revolution persisted well beyond his death. Even after a Stalinist incarnation of Soviet socialism was adopted near-wholesale in Mao's China in the 1950s, condescension persisted. My later borderland explorations would reveal whether or not the notional Sino-Soviet 'Friendship' that emerged at this time did indeed achieve the inter-people harmony speculated about by Vason. But clues as to the outcome, and the mirrored differences that would haunt Sino-Soviet and Sino-Russian ties, were already there in post-1917 Moscow.

Possibly as a reflex against Vason's condescension, Qu's admiration for the new socialist mentality was mitigated by his voluble complaints about the appalling food he was invited to force down at the Soviet Foreign Ministry canteen. Russia was a 'land of hunger' in strikingly personal ways. Tactfully blaming the situation on the supply problems of a war economy adapting to the elimination of private enterprise, Qu nevertheless expressed a view that, as Mr Zhao demonstrated, echoes down the ages: whether exacerbated by shortages or not, the contrast between hearty yet often stodgy Russian fare and the explosion of texture and flavour offered by Chinese food, even in its frigid northern borderlands, is a symbol of the inescapable cultural differences between the two sides. I never found my pie shop in Red Square, but culinary affairs would become a motif for my journey as a whole.

* * *

Debates over the ability of diverse populations to digest Soviet socialism were, given the USSR's own multi-ethnic Asianness, as widespread within the county's borders as they were with Chinese visitors. I would shortly be making a decisive leap into the arena of Russia's confrontation with its internal 'East', but before this Moscow offered one final foretaste of the entangled cultural worlds that lay ahead. Back in the capital's grand imperial centre close to a historic pedestrian street known by the Arabic-derived term 'Arbat' (meaning 'suburb'), the Museum of the Orient blurs the boundaries between the imperial and Soviet East and the countries and peoples lying beyond its limits.

A bespectacled *babushka* of the kind that staffs most museums across Russia sat behind the low glass window of the ticket office. Having sounded Russian enough to avoid paying the 'foreigner' price (here it did make a difference if you came from beyond the borders), I took the stairs to the upper galleries. In corridors sandwiched between the quadrants of wood-block flooring and polystyrene ceiling tiles there unfurled a creeping continuum of material cultures. The arts and crafts of people whose historic territories still lie within the post-Soviet Russian Federation abutted curiosities from the now-independent former-Soviet republics, and items from lands still more culturally and politically distant. Buryat, Nanai and Chechen rugs adorned walls next to Kazakh hats and Georgian paintings, Persian and Pashtun national costumes hung in cabinets along halls from Chinese Zhou-dynasty pottery and an imperious ivory eagle given as a coronation gift to Tsar Nicholas II by Japanese Emperor Meiji. This kaleidoscopic display suggested either a tolerant come-one-come-all approach to political boundaries, or a more problematic lumping together of anything considered generically 'Eastern'. Closer to the sources of some of these items, evidence of the latter view would often be apparent, alongside a similarly indiscriminate Chinese attitude to things 'European'.

The homogenisation of the east to which I would be travelling has resulted from Moscow's historical preference for retaining centralised influence over its continental hinterland. The transmission lines via which the capital, often referred to by Russians simply as 'the centre' (*tsentr*), projects its authority—all the more uncompromisingly in the Putinist era—are today mostly invisible satellite signals, radio waves and fibre optic pulses. But seen on a map, a set of older routes unspools from the metropole in hard physical form. Contemporary Russian rapper Guf, who lived for seven years in China and leads a hip-hop collective itself called 'Tsentr', introduces his second album *City of Roads* with an evocative paean to this physical infrastructure. Zooming from space down into the largest city in the world's largest country, we move past the Stalinist 'seven sister' skyscrapers and Moscow's nine main railway stations, through its underpasses and past its Khrushchev-era apartment blocks.[19] Much of Guf's music is suffused with similarly gritty imagery of his home city, the pulsing heart of the empire from which rings of roads and railways radiate out to Russia's Far East, south and north. But as I had seen, these conduits for Moscow to project a vision of itself do not run only in one direction: befitting the 'Rome' moniker of times past, the capital is also a place where roads converge. Every day, the city's highway junctions, airports and the nine termi-nuses disgorge innumerable passengers. Their arrivals are responses to the city's status as a Eurasian commercial, cultural and political centre. Some come from the colossal Asian empire forged by tsars and their emissaries, stewarded over for the twentieth century by a gerontocracy of general secretaries, and today governed by a former KGB agent and his diminishing coterie of musclemen and petro-billionaires. Also reversing the direction of an earlier period of domination and influ-ence, China is an increasingly common point of origin.

Yet for all the evidence of the Empire under Heaven's longstanding ties to Moscow, it nevertheless felt counterintuitive at this distance to think of China as a country neighbouring Russia. An old Soviet saying still used by Russians states that 'all is quiet on the Finland–China bor-der', a sardonic comment on Soviet Russia's stagnant atmosphere that implicitly plays on the fact that China feels much more distant than Europe. This distance had confronted me personally in Moscow, for from far away I espied just a part of the mirror, disaggregated glimpses like cracked tiles in an incomplete mosaic. Only blurry visions of Chinese life make it this far: 'China-Town' has nothing to do with China; Louis Vuitton-clutching tourists were drawn to Russia's shopping and its rugged image but not the bearded bald man who played a foundational role in their political system; snatched conversations in fur-girded shops revealed the contingent and dislocated lives of other outbound Chinese emissaries.

If these fragments had one thing in common, it was a relative lack of engagement with the host country. Raucous tourists trooping around in groups could perhaps not be expected to drink too deeply from the Russian cultural well. But with their dislike of Russian food, scant knowledge of the Russian language, and lifestyles permitting little meaningful contact with the place, longer-term residents hardly showed evidence of closer ties. Adapting to circumstances—primarily the need to make a better life for those back home—they understandably got on with their jobs. Mr Zhao had been to Red Square once or twice in his decade and a half, he thought, and thus in some respects resembled an inverted version of tragic hero of Russian author Venedikt Erofeev's *Moscow–Petushki* (1973), whose drunkenness, rather than busyness, prevents him from travelling from the centre to the outer suburbs. This lack of deeper contact with Russia and the Russians sets today's visitors apart from their scholarly leftist antecedents. But this, after all, is a very different political era whose challenges, thankfully, do not include the reconstruction of two entire countries.

Regardless, for me it was time to move closer to points of fuller contact, places where mirrored Russian and Chinese worlds would meet and intersect directly. Here it would be clearer how these countries had ended up sharing a border in the first place, and what effects this had had on each side's perception of the other. The Russian capital where I had started out has for centuries been pivotal to interfaces with both internal and external Easts, and the colonial conversion of the latter into the former. But although Moscow only reclaimed the status of Russian 'centre' a century ago—St Petersburg served as its capital from 1712 to 1918—its twentieth-century stint as fulcrum for global revolution was in many respects a reprise of a much earlier role. Well before Peter the Great's other capital arose out of the northern marshes, Moscow was the origin point of outward visions as expansive as international socialist dreams, if ideologically very distinct. Projecting their enterprise through space and time across Asia, and with the assistance of conquistador nobles and hardy Cossacks, those seated in the grandiose Eurasian-Italianate Kremlin embroiled themselves in eastern ventures that would lead them to the Pacific, to Alaska, and to confrontation with China itself. I set out to follow them.

2

MULTI-ETHNIC SIBERIA

THE EAST WITHIN

For all its reputational problems in the West, Aeroflot was voted China's favourite airline in 2017[1] and seemed preferable to the decades of hacking through impenetrable forest and drowning in swamps that would have made for a realistic historical re-enactment. The first centuries of Russia's eastward continental expansion (beginning in the sixteenth) involved struggles with Siberian khans, squelches through impassable marshland and tooth-grittings during sepulchrally cold winters. But six overnight hours was all it took a comfortable Airbus to fast-forward me to a region where a group of Buddhist Turks sits atop terrain stuffed with mammoth skeletons and diamonds.

The vast area known as the Sakha Republic, or Yakutia, would be a fitting secondary departure point for my China-bound journey. Long before socialism, this 1632-founded outpost of Moscow's influence was a historic base not for global revolution, but for the colonial projects that carried the language, culture and ultimately the sovereignty of the Russian Empire south to the Chinese frontier. Since then, Yakutia's indigenous Sakha inhabitants have also negotiated one half of a Sino-Russian mirroring between visions of 'Asia' and 'Europe' in each country's midst. The region thus made a doubly suitable overland trailhead.

On landing in the regional capital Yakutsk, conditions were immediately less oppressive than they had been in Moscow, and there was a balmy freshness about the town that perches here atop permafrost. Yakutsk's establishment, and Russia's distention across northern Eurasia more broadly, were driven by paranoia over western European efforts to find a northern passage to East Asia, and by the fur trade. Kremlin-building monarch Tsar Ivan IV gave his imprimatur to early expansive missions, proving as adept at eastward colonisation as he would later become at executing rival aristocrats, sacking rebellious towns and other 'terrible' activities. But despite this approval from higher up, and the involvement of a cast of nobles as keen as Moscow's Mr Zhao to sell expensive furs on European markets, the push was, like any colonial endeavour, mostly a demotic affair. Most of those who came to Siberia were trappers inspired by lurid rumours about fluffy sable and their valuable pelts, and the Cossacks who spearheaded the colonial endeavour.

The eastward movement of these adventurists marked a historic reversal in prevailing trans-continental trajectories. The Cossacks had originated as bands of frontier guardsmen defending Moscow against raids from restive bandit-filled areas on Europe's south-eastern fringe, a situation that was in turn a legacy of the earlier westward Mongol conquest of Russian lands under Genghis Khan. Therefore, as fighting groups under a Cossack named Yermak Timofeevich, alongside agents of the wealthy Stroganov family, chopped, hiked and slid their way east from the 1550s, they pushed back across hundreds of miles of formerly Mongol-dominated taiga and steppe. One early obstacle was the troublesome Mongol-remnant Sibir Khanate, whose pacification saw the death of Yermak in 1584. But after this the endeavour became more straightforward from a Russian point of view. The year 1613 saw the founding of Russia's last imperial dynasty, the Romanovs, and under their rule successive generations of *promyshlenniki* (the tongue-twisting name for the fur-trappers) and tsarist emissaries positively hared it across North Asia, rapidly establishing new stockades and trading outposts farther and farther east.

Yakutsk became a base and administrative centre for the final push towards the eastern ocean (not that the Russians yet knew it was there), but even when the Pacific was reached in 1639 this was not the end of it. Fur-drunk explorers pushed on, sailing, camping and fighting their way into realms of which they had scant knowledge. In 1644, a Cossack expedition wintered at the mouth of the Amur just as China's last imperial dynasty, the Qing, was taking power in Beijing. Peter the Great's unquenchable passion for forcing reluctant landlubbers into boats drove Russians on to the Kamchatka Peninsula by sea in 1716. By the 1740s, after Peter's death, Alaska was Russian, and amid an unhealthy number of further drownings, starvations, bouts of dysentery and ill-coordinated boat trips through thick fog and treacherous reefs, it remained so until its 1867 sale to the United States.[2]

Russia's age of Eurasianisation was a bloody and exploitative one, and indigenous populations, including the ancestors of the Sakha or Yakut people, Yakutia's main population, perished in their thousands in skirmishes, or from the new diseases the Russians brought with them. In a modest concession to equality, the colonists did also apportion some of their time to murdering one another, and between 1677 and 1697 the heads of the new stockades at Yakutsk, Albazin, Nerchinsk and Irkutsk all met violent ends. Others were killed by the wilderness itself. Russian-employed Danish explorer Vitus Bering, who left his name in the sea, met with a frostbitten death on a barren north Pacific island. But no amount of terrestrial or maritime suffering, or tragi-comic encounters with native peoples and British and Japanese sailors, proved able to halt the Russian advance. The Yakutsk fort's emergence as a setting-off point for dozens of expeditions and a centre for administration, Orthodox missionary activity and fur was accelerated by its location on the usefully enormous River Lena, which made it accessible for much of the year. Winter was the season to travel in these parts, as from Ivan the Terrible to the railway age (into which Yakutsk is just now poised to step), eastern navigation was easiest when the region's vast waterways froze into roads. Founded on blood, Yakutsk's expansion saw it become a site for complicated and traumatic cultural collisions whose effects reverberate to this day across the empire it helped make.

* * *

The Yakutsk flat of Dmitri, a Sakha IT developer in his mid-twenties, whom I had met via online spare bed portal Couchsurfing, was on the top floor of one of the rectangular Khrushchev-era apartment blocks that skirt cities from East Berlin to Chukhotka. Having once furnished the untold luxuries of enclosed space, cosy kitchens and private bathrooms to a generation raised in the socially fractious communal flats of Stalin-era housing shortages, many such buildings across the former Soviet space are today shabby and tired. Younger Russians mock them, combining 'Khrushchev' with the word *trushcheby* (slums) to form *khrushcheby*—'Khrushchev slums'. Yet Yakutsk is a diamond boomtown—its very name a corruption of the Sakha word *zhakut* meaning 'precious stone'—and Dmitri's building was getting a fresh lick of paint. Heaving my bag upstairs, I was struck by how cheerily the stairwell gleamed in lacquered tones of tan and brown. A new front door had even been installed, although in a tribute to the hazards that lurk in the dilapidated interiors of many Russian apartment blocks elsewhere, tangles of loose wires still dangled treacherously like artificial creepers along the corridors, ready to strangle ill-advisedly tall visitors.

Inside Dmitri's apartment, things were less prim. As he opened the door on to the spacious abode, we passed through low rooms clad in lumpy brown linoleum, surfaces strewn with curled documents, food wrappers and crockery. Something sugary coated the sideboards and tables, cloying at anything you put down and retaining papery fragments of the cover of any book injudiciously set aside. But permanently open windows encouraged a warm summer breeze to waft through the space, and so somehow the grime contributed to a comfortably welcoming atmosphere. Warmth of any kind, whether a product of meteorology or hospitality, is to be cherished in climes where winter temperatures hit–45°C as they do in Yakutsk. Aside from Dmitri himself, the welcoming committee consisted of his younger brother Kostya, who was permanently shut in his room filling the school holidays engrossed in violent video games, and an adopted stray dog, who was permanently shut in the bathroom, filling the already pungent air with every smell a canine can muster. There was also a cat brought to Dmitri as a gift by a friend from St Petersburg.

'I think she probably feels like a Decembrist's wife,' he joked as he showed me around the flat. This description of the cat was a reference to the urbane St Petersburg ladies who followed their dissident husbands into political exile in Siberia in the 1820s and was a fitting foretaste of many of the humour-tinged but intellectually informed quips

Dmitri would offer during my stay. 'Sent from the northern capital to this outpost. What an ordeal!' he added.

After putting my luggage down in as sanitary a corner of the apartment as I could find, and having evicted the dog from the bathroom, we headed straight out for an obligatory tour of the city. Plentiful tramping of Yakutsk's arrow-straight streets took us down avenues named after Russian literary luminaries including Lermontov and Turgenev, and along tiled pavements pushed into bulging mounds by tree roots that had expanded underground over successive winter freezes. At right-angled junctions and along long boulevards, I admired the intriguing mix of Soviet apartments and new-build palatial shrines to Yakutsk's jagged bling of hardened carbon. Yet Dmitri explained that all was not quite as it seemed.

'Lots of these buildings aren't new at all,' he said as he gestured towards the 'Rostelecom' office on the corner, a brown cuboid topped by radio prongs. 'They've just covered this one in those cheap Chinese panels to make it look better. I guess you could say it's Asian-style renovation!'

Similar observations followed as we passed other buildings in the centre of town, from the head offices of diamond trading firms Alrosa and EPL (whose name, when pronounced in Russian, fittingly sounds like 'Apple', another producer of shiny and inexplicably expensive goods), to local government buildings. 'Asian renovation', with its implications of fakery and façade, was the first of many times that the Asianness of Yakutsk and its people would inveigle itself into conversation, but for now there was more to be appreciated about the urban fabric. Aside from being in better shape than much of its architectural kin across the old Soviet world, Yakutsk's built environment boasts another atypical trait. The presence of permafrost under the city means that everything must be constructed on stilts to stop heat from the buildings melting the ground below and making structures unstable. This was the inspiration for a decidedly non-Asian reference from Dmitri:

'You could say that Yakutsk is the "Venice of the East",' he chuckled. 'Buildings have stilts in both places after all.' Not being especially familiar with Venice, I felt in no position to argue.

This led us on to discussion of Dmitri's passion for travel, and his tales of trips to China, Korea and Thailand offered a complementary internationalism to the nationalist paraphernalia around us. Much of Yakutsk bears evidence of the successive incarnations of Russian statehood that have imprinted themselves here. From the twee reconstructed 'old town' behind the main square, a cluster of wooden Siberian cabins—some incongruously bearing the logo of Putin's ruling United Russia party—to the imposing Yakutsk foundation pillar topped by an Orthodox cross, first arrivals here are commemorated by a mix of Disneyfication and vaguely threatening monumentalism. These are recent trends, for the wooden houses and the column alike were erected in the 2000s, symbols of a growing Russian taste for plumbing pasts deeper than the more recent but intractable Soviet legacy.

Yet signs of socialist times were also inescapable, and passing Lenin statues and shabby rectangular Khrushchev apartments, we arrived at Yakutsk's sprawling memorial to the Great Patriotic War, known outside the former-Soviet space as World War II. Over a wide expanse of austere grey tarmac, a gateway of square black marble girders framed an avenue flanked by benches. At the end of this towered a maroon column, which, decorated in curling golden Sakha patterns, rose over a man on a galloping horse, also a key Sakha symbol. Narratives of common participation in the Great Patriotic War, which have grown in prominence in the Putin era, were key to the Soviet authorities' efforts to foster a sense of shared national identity in the union's later decades. The monument was thus a statement of Sakha loyalty to the socialist state that had fought Nazism, and—orderly and well tended—implicitly asserted their attachment to its successor, the Russian Federation. Fittingly, it was also here, as we settled on one of the benches, that my host explained more about his own sense of belonging.

Dmitri had mixed feelings about his membership of the Sakha people, who, despite centuries of Russian influxes, remain around half of the population of Yakutia. Ethnic Russians form only 38 per cent, with the remainder comprising other smaller ethnic groups. Intimidatingly named 'Sakha Öröspüübülükete' in Sakha itself, the republic is hardly a crowded place—despite covering an area roughly the size of India, it is home to under 1 million people in total. In this empty vastness, many Sakha have remained unequivocally Sakha, but in the cosier quarters of the cities, Sakha/Russian boundaries are more blurred.

'My family has been in Yakutsk for a few generations,' said Dmitri, 'so I hardly know any Sakha language.' This Turkic mother tongue of a historically Buddhist-shamanist people stands out among its Turkish, Azeri, Uzbek or Kazakh confreres in having minimal influence from Islamic vocabulary, yet its demise in Yakutsk reflects similar processes underway for centuries across Russia's imperial domain. Like Almaty's non-Kazakh-speaking Kazakhs or Ulan-Ude's non-Buryat-speaking Buryats, indigenous residents of other important outposts have largely been linguistically assimilated. 'I guess like a lot of people I'm much more comfortable in the language of the colonists,' he continued, only half-joking. 'So many of us have been absorbed in the last few centuries. I mean, "Dmitri Fedorov"—that's not a very Sakha name is it? Even before Soviet times, everyone was baptised and given Orthodox Christian names. First there was the Russian civilising mission then the Soviet one, we didn't stand a chance ...'

Dmitri compared his situation to that of East Asian Americans, 'bananas', he said, who 'look yellow on the outside but are white on the inside'. But aside from the important implication that, to Russia's Asians, ethnic Russians and Caucasian Americans are equally 'white' expanders of bloated European colonies, there are still other confounding layers to modern Sakha identity. Unlike Chinese, Korean or Japanese US citizens, Russified Sakha live in a situation resembling that of Native Americans since they still inhabit their old lands. Yet despite having learnt Russian as a pragmatic or forced measure in order to succeed in the wider polity encompassing them, many nevertheless feel just as detached from archetypally 'Russian' affairs as they now are from their hazy Sakha pasts. As Dmitri explained, people in his position are caught in between, neither feeling part of the Slavic mainstream that dominates the region's diamond businesses and siphons off most of its wealth to Moscow, nor having much in common with the rural Sakha-speaking population. Many of the latter are today migrating to Yakutsk, drawn in from the republic's ragged countryside by the capital's wealth, and as we made our way back from the memorial to Dmitri's apartment he could hardly conceal his scornful detachment from these new arrivals. The raucous Sakha conversation on the loaf-shaped bus we took, which also had Sakha-language stop announcements, had him tutting irritably, and as we got off he pointed at a new housing development across the road from his own block.

29

'That one's for the peasants,' he said sarcastically as rickety Soviet-era cranes languidly moved panels of prefabricated concrete over mucky plots and shiny new heating pipes looped up high off the ground to avoid future frosts. These developments, along with the nearby corrugated metal Sakha-language cinema, seemed suggestive of an urban Sakha revival to compete with the centre's recent reassertions of Yakutsk's Russianness.

Returning to the flat, we sat in the kitchen for a cup of tea containing a bobbing slice of lemon, Russian habits having made their way into the innermost spaces of Sakha homes. 'Yeah, lots of those people don't really speak Russian well,' Dmitri continued disapprovingly, as I looked over his shoulder at a mouldering hunk of bread that was solemnly observing us from a wooden shelf. 'I mean, in many ways they're real Sakha people and that's important, and in a way I wish I did know more about our past. But at the same time, they need to realise that we're Russian now.'

Prone to only occasional Sakha-related sentimentality, as a citizen of Russia Dmitri had few doubts about where his people belonged and where their best interests lay. There was certainly much that he loved about Asia, and he confessed harbouring a secret passion for South Korean K-Pop and TV dramas: for many non-ethnically Russian Russians across the country, the 'Korean Wave's' exuberant recent explosion has offered exciting new ways of being both Asian and 'cool'. He had also made several backpacking trips throughout the continent to which Yakutia belongs. But in the end his travels had made him certain that, for better or worse, the Sakha had few options anywhere except the Russian Federation.

'Sure, Beijing is much closer to here than Moscow is,' he noted, 'but there's a general feeling among Sakha I know that even if some people don't like the Russians, at least we have centuries of experience dealing with them. We know how they operate. The Chinese are still very unknown to us, and we wouldn't want them claiming to be our masters.' On a recent trip to Beijing, Dmitri had found the place fascinating but also unfamiliar and exhausting. 'I couldn't breathe there, it was so crowded,' he said. 'It's much better up here where there's space. And the Chinese are just so different from us,' he went on. 'At least the Russians and the Sakha are both northern peoples. Plus, things haven't really been so bad for us under the Russians. We didn't suffer nearly as much as the American Indians.'

East of the Urals, the comparison is often drawn between America's gallop west and Russia's eastward drive, both of them having sought fur, freedom and gold in varying proportions over time. Both were projects that, whether their participants knew it or not, would shape the 'destiny' of their respective lands. But while the American frontier remains totemic in that country's identity, and its terminus in California is among the world's wealthiest and most celebrated places, Russia's spread across Eurasia with its baptisms and sable are less known, even to Russians themselves. As California's first Europeans marked their colonies with references to Catholic saints—San Diego, San Francisco, San Jose—Russia made similarly ecclesiastical allusions: Kamchatka's Petropavlovsk is named after St Peter and St Paul, Blagoveshchensk means 'city of the annunciation', and Russia's main settlement in Alaska was New Archangel, an ethereal transpacific twin to Los Angeles. Other locations received the names of the explorers who 'discovered' them, the Bering Strait taking the surname of the deep-freeze Dane, and Khabarovsk honouring seventeenth-century swashbuckler Erofei Khabarov. But for all this evidence of people and knowledge emanating from the centre, and despite Moscow's many eastern migrants, somehow little information about Russia's colossal backyard has filtered back to the metropoles in the European part of the country.

'Because I look Asian, lots of people don't believe I'm from Russia at all,' Dmitri said, slurping his tea. 'Obviously that happens abroad all the time, I've had it in Thailand and China. But I get it a lot when I'm outside Siberia too. Once I was in Moscow and I decided to go to a Japanese restaurant. I walked in, sat down and it soon became clear that all the Russian staff thought I was Japanese—they were even giving me free sushi! So I played up to it, put on an accent and said *arigato* at the right times and everything, why spoil their illusion?'

That Russia's 'Asian' territories and their inhabitants remain a mystery to many farther west reflects a brand of ignorance that has been somewhat traditional since the earliest days of imperial expansion. Moving through their newly acquired lands, and seeing the poorly understood locals as threats, inconvenient impediments or business opportunities, Russian colonists were also overwhelmed by North Asia's prodigious geography. Naming places after saints or explorers was one way of taming them, but some locations defied even these efforts, and distributors of imperial toponyms were left clutching at bald references to local geographical features. Many of Yakutia's settled places have old Sakha names, but the Russian Far East is also littered with settlements called 'Bolshoi Kamen' (large stone) or 'Dalnerechensk' (distant river), echoing Colorado's 'Boulder' or New York's 'Buffalo' in their subordination to nature. In choosing such names, Russian explorers were in fact unwittingly continuing practices laid down by local indigenous people whose shamanic and animistic beliefs imbued many features of the landscape with spirits whom they were more inclined to respect than the arriviste despoilers were. Native names adopted into Russian included 'Lena' for the Arctic-bound river on Yakutsk's outskirts, which, exactly like 'Mississippi' in Algonquin, means 'great river' in the language of the Siberian Evenk people. The river came up as a conversation topic when Dmitri and I met up with a friend of his named Katya a few days after my arrival.

'Yeah, don't imagine there's some romantic story behind the name,' said Katya as we sat in one of Yakutsk's several new craft beer bars with 1970s and '80s titans including Deep Purple and Scorpions blaring over the stereo. Whatever Dmitri's affections for K-Pop, in a beer-drinking environment more rugged genres were appropriate.

'It's not like some Cossack explorer loved a girl called Lena and named this river after her,' Katya continued with the sarcasm in which she specialised. A half-Sakha and half-Ukrainian beautician whose infectious humour and enthusiasm bucked the commonly held stereotype that peoples of the north are emotionally reserved, Katya also worked as hairdresser to a well known local Sakha politician. Yet she played down this important connection, possibly because she valued discretion but mostly, I suspected, because despite her grooming efforts, the politician was still widely known as 'Jabba the Hutt' by locals in honour of his inelegant appearance and gurgling be-jowled manner. After several glasses of tangy local 'red' beer served in Chinese-made jam jars, we moved on to the studio apartment of Nastya, a friend of Katya's. Perched around a recently installed lacquer breakfast bar, cans of dark Czech Kozel beer were served alongside dried squid to snack on.

'Do you know the Bloodhound Gang?' asked Nastya in the midst of an unrelated conversation, referring to a band whose tongue-in-cheek and sexually explicit lyrics were a source of covertly scandalized mirth to me and my friends at secondary school. She was unclear about some of the words to a 2000 hit about porn star Chasey Lain, and so I did my best to explain while she played the song's video through an enormous flat-screen TV brought from China. Fortunately, however, demands to parse other profanity-laced tunes were cut short by the arrival of more of Katya and Nastya's friends, including a Tatar called Raya and her fiancé. Perhaps such conversations were more likely to occur in the presence of a foreigner such as myself, but after mutual introductions, discussion soon moved from turn-of-the-millennium Americana to the topic of Russian ethnicities, which Dmitri and I had been discussing days earlier. With tongues lubricated and feelings freed by alcohol, things become frank very quickly.

'I get so much shit in Moscow,' said Raya. 'They look at me and say I'm dirty and "black" because I have dark hair.' To my non-ethnonationalist eye, Raya's pale skin and dyed-looking hair looked eminently Russian.

'People say I'm not really Russian too,' chipped in Katya, who had joked several times already that her Ukrainian grandmother had gifted her the inheritance of a large bosom. Katya grew up in almost the only Sakha family in Kirzavod, an outlying district of Yakutsk that is home to burly river sailors and is known as a 'Russian ghetto' full of *gopniki*, a loaded term applied to a much-discussed violent and tracksuit-clad alcoholic subclass.

'Once I was on the train from Vladivostok to Khabarovsk and there were a couple of older Russian guys in the compartment,' she continued. 'I was on the top bunk and they were talking about me right down there in front of me, speculating about whether I was Chinese or Japanese and about who would get to have the first go with me and who I'd be sleeping on top of. It was awful! Thank god the conductor came in soon after and said there'd been a mix-up and I was supposed to be in a different compartment. I turned to the men, said "thank you very much for such an edifying discussion" and left. They looked stunned.'

This was an uglier side to Russia's lack of awareness of its own peoples: Dmitri's free sushi was one thing, but being publicly demeaned on the assumption that one was an uncomprehending 'foreigner' was quite another.

The Russian language has two words for 'Russian'. One, the version of Russianness with which Dmitri felt the Sakha should identify, is *rossiiskii*, connoting 'pertaining to the country Russia'. Indeed, for

Dmitri, being *rossiiskii* meant belonging to the Russian Federation (Rossiiskaya federatsiya) whose very strength and greatness were precisely a function of its vast multi-ethnic character. Yet Katya's experience was a darker reflection of increasingly common collisions between *rossiiskii* and the other kind of 'Russian'—*russkii*—which usually marks 'ethnic Russians' out from, say, Sakha, Chechen, Nanai, Evenk or any of the other myriad peoples inhabiting the old imperial space. Often going hand in hand with the conservative revivalism embodied by Yakutsk's new Orthodox cross-bearing foundation monument, looser usage of *russkii* and twenty-first-century Russian ethnonationalist discourse has grown perturbingly more frequent. Vladimir Putin himself has been guilty of exploiting this trend, notably since 2014 when he began replacing his formerly habitual use of *rossiiskii* with *russkii* during a speech to the Russian parliament about the annexation of Crimea.[3]

Throughout three uncertain post-Soviet decades, the phrase 'Russia for the Russians' and mystical allusions to a 'Russian world' extending beyond the borders of the federation have flitted in and out of the country's national(ist) conversation. But in an era when the Moscow government is looking for new ways to garner popular support amid economic stagnation and a lack of fresh faces at the top (other than successive incarnations of Putin's own Botox-freshened one),[4] such ideas appear for the first time to have gained tacit official approval. Unencumbered by detailed knowledge of the country's imperial past or the non-Russian peoples who live in places like Yakutia, growing numbers of Russians have been tempted to equate *Rossiya*—Russia— with *russkii*, a view further stirred up by fear of Chechen terrorists, disdain for Tajik guest workers, and an atavistic inclination once again to see Moscow as an Orthodox 'Third Rome'. A paradox thus lies at the heart of Russia's contemporary relations with its East within, for while control over territory and people feed into visions of national greatness, that same purported greatness in turn breeds ignorance about the very imperial expansion that was necessary to have the territory in the first place. The equivocal position of Russia's 'Asians' embodies the insecurities of a country that looks in the mirror and is unsure what it sees.

* * *

Sometimes looking in the mirror means looking at China. Non-ethnic Russians may inconveniently complicate views of the Russian East's inherent *russkii* character, but in the paranoid nationalist imagination, China is a larger and even less well-understood presence than the Sakha. Long seen as Russia's main imperial rival in the region, and for decades the subject of largely baseless fears over its intentions to seize Russia's depopulated and resource-rich Asian backyard, China has nevertheless been a longstanding presence in Yakutia itself. Archaeologists sifting through the republic's loam have found coins from the Chinese Song dynasty (960–1279) buried alongside the republic's more famous mammoth tusks, although it remains unclear whether it was Chinese people themselves who brought them here.[5]

Better documented arrivals from the Middle Kingdom began to occur from the late nineteenth century when turmoil and deprivation in China, and a gold-rush in the Russian north, combined to entice significant numbers of prospectors across the taiga and tundra. New Chinese family trading houses in Siberia established links with larger firms in Harbin and Shanghai, forming commerce routes via which gold and furs travelled back southwards. Into the twentieth century and as World War I raged in Europe, Chinese numbers here increased still further. Industrial disputes and worker unrest fed by the eastward creep of Bolshevik agitation exacerbated labour shortages caused by the departures of men to the front, and so Yakutsk's mines recruited Chinese workers as strike-breakers. Alignment between the interests of the Russian and Chinese proletariats would later be a cornerstone of revolutionary internationalism, but in early socialist days capital continued to pitch them against one another.

Contact with the Chinese saw Yakutia's Russians heap praise on their work ethic, a positive impression buttressed as migrants readily adapted to 'European' ways, jettisoning their tunics for trousers, jackets and hats. While some left during the chaos of the Russian Civil War when gold mining activity reduced, as industry recovered under the new Soviet government from the late 1920s and '30s, the influx resumed, and many settled down to become citizens of the new avowedly internationalist USSR. Indeed, in the ideological fervour gripping the young Soviet Union, Chinese workers organised their own brigades to promote revolutionary ideas, while maintaining a keen interest in the social upheaval occurring back in their homeland. A Siberian branch of the 'Hands off China!' society formed in the mid-1920s and collected donations to send to compatriot revolutionaries back home. These were precisely the people whom young intellectuals Qu Qiubai and Hu Yuzhi sought to awaken. Showing less class solidarity, some Sakha-based Chinese still preferred to operate covertly, dealing in contraband, smuggling gold and forming banks which went underground as such practices became illegal under socialism. But whatever their political affiliations, many members of the mostly male Chinese population of the time stayed, marrying local Russian or Sakha wives, enduring the same hardships as other Soviet citizens, including racially targeted Stalinist purges, and emerging as an integral part of Yakutia society. Descendants of these early settlers remain recognisable today from their trisyllabic Chinese names rendered in idiosyncratic ways in Cyrillic.[6]

The twenty-first century being a new era of Chinese labour migration, interest in Yakutia's gold—always a treasured commodity in China—persists, and groups of informal miners are periodically rounded up by the local authorities and deported.[7] Curious myself to meet some more recent Chinese arrivals, although hopefully without being sent to prison for the deed, I headed on Dmitri's advice to Stolichny Market on the road out towards Yakutsk's airport. Like many urban markets of its kind, Stolichny was a place where Russia's internal and external Easts meet across lines of carefully inscribed hierarchy. In the central covered hall were ethnic Russians (middle-aged women selling chunky tubs of squeaky *tvorog*, tangy *kefir* and other products along Russia's rich dairy spectrum), non-Russian citizens of Russia (rural Sakha migrants behind tables of river fish), and 'Asians' from now-independent former-Soviet republics (Uzbek stallholders with bright arrays of colourful fruit and vegetables). The Chinese, by contrast, were all outside, running more improvised stalls out of shipping containers or awnings propped up by wooden struts.

They seemed unperturbed by their spatial marginalisation, however, and as I approached, several families were standing around, parents chatting animatedly while their children scooted small electric go-karts around the mud and gravel forecourt. From their accents, it was apparent that they were mostly north-easterners, a suspicion I confirmed by asking a group of mothers who were conversing, studiously ignoring their children's antics. As one often hears from proud locals in Manchuria itself, north-eastern Chinese people speak dialects that are very close to the national standard Mandarin, and so fewer of the regional accents I had heard at Moscow's Novocherkizovsky Trade Centre were present here. As I approached China, it seemed, it was also approaching me.

I spoke to a shoe-seller who introduced himself as Mr Li. Dressed in jeans and a tight-fitting fake leather jacket, Mr Li had a large nose, thick shaggy hair and a long fringe that almost covered his eyes. Aside from this ensemble, which made him somewhat resemble an '80s rock musician, his rugged features also made him appear not to be a member of the Han—China's ethnic majority who have played a similar role in that empire as the Russians have in theirs. Probably over-keen to explore complex ethnic origins, I asked if he might by any chance be Manchu, north-east China's historical inhabitants, founders of the Qing dynasty, and still a notable population in the region.

'No of course not,' he said defensively. 'I'm Han.' As earlier with Mr Zhao, I wondered for a moment whether I had unwittingly discovered in myself a knack for making Chinese market traders indignant. But, more likely, people whose lives are dedicated to selling fur coats or footwear simply feel they have little time for idle chats with foreigners on obscure subjects. I asked Mr Li how he found Yakutsk. 'The Russians are quite severe,' he said, 'and it's cold—much colder than north-east China.'

That day was warm, but he crossed his arms and rubbed his leather elbow pads as he imagined the bitter winters to which Yakutsk is annually condemned. Oymyakon, the coldest inhabited place on earth, is not far away. Mr Li's sensitivity to the cold was hardly surprising, for he and the other traders, he told me, lived in a row of two-storey prefabricated huts that poked up behind the market. 'I'm not sure how long I'll stay,' he said, 'maybe a year or two.' Few Chinese arrivals remain in Russia as long as Mr Zhao, who played a kind of anchor role for his own family business. For most, a spell in the northern country is a chance to earn some extra money, to see something beyond China's borders—however limited their contact with locals—and to play a part in the familial webs of *guanxi* (relations) around which such international trade arrangements are based.

I tried to ask more questions, but Mr Li seemed distracted and uncertain. Perhaps recollections of bitter −50°C winds and feet of snow had chilled him, but equally likely anyone of European appearance asking too many questions was something of which to be wary. Many in his position arrive on tourist or group visas whose provisions do not necessarily include shoe-dealing. Their precarious position here mirrors that of the much less numerous Russians—including pensioners—who move to north-east China to eke out a living.

Leaving the market, I returned to town, passing on my way several large advertisements for a 'Restaurant with Dance Floor' called Kitaisky Stil (Chinese style). Sakha locals may have mixed feelings about the Chinese, finding them less familiar than the Russians and disliking being mistaken for them. But as providers of 'exotic' evening entertainment and footwear, they evidently had a role to play here.

* * *

Rounding out my encounters with Yakutsk's major national constituencies was a trip to a local tourist attraction named the 'Permafrost Kingdom' in the company of Dmitri's friend Katya and Grigory, a local ethnic Russian. A kind-faced forty-something accountant with a bounce of combed-back grey hair, a brown-and-white striped T-shirt and a slim briefcase that seldom left his left hand, Grigory was introduced to me with a brief flourish of English from Katya, who referred to him simply as her 'man-friend'.

For Grigory, Yakutsk's Russianness was beyond question, although not necessarily in a good way. The trip to the 'kingdom', an ice sculpture-stuffed series of tunnels hewn into a hill near a traffic police station on Yakutsk's rural fringes, occurred on my last day in town, and, everyone had assured me, it was certainly a place worth visiting. Even in the height of summer, the permafrost means that frozen ground lies just 10 metres below the surface of the city, and so however green the grass on the surface, ice can be reached simply by burrowing sideways into a steep slope.

After arriving and paying, Grigory, Katya and I were told to wait in a rustic wooden shed, donning the reflective thermal capes we had been handed unnecessarily early, spurred on by enthusiasm for the impending deep freeze. Yet after forty minutes of increasingly sweaty conversation, a Sakha employee of the kingdom entered the waiting area to tell us in rapid-fire Russian that, despite our patience, we would not be able to visit today after all. A group of local dignitaries had just turned up in a minibus and so, he reported improbably, they had to be let in first since they had a prior booking. We protested for a while but, as is usual when one is confronted with the arbitrary power of dignitaries in minibuses in Russia or China, resistance was futile.

'Do you know what that man is?' asked Grigory as we trudged away. 'He's an *urod*, Russia's full of them.' *Urod* means something between 'bastard' and 'monster', and Grigory was deeply dispirited by what he saw as a surfeit of *urods* holding his nation back.

'Our country barely really exists these days,' he sighed. 'England, America, that's power. But we just have these fucking *urods*.' I keenly assured Grigory that the other side of Eurasia was hardly an *urod*-free zone, and after some thought he recalled having watched the British football film *Green Street Hooligans*, which seemed to corroborate this in his mind.

Grigory's spirits were lifted, however, as we decided to go and eat instead. Not far from the Permafrost Kingdom is Chochur Muran, a Sakha crafts centre and restaurant where we were treated to a traditional meal of *stroganina* (uncooked strips of frozen fish dipped in salt and pepper), reindeer meat and soft loaves of flat bread. His mind drawn away from the powerful cocktail of anger and despair that it is the *urod*'s unique capacity to inspire, and after a few shots of pleasantly chilled local vodka, the pride Grigory evidently felt in this distant Russian outpost was restored. As we talked, he pointed out some local curiosities displayed around the grand timber cabin where we were sitting.

'International science does not recognise the Sakha husky as a distinct breed, but one day it will,' he assured me and Katya, pointing at a stuffed canine lurking under the wooden staircase. In another corner was a traditional Sakha bivouac draped in the pelt of an Arctic wolf, observing which Grigory was led to muse, 'this is no ordinary wolf skin …' We left more contented than we had entered.

Whatever Grigory's feelings on the matter, however, the next stage of my journey would not take me to the land where the unique Sakha huskies roam. There on the shores of the frozen ocean, Sakha men evade the Russian authorities to hew massive mammoth tusks from the frozen soil and sell them to Chinese smugglers. Instead, I would be travelling south to China, ultimate destination for the teeth of the ancient hairy elephants that are later carved into wondrous shapes as ornaments or ground up for traditional medicine. Time in Yakutsk had given me a sense of its position at the intersection of several cultural worlds. For many Sakha it is capital and centre, an Asian city looking to Central Asia for kinship, Korea for cool, China for consumer goods and Moscow for a reluctantly accepted brand of insensitive political stewardship. Seen from the Russian centre, the Sakha Republic remains a Siberian outpost, a base for expeditions that today burrow downward towards diamonds rather than pushing horizontally across territory. Ahead lay other parts of 'Russian Asia' where lateral movement— mostly along railways—is still the dominant trajectory, and from there I would continue to locations where the experiences of 'European' Chinese people would mirror those of Russia's Sakha in striking ways. But first there was Yakutia's own hinterland to traverse.

* * *

The road to Neryungri, the Sakha Republic's second city and a 1970s Soviet coal-mining town of rectangular apartment blocks, is a 500-mile forest track with an official status belying its potholed and rutted condition.

'This is a federal-level highway!' Ivan to my left bellowed with gleeful cynicism as we barrelled south. I was sitting in a backward-facing middle seat wedged between the mercifully slim Ivan, a Russian mechanic in his mid-forties, and Anton, a twenty-year-old Sakha student of public relations, self-identifying hipster and modern dance enthusiast. Our ten-seater Korean SsangYong minibus was being deftly piloted between the road's deepest divots by a rotund middle-aged Kyrgyz man with a face burnished deep red. As we had swayed our way out of Yakutsk, he had had dire prophecies for the journey ahead. 'There is rain. It could be bad. At least seventeen hours,' he noted laconically.

An early feature of the journey was the ferry over the River Lena. Although a road and rail bridge across the mighty waterway has been planned for years, construction as yet remains in a logjam over a controversial tender process involving sundry national oligarchs and more local 'minigarchs', all squabbling among themselves. Suggestions in

2015 that a Chinese firm would be completing the multi-billion-rouble project without any bidding process at all came to naught,[8] and since then local media have dutifully reported on a parade of Chinese and Japanese delegates visiting Yakutsk, despite nothing more concrete emerging from their sessions than lots of photos of men peering earnestly at maps and charts.[9]

But the ferry crossed smoothly, and the lack of bridge and even the appalling quality of the road soon sank into the background. For much of the journey to Neryungri, all aboard the SsangYong were deep in conversation. Eclectic and often simultaneous discussions in the cramped space roamed between the need to be adequately insured (the kindly peroxide-haired Varvara opposite me worked for an insurance firm), the relative merits of English and Sakha horses (Maria next to Varvara wondered whether the former somehow resemble the gentlemen who supposedly ride them), doubts over whether the West adequately admires Yuri Gagarin (one of Ivan's main concerns), the sizes of various local fish, the nature of the true spirit of hip-hop (Anton), and how the Soviet Red Army had worked out where best to fight its battles with the Nazis.

From the very back row, Sasha, a beefy Russian who was rarely without a bottle of beer in his thick fist, intervened to shout about the merits of chum salmon and mandatory military service, the latter still an obligation for Russian boys. Anton, clearly more of a peacenik, and possibly deterred by the dark tales of violence and abuse that emanate from the murky world of conscripted service, squirmed uncomfortably, or would have done if there had been room. Sasha himself claimed to be on his way to Moscow, a journey of at least a week, and like me was heading to Neryungri to meet the railway that—awaiting completion, or even commencement, of the Lena bridge—does not yet offer passenger trains as far Yakutsk. All the while an enigmatic bespectacled Sakha man sitting on Sasha's right looked on, a thin smile hovering on his lips. Throughout the journey, he remained demurely aloof from the hilarity into which conversation frequently descended as we lurched south, plunging deeper into southern Yakutia's pine forests.

As night drew in, the good-natured badinage between people belonging to two countries and three peoples distracted most of us from the bone-jarring ride, and only occasional grimaces or shouts of 'oppa!'

marked the most vertiginous sways into and out of ruts. Yet for Ivan, the ride itself seemed to be the primary reason for going to Neryungri. He was a man who prided himself on knowing precisely what was going on at all times, and would often poke me to point out local curiosities by the roadside. While I was awake this was interesting, and although everything he wanted to show me looked a lot like pine forest, I was gratified to know when the trees were concealing particular villages or military bases. Yet, more invasively, this unsolicited tour-guiding continued through the night as our fellow passengers gradually dropped out of the conversation to attempt sleep, heads lolling wildly from side to side but faces somehow carrying deeply peaceful expressions.

'Look, a gold mine!' Ivan whispered urgently around 1 a.m., jabbing me in the arm to wake me from feverish stiff-necked slumber. He gestured into the still rose-tinted gloom of the northern summer night; it never quite gets dark here at this time of year.

'Yes,' I mumbled, squinting through the twilight. 'Thanks.'

Our Kyrgyz driver's estimate of seventeen hours turned out to have been rather conservative, and after the twenty-hour transit during which we stopped only briefly for fuel, we reached Neryungri in the early afternoon of the second day (Image 2). Provided with a merciful chance to escape Ivan and stretch my compressed limbs, I said goodbye to my fellow voyagers and prised myself out of the minibus on to a long street lined with turquoise and brown housing blocks.

The train was not until the next day and, perhaps seeking symbols of my approach to China, I found lodging at a small private hotel on People's Friendship Street seductively named Lotus. Its proximity to Neryungri's main Lenin Avenue also appealed to my exhausted brain.

'You're going to Mongolia?' asked Valeria, the kindly Russian lady at reception.

'No no, Manchuria,' I repeated. She smiled knowingly, although it was unclear whether she did know.

'You're from the Baltic?' she continued, posing a question commonly put to European-looking people speaking fluent but not entirely Russian Russian.

Valeria was amazed that I had come all the way from cloudy Albion (*tumannyi Albion*, a stock Russian moniker for England), yet her own story was equally epic. Her family, she said, was originally from

Russia's south-western Volga region although she herself had grown up in Kazakhstan. 'I've been here twenty years now, though,' she chuckled, 'I'm basically a local.'

For Soviet citizens, the USSR's territory was a relatively smooth expanse over which to move, and move people did, either coerced during the Stalin age or subsequently motivated by job incentives, love or simply desire for change. To all the country's scores of Eurasian peoples, the vast distances involved perhaps seemed less significant than to islanders such as myself. The Kazakh Soviet Republic where Valeria's family had gone was a case in point, and both before and during socialism it served as destination for both voluntary and forced Russian migration on a vast scale. By the time the Soviet Union collapsed, ethnic Russians made up almost half the population of now-independent Kazakhstan. Yet with the breakup of the USSR, the once-smooth territorial expanse became as uneven as the Yakutsk–Neryungri highway, and in a post-Soviet world of tangled borders, diverging identities and rising travel costs, trans-continental migrations such as Valeria's Volga–Kazakhstan–Yakutia path now seem increasingly improbable. These days many people are more rooted than ever in single locations such as Neryungri, which, despite internet and mobile phone access, are in many ways more isolated from one another than they were 'under the union', as people call the old times. Consequently, unexpected arrivals such as mine from beyond the fringes of the former empire are impingements from a world that is as spatially and conceptually distant as it was during the Cold War. Valeria seemed delighted that I had appeared.

We chatted for a while longer as she bustled me into one of the hotel's tidy rooms and made the bed, which included the familiar feat of stuffing a prickly blanket inside a double-layered square sheet with a hole in the middle. Then, after a shower and an improvised dinner of sausage, fruit and instant noodles bought from a down-at-heel *produkty* convenience store (evening dining offerings in Neryungri were few, although a stroll around the town whose somnolence verged on desolation suggested daytime would not be much more bounteous), I slept off most of the minibus ride.

The next morning, however, I found myself caught up in my own struggle with Russia's spatial vastness, its many frictions and time zones. The Sakha Republic greets each day six hours ahead of Moscow, but lost in a mental whorl of planes, trains and SsangYongs, I had managed to confuse this six-hour time difference with the nine-hour gap between Neryungri and London. My consequent arrival at the railway station three hours late for the southward train I had booked was disorienting. The situation was only made more complicated when I found myself standing in the queue at the ticket office behind Sasha, the Moscow-bound fan of salmon and conscription who had, perhaps unsurprisingly, made it no farther than I had.

'Fancy seeing you again!' he boomed, proffering a comradely paw.

I kept things brief, wished him luck on his quixotic journey, and having made the necessary modifications to my ticket limped back to the hotel to wait for the next train. As surprised to see me as Sasha had been, Valeria greeted me with a gentle scolding, but soon cheered me up with a rich tray of bliny, fruit conserve, cheese, ham and sugary black tea. Such unstinting generosity, often from people putting up with grim surroundings, is a hallmark of encounters across the Russian Far East, and as I returned to the station later that afternoon I felt invigorated for the road ahead by the hospitality, warmth and humour I had been treated to by all the Sakha Republic's peoples.

3

SIBERIA'S RAILWAYS

EURASIAN ARTERIES

The railway running south through Yakutia towards the Chinese border, and the wider network of which it is a part, serve as both blood vessels and creaking iron skeleton for Russia's emaciated east. After the initial hiccup in Neryungri and happy avoidance of a third encounter with the overbearing Sasha, I was bound for the town of Tynda. At only five hours, this was a modest journey in these parts, a short trundle down the Amur–Yakutsk Mainline (or AYaM), which—if the bridge is ever built—will eventually reach Yakutsk. Tynda marks the AYaM's junction with the west–east Baikal–Amur Mainline (or BAM), and, sticking close to the rails that today sustain life here, I spent the night in a four-bed dormitory with some pungent men somewhere deep in one of Tynda station's twin towers. By far the grandest building for miles around, this striking edifice in white tile and rusty metal is said to resemble a futuristic bird, and even if this railway junction is in a dreary state today, forward-looking futurism still flits through the town known as the 'Capital of the BAM'. When set alongside later observations from Manchuria, the BAM's past and present would reveal the mirrored ways in which both Russia and China have pursued massive popular mobilisation projects at their imperial fringes. However, equally evident on each side would be signs of the human and industrial damage left behind when the ideological and economic zeal behind such endeavours evaporates.

'Take a shower if you dare,' the receptionist warned me with a resigned shrug. All of Tynda was without hot water for the summer while the system underwent unspecified 'repairs'. It seemed odd for the capital of anywhere to lack non-heart attack-inducing washing facilities, but Tynda clings to its railway heritage more tenaciously than it does to functioning plumbing. Tracing much the same route as Russia's early sea-bound Cossacks, the BAM sprouts off the Trans-Siberian mainline at Tayshet far to Tynda's west, traversing lands north of the great water-filled rift in the earth's crust that is Lake Baikal, and passing through Tynda midway en route to Sovetskaya Gavan, 'Soviet Harbour', on the Okhotsk Sea. The original reasons for building the BAM, the very last Soviet mega-project, now appear obscure to many. But important among them were resource exploitation and a potent double desire to 'civilise' distant lands and manufacture revolutionary zeal. A 1974 declaration by then-Soviet leader Leonid Brezhnev stressed the first point. As my minibus neighbour Ivan had sagely pointed out between Yakutsk and Neryungri, the vast tracts of Russia lying north of the Trans-Siberian are home to most of its resources: Yakutia's diamonds, Kolyma's gold, Khabarovsk territory's coal, Sakhalin's oil and many other scattered treasures. These alone might have been sufficient inducement for the laying of this 2,300-mile single-track rail line, including nearly 30 miles of tunnels, through picturesque but nearly impenetrable taiga.

However, security concerns relating to China were also paramount in Soviet minds, for despite the country's earlier 1950s status as an official socialist 'friend', relations had soured during the 1960s. Following a brief border war in 1969, things remained tense over the next two decades and consequently the eastern Trans-Siberian suddenly felt very close to the Chinese frontier. Running around 450 miles to the north of the old Trans-Sib, the BAM would therefore provide a less exposed parallel to the existing line and would also allow for troops to be moved east should Mao Zedong—who was condescendingly considered by the Soviet establishment to be an agriculture-obsessed, Sino-centric non-Marxist[1]—decide to invade. Yet these strategic considerations in turn raised difficult questions, for while BAM would notionally serve as a demonstration of Soviet technical capabilities in East Asia, it was also important not to make it look too much like a Beijing-directed provocation. In order to give the project a non-threatening gloss, therefore, official speeches would vaunt the ongoing 'fraternal' connections between the Soviet and Chinese peoples, and BAM workers would be made to attend mandatory lectures on Chinese history, language and culture.[2]

The organisation charged with undertaking the, as it turned out, disaster-ridden and achingly slow BAM project was the All-Union Leninist Communist Youth League, more commonly known as the Komsomol. Whether or not its members were particularly enthusiastic about studying Chinese culture, or indeed about anything, is debatable. By the 1970s, Soviet youngsters had experienced little of the grand campaigning or mobilisations that their parents and grandparents had seen, and amid a broader climate of ideological drift, crime and 'hooliganism' (*khuliganizm*) appeared to be on the rise. With the authorities fearing 'Communist morality' to be in decline, building the BAM seemed an ideal way to infuse the young with revolutionary spirit. As 1920s–30s Chinese visitors to Moscow had noted, the entire Soviet project had from the beginning envisioned refashioning mankind in a new image through productive socialist labour. Asking a poorly equipped organisation that had never previously built a railway to build a railway through some of the empire's most ferocious terrain might just do the disaffected late-twentieth-century youth a lot of good.

From 1974, young people from every corner of the union were dispatched to the Russian Far East, encouraged by promises of priority allocation of apartments and cars under the centralised command economy. BAM construction was an avowedly multi-ethnic endeavour, continuing age-old efforts to make participants see past distinct identities as Russians, Ukrainians, Armenians, Jews, Sakha or anyone else, and be melded together as a single Soviet people. In the event, however, the railway-laying brigades were riven with ethnic strife, and while the contributions of all minorities were lauded by the official press (which loved lauding things that were not really happening), many non-Slavic 'Asian' workers received substandard equipment and were condemned to the construction zone's most remote locations. What had been conceived of as a microcosm of the happy patchwork of equal Soviet peoples thus ironically succeeded in portraying in accurate miniature all the internal tensions and Russian chauvinism that would see the entire USSR slide apart with relative ease just over a decade later.

Today, four decades after BAM construction commenced, only ragged traces of those already ragged early years are evident. As I walked around under grim steely skies and spitting rain, Tynda's morning atmosphere conjured up the Russian East's worst associations of depopulation and decay. Reflecting a regional trend, Tynda's population has plummeted since the end of empire, and now stands at under two thirds of its 1991 peak of 65,000. Brezhnev had emphasised the BAM's role as a civilising influence on these eastern lands, a telling indication that 1970s Moscow still saw most of its territory as wild and uncultured, even three and a half centuries after Slavic explorers first got here. The size of, and lately the resources underneath, this Asian hinterland have given Russia a sense of greatness, but this expanse is also a burden to the centre, an undefendable and unknowable space whose nature and people seem to require constant taming.[3] Whether or not Brezhnevian notions of civilisation had ever succeeded in reaching Tynda, my arrival well into the twenty-first century revealed a place that seemed to have returned to about as feral a state as Brezhnev's eyebrows attained in his later years. Like so many Far Eastern towns, a place suckled on Soviet subsidies was now subsiding under the erosion of market-driven emigration and underinvestment, its physical and social fabric fractured and frayed. Boarded-up windows in crumbling brick apartment blocks, overgrown pavements and derelict industrial buildings all spoke of the retreat of state and inhabitants alike.

But the decay was reflected little in Galina's cheery attitude at the BAM Museum. A retired school history teacher and now a museum guide, she enthusiastically led me from hall to hall, doting solicitously over each exhibit as though the collection were her own. Galina's favourite was the ethnography section where she revelled in enriching otherwise stale descriptions of the costumes, dwellings and traditional beliefs of the Evenk, a local reindeer-herding people. I had already seen one condescending 'progress'-oriented reference to this people on my way into town, as a nondescript rock on a plinth by Tynda's main road bridge had stated: 'From reindeer tracks to the capital of BAM! Tynda is 100, 1907–2007'. 'Tynda' itself means 'a place for unharnessing reindeer' in the Evenk language, and along with camels from the Gobi these ungulates were used as beasts of burden to build the original wooden settlement at Tynda in the last years of Romanov rule. Galina pointed to some curling black-and-white photographs of Bactrian camels hauling thick beams as she explained her fascination for the indigenous herdspeople.

'The Evenk remember the age of the mammoths in their legends,' she confided to me in quiet awe. 'And they practised shamanism.' She rested her hand wistfully on a replica of a carved wooden stump used in shamanic rituals. But then she changed tack, observing, 'of course, that all ended when they became Soviet. But that wasn't a bad thing. The Soviet Union tried to transform the native people here, to educate them, not kill them like the Americans did.' Genuine curiosity for indigenous far easterners was not mutually exclusive with a sense of a need to remake them. The Evenk, Galina told me, were well understood by the Soviet authorities, who offered them assistance in developing their cultural and economic practices to fit modern visions of progress. Collectivisation of the reindeer herds, she said, had breathed new life into the ancient symbiosis of man and beast.

Yet while Galina's words may have echoed the perspective of an often-overbearing Soviet/Russian centre, hers were not mere parroted reflections of official dogma. For Far Eastern Russians of all ethnicities, any reference to Soviet times carries deep emotional resonance, as nostalgia for this bygone age is driven by sense of lost purpose to life, the demise of bustling towns, and the disappearance of an entire superpower homeland that purported always to be on a forward developmental trajectory. It is hard to blame residents of Tynda, and others surrounded by the physical detritus of a stalled history, for feeling this way. As we walked around the outside of the museum, Galina showed me one of the original dwellings used by the BAM workforce, which stood under a tall tree. Youthful Komsomol toilers had spent their sojourn in the taiga in long red-and-white metal tube-houses known as 'Diogenes Barrels', a reference to the mythical Greek philosopher who lived in an actual barrel. But this classical reference seemed only another high-minded idea that was doomed to be dashed on the rocks of late Soviet reality. Brighter weather greeted me as I left the museum and strolled down Tynda's Krasnaya Presnya Street, but even blue skies and Galina's valiant generosity and good cheer only partially filled the melancholy void of this emptying town.

* * *

The sense of futility around the BAM's civilisational mission was hardly unique in this part of Russia. My route southward to the more antique, if equally tragedy-tinged, majesty of the Trans-Siberian would take me along another memorial to the human cost of Soviet internal colonialism. Decades before the Komsomol began their hack through the taiga, a shorter line known as the Little BAM was laid from Tynda directly south to the small settlement of Skovorodino, which lies on the west–east Trans-Siberian route. One potent, and self-perpetuating, reason for Russia's complex relationship with its eastern reaches is Siberia's longstanding role (mirroring Manchuria) as a repository for criminals, exiles and political undesirables, from the tsarist penal colonies visited by doctor-playwright Anton Chekhov to the GULAG whose archipelago stretched from Kazakhstan to Kolyma.[4] As Stalin's political repressions of the revolution's notional class enemies, landlords and wealthier peasants known as *kulaks* gathered pace during the 1930s, the Little BAM was built by forced prison labour. A corner of Tynda's BAM museum had described this grim episode of local history and, to judge by her discomforted efforts to move past it as quickly as possible, this had been Galina's least favourite section.

'My own family were persecuted as *kulaks*,' she had said, adding with a grim smile, 'some of my friends remind me of this if I ever express an opinion which seems too bourgeois.'

Russian humour has a way of defusing painful pasts. Yet Galina's wry grin was a brave face put on the haunting personal impact of this region's history of punishment and banishment. Grainy photographs of bones dug out of the Little BAM's embankments were mostly too vivid a reminder for her. The museum director, she told me, was on Tynda city council and had taken a personal interest in unearthing these skeletal remains. But things had become much more difficult in the restrictive environment of post-2012 second-wave Putinism, and little work had been undertaken recently. Similar fates have met others seeking to delve into the Soviet past's darker chapters of late, particularly the Stalinist repressions. After a flurried spell of archive-opening and research permit-granting during the chaotically liberal 1990s, the climate has chilled as archive doors have slammed shut again, to Russian and foreign scholars alike. Some suggest this is because Putin himself relies too much on the same great power and Russian nationalist narratives that buttressed Stalin's murderous rule to allow the USSR's record during this period to be undermined. But whatever the reason, researchers are left cursing themselves for not having pulled more out of the records while they still could, and, more poignantly, those hoping for an adequate account of their own family histories are met with nothing but stony silence. Nationwide offices of the well-established human rights group Memorial, which works with victims of Soviet political repression, have been raided by police, with 2008 and 2013 confiscations being followed by calls from the Russian Justice Ministry in 2014 for the group to be shut down altogether.[5] The organisation limps on, but it was small wonder investigation into Tynda's shadowy past had stalled.

My own evening train along the Little BAM's railroad of bones took me to Skovorodino, only 35 miles from the Chinese border. A gap between trains afforded a brief stop here, and as I disembarked the place resembled little more than a forgotten village in the ethereally glowing Siberian dusk. A light evening mist hung in the air, mingling with the distant shouts of larking children that rose up past the ornate eaves of wooden houses into the reddening sky. But belied by this unprepossessing appearance, Skovorodino is a significant administrative centre, being both a critical rail junction and a key locus in Russia's oil pipeline network. As another kind of capillary giving life to eastern locations, a pipeline spur here takes Russian oil over the border to the northern Chinese city—and iconic centre of Communist China's oil industry—Daqing, contributing to a Russia–China resource marriage that ought to be a perfect match between the former's vast reserves and the latter's vast needs. But although the Skovorodino–Daqing line has been operational since 2011, supply volumes remain anaemic compared to the potential torrents that ought to gush between such an apparently perfect pair. This is only one example of a wider dynamic: elsewhere, a feted 2014 agreement worth $400 billion between China National Petroleum Corporation and Russian gas giant Rosneft spent years mired in obscure wrangling over price,[6] while sales such as the 2017 transfer of a $9 billion stake in Rosneft to CEFC China Energy are usually suspected of being concluded mainly to benefit the Putin government and its cronies.[7] Deals done in Moscow and Beijing may determine the role localities like Skovorodino play, but, dogged by mutual distrust, corruption allegations and geopolitical jostling, they also serve as symbols for a more widely problematic relationship. While one declining power—Russia's economy in 2018 was smaller than that of Italy, California or Texas—counts resources alongside nuclear weapons as its main remaining strategic asset, the other state's thirst for fuel symbolises its continuing advance to global pre-eminence.

But official acrimony brewing in distant capitals would have little direct bearing on my presence here, and I was excited rather than anxious about the proximity of China. Passing through the Skovorodino railway station, a large single room with a timetable simply listing 'Trains East' and 'Trains West', I stepped outside to be confronted by a squat white Lenin statue standing in the middle of an overgrown thicket. With a few hours here until my connection, I strolled up the hill past this watchful figure and, seized by the frisson of being so close to China, stepped into a restaurant whose red backlit sign promisingly declared 'Tianlong Joint Stock Company Oriental Dragon Café'. A plate of sweet and sour pork and fried rice seemed the best choice on the bilingual Chinese/Russian menu, as the culinary in-betweenness of this gloopy Russified dish befitted the not-quite-China setting. The meal plonked down before me could have fed a family of four, and although I managed most of it I soon began to feel quite sick and so, as Tianlong Joint Stock Company Oriental Dragon Café slipped into its evening role as Skovorodino's local nightclub, I hauled my newly acquired bulk back to the station to digest things there.

* * *

Boarding the Trans-Siberian proper meant entering another, also rail-dominated, chapter of Russia's storied experiences in the East. Together with the China Eastern Railway (CER) across Manchuria, the Trans-Sib sounded an infrastructural death knell for the tsarist Russian Empire much as the BAM had for the USSR. Both empires had foundered in Asia, matching their rail-laying enthusiasm with ill-advised Asian wars against Japan and the mujahideen in Afghanistan respectively. (Significantly, the Soviets' Afghan campaign had seen them face guerrillas inspired by Mao Zedong.)[8]

This would be the first of two encounters with the famous railway on this journey, and I was getting on in an unorthodox place travelling in the opposite direction from that usually taken by those coming from Moscow. But the westward stretch from Skovorodino to Chita would nevertheless provide a taste of life on this continental route, which, having its own customs, vital rhythms, and indigenous population of travellers, carriage attendants, engineers, restaurant car staff and loco-motive drivers, in many ways resembles a separate state within the wider Russian imperial space. Indeed, the Russian Railways company may not have its own court system as China's Railways Ministry did until 2012, but with almost 1,000,000 employees, its population is larger than that of many of the European countries away from which its ferrous tendrils stretch. On board, I would also be resuming my dialogue across time with several historical travel companions, some of whom I had already exchanged notes with back in Moscow, some new.

One of these first-time partners was playwright, poet and journalist Sergei Tretyakov who, on leaving the Russian capital in 1924, was urged by a fellow-leftist friend to take careful note of all he saw on the way. This instruction he followed in an impressionistic, experimental and irony-laden travelogue entitled *Moscow–Beijing*, which is divided into various thematic and geographical sections.[9] In an early part of the diary dedicated to waving farewell, Tretyakov notes that aboard the train, 'you have started a new life—that of a comrade-passenger'. Tretyakov's own life on board the Trans-Siberian involved sharing a carriage with a melancholy attendant who barked orders in various European languages, and a compartment with a German businessman who had brought vast quantities of medicine with him and who appeared to support Bolshevism with the provision that it came into effect after his death. Slyly jotting down such observations, Tretyakov also remarks matter-of-factly that he never bothered learning the German's name. The man is imaginatively referred to throughout sim-ply as 'the German' or sometimes 'my German'.[10]

Like Boris Pilnyak, Tretyakov had been dispatched by the Soviet authorities and was on his way to work as a Russian literature lecturer in Beijing. Mirroring Qu Qiubai, he would also serve as a correspondent for *Pravda* there. For anyone on such assignments, the railway was among few viable modes of transport to or from China in the revolutionary, pre-Aeroflot age. Yet ever since the Trans-Siberian's completion in the 1910s, many visitors to Russia have also dived into new lives aboard this Victorian *grand projet* with a sense of romance, carried away by the immensity of the landscape it traverses, and the intimate communities that form on board. Even pragmatic revolutionaries were not immune from this.

In a wagon heading from Moscow to Manzhouli in 1935, Esperanto scholar Hu Yuzhi struck up a slow-burning acquaintance with his fellow-travellers during their long, languid eastward ride. As today, much socialising occurred in the train's restaurant car, which, Hu noted, was daubed with posters explaining railway construction projects under the latest Soviet Five Year Plan. The diverse coterie surrounding the author included a Polish businessman on his way to Shanghai, a wan young German professor going to work in Nanjing, an Austrian husband and wife who kept themselves to themselves, and a middle-aged German couple—the man, Hu notes laconically, 'three times fatter' than his professor compatriot—with their small child.[11] The Pole and the young German were full of questions for Hu about 'oriental life', which he did his best to answer, managing their perceptions of a destination that had little in common with their European homes. Yet the clearest indication of Sino-Russian separateness emerged as two Chinese manual labourers climbed aboard along the way. Yakutia's gold mines were far from the only branch of Soviet industry to employ Chinese workers at this time of rapid Stalinist industrialisation, but despite the country's reliance on this manpower from the east the pair appeared to be having difficulties. These mainly revolved around repatriating their earnings back to China.

'Our money's trapped here!' they complained bitterly to Hu after boarding. 'Even in Harbin you can't exchange it for anything.' During my own years living in China, I had experienced inverse headaches expatriating my modest earnings in non-convertible *renminbi*. I could only imagine what currency struggles befell Soviet foreign workers eighty years ago, particularly if even the bustling Sino-Russian entrepôt of Harbin, a city on my route, could not help them.

'Why don't you just become Soviet citizens and stay here?' asked Hu, ever-brimming with Esperanto-glossed internationalist fervour, but also alluding to a common Chinese practice of the time, in Yakutia as elsewhere. 'Then you'd be able to use your money.'

The two scoffed and replied bluntly, 'We can't do that. We're Chinese.'[12]

Both this statement and the young Europeans' questions about the distant and mysterious 'East' were indicative of the cultural gulf that the Trans-Siberian has been seen to bridge. Indeed, whether leaving home or returning, many passengers in the early to mid-twentieth century travelled this route the whole way from one end of Eurasia to the other, and so what mattered were the contrasting 'European' and 'Asian' locations at either end. Transit times were long in the decades after the Civil War when Russian infrastructure was at its most decrepit, but what lay in between was often seen as a void. For his part, Sergei Tretyakov reported feeling extremely bored as 'the train threw out behind it fields and forests, provinces and days'. Rare episodes of diversion came only during chances to play chess, buy cheese from trackside vendors, or observe 'the German's' animated excitement at having the chance to dump a huge pile of anti-insect powder on a flea found in a neighbouring cabin.[13]

Unlike Tretyakov who only briefly disembarked in Siberia and Manchuria to change trains, Russophone journalist Qu Qiubai was atypical in making several fuller stops during his journey west from China in 1920–1. These were often mandated by the chaos of war, yet while he spent longer at various points en route, Russia and China's intermediate spaces still appeared to him somewhat empty: for him, the Trans-Siberian was 'Eurasia's artery' (*ouya dalu de xuemai*) running through an otherwise barren landscape whose only variations were shifts between wide plains, dense snow-filled forests, and the occasional factory chimney spied in the distance.[14] Cocooned away from this inscrutable vastness on a journey that took almost four weeks from Harbin to Moscow, Qu had plenty of time to study his fellow passengers. Among these were an Englishman and his Cantonese wife who spent much of the early journey chatting away in her language until, at a station close to the border, they were approached by a Chinese beggar. Dissatisfied with how much money the Englishman offered him, the beggar asked for more, and, suddenly becoming animated, the passenger switched from his fluent Cantonese to the Shanghainese dialect the beggar was using, dressing him down for his greed.[15] The anti-imperialist Qu was impressed despite himself: seemingly a few of the colonists busily carving up China were learning something of the country's ways.

More typical of European journeyers were the linguistic limitations of intrepid aristocrat Ethel Alec-Tweedie. She and her travel companion undertook their fourteen-day Moscow–Manzhouli journey in 1925 alongside four German, seven Japanese, one Chinese, two Polish and two Russian co-passengers. Making much of her facility in German, but undoubtedly impeded by her inability to talk to any actual Russians, Alec-Tweedie spent the train ride in a state of perpetual confusion about what was happening on board. This only seemed to lower her estimations of Soviet life, which, as had already been clear in Moscow, had started from a subterranean base. Siberia, she opined, was 'one huge land of lonely despair' in which she experienced only 'unmitigated, unnecessary misery'.[16] The last straw came when her train crashed and derailed near Omsk, leaving the bourgeois explorer writhing around on the compartment floor in a pile of her own hatboxes.[17] This ordeal, coupled with other organisational problems and intransigencies of the new Bolshevik state, led Alec-Tweedie to the problematic but revealing conclusion, 'the Russians are Asiatics'.[18] Whatever her linguistic abilities, the author was evidently not exempt from the same binary Europe/Asia thinking that had undergirded both Boris Pilnyak's musings back in Moscow and centuries of debate over Russia's continental destiny.

My train ride, perhaps less eventful and certainly involving fewer hatboxes, continued westward from Skovorodino with carriage-mates that included a compartment of extremely inebriated Russian men and a Chinese student in his twenties named Liu Zhe. Zhe was travelling with his father during a break from studying for his master's in Blagoveshchensk, a large Russian border city to Skovorodino's east. The two of them were heading to visit Lake Baikal, he told me. I was not surprised: having beheld a few years previously this azure container of one-fifth of the earth's unfrozen fresh water, and its deepest lake, I understood the appeal. But conversation soon turned from distant destinations (Baikal was still at least a day away) to more immediate on-board concerns.

'This train is very slow,' opined the elder Mr Liu as we rattled through the gleaming green meadows and over the rushing rivers of Siberia's verdant underbelly (Image 3). As a resident of Zhejiang province outside Shanghai, Mr Liu presumably had impeccable standards, since while China's post-2007 high-speed rail boom has sent lines stretching to the country's very edges (including to the Russian borders, as I would see), the network is especially dense in the wealthier eastern provinces. In fact, China's newfound expertise in very fast trains has led to discussions of a Sino-Russian project for a high-speed line between Moscow and the Russian Tatar capital of Kazan, a mooted first link in a new route running all the way to Beijing. It is striking to reflect that if the Trans-Siberian were as blisteringly quick as China's superfast new G-Trains, it would take just a day to cross Russia rather than a week as it does in 2018. But in view of the situation with Yakutsk's bridge over the River Lena, or indeed the BAM, which was not actually finally completed until 1999, it would seem premature to be making dinner reservations at Tianlong Joint Stock Company Oriental Dragon Café to fete the plan's realisation.

Zhe, more accustomed to life at a Russian pace, was content simply to enjoy the ride. 'Do you know Genghis Khan?' he asked me enthusiastically as we swigged on bottles of Baltika 7 beer he had brought aboard and shared our impressions of the striking landscapes of this corner of south-eastern Siberia. 'This is Genghis Khan's country!'

It seemed churlish to point out that from the early thirteenth century vast swathes of Russia had belonged to the khan and his successors, as part of a Mongol space stretching from Guangzhou to the outskirts of Vienna. The eastern Slavic heartlands fell within a subdivision of the empire known as the 'Golden Horde', whose legacy lurks beneath longstanding debates over Russian 'Asianness'. Bygone Mongol domination also serves as a menacing precursor for anyone given to paranoia over Chinese intentions in sparsely populated Siberia. But it seems difficult to imagine what benefit Beijing, a city that itself owes much to Mongol invaders, would see in seizing eastern Russia. Negotiating favourable prices for its resources without having to shoulder the responsibility for defending this 'huge land of lonely despair' seems a much preferable option.

Yet Zhe and I did not spend long contemplating such momentous matters and leant on the window rail sharing the idyllic view. As we evaded emissaries of the drunk Russian party who would periodically sway semi-naked down the stiflingly hot corridor, we discussed Zhe's life in Russia. The place was full of business opportunities for Chinese people, he said, and Russians were fun, party-loving extroverts compared to Chinese people. But, he added slyly, they did have terrible food. We felt immediately close, drawn together as generations before us had been by the intimacy of the Trans-Siberian setting. In this warm narrow space, people are more given to frankness than when exposed in the enormous landscape outside. But disappointingly soon my intermediate stop before Chita was approaching, and so, after adding each other on the Chinese messaging app WeChat and promising to meet again in Blagoveshchensk, I bid Zhe and his father farewell and leapt off the train.

* * *

My detour was to a place that—unlike Tynda and Skovorodino—was never an infrastructural hub, having long ago been bypassed by the railway. The 1890s decision to route the Trans-Siberian 6 miles to the south of Nerchinsk marked the onset of the town's decline, but in today's depopulated post-Soviet age disconnectedness represents a still more fatal condemnation. Concealing its historical centrality to another of Russia's key concerns in Asia—relations with China—Nerchinsk now lies hidden from direct contact with the outside world, isolated behind low rolling hills from the vital currents of money and power that, with President Putin having curtailed regional autonomy, mostly flow eastward from Moscow. For towns along its eastern reaches, the Trans-Siberian today resembles Qu Qiubai's life-giving 'artery' more than ever, and those left behind are dying.

Founded two decades after Yakutsk in 1654 as explorer-imperialists pushed south from the land of the mammoths, the Nerchinsk stockade initially served as a base for Cossack and Russian outriders to subdue local Tungusic clans. These groups, relations of the Evenk, lived along the Nercha River from which the town gets its name. Those among them who did not flee southward when faced with their new hirsute foe were forced to offer tribute (known as *yasak*) to the tsar, handing over furs at Nerchinsk for transportation back to Moscow. Yet this reconfiguration of local economics set off a chain reaction, drawing the ire of the Khalkha Mongols to the south who, as the Tungusic clansmen's previous overlords, expressed their displeasure by means of a thirty-year siege of Nerchinsk late in the seventeenth century. The Mongols were growing particularly desperate as, with a young, thrusting Manchu Qing dynasty advancing on them from China to the south, the last thing they needed was to be caught in an inter-imperial sandwich. But in time the Qing dispatched the Mongols, and in the process drove some indigenous groups, many of them precisely the same people who had earlier fled the Cossack advance, back northward into the arms of the Russians. These twice-harried refugees found little sympathy at Nerchinsk, and one local commander, Pavel Shulgin, distinguished himself in the 1670s by greeting them with demands for hefty bribes before promptly driving them back towards the Qing again pursued by Cossacks.[19] The width of the mirror-border was growing ever narrower.

The Mongol rout left the Manchus and the Russians face to face, although at this stage neither was entirely sure who the other was. Since the 1650s, Qing scouts along the Amur River to Nerchinsk's east had been dispatching increasingly alarming reports to Beijing of the activities of mysterious 'man-devouring demons'. These were actually Russian generals Khabarov and Stepanov and their ne'er-do-well tagalongs who, vexingly, were extracting *yasak* from local Daur and Jucher clans once loyal to the Manchu emperor. Such were the riches acquired by the ragtag Russians that a third of Khabarov's Cossacks had already abandoned him, absconding downriver with armfuls of booty. Much of Russia's eastern imperial activity was at best under only partial central control, and so even after the Qing managed to put a stop to the Moscow-backed raids by the late 1650s, haphazard marauding continued. One corollary of the wildness that made Cossacks good explorers and fighters was their propensity simply to strike off on their own, and mutineers from Yakutsk, Nerchinsk and elsewhere established a new base named Albazin in the fertile and mythologised region known as Dauria in 1665. Commanded by exiled Polish noble and serial murderer Nicefor Czernichowski, the Albazin stockade lay directly south of today's Skovorodino and, by inundating the tsar with furs extracted from the locals, its absconder residents earned themselves a royal pardon and official integration into the Russian Empire by 1684. Yet favour from Moscow was exactly proportional to Qing exasperation, and this was the last straw as far as Beijing was concerned. The Manchus responded by launching a series of attacks on this northern infestation and crushed Albazin in 1686. Most residents fled, although, as I would later see in the Chinese capital, several dozen Cossacks characteristically decided to abandon their former masters and return to Beijing with the victorious army, setting down the roots of a Russian community whose traces remain there today.

Any Russians who decided not to switch sides were pushed back from Albazin to Nerchinsk, where a stop was finally put to this first round of competitive Sino-Russian tribute-levying and native-terrorising. The 1689 Treaty of Nerchinsk which followed may have been dogged by the month-and-a-half-late arrival of the Russian delegation from Moscow—an early foreshadowing of Vladimir Putin's reported habit of making other foreign leaders wait for him—but the agreement was the first of its kind in global diplomacy. Negotiations were conducted in part via Mongolian-speaking allies on each side. More remarkably, an important role was also played by a Russia-loyal Polish Catholic translator and a pair of Jesuit priests (one French, one Portuguese) based at the Qing court who shared the most improbable of all cameo languages of Asian diplomacy, Latin. Just as the Manchus had been confused over the identity of their new northerly neighbours, it was only as the treaty negotiations progressed that the Russians understood that the 'China' they had read about in the annals of early European visitors was the same realm ruled by the Qing forces they were now confronting along the Amur.[20] At this early stage of contact, the mirrorlands reflected mutual ignorance.

The rather shocking realisation that a vast, newly ascendant eastern empire now lurked at the bottom of their admittedly enormous back garden, as well as exhaustion from a very different theatre of Eurasian conflict with the Ottomans, meant the Russians were content merely to hold on to Nerchinsk, even if it meant losing Albazin and its surroundings. A new China–Russia border thus unspooled across the vast and at best hazily understood tracts of rivers, forests and ridges north of the Amur basin running as far as the Okhotsk Sea. That neither side had much of an idea of the terrain they were apportioning made the final wording of the treaty somewhat open to interpretation, but the

Russians broadly respected the stipulations laid out in Manchu, Russian and, yes, Latin (the text was not translated into Chinese until the nineteenth century), and gave up Amur-based marauding, at least for the next century and a half.

Having followed this 300-year-old Russian trajectory south from Yakutsk to Skovorodino and then back west to Nerchinsk, I walked from the low railway platforms—little more than strips of concrete between wide Russian tracks—to the dusty forecourt of Priiskovaya station, the closest stop to Nerchinsk. A cluster of middle-aged locals were waiting hopefully by their cars, and I teamed up with another disembarkee to take a lift into town with a slim suntanned man named Aleksandr. As we followed the tarmac road winding high along the bank above the River Nercha, the town gradually revealed itself.

'Ah, a visitor from afar!' said Aleksandr when I disclosed my origins. 'What have you come to Nerchinsk for?'

The question seemed as much a reaction to my surprising provenance as it was to the drab vista distending itself along the other side of the river. Dilapidated remains of Soviet factories, water towers and red-and-white chimneys clustered on the town's outskirts. Why would anyone want to come here, he seemed to imply.

'For history,' I said. 'I heard about a treaty with China.'

'What about the Decembrists?' asked Aleksandr, 'they were important too.' As a destination for forcibly resettled peasants, convicts and political prisoners since the early eighteenth century, Nerchinsk had indeed been among several Siberian locations to welcome the banished Decembrists. After a failed 1825 rebellion against Tsar Nicholas I, whom they accused of usurping the throne from his brother, 105 of these St Petersburg nobles arrived here and were put to work on the town's recently opened silver mines.

'We are all grandchildren of Decembrists here,' chipped in Vasya, my fellow passenger, leaning over the back seat of Aleksandr's four-by-four and grinning a proud and grubby grin. A local on his way home, Vasya too had come down from Yakutia, a seasonal migration for him since he spent several months of each year in the northern republic working as a guard in the mines towards the Arctic. His and Aleksandr's invocations of distant exiled ancestors reminded me of Galina's mention of her *kulak* forebears in the BAM Museum. Whether originating in the 1820s or the 1930s, and whether rebellion had been perceived in one's explicit views or merely one's unfortunate social standing, an inheritance of political banishment seemed to have left some Siberians with a longstanding scepticism and lack of trust in the centre. I had the feeling that with Moscow controversially using expensive prestige gambits such as Crimea and the 2018 World Cup to bolster its 'greatness' of late, easterners were keen to revel in their anti-centrist pasts. Besides, as Vasya's epic journeys for work and Tynda's empty apartment blocks showed, many places to which the Decembrists or *kulaks* were sent offer little inspiration or opportunity today.

Once denied the benefits of the Trans-Siberian and now deprived of Soviet subsidy, Nerchinsk bears the scars of a double decline: post-Soviet rust sits on a crumbling bedrock of *longue-durée* post-nineteenth-century neglect. In such a gloomy present, there are many reasons to remember history here. Having dropped Vasya off outside a wooden cottage on a hillside behind the town, we returned to examine some of the remains of the town's bourgeois heyday. As fierce gusts of wind whipped up the dust along the deserted streets, crumbling merchants' houses stood sombrely around a scrubby football field where a slim Lenin statue raised one arm as if celebrating scoring a goal on the pitch in front of him. Nearby, a blue Lada groaned past the half-collapsed neo-Moorish remains of Butin's Palace, once the home of a nineteenth-century gold magnate who conferred great glory on Nerchinsk by purchasing what were then the world's largest mirrors at the 1878 Paris World's Fair, and miraculously shipping them here intact. On the façade of the grand but graffitied local Trading Arches was pasted a notice, itself made indistinct by age: the building needed serious renovation and must not be climbed on, the local government declared despairingly.

Yet as Aleksandr drove me around, offering a sparse commentary on the faded pasts of some of the single-storey wooden houses we passed, it turned out not all was neglect and dilapidation. On Sovetskaya ulitsa—Soviet street—several doors down from a house where Chekhov once stayed with a merchant friend on his famous 1890 trip to the Sakhalin penal colonies, was a gleaming new building. It turned out to be a branch of Sberbank, Russia's largest bank. Chekhov had not been excessively complimentary about Nerchinsk, reserving for it only a single sparse line in which he stated that it was 'not exactly a great place, though you could probably get by here'.[21] But the mock-tsarist red brick Sberbank seemed, if not great, then at least very striking given its incongruity with the down-at-heel surrounding buildings.

'The Chinese built this one,' Aleksandr said without much interest. 'There are lots of them here now.' I pressed him on the Chinese: did he know much about their past involvement here? He had heard of the treaty, he said, but had little interest in it. Russia lost out to the Chinese then, he thought, and it was losing out now too.

Besides, Aleksandr's feelings about Nerchinsk had little to do with geopolitics. Born in Ulan-Ude to the west and transferred here under a system of Soviet job allocation that swept people far and wide across the vast empire, his twenty years here had been enjoyable mainly for the place's open space.

'Cities are all the same. Ulan-Ude, Chita, what's the difference?' he intoned quietly. 'I love the hills, the fresh air, the skies.' His was an old Siberian family, and the deep attachment to the vast eternal landscapes that this inheritance had conferred on him seemed a robust source of human warmth amid the decay. This attachment to these hills and rivers, more personal than Zhe's outsider visions of 'Genghis Khan's country', reassured me as Aleksandr dropped me back at the railway station. Here the feelings of an old man who cared deeply for his surroundings mitigated against the past of this place, so bound up in tragedies of loss and relinquishment. Since the concessions made in 1689, Nerchinsk had lain at the centre of serial stories of abandonment and, after only a brief visit, now I too was leaving.

* * *

As the biggest city I had been in since Moscow, Chita promised some of the cosmopolitan comforts—or at least running hot water—that were lacking farther north. Anton Chekhov, with a nonchalant brevity characteristic of many of his dispatches from these parts, had written Chita off in 1890 as 'bad, quite similar to Sumy [a small city in northeastern Ukraine]'.[22] I had never been to poor Sumy, and while the town had still not improved much by the mid-1920s—Sergei Tretyakov noted, 'Chita is all the same. In winter there is sand, in summer there is sand'[23]—it seemed reasonable to hope that the intervening century might have been enough time for it to get its act together. I found a hotel a short distance from the railway station up one of the town's perpendicular streets and set out to explore. Crossing Lenin Square, I noticed that all the green and red tiles beneath my feet bore the small Chinese characters '万里' (Wan Li). The name of a Chinese tile-manu-facturing company, literally meaning '10,000 miles', was thus sprinkled thousands of times between the unambiguously Russian symbols of the Soviet neoclassical military headquarters to the square's south and the robust sandstone Lenin at its centre.

The sense that an assertive 'Russianness' was seeking to mask inevitable Chinese influence would be a feature of much of my later journey through Russia's farthest east, and here Chita's very layout expressed its identification with the empire that founded it. The central part of the town follows a strict grid pattern reflective of the notional order and civility that an influx of Decembrists, more numerous here than in Nerchinsk, reputedly brought when they arrived in 1827. The efforts of these intellectual prisoners to improve local urban planning, land cultivation and education were given new energy when they were joined by their wives and mistresses who, in a pattern reproduced in various global histories of colonisation and exile, wisely followed only after their menfolk had first spent a few years stewing and cobbling together the basics of existence in unfamiliar surroundings. This was the group to whom Dmitri had compared his cat back in Yakutsk.

Along streets running parallel to the westward-stretching rails of the Trans-Siberian, I left the grand centre of town behind for now and entered a quieter and less perpendicular quarter. Clustered mostly forgotten between the railway sidings and a questionable looking night club named 'Pyramid' were a few ornate log houses on a quiet curved stretch of what was once called 'Damskaya' (Ladies') Street. These buildings known as *izby*, also ubiquitous in Nerchinsk and throughout the older Siberian and Far Eastern towns along my route, are often among the more elusively attractive features of Russia's remote urban centres. Delicately carved eaves, window frames decorated in wood-work that resembles lace fabric, shutters in bright blue, purple, red and green, and sometimes small upper attic floors with windows peeking over porches, all pay vivid tribute to the carefully attentive home-making that followed tsarist conquest of this incorporated east. Here in Chita, these houses attested to the flecks of aristocratic colour and vibrancy brought to the Chinese borderlands by co-exiled ladies and gentlemen, required to inhabit more modest dwellings than they had been used to in 'Europe'.

Back in the demure town centre, Chita's Regional Museum offered a trove of information on the town's Decembrist years, but accorded much more attention to the male malefactors than their spouses. Solemn portraits of the men whose St Petersburg-based misdemeanours brought them here glowered out from the walls. The museum's linear historical narrative suggested that, for all their wrongs, these men had managed to establish a whole mercantile tradition here. Chita and Nerchinsk had become thriving nineteenth-century trade centres dealing in tin, furs and Chinese tea. As I had seen, gains from this brisk commerce had even permitted some locals to embark on frivolous trips to Paris to purchase enormous mirrors. Dark wooden cabinets lining several of the museum halls also displayed the extensive collections of Chinese and Japanese porcelain that other Siberia-based merchants had amassed from their geographically advantageous position: carrying a vase a few hundred miles seemed easier than floating huge panes of reflective glass across seas and down continental waterways, but such objects were nevertheless valuable adornments in early Siberian settler homes.

Also among these older eastern wares was an interloper from an age when commercial activity was much less celebrated. Behind various Ming and Qing treasures hung a decorative cream-coloured rug with a dove spreading its peaceful wings above the florally embroidered legend 'Long Live Sino-Soviet Friendship'. Lower down, more stitching in red Chinese characters read 'A Gift from All the Youth of Hohhot Carpet Factory, Inner Mongolia'. Yet local, evidently non-Chinese-speaking, curators had overlooked the rug's stylistic incongruence with the exhibits around it, and so this stitched paean to socialist brotherhood bore the sober Russian label: 'Chinese gift rug. Nineteenth Century.' Was this a magic carpet with the ability to predict the 1950s Sino-Soviet friendship a century in advance? Stranger things had happened in eastern Siberia.

The long chain of twentieth-century revolutionary events that ultimately brought rug-exchanging socialist governments to power in both Moscow and Beijing saw Chita assume an international prominence hard to imagine in the quiet town today. The Bolshevik victory may have been named for October 1917 when the Cruiser Aurora fired its signal shots starting the revolution in St Petersburg, but it took five further years of bloody civil war with 'White' tsarist loyalists and foreign interventionists—British, French, American, Japanese and others—before Soviet power was established over the whole Russian imperial space. In the east, the proximity of great powers who were none too keen on the new red regime, particularly Japan, which was in the throes of its own era of imperial Asian conquest, led to the decision to create a buffer state. The Far Eastern Republic (FER), as it would be called, existed for the final two years of the Civil War before the November 1922 seizure of Vladivostok, and had Chita as its capital. Officially a neutral and independent country, the FER in fact became a petri-dish for all manner of political and military machinations among Tokyo, the young Moscow government, proxies of both, and numerous other regional actors.

It was into this fray that Qu Qiubai arrived on his way to Moscow in the last days of 1920 and, with wartime unrest disrupting railway traffic to the west, the young thinker spent several days held up in Chita pacing the same streets where I was enjoying cups of coffee and readily available Wi-Fi a century later. When rendered in Chinese, the name 'Chita' makes for an orthographic coincidence that would have pleased Qu. Most Chinese transcriptions of foreign names mimic sounds, paying less attention to the precise meaning of the characters used: the syllables making up Mosike (Moscow) thus bear the nonsensical meaning 'do not this science', while other mouthfuls such as Fuladiwosituoke (Vladivostok) would, if separated, translate as 'symbol pull edify fertile this care gram'. By contrast, 赤塔 (Chita), literally meaning 'red tower' and employing the same *chi* as Qu used in his label for the USSR—'red country' (*Chiguo*)—presents a satisfying harmony of sound and meaning, especially to someone seeking a Communist beacon to light the way forward.

Qu spent his time in the republic's capital interviewing various local figures who described the hardships of this interstitial period in Chita's history. Particularly vociferous was the head of the East Siberian Overseas Chinese Union who set out in stark terms the ordeal that his 4,000 members were experiencing. Once trusted by all the various belligerents bogged down in the Civil War quagmire—from the Bolsheviks to White General Ataman Semenov, the Japanese forces propping him up, and even a band of stranded Czech legionaries who were forced to take a 6,000-mile Siberian detour to Europe after the revolution—the union now found itself harassed on all sides. The FER's weak economic position was making business impossible, and many feared for their personal safety as raids by Communist-sympathising Chinese bandits known as 'red beards' (*honghuzi*) were on the rise. The region's storied commercial history was fading fast, and few were inclined to protect the trading classes, particularly if they had come from over the Chinse border.

Qu and his travelling companion Song Hua also gained an audience with several of the FER's politicians. Having grilled the minister for transport about the fate of the CER, the Russian-built line across north-eastern China on which I would soon set out from Chita, and after a rather surprising encounter with the minister for food supplies during which he declared that the FER wished to join China, they managed to meet the foreign minister. This was a considerable coup, both because it was 2 January 1921—the day after the New Year, which today is Russia's most important holiday and vodka-drinking occasion—and because the foreign minister appeared to be laid up with a serious illness. Qu does not speculate whether this 'illness' had anything to do with the recent festivities, but the minister in any case managed to croak out a few statements from his bed in a dingy, heavily curtained room. To the ever-attentive Qu's nervous questions he corrected the errant food minister's bizarre claims, declaring that of course the FER was bound to Soviet Russia. After a few more awkward minutes of ministerial wheezing and indistinct spluttering, the pair shuffled hurriedly out of his house.

Old Russia may have been in a state of disintegration at this time, but China was hardly faring any better. The 1911 overthrow of the Qing dynasty, inspired in large part by the political ideas of 'father of Chinese nationalism' Sun Yat-sen (in whose name a university would open in Moscow in 1925), had failed to produce a coherent new state. Entrenched military interests in Beijing had ensured that the 1912-founded Republic of China quickly gave way to army rule as first president of the republic Yuan Shikai attempted to enthrone himself as emperor and the country broke up into warlord-ruled fiefdoms. It was thus on a background of mirrored post-imperial fragmentation that Qu's busy schedule in Chita also included a maddeningly frustrating final audience with the Republic of China's ambassador to the FER. Offering little hope concerning China's future direction, the man communicated mostly in bouts of official-speak that would make modern Chinese Communist Party cadres proud. Much of their conversation was dominated by him bloviating vacuously about the importance of patriotism, and bemoaning the failure of local Russians to invite him to dinner often enough. In relating this, Qu's ordinarily measured prose slides into irate railing against the ambassador's intolerable mix of excessive abstraction and ridiculous pettiness, and the writer was left with the impression that the Chinese foreign ministry had little idea about any of the monumental events occurring in its own country, let alone in its vast northern neighbour. Qu was therefore relieved to escape not only the clutches of all these eccentric characters but also Chita in general. Having collected a stash of fresh texts on internationalism and socialist theory from the local Soviet Communist Party office, he at last managed to secure a train ticket west towards Irkutsk.

Three years later, and only two years after the FER's demise, Sergei Tretyakov arrived and found a Chita wallowing in nostalgia for 'those magisterial times when it was capital of a powerful state'. 'The Far East has inherited one thing from that great power,' he added in an unusually sarcastic passage even by his standards: 'proper forty per cent vodka. Although I'm just mentioning this for context—I don't drink, so it makes no difference to me.'[24] Today too, while local far easterners occasionally cite the FER's brief existence as evidence that they can manage their own affairs without Moscow's interference thank you very much, few significant remnants of the buffer era remain. A diminutive plaque on a grand salmon-pink and white-tile building in central Chita indicates that it once housed the FER government, but the signs and insignia of its present role as a branch of Russia's Federal Cartography Service crowd out this inscription. More enduring among the phenomena witnessed by Qu is the considerable Chinese presence in the town, and so, before crossing the border myself, I went to my third Sino-Russian market in search of the twenty-first-century Chinese trading community.

The small stalls surrounding the main building of Sya Yan International Trade Centre, known locally as the 'Chinese Market', had a more convivial and integrated atmosphere than I had seen in Yakutsk. Along narrow lanes between boxy shop spaces in the outdoor section, traders of numerous ethnicities chatted and joked in varying levels of Russian. Above the entrances to their cosy emporia small name plaques with registration numbers told of their diverse origins: Ivanov— Russian, Babaev—Uzbek, Nguyen—Vietnamese. None of these came from the near neighbour to the south, however, and so I headed into the main building, a confection of green walls and pyramid-shaped red roofs whose gaudy yellow advertisements for children's toys further augmented the Disney-esque feel of the place. Here things were more uniformly Chinese. As I slid down the narrow corridors between shops selling mobile phones and outdoor equipment, the cross-hallway conversation between vendors about deliveries or sales figures was in Chinese, with occasional breaks into Russian as sellers sought to entice me into their booths.

'*Kurtka nado? Telefon nado?*'—Need a coat? Need a phone?—I was repeatedly asked. As in trading posts all along the border, the salespeople here spoke their survival Russian to me, there being no reason to believe that I was anything but a local. To the evident shock of one mobile phone salesman, I responded in Chinese, a language that, if the rug in the museum had been anything to go by, has made little headway among Chita's native population. Here in the market, economics dictates that those selling learn the customer's idiom.

Mr Peng was standing in his shop methodically rearranging various plastic-wrapped phone protectors in a glass cabinet. A colleague, also Chinese, sat at a table in a corner under a powerful light, poking at the circuit board innards of a broken Samsung. 'I'm from Dalian and I'd love to go back,' Mr Peng replied when I asked where he was from. 'I've been here fifteen years already. To be honest I've had enough.'

I asked whether he couldn't just make frequent visits. Unlike Mr Zhao in Moscow, or even those I had met in Yakutsk who are thousands of miles from China, surely popping back occasionally was an option—the border was only 250 miles away and the journey relatively straightforward by Eurasian standards. 'It's my Russian wife,' he sighed, reaching into a high cupboard to pluck down a charger for a customer's Nokia. 'She won't let me go anywhere.'

I had heard from other non-Russian men with Russian wives that persuading their spouses to leave Russia could be difficult, but to hear it in the Chinese context was interesting. Although arguably sensationalised and over-reported in media on both sides, marriages between Chinese men and Russian women have long seemed a good demographic match. The ravages of the twentieth century—over 20 million Soviet casualties in World War II and, conservatively estimated, another 30 million dead in Stalin's bloody internal conflicts—left the USSR with a considerable man-deficit. By contrast, China's longstanding cultural preference for male offspring and the resultant surfeit of single men—selective abortions under the PRC's one-child policy have purportedly exacerbated this, creating a 'bachelor bomb' of 20 to 30 million men who will be unable to find wives in the coming two decades[25]—has seemed to offer an answer to many women in Russia's east. Long after Stalin, gender ratios are now more balanced among Russians of marriageable age, but popular opinion along the border continues to hold that there is a surplus of Russian women who prefer Chinese men's purportedly strong work ethic and lower rates of alcoholism.

'So you'll be here forever?' I asked.

'Looks like it,' Mr Peng answered with resignation.

But if this vendor and many like him were staying put for now, I was poised to enter the land from which they had arrived. That same evening I climbed aboard the *Dauria*, a special train named after the semi-mythical region of early Sino-Russian contact and friction, a province appearing on maps of the tsarist empire and FER that disappeared during Soviet redistricting. My journey would carry me south-east via the border town of Zabaikalsk to China, where much that mirrored eastern Siberia's quandaries over identity, migration, territory, politics and history would loom large in local lives.

4

INNER MONGOLIA'S LOST RUSSIANS

RUSSIA ON CHINESE TERMS

The ride on the *Dauria* was quiet and smooth, grassland mounds slid by the train windows as night drew in and, if one version of the legend is to be believed, somewhere in the dark we passed Genghis Khan's birthplace. This was his country, after all. I was trundling towards the border with Inner Mongolia, a part of China hived off from other Mongol lands around the time that the Qing dynasty drove the Russians back from their first late seventeenth-century advance. Generations after their initial retreat, the bearded Slavic visitors from the north had eventually returned to this region of undulating grassland and steppe plain. It would be as I crossed into China and sought out the past and present consequences of their return that the mirror-like qualities of Sino-Russian life would begin to become clearer. Just as Yakutia had offered Russified versions of 'Asia', so Sinicised visions of 'Europe' would be a pervasive feature of northern Inner Mongolia, where local populations have had their existences shaped by Chinese-inflected echoes of successive trans-Eurasian cataclysms.

At 4.40 a.m., I was vigorously shaken awake on my upper bunk by the carriage attendant, who was on his rounds alerting people that their stop was coming up. Mumbling groggily, unable to hear what he was saying because of the earplugs I was wearing, I eventually surmised that he had decided it was my turn to get off.

'Oh sorry, I thought you were someone else,' he said as I grumpily reconfirmed that I had no plans to disembark arbitrarily in a remote village between Chita and the border. Irritation did not last long, however, and I was soon asleep again, lulled by the gentle swaying particular to Russia's unhurried and spacious overnight trains.

Two hours later we arrived at Zabaikalsk's high Stalinist railway station, a square lump of faux-Grecian imposture that juts out of the steppe with a grandeur disproportionate to its modest surroundings (Image 4). From the hand-me-down South Korean bus that took me and other border-crossers through the ramshackle centre of Zabaikalsk, I made out rectangular grey-brick apartment blocks peering through the early morning gloom. One boasted a small restaurant called Santa Barbara: the 1980s US soap opera retains widespread popularity in Siberia, and, inspired by the show's reliably outrageous storylines, its name has entered colloquial Russian as a term describing affairs of a dramatic or scandalous nature. But despite such exotic curiosities I did not tarry on this side of the border: the crumbling façades and cracked pavements in towns like Zabaikalsk may tell stories just as interesting as the gaudily renovated centres of larger conurbations, but most of Russia's frontiers are designated as highly securitised and reduced-access 'border zones', so loitering is ill-advised. Around Zabaikalsk, the 'zone' is a 15-mile long strip abutting China, officially closed to both Russian and foreign visitors who lack the correct permit. In other places, these restricted areas, which swallow all the settlements within them, can extend up to 25 miles deep into Russia.

At the bus station for cross-border transport, really just a cuboid brick hut next to a car park, I bought a ticket for the first bus to Manzhouli, the neighbouring Chinese town known to Russians as Manchzhuriya—'Manchuria'.

'Are you Mongolian?' asked the lady in the linoleum-floored ticket office after leafing through my passport for a confusion-betraying number of minutes. Seeing the Russian and Chinese visas that the two London embassies had helpfully placed opposite one another, she had presumably concluded that the only kind of person crossing here who would need both must be from Mongolia. But although Zabaikalsk–Manzhouli admittedly lies only 30 miles east of the three-way Russia–China–Mongolia border, this still seemed a farfetched guess, particularly since my eminently un-Mongolian frame was standing in full view.

Outside again, and with flocks of screeching crows wheeling over-head, I waited next to a field of dormant concrete shells wondering whether they were building sites or ruins. The slow pace of construc-tion in the Russian east tends to mean projects crawl upward, meeting the downward slouch of decaying Soviet buildings halfway. As the red sun rose into a cloud-streaked sky over quiet conversations in Russian, Chinese and Buryat among the other passengers, a goods train rumbled by, spouting a billowing plume of black smoke as it passed under the towering gateways that each country has erected over the track here. While Russia's bears a simple label, tall white Cyrillic letters spelling out 'Russia' on a blue background, the Chinese construction is a more monumental symbol of a nation on the rise, resembling the colossal tiled buildings that serve as Communist Party headquarters in towns across the Middle Kingdom. Known as the *guomen*, or 'national gate-way', this is one of Manzhouli's primary tourist attractions, two vast grey towers topped by points in the shape of stepped Aztec pyramids, joined by a central span of glass panels. Red characters under the national crest declare 'People's Republic of China' as a flag flutters high on a pole like the flame of a single candle atop this grand nationalistic wedding cake. The view from the top over the wide-open steppe plains is the gaze of a country confident in its position here.

The bus eventually arrived and we filed on board. Unlike the baffled Zabaikalsk ticket-vendor, the middle-aged Russian lady responsible for herding China-bound passengers to Manzhouli was taking no chances when it came to my identity. 'Who are you?' she barked, squinting at my passport, whose lack of Cyrillic gave me away.

'A foreigner,' I replied, feeling facetious after the early start and the identity confusion with which the day had begun. This seemed to pla-cate her, and she continued to bustle up the aisle, checking everyone was fit to cross. But I was clearly a headache: Russians do not require visas for short shopping trips into China, so my presence added annoy-ance to her usually routine job.

'Young man, you get off first,' she commanded as we rolled into the customs area between the border posts, which also had a duty-free shop. 'Everyone else, now it is time to buy alcohol. Two bottles each. Buy them fast or we'll be stuck here till midday.'

Most of the sleepy passengers seemed only too happy to submit to these orders and disembarked, spending a few suddenly animated minutes browsing, and then clambering back aboard clutching thick plastic bags of clinking bottles. The rest of the crossing was less problematic than the bus manager's tone would have implied, however. Leaving Russia presented no issues, and while the Chinese border guards appeared momentarily confused at the arrival of a non-Russian European, they quickly unwrinkled their brows and ushered me through with a smile and a cheery English 'hello'. Mirroring the difference between the gateways over the nearby railway, the Chinese border compound contrasted markedly with its Russian counterpart, being a grand multi-storey edifice with slick tiled floors and electronic signs with information on import limits scrolling at great speed in Chinese and Russian.

Crossing at this same location in 1925, although under very different circumstances, aristocratic wanderer Ethel Alec-Tweedie was also impressed by the Chinese side's cleanliness and order. This she contrasted favourably with the horrors through which she had winced on the Soviet side.[1] In the twenty-first century, the difference in physical conditions between well-invested Chinese infrastructure and its down-at-heel Russian equivalent was only part of a wider contrast between atmospheres. We were poised to enter an arena of licentious behaviour and bustle entirely the inverse of the forbidding Zabaikalsk 'border zone'.

In Manzhouli, my fellow-passengers were met off the bus by local Chinese agents who were to help them navigate their shopping lists of car parts, soft furnishings, children's toys and household electronics. Such consumer goods are cheaper and more available in China than in Russia, and while many Russians visit border towns to shop for personal items, some also come as entrepreneurs running small cross-border trade operations, heaving bulk purchases back home to sell. Relieved to be liberated from the hail of instructions that had filled the bus ride, I left the shoppers to their business, found a hotel room with a view of the railway tracks, and set out to explore.

Manzhouli's streets were graced by the same Wan Li tiles as I had seen in Chita's Lenin Square: the company was evidently hoping to live up to its 'ten thousand miles' name by covering as much ground as possible. Along the red-and-green pavements, garish signage in iridescent neon lettering advertised the cornucopia of wares on offer to visitors, Cyrillic capital letters taking priority over smaller Chinese characters, which were generally relegated to the margins. 'YU XIANG CARPETS AND PICTURES TEA GOODS FOR THE HOME TEA,' shouted one. As a marketing strategy, many borderland shop owners have adopted Russian first names to serve as memory-aids for their clients. Another boasted, 'FRIENDSHIP SHOP ANDREI MOBILE PHONES LAPTOPS' and, lower down just to make sure, 'ANDREI SHOP', 'MOBILE PHONES'. Manzhouli's efforts to cater to its northerly visitors have included the erection—much faster than anything occurring in Zabaikalsk—of a gaudy array of faux-European buildings with pronged towers, jagged crenellations and jutting buttresses. Parts of the centre of town resemble an effort to reproduce the streets of Paris with only Disney's cartoon *Hunchback of Notre Dame* as a source. On the outskirts of town, a complete reproduction of Berlin's Reichstag sits lonely in a field, complete with a swollen clone of Norman Foster's glass dome, while in more directly Russian-aping style, the local branch of Inner Mongolia State University is housed in a boxy reincarnation of the iconic Stalinist Moscow State University building. The proportions of many of these constructions are slightly awry, and so one has a queasy feeling wandering in the shadow of towering pink, yellow and orange mirrorings of a fantasy Europe (Image 5). To locals, the speed at which all this has arisen is equally disorienting: almost every building has appeared from nothing in just two decades to meet the demand of post-Soviet cross-border shoppers, the town's population expanding even more rapidly than that of many eastern Russian locations has shrunk.

Browsing the emporia housed in the ground floors of these destabilising Sino-tsarist monstrosities, I sought to steer conversation with vendors away from sales patter towards more general topics.

'Ah yes, I can tell you're English or American because you have clean shoes,' I was told by one souvenir-seller. 'Russians' shoes are dirty.' This was a confusing statement for several reasons. For one thing, I had personally never perceived Russian footwear to be any grubbier than average, and, more relevantly, my own Adidas trainers were themselves covered in layers of transnational dust I had picked up trudging Yakutsk's dry summer streets. Indeed, Manzhouli's commercial pull draws in much more than dirt from Yakutia, for Russian shoppers come here not only from locations directly on the border but also places hundreds of miles 'inland'. My Yakut and Russian fellow-minibus passengers between Yakutsk and Neryungri had offered various reports on how things were in Manzhouli, with consensus emerging that vendors here had become much less friendly of late.

'Prices are higher and the Chinese are getting more and more mean,' the insurance worker Varvara had opined. But I found everyone, including this shoe-gazing curiosity-seller, to be very welcoming and willing to chat. He seemed unperturbed when I voiced doubt about the veracity of his footwear claims and, having confirmed that I was not Russian, enquired as to whether I would be interested in buying any Russia-themed souvenirs. A model tank, perhaps, or maybe a brown leather wallet bearing an inaccurate outline of Stalin's head.

These goods were signs of how Manzhouli, in many ways the quintessential border-mirror, faces both into and out of China. As well as Russian shoppers here to pick up key purchases for everyday life, the town also bustles with Chinese tourists who come to soak up the 'European' ambiance of the place (including the absurdist buildings) and to catch a first-hand glimpse of real live Russians. International Chinese tourism may have boomed in the 2010s, hence Red Square's Burberry-buyers, but this has been outstripped over the past decade by the stupefyingly rapid growth of domestic travel within China.[2] Most Chinese citizens still lack the means to travel abroad, and so the chance to sample a foreign culture without leaving home soil is an enticing one.

Correspondingly, Manzhouli's shops are an intoxicating gallery of intersecting international wares. Ranks of Russian *matrioshka* dolls line up on shelves above packets of *aaruul* (a hard Mongolian cheese in pebble-sized balls), busts of Marx and Lenin in fake bronze, shoulder bags bearing the words 'Russia' or 'Muscovite' in error-ridden Cyrillic under hammer-and-sickle logos, cheaply produced garments of Mongolian national costume, 'Stalin'-brand vodka, playing cards depicting female spies from Lona Cohen to Anna Chapman, Soviet coinage, 'Lenin'-brand vodka, hip-flask and shot-glass sets, pipes and lighters. As I searched in vain for souvenirs that actually had something to do with Manzhouli itself and was told 'Russian souvenirs are Manzhouli souvenirs!', this swill of Soviet, Russian, tsarist and Mongolian paraphernalia seemed a fitting reflection of modern China's status as a product of numerous global influences. Illustrating this in a different way, dusty corners at the backs of many shops displayed faded wall hangings wishing prosperity for the Chinese New Year, grandly depicting an incongruous array of images of Mao Zedong, Daoist wealth god Cai Shen and the benevolent grin of Benjamin Franklin. The blending here of genuinely 'foreign' Russian and Mongolian goods alongside fake Sinicised items in some ways created a 'foreign' atmosphere, but their combination and presentation could not have been anything other than Chinese.

I continued my tour of these blurred Eurasian visions to the outskirts of town where, midway between Manzhouli proper and the Russian border, a park filled with enormous *matrioshka* dolls is a popular draw for Chinese domestic tourists. Under intense sun beating down from a cloudless sapphire sky, I joined umbrella-wielding visitors from the nearby provinces of Heilongjiang and Jilin as they snapped pictures and prodded at the goods on sale inside the belly of the colossal central doll—a five-storey monster housing a café and souvenir stalls (Image 6). Surrounding this were more modest 5-foot miniatures depicting famous figures from all over the world, and since there was a doll representing most of the better-known countries in Asia, Europe and North America, it turned out that the Chinese, Mongolian and Russian flags flying at the park's entrance considerably undersold the worldliness of this location.

Each doll in the park carried an explanation of the character it depicted in English, Chinese and Russian. 'Russia royal court were full of magnificence and messiness, the color were dark and strong, complex in image,' read the English inscription on a doll displaying a nineteenth-century St Petersburg aristocrat. Greta Garbo appeared on the Swedish doll: 'Her works was Anna Karenina,' I read and, on the Spanish one: 'Spain is located on Liberia peninsula of southwest of Europe. Bullfight is the quintessence of Spain.' Judging from the reactions of most locals I spoke to, few Anglophones ventured this way, so the confusion that might have arisen from these signs seemed unlikely to cause an international incident. The Chinese versions were both more grammatically and more factually coherent, keeping Spain away from West Africa and Garbo out of Tolstoy's writing chair. The *matrioshka* park was yet another indication of how, while promoting a version of Russian- or Europeanness, Manzhouli largely succeeded in creating an unmistakably Chinese cultural atmosphere. Russian territory is close at hand but, given the monotonous flatness of the surrounding steppe, lies invisible at an indistinct distance. Correspondingly, in a town that exerts economic pull from here to Yakutia, visions of the Slavic neighbour, and indeed of the world at large, emerges on largely Chinese terms.

* * *

From a historical point of view, Manzhouli's boom as a site of China's free engagement with the northern neighbour represents a marked change in fortunes, for a century ago the town was under Russian control. Although Manzhouli was the first 'Chinese' stop on the China Eastern Railway, this was a Russian-built line laid via Harbin and Suifenhe to Vladivostok, on a strip of territory forcibly leased from Beijing in the late nineteenth century. Like the Trans-Siberian off which it branched, the CER was initially run like a sovereign entity in its own right, and with Manzhouli being home to the Russian signal workers staffing much of the rest of the line, business initially thrived in this crucial communications and transit hub. As I would be exploring further on in my journey, topsy-turvy political fluctuations across Manchuria saw the CER switch hands many times over the first half of the twentieth century between Russian, Soviet, Japanese and Chinese owners. But throughout this Manzhouli remained an important stop for trans-Eurasian trains and all aboard them: among my historical travel companions, Hu Yuzhi, Qu Qiubai, Sergei Tretyakov, Boris Pilnyak and Ethel Alec-Tweedie all changed trains here. Pilnyak had most of his leftist books confiscated since they seemed liable to spread the 'Bolshevik virus' into China,[3] and Tretyakov's 'German' endured a harrowingly thorough inspection of every last piece of his luggage.[4]

When Qu passed through in 1920, Manzhouli was in a much-diminished state with cross-border commerce having almost dried up with the arrival of the new, business-hostile Soviet government.[5] Yet even with socialist regimes on both sides the town remained important, and here in September 1953 the PRC took delivery of its entire second-generation run of banknotes, the money having been minted in Moscow because of manufacturing weakness in the young communist Chinese state.[6] Today, as I had observed, private business is booming again, and this vigorous commercial drive has effaced many traces of events of past decades. Manzhouli railway station has a new elongated façade in light grey panels and tinted glass topped by a golden dome. Yet, on the opposite side of the rails from the downtown's gaudy kitsch, remnants of the late nineteenth-century Russian settlement still remain.

Crossing a crumbling concrete footbridge on which hawkers spread out mats offering plastic children's spinning tops and rusty collections of Mao-era medals and pin badges, I picked my way across some trackside scrubland to a cluster of old wooden houses resembling those I had seen in Nerchinsk and outer Chita. The green-and-yellow painted panels and red roofs of some were presumably supposed to give the subsiding dwellings a cheery air, but even this attempt at renovation had long since been rendered antique by neglect. Stacks of dismantled wooden pallets leant up next to front doors, destined for the small spluttering hearths that released bobbles of puffy smoke into the hot outside air. This was a world apart from the thronging emporia I had just visited, and this urban village was separated from the new centre and its commercial bustle by a broad rank of railway sidings. Long trains of Siberian timber and shipping containers bearing the logo of Russia's Far Eastern Shipping Company acted like concentric fortifications blocking the old from the new, and while locomotives occasionally hissed and clanked down the tracks—resources away from Russia, containers of manufactured goods into it—there were always at least five ranks of wagons between here and central Manzhouli. Next to a nearby statue of Chinese Communist revolutionary and erstwhile foreign minister Zhou Enlai signs warned against crossing the rails.

I wandered through the dusty yards between the low dwellings, ducking under washing lines and skirting around modest kitchen gardens hemmed in by fences of dry twigs. In clearer patches, the stalls of communal toilets showed signs of recent attention, but they sat alone in their newness. An elderly lady and her daughter were sitting outside one of the more substantial looking homes, a brick building displaying an ironic-seeming silver plaque that stated that it had been under the protection of the local government since 2006. I said hello and, again grateful for how intelligible China's Mandarin-resembling north-eastern dialects are to the foreign listener, was soon in conversation. The two ladies were from the city of Qiqihar in next-door Heilongjiang province and had come to Manzhouli to find work.

'There's much more happening here than back home,' said the daughter animatedly. 'Manzhouli is becoming a rich city!' The statement seemed out of kilter with the modesty of their surroundings. Despite moving here six years ago, my interlocutors were yet to profit significantly from the border town's progress, as their living situation showed.

'We're here because the rent is very low,' the daughter continued, 'but actually we don't have much choice.'

Wasn't there a charm to the old Russian style of the building, I asked in a moment of romantic self-involvement, but the answer was pragmatic, and condemnatory: 'it's horrible,' she said. 'Not even slightly beautiful.'

Seeing that further questions about their fortunes were likely to be unwelcome, I made my excuses and walked away reflecting on the topsy-turvy historical dynamics at play in edge-space Manzhouli. Here hard-pressed Chinese migrants in a city whose present-day success is based on a Russian presence were obliged to live in housing built, but later abandoned, by earlier generations of people from that same country. Moreover, while these dilapidated but authentic properties lay neglected, the local construction industry was intensely focused on reproducing a version of Russianness that made no use of the actually Russian remnants in its midst. The focal point of Manzhouli's urban life had only shifted a few hundred yards over the tracks in the decades since this patch of land was the CER-oriented centre of activity here. But more than local events, it had been the 3,500-mile sweep of sovereign control and commercial ascendancy from Moscow to Beijing that had made the difference between quaintness and decrepitude for these houses and those who live in them.

That evening provided further cause to wonder about the delicate ironies that such changes in fortune have thrown up. As I walked down Zhongsu Street, I was approached by an enthusiastic man offering his services as a *pomogaika*, a term meaning 'helper' that has emerged in the Sino-Russian borderlands to refer to the Chinese locals who work as translators and general fixers for Russian visitors. I politely declined but asked the man about the name of the street we were on, which literally means 'Sino-Soviet'.

'It's called that because this is where Chinese and Soviet people stroll together!' he enthused. The *pomogaika* was young, perhaps thirty, but people of all ages in north-east China continue to refer to the northern country and its people as 'Soviet', at least when they are not conspiratorially labelling them with the longstanding term *maozi* (hairy ones). As the neon lights of central Manzhouli's cosy emporia began to blaze in the growing gloom, plenty of Sino-Soviet strolling was in evidence, although little of it seemed entirely in step. While groups of Chinese tourists posed for photographs next to the bronze statues of stereotypical 'Russians' that decorate the streets, smaller clusters of Russian shoppers made a few late purchases before moving on to local restaurants specialising in gloopily Russified Chinese dishes. Each side seemed to prefer a simulacrum of the other over direct contact.

Manzhouli does—like many border towns—offer more illicit nocturnal attractions, and thus opportunities for intimate international encounters. But out on the street Sino-Russian connection was all about fakery and performance. In front of the town's Shangri La Hotel, an imposing stage bearing advertisements for Chinese real estate giant Wanda formed an arena publicly celebrating supposed international camaraderie. With the South Korean global hit 'Gangnam Style' bouncing off the gleaming shop fronts opposite, a row of scantily clad Russian girls pivoted and dipped in time to the song's thumping beat and electronic swoops, observed with a blend of enthusiasm and confusion by a mixed group of Chinese tourists, street peddlers and migrant workers in grubby overalls. This display proved to be the high point of the show, a nightly feature of Manzhouli street life, and interest waned considerably as the strutting troupe was replaced onstage by a Russian man in a khaki baseball cap, who launched into an atonal and deeply emotional croon of 'Moscow Nights'. An echo of the 1950s socialist 'friendship' period between the two countries—an age when Beijing trusted Moscow to manufacture its banknotes—this Soviet classic also has a Chinese version that remains popular south of the border.

In combination, this at-best-equivocal display of warm relations between Chinese and Russian people, and the slowly collapsing piles of brick and wood on the wrong side of the tracks I had visited earlier, testified to Manzhouli's enthusiastic engagement with a new internationalism on Chinese terms, and its non-committal approach to the more distant past. As I returned to my hotel with the receding thumps of techno muffling the mournful hoots of cross-border trains, it was clear that a distinctly Sinicised twenty-first-century version of Russianness was in the ascendancy here.

* * *

Mirror visions of a Sinicised Europe emerged still more strongly as I headed east to the regional centre of Hailar before looping northward again to visit a group of frontier 'Russians' very different from Manzhouli's. A string of minibuses took me across grasslands made solemn by heavy brown rains, and after a few hours spent peering at *Men in Black II* and several Hong Kong kung-fu films on distant on-board TV screens, I entered Inner Mongolia's north-easternmost marches. Muddy turnings off the main road led alternately to tourist yurt camps and coal mines, demonstrating the difficult balancing act in which this region is engaged as it struggles simultaneously to draw visitors and also slake China's industrial resource thirst: Inner Mongolia promotes itself as a grassland wilderness, but it also has some of the country's most polluted cities. A message from the local authorities by the roadside captured this contradiction well: 'Protect the grasslands, protect the highway,' it declared sternly.

My fellow-passengers, which included three families from cities in China's south-western Guangxi province, were as fixated on the increasingly verdant scenes unfolding outside the bus windows as I was. As the weather cleared and we neared our destination, excitement reached fever-pitch. Fascinated shouts erupted as herds of Friesian cows were spotted grazing in the distance, while a flock of sheep browsing by the roadside elicited hushed gasps. For many residents of rapidly urbanising China, such scenes are an increasingly exotic sight, wildness of a kind forgotten after only a generation or two of city life. I, as a specimen of on-board fauna, also attracted attention and was questioned about what I might be doing in this distant land. As I did my best to answer, struggling with the accents of the grandparents—Guangxi people speak several languages, some entirely unrelated to Chinese, and none mutually intelligible with Mandarin—it was curious to me that I seemed so much more foreign here in the steppe than these southerners. We had all travelled thousands of miles across intersecting linguistic and cultural spheres to get here, yet the power of the idea of 'China' as unifying entity covering locations as diverse as subtropical Guangxi and quasi-Siberian Inner Mongolia is strong. And in an era of high-speed rail and ever-greater interconnection, the PRC is arguably a more unified incarnation of China than any that has existed since the nineteenth century. Just as the Soviet Union once created a smooth multi-ethnic space facilitating trajectories like the Volga–Kazakhstan–Yakutia route of Valeria in Neryungri, so the vast Chinese world is now a relatively frictionless whole, and the reigns of Chinese Communist Party (CCP) leaders Hu Jintao and Xi Jinping have seen consolidations of Chinese lands perhaps as significant as those achieved by dynastic founders Qin Shihuang or Mao Zedong. Consequently, even if these tourists were here to see people and places identified as 'Mongolian' or 'Russian', such things would remain unambiguously 'Chinese' in ways I certainly was not.

Also aboard the minibus were Langjuan and Dingding, two sisters in their twenties from a small fishing town in Guangdong, another southern province. After getting to know each other, we disembarked together in Labudaling, a modest town of square low-rise buildings surrounded by rolling hills. Labelled on maps as 'E'erguna', the Chinese transcription of the nearby Argun River that forms the China–Russia border here, Labudaling offers a microcosm of the tussle between tourism and industrial development at play in Inner Mongolia, and China at large. While the town serves as a jumping-off point for domestic visitors to the Russian borderlands farther north, foreign investment is also a priority for the authorities, and in addition to nearby mines, a towering Nestlé dairy products factory has jutted out of the local countryside since 2007.[7] Driven by both economic vectors, internationalisation here has taken on a haphazard and abstract form, with a local directive decreeing that all shop signs be in Chinese (the national language), Mongolian (the regional language), Russian (the language of the neighbours) and English (the global language). Less attention has been paid, however, to whether or not labels in each of these tongues is intelligible, and Labudaling's shop façades are thus a jumble of inscrutable Cyrillic, tiny vertical Mongolian script and English renderings. These include 'Mariachi Hotel', 'Dumpling Museum' and 'Donkey Meat Hotel' on establishments that are certainly not hotels or museums, nor have any connection with sombreroed Mexicans strumming *guitarróns*. Only the

Chinese characters are generally correct, and local globalism thus bends once again to distinctly Sinitic priorities.

Understandably, the sisters from Guangdong were paying less attention to such things than I was, and their first thought was to find Labudaling's nearby grasslands and experience them first hand as quickly as possible. Dingding was an experienced traveller and had journeyed across much of China's newly accessible touristic terrain including all the way to Tibet, something of a holy grail destination for a new generation of domestic backpackers. This time around, she was accompanying her younger sister to another quasi-mythical location 2,000 miles due north of their hometown: the invigorating lushness of the grasslands have a deep resonance in China's long history as a steppe-influenced empire, as well as in the imaginations of young explorers.

But despite surrounding Labudaling on all sides, this longed-for terrain began to seem frustratingly elusive as we headed to the town's ramshackle outskirts. Part of the problem was that a large swathe of the most pristine hills lay behind a high meshwork fence permeable only via a paid entrance gate.

'Chinese tourist sights are always behind walls with high ticket prices,' complained Dingding bitterly. 'These places should be open for everyone.' Having often experienced the strange blend of artifice and natural splendour that characterises the formal 'scenic spots' across China, from hemmed-in sacred mountains to old villages, I was inclined to agree.

Langjuan and Dingding's quest for a piece of true wilderness was therefore an arduous one and involved multiple wrong turns up steep concrete tracks that petered out after a few hundred yards, and a liberal dose of wading through mucky fields specked with litter and straggly weeds. Several times on our search for a barrier-free tract of grassland we passed the same group of Hui—Chinese Muslim—men who, distracted from their attempts to string up an electricity cable in a tree outside a local mosque, cast increasingly quizzical looks on our curious vagrant trio. As prospects of accessing the surrounding slopes waxed and waned, Langjuan and Dingding slipped between Mandarin and Cantonese, encouraging each other in their more intimate mother tongue not to give up hope. Our explorations had started in high spirits with Langjuan chatting excitedly about how pleased she was at her recent result in the *gaokao*, the nationwide university entrance exam. But the challenge of finding a piece of China not laid claim to by someone wishing to make money had put paid to much of this. We were all momentarily encouraged when, at one point near the perimeter of the fenced-in 'scenic spot', Langjuan spotted a gap under the tall green mesh. All of us squeezed frantically through, but our euphoria was short-lived as an elderly man in a red armband approached at great speed and shooed us away.

'You're not allowed in this way,' he said, 'park regulations. Not my choice.' He looked down at my legs, a frequent source of fascination for relatively hairless Chinese people. 'What are you wearing shorts for?' he asked, in something of a non sequitur.

'It's hot,' I said.

'You'll get bitten,' he admonished.

Dingding attempted to remonstrate with the man, but he was clearly struggling with much of what she was saying. This was a problem she was suffering from wherever she went in these northern parts, she later complained. Even when she was speaking Mandarin, her Cantonese accent caused difficulties for locals with only recent exposure to visitors from across the broader Sinosphere.

Sliding back under the fence felt like a deflating blow to the sisters' libertarian instincts, and I wasn't sure whether Langjuan, whose mood had been dipping all afternoon, could put up with much more. But a short last burst of exploration some distance away finally swept all of this aside, and, as we reached the summit of a bluff topped by a radio mast, a glorious view of the grasslands, and some wetlands beyond, finally opened out below. Lush grassy hummocks rolled off towards Russia like a pea green desert. The sun was setting in a valedictory blaze, making distant wind turbines cast huge slender shadows and, as a shepherd led his flock between some Hui graves lower down the hillside, the whole struggle against rampant private interest seemed worthwhile. We fell on our backs and rolled around to soak up as much as possible of this elusive landscape.

* * *

The following morning the three of us rose early, excited about continuing towards places whose interest was more human than environmental: to the north lay villages that because of their inhabitants carry an official 'Russian' designation. Across China, areas with significant populations of one of the country's fifty-five official ethnic minorities have been given similar labels. Both the system for classifying ethnic groups and this practice of territorial allocation were borrowed from Soviet antecedents. Not unlike Kazakhstan or Georgia, therefore, whole province-level units such as Inner Mongolia, Tibet and Xinjiang are formally 'autonomous' territories for China's Mongols, Tibetans and Uyghurs, while hundreds of smaller divisions of territory from prefectures to counties and even villages also notionally belong to one or other group. The extent to which 'autonomy' is actually enjoyed in these places is questionable in a political system intolerant of pluralism. Watching the USSR collapse also reduced Beijing's already debatable tolerance for regional separateness. Nevertheless, learning what purported 'Russianness' really meant here was why we were going, so the day's travel was an enticing prospect.

Breakfast in Labudaling with Langjuan and Dingding provided a foretaste of the multi-ethnic stories I would hear along this section of border. Settling down to a plate of large steamed *baozi* dumplings, we fell into conversation with an Evenk sheep farmer sitting at the next table who was enjoying an early morning fillip in the form of a deep steaming bowl of congee, and several tall green bottles of Qingdao beer. Grinning confidently from under his ragged flat cap, the man, who told us his name was Batu, toyed with me when I asked where he was from, asking me to guess.

'Do I look Han, Mongol, or something else?' he asked.

I had to confess ignorance, for despite Galina's enthusiastic introduction to his cross-border people back in the BAM Museum in Tynda, I was not yet an expert.

'I am Evenk!' he eventually said with pride, rummaging through the inside pocket of his black coat, fishing out his ID card and gesturing with a gnarled finger at the place displaying the 'ethnicity' category. 'You know,' he added, turning suddenly to point at the startled restaurant owner who was serving him another beer, 'I'm not like this man. And I'm not like these girls either!' he pointed at the sisters. 'They are Chinese.' In his inebriated morning enthusiasm, and possibly encouraged by my obvious outsiderness, Batu was keen to impress his distinctness upon me. 'We Evenk are Tungus people! Look at my boots!' he continued. Recalling conversations in Manzhouli, I began to wonder whether there was some sort of tacit footwear-based identity code in operation throughout Inner Mongolia. Batu calmed down slightly and finished, 'My grandfather fled Russia after the Revolution. Don't I look like a Soviet person?'

The global Evenk population numbers between 60,000 and 70,000 distributed across Russia, China and Mongolia, with pockets of these distended communities stretching from the Arctic through Yakutia all the way down to the grassy surrounds where we were now having this disjointed conversation. Inner Mongolia even has its own areas officially granted Evenk 'autonomy'.

I told him he did look quite Soviet, whatever that might mean, and Batu explained that a century ago his family had fled the October Revolution to China from somewhere east of Lake Baikal. This fateful journey had meant that here he was now speaking Chinese instead of Russian, eating *baozi* instead of *pelmeny* dumplings and drinking Qingdao instead of Baltika beer. In fact, Evenk experiences of ethnic separation are echoed among dozens of other indigenous North Asian peoples. The seventeenth- to nineteenth-century collision of Russia's eastward sweep and the Manchu Qing surge through Mongolian and Turkic lands imposed new borders between populations of Mongols, Buryats, Tuvans, Kazakhs, Tajiks, Nanai, Oroqen and many other native populations. Contact with the larger Russian and Chinese polities that have swallowed them has brought cataclysmic yet often parallel changes to the livelihoods of these groups. As Galina had explained to me, in Russia the Evenk were once especially known for their prowess as reindeer herders, but had since been 'modernised'. I mentioned this to Batu and asked if he knew anything about the ungulates.

'Reindeer?' he replied thoughtfully. 'I think I might have shot one once!'

Chinese Evenk perspectives on traditional ways of life had evidently also shifted significantly.

The longstanding indigenous residents of this region were not the only people to have been divided by inter-imperial borders, and like the Chinese migrants moving northward, Russians had also come the other way in centuries past. With breakfast over, and Batu now in conversation with the owner, Langjuan, Dingding and I went to find a bus to take us on to villages inhabited by their descendants.

Most of China's officially designated Eluosizu—ethnic Russians—are distantly descended from roving woodsmen, pastoralists and later gold-prospectors who settled in a sort of grey zone between empires. The 1689 Nerchinsk Treaty had formally banned such migration, and so the modest numbers of early arrivals were independent actors rather than formal Russian colonists. They likely did not even realise that they had crossed the hazily demarcated boundary in what, then as now, was a lush green landscape of rolling hills and cascading rivers. But in contrast to today's pine forest roads, along which our bus passed tourist rest stops and picnic tables, in centuries past the area was very difficult to reach. Consequently, the Qing authorities only gradually became aware of the 'illegal activities', as Chinese sources term them,[8] of the new Russian arrivals here. Having paid scant attention to the Argun region in the decades following Nerchinsk, from 1727 the Qing government felt obliged to return and establish sentry posts along the river. But policing the thousands of miles of open frontier that lay between the two empires was a daunting task, and these scattered outposts were unable to stop Russians who within a decade or two numbered in the thousands.

When gold was discovered in the nineteenth century, settlement accelerated further, and Russian motivations for flocking here thus mirrored those of the later wave of Chinese migrants who trekked up to Yakutia. But this pull-factor was not the only reason underlying the migration, for crises back in the western regions of the Russian Empire, including its 1856 defeat in the Crimean War and rural overcrowding, had also sparked enthusiasm in St Petersburg for renewed expansion into East Asia on a grand scale. Ultimately leading to two new Sino-Russian treaties and large territorial gains for Russia, whose consequences I would be exploring when I myself moved farther east, these developments drove further colonisation into northern Inner Mongolia. Tsar Alexander II's 1861 Emancipation of the Serfs had given peasants greater freedom to migrate to all points from here to the Pacific.[9] By 1884, the gold- and timber-endowed area we were entering hosted up to 15,000 Russian border-crossers, who greatly outnumbered the local herding population.

In typical mirror-fashion, however, this was only half the story, for the Russian Empire's mid-nineteenth-century ills were matched, and arguably exceeded, on the Chinese side. Russia's was only one of many foreign encroachments occurring all around China's edges at the time. The Chinese heartlands were, moreover, beset by famine and uprisings, including that of a group of Christians known as the Taiping who sparked the world's bloodiest ever civil conflict and left up to 30 million dead. Faced by such crises, the Manchu Qing authorities enacted reforms that included lifting a centuries-old set of prohibitions on settlement of the north-east—the traditional Manchu homeland—by anyone not from the native Mongol, Manchu or other Tungusic groups. Although a few Chinese bandits and exiles had defiantly made their homes here during earlier times, both they and the indigenous population soon dwindled into insignificance as vast numbers of Han people responded to the lifting of the ban by flooding here from the 1890s, mostly from the northern provinces of Shandong and Hebei. In one of the greatest migrations in human history, known as 'Bursting East of the Pass'—in reference to the Great Wall's Shanhai Pass through which migrants passed—over 25 million Han Chinese came to Manchuria and Inner Mongolia between the 1890s and 1930s.[10] Many arrived in the very same stretches of verdant rolling terrain along the Argun River to which Russians were coming from the west.

By the turn of the twentieth century, therefore, Chinese and Russian imperial populations were brought face to face in northern Inner Mongolia by the sweeping forces of imperial demise, war, revolution and natural disaster. The 1911 collapse of the Qing dynasty made it still easier for Russians to cross in search of mining and logging opportunities, and the October 1917 Revolution and the ensuing Russian Civil War brought 'White' supporters of the tsarist *ancien régime* fleeing here as they were pushed deep into Siberia by the Bolshevik advance. Those retreating included subjects from across the Russian Empire, and Ukrainians, Poles, Tatars and Czechs all spilled over the border here alongside Russians themselves. All had epic stories to tell, but a certain group of Czechs in particular embodied the extraordinary fates of those living through these tragi-heroic times. Originally forming a legion fighting for the tsar in Europe, the men had been cut off from their home continent when the Bolsheviks pulled Russia out of World

War I, and so decided to seek a roundabout return to their homeland east via Vladivostok and then to Europe by sea. Qu Qiubai had heard indirectly of the group's progress in Chita in 1920–1, and many remarkably achieved this feat by the early 1920s. But on their way east some found the draw of the rolling Inner Mongolian grasslands irresistible and settled here instead of continuing their cross-continental fight.

But if the events that brought Russian and Chinese settlers here were of cosmic historical scale, then the interactions which resulted were of a closer, more intimate nature. Before the Bolsheviks withdrew Russia from the war to end all wars, conscription took many Russian men far away to the European front, leaving a surplus of Russian women in the region. In a harbinger of the cross-border Soviet gender imbalances mentioned earlier, the female population came to outnumber the male by two to one according to some estimates,[11] and the predominantly male Chinese migrants thus found themselves in a unique social environment. As nature took its course, each side grew familiar with the other in part as a way of easing the hardships of frontier life. In many of the partnerships that resulted there was a good chance that at least one party was already spoken for, but local needs prevailed, and spouses or betrotheds thousands of miles away in Shandong or on Russia's grizzly western front were forgotten. The grand events of Sino-Russian history thus played out here in very personal ways.

As further conflict and political repressions prolonged the twentieth century's brutal onslaught on Russian men, a pattern of Chinese men marrying cross-border Russian women persisted. The children resulting from these matches came to be known officially as 'Sino-Russian Descendants' (*Hua'e houyi*), or less officially as *ermaozi*—the offspring of the abovementioned *maozi* and thus 'second-generation hairy people'. Throughout the twentieth century, this unique and comparatively isolated population continued to grow and intermarry. Now in its fifth or sixth generation, many of the approximately 8,000-strong community of Eluosizu still live in villages along the east bank of the River Argun, and here we eventually arrived a few hours north of Labudaling.

The bus stopped at a crossroads off the main highway, and we disembarked next to a wooden gatepost that bore one peeling Russian sign declaring 'Enhe's ethnic Russians welcome you!' Another bilingually advertised the 2006 'Year of Russia in China', accompanied by a cartoon brown bear and panda standing merrily hand-in-hand. After we had wondered momentarily what would happen next, a small multi-seat vehicle—known in Chinese as a 'bread van' (*mianbaoche*) given its resemblance to a stubby loaf of bread—rolled up and the driver offered us a lift into Enhe. Langjuan, Dingding and I climbed in, and it turned out that the man shared Batu's enjoyment of dancing playfully over China's patchwork of borderland identities. Dingding had for hours been expressing her excitement at meeting European-looking people speaking 'pure standard north-eastern Chinese', and, carried away by the same spirit, I asked the driver, who I thought looked sufficiently non-Han to justify the question, whether he was such a person.

'Yes, I am an ethnic Russian,' he replied.

'Do you speak Russian?'

'Yes,' he affirmed. 'Do you?'

I said I did, and his face suddenly assumed a somewhat pained look. 'Ah, then I do not speak Russian,' he corrected.

'So you never learnt?' I asked.

'Er, actually I'm not Russian at all,' he mumbled slightly sheepishly, although clearly not dispirited. 'I'm Han.'

Dingding and I were both likely guilty of falling victim to a naïve desire for borderland exotica, something I would find many Chinese tourists sought here. This encounter made me wonder whether I should henceforth try harder not to treat ethnicity—often seen in the West as a sacrosanct and inviolable component of self-identity but at times treated in China as a sort of mutable plaything—with such levity. Yet my driver's act, performed to please me and, I imagined, any number of other Chinese tourist passengers over the years, was a useful clue to what ethnic identity means in Enhe and farther north. Conversations with locals and travellers alike would reveal a stark mismatch between my own expectations of what being 'Russian' here might involve and various local Chinese understandings of it.

* * *

Enhe's primary places of interest for the Chinese domestic tourist are clustered along a gently sloping street leading down to a small river. On the riverbank, large earth-moving vehicles were marshalling piles of pebbles and mud, laying a flat foundation for new additions to the town's modest accommodation options. Plans were afoot to fill Enhe with enough attractions to justify charging an entrance fee for visitors to the village. Here too the logics of China's touristification of the borderlands, resented by Dingding in Labudaling, were creeping in, and Enhe would certainly not be China's only village whose population would be fenced in like exotic zoo animals. To make its 'Russian' identity clearer, many nearby cement and brick buildings had been clad in resplendently shiny panels of varnished wood, apparently emulating the style of traditional Russian cottages. As well as ordinary people's houses, this practice had been applied to the two-storey local government offices, which consequently looked like a sort of monstrous sauna cabin.

After dubiously admiring these architectural stylings, Dingding, Langjuan and I settled at a local youth hostel. Leaving them to freshen up after the journey, I set out for a brief exploration of the village streets, soon attracting the attention of a toothless man in an off-white shirt who came out of his lopsided wooden cottage—this one really was made of wood—to greet me.

'Zdravstvuite,' he said. The thick consonant clusters of the formal Russian word for 'hello' are difficult for most foreign learners of the language, and speakers of Chinese, which intersperses every consonant with a vowel, often struggle especially. But Ivan was in fact a mother-tongue Russian-speaker, and his linguistic troubles turned out to be more a result of his near-total dental deficit and the fact that he had very rarely used the language in recent decades. Ivan told me that he himself was not from Enhe, as his original home lay to the west in an area directly on the Russian border. Local settlements there still bear the names of the Qing sentry posts erected to forestall the creeping Russian arrivals, and villages named Fifth Watchtower (Wuka), Sixth Watchtower (Liuka), Seventh Watchtower (Qika) reel off as they run northwards along the Argun's looping bank.

'We are poor,' Ivan said as he gestured me into his yard to sit on a tree stump, explaining that he had only come to Enhe as an old man so that relatives could look after him. 'Because I can't work anymore I have to live here now with my son. There's not much to do if you can't work, although I still help in the garden,' he pointed smiling at the neat lines of carrots that grew in front of the house, resembling the shriv-elled ranks of a defending army. He explained more about his family past—a Russian mother and a Chinese father who had met and mar-ried back in the 1920s. But, frustratingly, many of the details were lost as I strained to understand his phonetically indistinct cobweb of words. As I gently asked for clarifications or further details, we seemed to understand each other less and less: his largely forgotten Russian was not up to describing fading memories, and my efforts to switch the conversation into the Chinese he had used for most of his life drifted by ignored. Perhaps he was glad simply to have the chance to speak Russian to someone who looked the part, or perhaps even in this space of overlapping worlds, I was too physically unlike a Chinese-speaker for that language to seem appropriate. Whatever the blurring and mixing of times past, linguistic, ethnic and national identity today seemed as closely linked here as ever.

I left Ivan to his carrots and continued away from the river. A little farther up the hill, Irina and Katya—Russian names given at birth rather than chosen as in Manzhouli—were sitting on their shop veran-das in the sun. I bought a bottle of iced tea and joined them. A genera-tion younger than Ivan, their Russian was almost non-existent, but their faces still bore the unmistakable trace of their mixed heritage. Joking about the Slavic origins of her protuberant ears, Katya lamented the poor state of her Russian language.

'We used it a bit at home when I was a child,' she said, 'but both my parents are mixed so their Chinese was always better. We learnt it at school at the beginning too,' she added. 'But that was before the Cultural Revolution. It all stopped after that, things got really bad.' During the murderous bedlam and fits of denunciation that dominated Mao's 1960s and '70s campaign to reform China's traditional culture, perceived 'foreign' elements within the country were just as reviled as remnants of the imperial past. For residents of these borderlands, the situation was all the worse because the Cultural Revolution (1966–76) coincided—and was in many ways part of the same burst of PRC political extremism—with a cooling in once-friendly Sino-Soviet rela-tions. Mao had greatly admired Stalin, but he felt much less positive about his successor Khrushchev, and suspicion between Beijing and Moscow metastasised throughout the 1960s into full-blown enmity.

This led to a near-complete shut-off of contact with the northern neighbour, and the USSR was now designated a 'revisionist' power practising a deviant form of 'socialist imperialism'. In this poisonous atmosphere, Chinese citizens with a Russian background were accused of being members of 'oppositionist cliques' (*zaofanpai*), serving as operatives for Soviet special forces or, most curiously, plotting to found a 'mixed blood republic' (*mijisi gongheguo*). This latter slur carried both linguistic and political barbs, the first word *mijisi* being an adaptation of the Russian word *meshat'*, 'to mix'. As applying these dangerous political labels became a way of settling local as well as national scores, imprisonments, beatings and worse were *de rigueur* for many unfortunate Enhe residents during these dark days.

Yet in a happier present with the borderlands transformed from a zone of stigma and suspicion to a place for domestic tourists to explore China's internal exotica, this very same 'mixed' background is a revenue-generating asset. Many local homes in Enhe offer homestays to visitors wishing to lodge in 'traditional' Russian fashion, and Irina and Katya's shop offered versions of the 'Sino-Russian–Mongolian Souvenirs' available in Manzhouli. As we discussed Enhe's past and present, we were surrounded by racks of guidebooks. Their accounts of the complex history of the region mostly gloss over the Cultural Revolution, placing stronger emphasis on how its inhabitants have long been loyal to a multi-ethnic China, a selective account suggesting how much had changed here.

I bought one of these books and, browsing it later back at the hostel, I came upon the tale of a half-Russian, half-Chinese hero named Nikolai Gromov, or Wang Jiarong in Chinese. Gromov's story unfolded in the winter of 1944 as he was spying for the Soviet Red Army on the Japanese, who at the time were occupying north-eastern China. Approached one day by a sympathetic Han Chinese policeman, Gromov was warned of Japanese plans to force him to betray his colleagues, and, sure enough, he was accosted the following day and led into a sparsely furnished room by a moustachioed Japanese interrogator. As the questioning began in Chinese, the quick-thinking Gromov feigned misunderstanding and claimed to have no knowledge whatsoever of the language—one of his mother tongues. He insisted instead that his Japanese tormentor stick to more challenging Russian, putting

his captor on the back foot with this act of linguistic shapeshifting.
Gromov then refuted all accusations that he was a secret operative,
claiming instead to be a Russian farmer who had simply wandered over
the nearby border while drunk one night.

'You are lying!' shouted the Japanese agent, pulling out a cigarette.
'You think you can trick me?!' As he fumbled for some matches,
Gromov saw his chance and, picking up the stool he was sitting on,
thumped his foe over the back of the head before fleeing out of the
building towards the border river, which, this being winter, was frozen.
By luck, the interrogation had occurred at precisely the time when the
Soviet Red Army's horses were down on the opposite bank having their
morning drink. Nimbly crossing the river, Gromov therefore managed
a successful escape since the pursuing Japanese forces were unwilling
to open fire on Soviet troops. The narrative concluded by noting that
after a spell back in the USSR working in forestry, Gromov returned
to China and the 'bosom of his ancestral land', living to the ripe old age
of ninety-three.

Besides these nationalism-affirming biographies on sale in Katya and
Irina's shop, other local products included sets of postcards depicting
local Russian-looking people and bearing the English label 'Mysterious
Sino-Russian Descent Groups'. Yet for all their complex origins, there
was little mystery here about how their legacy was being mobilised to
forge an image of a peaceful China in which all ethnic groups live in
perfect harmony.

Did the women mind this?, I asked, was it not a bit strange to have
one's background used for political purposes, not to mention legions of
new visitors arriving to gawp at people seen as semi-foreign curiosities?

'Economic development is generally good,' says Katya. 'People are
better off here now, and the tourists are pretty friendly. We don't mind
too much being seen in this way as we're proud of our heritage.' This
greater sense of enfranchisement among China's northern 'Europeans'
was a notable contrast with the resentment felt back in Yakutia at being
seen as exotic foreign Asians. China was on the up, and so the 'Sino-
Russian descendants' seemed happy to be involved in this progress
however they could.

'My main worry is the local environment,' continued Katya. 'Too
many visitors can really spoil things, and this landscape is so beautiful.'

The digging and shunting on the riverbank, the plans for a village entrance fee, and the numerous tour buses I had seen thundering their way up the narrow roads to Enhe seemed to justify her concerns. Environmental efforts were being made, and solar panels and miniature wind turbines perched atop lampposts along the village's main streets. But growing piles of rubbish were accumulating in the outskirts, and heading back to the hostel I was confronted by a scraggy black mutt with bleeding eyes rooting through one of these. Enhe, I thought, might not yet have found the kind of mirrored equilibrium attained in its earlier Sino-Russian decades.

Similarly sensitive to environmental concerns were the other back-packers where Langjuan, Dingding and I were staying. The hostel, where I was the only non-Chinese guest, was housed in an eco-friendly complex of low log cabins surrounding a central yard with most shared facilities, including composting toilets, located outdoors. Energy-saving light bulbs, a pin board for leaving travel tips on neon Post-it notes, and an honour-based system for paying for small items such as washing powder and snacks by leaving money in a box completed an overall picture of low-impact communal life. Contrasting vividly with the grasping atmosphere of individualistic urban China to which I would later be heading, such an ethos reflected the aspirations of a new generation of young, independent middle-class Chinese travellers. The common rooms in hostels that have sprung up nationwide over the last decade offer backpackers like my own travel companions a forum for meeting friends from across this huge country. Here one can share both youthfully idealistic visions for China's future, and lament the lack of community and environmental values in today's society.

I rejoined Langjuan and Dingding, and we quickly fell into conversation about such matters with a group of other travellers in their twenties. After a time, we moved on to a local Korean-style restaurant where we ate fried meat and vegetables over a central hotplate. Initially, travel stories formed the backbone of discussion as we shared tall bottles of Snow Beer and dipped slices of pork, beef and aubergine into small pots of ground sesame, cumin and pepper seeds. Fiona from Hebei province was the eldest of the group, and had been alone in introducing herself to me using an English pseudonym, despite the fact that we were speaking Chinese. This marked her out as a member of the 'post-1980-generation' among whom adopting alternative names for use with 'foreigners' remains common. By contrast, everyone else was a 'post-1990' child—social change in China since Mao has been fast enough for each decade to spawn a completely new generation—and were all content to use their 'real' names, as though reflecting greater self-confidence in China's global interactions.

Fiona was on vacation from her secretarial job in a big company in the northern town of Shijiazhuang and was hoping to make use of her precious travel time by heading west to the distant Xinjiang–Tibet highway. She was reluctant to go alone, however, and was trying to entice Weixie, a handsome communications student from Zhejiang, to go with her. Much to Fiona's frustration, Weixie remained noncommittal and, like the others, had a laid-back live-in-the-moment attitude that discouraged him from making grand plans. Many of the group had come to Enhe looking for the same grassland paradise that Dingding and Langjuan had sought in Labudaling. Destinations had been researched online, tickets bought, and long trains up to the north-east boarded. To save money, several of the group had elected to spend fifteen or more hours sitting on extremely cheap bench seats rather than getting a sleeping berth or taking the high-speed lines that now stretch increasingly close to China's edges.

Conversation about Fiona's plans led us to discussion of the destinations in question, and then to debating China as a whole. Xudong, an architecture student living in Shanghai, was first to relate the adventures sought by young Chinese backpackers to her wider discontents with contemporary society: 'Xinjiang and Tibet are such amazing travel locations, but they're always made to seem so dangerous on TV,' she said. Since unrest in Tibet in 2008 and intensifying conflict in Xinjiang since 2009 where the Chinese state is now engaged in a campaign of mass repression and imprisonment of the local Uyghur population, China's western territories have come to seem problematic to the country's own population, despite official government efforts to portray both places as just as calm and harmonious as Enhe. Young people in particular are attuned to a sense that if the government insists people are living in blissful harmony, then something is probably amiss. Such complex issues were close to Xudong's heart, for although studying in Shanghai, she had grown up in Xinjiang, her parents having worked on the railway to the regional capital Urumqi, which opened in 1999. The others murmured assent and conversation quickly moved on to more general gripes with the PRC's propagandistic media environment and government corruption.

'What do you think of our Communist Party then?' asked Weixie, turning to me with a sudden directness amid the more impersonal discussion.

Throughout the evening, I had tried to remain ingratiating and peaceable, for foreigners' complaints about China always have a different ring to those of citizens. In a country where outsiders are treated comparatively well and there is so much to inspire admiration and wonder, negative views are understandably taken badly. I therefore attempted to remain diplomatic, mumbling something about the contradictory feelings many Westerners have when observing the developmental advances made recently in China, while also knowing it has occurred in a one-party Communist state. But if I did have stronger feelings, I perhaps need not have concealed them.

'I hate those bastards,' rejoined Weixie. 'To be honest it would have been better if we'd ended up like Taiwan, if the Nationalists had won the Civil War. Don't get me wrong, I'm proud of being Chinese and all we've achieved, but it isn't because of the Communists.' No one around the table seemed inclined to disagree with this statement.

'Yeah, they're just all out for themselves, the Party is basically a way for people to steal,' chipped in Heng, another student. 'All this anti-corruption stuff lately is just dog farts,' he added, using a colourful expression essentially meaning 'shit'.

Further conversation made clear the extent to which views ranging from suspicion to revulsion of the Party were standard among these chance fellow-travellers. Despite coming from quite different parts of the country, they were united by age cohort, by experience of an ever-more standardised national education system, and by membership of China's hundreds-of-millions-strong urban middle class. Arguably having as much in common as any previous Chinese generation, they also had the means and the inclination to explore the vast Chinese world on a much grander scale than was possible when only intellectuals such as Qu Qiubai or Hu Yuzhi could wander the country. There was therefore an irony in their opposition to the Party and its venality, for they owed much of their capacity for mutual empathy and connection, not to mention their shared command of standard Mandarin, to the very same political situation they found so objectionable. In a contradiction that continues to puzzle many observers of China, the CCP has managed simultaneously to create a system with profound flaws, and to provide its subjects with the tools via which to share their discontents. Negative comments are sharply policed online, but face to face in this freewheeling backpacker setting, 100 candid flowers could bloom unchecked.

We were offline, but the internet itself nevertheless featured high among my dining companions' shared cultural repertoire, both as the means via which they had discovered Enhe, and as the place they went to read about Party misdeeds and local scandals before such 'sensitive' information was censored. As conversation moved from matters political to the online realm, Weixie, Xudong, Fiona, Heng and others exchanged WeChat contact details using smartphone QR-codes, swapped tips about new bands they had discovered on social networking site Douban and checked train times for their onward trips to all points of the compass.

In another of the restaurant's private rooms next to ours, a raucous Chinese rendition of the Sino-Russian song 'Moscow Nights' was underway as a group of somewhat older tourists indulged their Soviet nostalgia here on China's Russian fringe. As though inspired to compete, Fiona decided it was time for us to have a singsong and, asking everyone to put down their phones, told each of us around the table to perform a favourite tune. While Langjuan and Dingding managed a nervous rendition of a tune by Cantonese megastar Andy Lau, I at first dredged up from memory a song by Singaporean singer-songwriter Tanya Chua, but was quickly told I should do something English. Perhaps, Weixie suggested cheekily, the national anthem would be good. References to God and queens seemed strangely apt after our discussion of authoritarian politics, and I awkwardly managed a few bars. Mercifully, this seemed to placate my karaoke-loving companions, and it was soon suggested we pay the bill. Following one Maoist dictum about the benefits of taking a stroll after a meal ('after eating walk 100 steps and you'll live until 99', he is supposed to have uttered), we made our way out into the balmy evening, roaming the pitch-black village streets with the Milky Way arching overhead. Full of barbecued meat and mildly inebriated, the group seemed content to have set the world, or at least a Chinese part of it, to rights.

* * *

While ambitious long-distance itineraries were being hatched back in Enhe, I would be continuing my more step-by-step borderland route, and, leaving Langjuan, Dingding and the others the next morning, I took a rainy three-hour bus ride through birch forests and over lush plains to Shiwei. Households in Enhe had only recently adopted the vogue for offering 'Russian'-style homestay accommodation, but Shiwei was ahead of the game, and everyone seemed to have beds available for fresh-off-the-bus tour groups. Once home to a Mongol clan, the Mengwu, who gave the Chinese language Menggu, its modern word for Mongolia, Shiwei is a more established stop for the sort of trippers I saw being disgorged from buses as I arrived.

I lodged with the Bian family, and on entering their courtyard was greeted by Lyuba who was one of the most Russian-looking Chinese people I had yet met.

'I'm fifth generation, so there's plenty of Han in me,' she said cheerily in Chinese as she ushered me into the dining room. 'But when I go to Manzhouli, or even Beijing, everyone tries to talk to me in Russian or English, thinking I'm foreign.' Like Dmitri and Katya back in Yakutsk, Lyuba had been linguistically misplaced by fellow-citizens unaware of their own country's ethnic diversity.

Lyuba bustled off to see to a newly arrived tour group and left me to a late breakfast of home-baked Russian bread, clotted cream, jam and milky tea. The bread—locally called *lieba* derived from the Russian *khleb*—was, like many such doughy items in China, somewhat sweeter than its true Russian counterpart. But this was nevertheless evidence of culinary habits quite different from those of the surrounding Han or Mongol populations. Mr Bian, Lyuba's husband, joined me. With his scruffy black hair and slight features, he looked somewhat less Russian than she did and also seemed to have less time for his family's Russian past than his role running a 'Russian'-style homestay would have suggested.

'My name's Bian Yikan,' he said. 'And of course I don't have a Russian name, I'm Chinese, even if my grandpa did come from Irkutsk.' His own identity established, we moved on to me. Was I from the Soviet Union, he asked. No, I answered, declining as before to point out that it would be difficult to be from there these days.

'Aha, English!' he said, mischievously. 'You bullied China during the Opium Wars!' Britain's mid-nineteenth-century imperial belligerence, during which it seized Hong Kong and forced China to open up to trade at the point of a gun, often comes up as a topic of conversation with more combative Chinese interlocutors. But Mr Bian meant nothing by this light-hearted mention of events, which, coinciding with Russia's annexation of many of its own eastern territories, marked the dawn of an era known of late in China as the 'Century of Humiliation'. Everything was fine between the English and the Chinese now, Mr Bian thought, and for him at least there were no hard feelings.

'I think it's all been ok since Hong Kong was returned in 1997,' he said, 'China was united again and now we just have Taiwan to deal with.' I admitted that at school we had learnt little of the Opium Wars, or indeed about any aspect of Britain's imperial past. 'Of course, of course,' Mr Bian nodded, 'every country just teaches the good bits of its history.'

I said I admired his balanced perspective and, possibly still looking for ethnicity that was not there, asked if this relativism had anything to do with his mixed heritage. Mr Bian quickly dispelled any such idea. 'Bah, none of that means anything to me, to be honest,' he said. 'I don't speak a word of Russian and we have no contact or communication with them.' He gestured offhandedly through the window towards a nearby hill, which, visible over the vegetable patch, lay on the Russian side of the obscured Argun River.

Had he been to Russia ever, I asked. Or did he want to?

'No, I haven't,' he said. 'You have to go all the way down to Manzhouli—over 300 kilometres away!—to cross the border. Even when the river's frozen here and you could just walk across, they're still watching us from the hills. But anyway, things in the Soviet Union aren't good now. Of course, they came through here in 1945 to liberate us from the Japanese, but their situation is bad these days. The Soviet Union isn't developed like China is.'

I asked why this might be.

'They don't have good fertiliser,' he said, perhaps revealing the agricultural prism through which village life had made him see the world.

'Plus Russian people don't know how to work. They just want to earn enough to eat that day, then they stop and relax. Chinese people are different—they want money to save up, buy a car, an apartment, things like that. They keep working.'

So they shared nothing with the other side of the river?, I asked.

'Look,' said Mr Bian, evidently trying to put this topic, about which he was likely asked by every difference-seeking domestic tourist, to bed. 'China definitely has its problems. The country is huge and the leaders have a real task on their hands to keep it all going. But we feel fully Chinese, we love our country. As for here and us Russians, well yes, the geography is the same on both sides of the river, but the people are completely different.'

Mr Bian had brought up a familiar set of contrasts between the national characters of each nation, from orderly versus chaotic to hard-working versus lazy, and this boundary-drawing, I reflected as I went out to explore the village, was consistent with a whole historical perspective. The Opium Wars, which took place 2,000 miles away and 150 years ago, occupied a much more prominent place in his mind than any ideas about past cross-border ties, a fact running counter to the current efforts of local tourism agencies to rehabilitate Sino-Russian stories like that of Nikolai Gromov. The Chinese Cultural Revolution and its Russian equivalent under Stalin, had been disastrously destructive social engineering campaigns, but there was no doubt that they had had many of their intended effects in removing the possibility of loyalty to another state over the river. Today's wedge between communities either side of the border is difficult to imagine removing, and while the Yakuts are stuck with the Russians, these 'Russians' are stuck with the Chinese.

In this climate, even the most fervent attempts to forge cross-border linkages can become almost comically ineffective, as I discovered on a nearby stretch of the Argun riverbank. On Shiwei's north-western edge, a sloping concrete track led down to the 'Friendship Bridge', a crossing-point to Russia, which, Mr Bian had told me, is not open to passenger traffic. The road is used mainly by lorries transporting quarried stone from the Russian side to the Chinese, a young People's Liberation Army guard explained as he loitered outside a wooden sentry box in an ill-fitting dark green uniform. Originally from Xi'an, the guard had been in the army two years and, hands barely poking out of his long sleeves, stood idly chatting to the cluster of tourists that had just stomped off a bus to snap pictures of the bridge and nearby Chinese border marker. A few members of the group who were not wielding cameras or smartphones stood watching some decrepit Russian cars and military jeeps which were crawling along the opposite bank.

'There's a Russian car. That one's called a Lada!' a man shouted, adding, 'Those cars are terrible!' for good measure.

A short way along from the sentry box, I spent a while chatting to a souvenir vendor whose small hut stood on the riverbank almost directly under the bridge. He was from Heilongjiang province and was keen to stress the authenticity of his wares, which, it was fairly obvious, were not very authentic. 'I go to Russia all the time!' he said with exaggerated sincerity. 'Where else could I buy all this stuff?' He swept his arm emphatically over a shelf that included packets of chocolate dotted with random Cyrillic letters and bottles of the same Chinese-made 'Stalin' and 'Lenin' vodka brands I had seen in Manzhouli.

On my way back from the bridge, I was stopped at the roadside by a Chinese man in oily overalls, his muscly arms smeared in tar up to the elbows. He looked expectant, and made a gesture that looked a lot like he was downing an imaginary shot. 'Drink?' he enquired hopefully.

It took a second, but I realised he must have assumed from my appearance that I was coming from the other side of the bridge and had brought a gift. I asked if this was the case, explaining that I was not, regrettably, doing any such thing. 'Oh,' the man said with disappointment. 'Yeah, the truck drivers often bring us alcohol. We love it. Sorry, I thought you were from the Soviet Union.' Quarried stone was evidently not the only Russian product making its way over the Argun.

This hint at human contact was a welcome glimmer in what was otherwise a vivid mismatch between the rampant touristic rambling of the Chinese side and an atmosphere of dilapidation and steely militarised sternness that drifted over from the Russian bank opposite. Upriver, this contrast between joviality and foreboding was especially stark. I joined a group of Beijing and Shanghai tourists looking across at the Russian village of Olochi, a literal stone's throw's away opposite Shiwei, and we observed a small group of youthful-looking Russian soldiers moving despondently in and out of a metal guard shack near some patrol boats and a rusting half-submerged barge. Olochi's cluster of low wooden buildings interspersed with the occasional rectangular Soviet apartment block made a dispiriting backdrop, and as the soldiers finished whatever it was they were doing and plodded in a desultory file back towards the village, one of the Beijing tourists shouted, 'Where are you going?!' in Chinese. 'Come back!'

Haloushou, another man to my right ventured, attempting valiantly to pronounce the Russian *khorosho* (good). But these entreaties failed to gain any attention, and once the soldiers had disappeared, many of the tourists lost interest and seeped back towards their waiting buses. A rhythmic Chinese ditty *xiache paizhao, shangche shuijiao* 'get off the bus and take a photo, get on the bus and go to sleep' is often used to describe group package tours, and these visitors were sticking closely to the script.

Once the tourists had rumbled off, I turned around and noticed that we had been standing in front of a tall stage, which, facing across the river, was erected so that song and dance performances could be projected over the Argun's sludgy brown murk to any Russians who cared to watch from the other side. Russian and Chinese flags decorated a backdrop decorated in whimsical quasi-Mongolian patterns. There was some balance here, however, and looking again at Olochi I realised that the Russians too had set up their own timber stage. In an echo of the ursine iconography seen at the entrance to Enhe, large photos of a brown bear and a panda were visible on a background that bore the legend 'strengthen friendship between Chinese and Russian peoples'. Yet there was a key difference between the two stages, for while the Chinese construction was both visible to the Russian side and had stools laid out in front of it so that Chinese tourists might share the enjoyment of the spectacles performed here, the Russian stage merely fronted on to a steep patch of slippery-looking mud sloping town towards the river. No Russian tourist would dream of venturing to remote and crumbling Olochi, which in any case lies bureaucratically sealed off within one of Russia's many restricted border zones. Watching a dance show there was even less of an option. Shiwei's greater activity and openness and its attempts, however misdirected or Sinicised, to bringing together cultures seemed to be captured well by the Chinese stage's dual purposes.

Back in the centre of the village too, the real entertainment was by the Chinese for the Chinese. That evening, amid the neon lights and bright shopfronts of Shiwei's slickly paved central square, a huge bonfire was blazing and, accompanied by thumping techno music, a free-spirited air of revelry reigned. Many of the tourists I had encountered throughout my stay were here, and the somewhat harried air they had had earlier as they followed packed itineraries had now dissolved. Conga lines and Riverdance-imitating rows of kicking dancers formed spontaneously as sparks flew up into the clear night air. I made my way beyond the fire to look again at the Russian side of the Argun, but it was dark, completely invisible in the sable night. The flashing bulbs and leaping shadows must make a bizarre nightly spectacle for Olochi's few residents, but the blackness and the light seemed like a suitable metaphor for the difference between these two places, which, though united by history and only 150 yards apart, now seemed like perfect opposites.

5

THE RUSSIAN FAR EAST

AN EMPTYING BREADBASKET

Cutting eastwards from Inner Mongolia to the next, very different point of border contact in Heilongjiang province meant lopping off China's northernmost tip. A series of buses rumbled me along rutted roads through dense birch forests and alongside seething rivers thick with summer swell. Brief stops for meals occurred in settlements, lying on sites where Mongol and Manchu military brigades once overnighted on cross-country campaigns. The wild tracts of the Greater Khingan Mountains have long awed anyone choosing to live here, and the names of small towns such as Genhe and Yitulihe through which we passed refer to the local rivers (*he* meaning 'river') that have subjugated man's presence to their natural force. After a brief overnight stop in the gritty railway and lumber hub of Jiagdaqi, which takes its own toponym from a kind of pine tree in the indigenous Oroqen language, it was time to move on to another river-named location—Heihe or 'black river'. The floodplains of this black river, more properly 'black dragon river', or Heilongjiang in Chinese, is a borderland space where China and Russia are separated more widely than across the sluggish Argun. No international bridge yet spans the mighty Amur, as it is called in Russian, though two are under construction—more enthusiastically from the Chinese side. But despite the spatial divide, the Sino-

Russian stories awaiting me would be of myriad cross-border links and a mirrored interdependency unlike the divisions I had encountered in Russian Inner Mongolia.

As we trundled into Heihe, Mr Ren, who was sitting next to me on the bus, poked me in the leg. A Han Chinese coal miner travelling for his annual visit to see his ailing mother, Mr Ren professed to be 'a man without culture'. He had never studied, he said, which was why he now had to spend his days in the darkness of the pit, yet this had not narrowed his horizons entirely. Before mining, he had sojourned as a timber-worker on the other side of the fast-approaching border, spending blurrily recollected nights drinking with Russian co-workers on the outskirts of Irkutsk. As a result, Mr Ren had picked up some of the language.

'*Prrrivet!*' he said, offering the Russian word for 'hi' by way of an example. His accent—particularly his mastery of the trilled 'r'—was much better than that of many Russian-speaking Chinese people I had met.

'*Orrrchen khoroshorr!*' he then exclaimed, giving a thumbs-up before adding, 'that means "very good"!' His command of the 'r' was indeed itself 'very good', but his swell of pride at this talent seemed to have got the better of him, and much of his vocabulary rolled around coated in an unnecessary rhotic gloss.

'*Pivorr!*—that means "beer"!' he said. There is not, strictly speaking, an 'r' in *pivo*.

Heihe was the first Chinese city of any substantial size that I would be visiting, but I was unable to pay much attention to our approach as Mr Ren continued to reel off his impressive string of contextless Russian words.

'*Vodka!*—that's Russian *baijiu!*'

We sped past some billboards advertising the town's latest luxury villa development.

'*Mashinarr* means "car"!'

Up ahead, another coach had stopped by the roadside, and the driver was standing hopelessly at the back of the vehicle looking into the engine. Traffic was light, but our driver ignored him and sped past.

'*Devurrrshka* means "girl"!'

This last example had given Mr Ren an idea. He leaned over conspiratorially: 'I know some bad words too, you know.'

'Really?' I answered, trying not to sound too curious. Initially startled at having unsolicited pokes directed into my leg, I had warmed to Mr Ren's irrepressible cheerfulness and its sudden transition to vulgarity.

'Yes …' he said, still in an earnest whisper before quickly blurting out, '*Suka! Yebat!*', gleeful in the rest of the passengers' incomprehension. 'You know what those mean, right?' Yes, I said, I did, slightly embarrassed that such profanities, however unintelligible, were being bellowed in front of a busload of curious onlookers.

'Right!' chuckled Mr Ren. '*Orrrchen Khoroshorr!*'

But if I seemed prudish to Mr Ren, he need not have been concerned about the rest of Heihe's population, for despite its size, this city facing Russia's Blagoveshchensk across the Amur had few genteel pretences about it. Amid the biblical rainstorm that greeted our arrival, I heard plenty of the invective admired by Mr Ren as several groups of Russian visitors dashed around the streets in ponchos cursing the deluge. As this boisterous clientele in flip-flops and crocs waddled through puddles, entering and leaving shops, it was impressive how little the adverse weather was inhibiting Heihe's trans-Amur commerce. With all the city's bilingual signage along its tree-lined streets, and even route maps on local buses in Russian, Heihe is well appointed to serve its visitors. All post-Soviet ideological needs are also catered for, and restaurants I passed on the way to my hotel were named to honour both Presidents Vladimir Putin and his less authoritarian, and less sober, predecessor Boris Yeltsin.

Such are Heihe's adaptations to the visitors that some Russian retirees have even chosen to live longer term here in recent years, attracted by a higher and more affordable quality of life. The proximity of Blagoveshchensk has made it possible to pop over the river to draw one's monthly pension and then return to spend it on cheaper Chinese goods and accommodation. Yet while media both sides of the border, and indeed Dmitri back in Yakutsk, have implied that this has occurred on a vast scale, in reality it is a phenomenon more widely discussed than practised. The dozens or at most hundreds of trans-frontier pensioners who have settled in Chinese border towns are still dogged by visa troubles and fluctuating exchange rates—brought to the fore in 2014 when an oil price drop caused a crash in the rouble—meaning they rarely imagine staying forever.

Having located my hotel, a cheap family-run affair near the centre of town with grubby off-white concrete walls and tiled floors, I walked through the rain to Heihe's riverbank promenade (Image 7). Slushing and sliding along this grand walkway whose grey and red granite surface had become almost frictionless in the wet, I peered across the roiling water trying to make out Blagoveshchensk on the other side. The proximity of substantial Russian and Chinese population centres here, while useful to pensioners, is unusual: as I had seen, Zabaikalsk and Olochi make decidedly dreary and depopulated neighbours for Manzhouli and Shiwei respectively. But I was barely able to discern the Russian side through the storm, as the Amur proved too broad. This was fitting, for the river has long been a powerful natural obstacle whose impression on the minds of nearby inhabitants has been as deep as its channel through the landscape.

The Russian 'Amur' is taken from a word for 'large' in languages of indigenous Tungusic peoples, whose legends say that the surface of the earth was once flat until vast snakes came and carved out rivers. Whether or not these snakes were like the black dragon itself, the Chinese name 'Heilongjiang' arguably has still more menacing implications, at least to Europeans, who, unlike the Chinese, see dragons as bringers of misfortune rather than luck. But menace and promise often go hand in hand during colonial projects, and in the nineteenth century the Russians saw in the Amur a key exploration route and winter road, which, like the Lena towards Yakutsk, would aid new expansive forays. I had already seen dusty Nerchinsk where the Cossacks' first seventeenth-century advances here had been rebuffed by the Qing. But when dreams of eastward expansion re-emerged in Russia in the 1840s, the Amur regained its appeal. Late Qing weakness, and a desire in St Petersburg to compensate for loss in the Crimean War by joining the competition among European empires in Asia, ignited a quest for 'rediscovery'. The region east of today's Blagoveshchensk thus became a vast canvas for projecting every conceivable imperial fantasy. Dreams abounded about the Amur basin as an Asian 'El Dorado' or 'Mississippi', an arena for adventure and enrichment and sacred civilisational quests that would soothe Russia's late imperial ailments. Perhaps this would be a fertile agricultural region, a new imperial 'breadbasket' (*zhitnitsa*) to replace lost lands in Crimea. Nimbly skirting around the geographical inconvenience that, lying well north of the Mississippi, and indeed the entire continental United States, the Amur is frozen for half the year, metropolitan commentators who had never been here whipped one another up into a frenzy around the 'almost entirely empty' land ripe for conquest.[1] Everyone from anarchist revolutionary Mikhail Bakunin to agrarian philosopher Alexander Herzen was borne away on an imperial romance that echoed on for decades.

Passing through Blagoveshchensk on his way east to Sakhalin in 1890, Anton Chekhov was still singing the region's praises: 'I am in love with the Amur and would happily stay here for a few years,' he enthused in a letter home. 'It is beautiful with vast open spaces and freedom, and it's warm. Switzerland and France have never known such freedom.'[2] This yearning for 'freedom' spoke of the desperate destiny Russia sought to enact along the river. Imperial ambitions stirred plans to bring 'civilisation' to apparently benighted natives, and realise pan-Slavist fantasies of a new Eurasian homeland. Consistent with these goals, the man responsible for the formal annexation of territory along the Amur, which followed years of de facto expansion and settlement from the 1850s, was a swashbuckling statesman named Nikolai Muravyov, then governor of Irkutsk and Yeniseisk territories. His track record of conducting 'civilising' missions in Russia's Asian colonies, including by forcing Sakha subjects like Dmitri's forebears to learn Russian, symbolised the impetus underlying the drive along the Amur.

After the Nerchinsk setback of 150 years earlier, thoughts of China also inevitably featured prominently in Russia's feverish expansionist dreams. The Qing had some level of control over the land that would become the Khabarovsk and Primorsky regions, and treaties were signed by Muravyov (who subsequently had the riverine title 'Amursky' appended to his surname) and Beijing representatives at Aigun (1858) and Beijing (1860). This occurred as broader European interference in the Middle Kingdom was reaching a high point. Around the Second Opium War (1856–60), over which I had been chided back in Shiwei, exploiting Qing frailty was very much in vogue, and Russian 'patriots' promoted the new East Asian territories as a means of dominating China beyond anything British, French, Japanese or American rivals could dream of. Russians would henceforth not be 'strangers from across the ocean' like the other Europeans, but 'old neighbours' of China, ready to benefit from everything that such a status might confer.[3] This ambition astonished many contemporary observers, including Friedrich Engels who noted in 1858 that as a result of Aigun China had 'been despoiled of a country as large as France and Germany put together and a river as large as the Danube'.[4] Needless to say, this was not a part of the thinker's written cannon, which was celebrated during the later, and otherwise Engels-rich, Soviet period.

As it turned out, Russia's California dreamings about the Amur were disastrously misplaced. Waves of peasants making the government-incentivised journey eastward, which in pre-Trans-Siberian days could take two to three years, arrived to find squalor, bleakness and unprofitability. Convicts also dispatched here mingled with and menaced the new population, crops failed in the inclement climate and rumours of cannibalism circulated as the region was deemed 'cursed' by one visiting dignitary.[5] The Amur itself, touted as a key artery for maintaining Russia's north Pacific and Okhotsk Sea colonies, turned out to be much shallower and siltier than initially thought, and navigation was thus impossible for anything except small flat-bottomed craft. Furthermore, far from lording it over China from across the river, Russian settlers relied heavily on the Manchurian population to their south for trade in badly needed cattle, alcohol and food. Chinese weakness might have presented Russia with a golden opportunity, but misapprehension of local conditions, inept management, misallocation of resources, and a failure to grant migrants the freedom they were promised all left Russia in a position of embarrassing reliance.

However, the Qing side, who had been coerced into signing over the Amur lands, were hardly more familiar with the river than the Russians, the 'black dragon' moniker speaking of its murky presence in Chinese minds. The river's wide bends and surrounding taiga formed the northern limits of the empire's territorial consciousness and were largely left to indigenous groups such as the Evenk, Oroqen, Ulchi, Nivkhi and Nanai/Hezhe people, whom I would be meeting later. From the seventeenth century some of these groups had been persuaded to offer tribute to the emperor in Beijing or, if living closer to Qing power, to integrate further by receiving military honours and intermarrying with dynastic families.[6] But this remained a poorly understood space, which in many ways only became the China–Russia boundary because of weakness and turmoil on both sides. The implications of the new collision of Russian and Chinese interests would only gradually become clear, and the Amur itself would continue to defy 'civilising' efforts to subdue it. The province surrounding Heihe where I now was is named Heilongjiang, a territorial division created by the Qing in 1683. Blagoveshchensk is similarly situated in Amurskaya oblast—a Russian region since 1948. Here this huge waterway dominates efforts to make sense of this joining of imperial edge-spaces.

Between Heihe and Blagoveshchensk the Amur shifts on its broadly west–east course and runs north–south, and as I continued my walk water was moving in still other unexpected directions. The rain had not abated, and so gravity-defying dampness crept slowly up through my shoes, socks and trousers. But the tempestuous gloom was receding a little, and I was soon able to discern more of Blagoveshchensk's tower blocks looming in the heavy pall of fog and cloud, darker patches of grey on grey. Behind me too were tall buildings, more numerous here on the Chinese side, which mirrored the Russian towers. These ones had banners offering a 'high-level lifestyle', pun presumably intended, to Heihe's growing middle class. The sense of balance here was striking as city faced city, apartments faced apartments. Heihe's riverside promenade was admittedly decorated with un-Russian novelties— figures of dancing pandas, misshapen Russian dolls and signs saying 'China–Russia border' for tourists to pose with—but this was still a far cry from Shiwei's atmospheric clash of touristic versus brooding. Dryer times would offer more chances to take this in.

'Why didn't you take a taxi?' I was reprimanded on my return by the permed north-eastern Chinese woman who ran the hotel.

'I wanted to walk,' I explained inadequately, questioning the decision myself. Unbeknownst to my host, much more unseen moisture had made its way outward from inside my excessive layers than had visibly soaked its way in from the storm around me. Squelching back to my room, I spent the rest of the evening arraying my clothes as best I could around a rattling air conditioner.

There were several more days of deluge as Yu Shi, the Chinese rain god who is often depicted cavorting around holding a dragon or snake, toyed with the Black Dragon. I mostly sheltered indoors, reading books

I had bought en route. But eventually blue skies flecked with bobbly clouds provided an auspicious backdrop for moving on and making the second of my Sino-Russian border crossings. I spent a morning talking to vendors in the gaping neon Aladdin's cave of Heihe's Huafu Trade Centre and browsing the trinkets on display on the town's main commercial avenue, 'Central Business Pedestrian Street'. Because of a weakened rouble, vendors told me, Russians were getting unacceptably good at bargaining and so profit margins were depressed. But as elsewhere along the border, Chinese tourists seeking a taste of Russia were stepping in to pick up some of the slack. A caricature painter, whose sample works incongruously included Jackie Chan, Kofi Annan, Marx, Engels, Lenin, Stalin and Mao, offered to sketch me, but I resisted the urge to have my features bulbously refashioned in the style of a world leader, and headed for the port.

As though still ruing the 1858 Treaty of Aigun, signed nearby, Heihe keeps much of its cross-border business and its ferry terminal confined to an Amur island named Daheihe. During my precipitation-dominated first stroll, the place had seemed desolate. Over an asymmetrical arching bridge from the town centre, bilingual advertisements for China Telecom, a truck dealership and a cavernous furniture showroom had stared bleakly at their own reflections shimmering in oceanic puddles in the car park. The sweeping curved front of the Yuan Dong Free Trade Commercial Centre had been shuttered for the evening, its automatic doors gritted like teeth. Even the cheery yellow marigolds and crimson geraniums around the customs building had looked depressed, buffeted by wind and cowering below hoardings advertising lampshades, wallpaper and local hotels.

But now things were much cheerier. The Yuan Dong, whose name— 'Far East'—reflects how contact with Russia and other European powers caused China to contort its worldview into paradoxically seeing itself as 'oriental', was now bustling, and the funfair alongside Daheihe's warehouse-sized commercial outlets was whirling in the sun. Before crossing to Russia, I made for the Ferris wheel, evading the eagle-eyed hotel room touts brashly shouting '*paren*' (guy) at anyone European-looking who seemed fresh off the boat. As well as allowing for a bird's-eye view of a go-karting Russian couple being berated by an attendant for repeatedly ramming their kart into a bank of protective tyres, the wheel's loft afforded a commanding cross-border per-spective. Upriver, before dividing around the island, the grey-brown Amur wound its way out of a blue mist of low hills, barges specking its shimmering surface as it passed Heihe's northern suburbs. A short while later, reaching the tall white-and-red radio mast that marked the onset of Blagoveshchensk's urban sprawl, the main channel straight-ened out, thrusting in a broad corridor between the Russian and Chinese banks, the spume-flecked wakes of international ferries criss-crossing in the channel. The waterside frontages of the two similarly sized cities are slightly offset, so Heihe petered out first as the river proceeded, the urban embankment dissolving abruptly into neat par-cels of farmland embraced by thickets of deciduous forest. Blagoveshchensk stretched farther, the level of the skyline falling step by step as a last burst of pink apartment blocks gave way to the crick-necked cranes of the town's boatyards and then nothing. As though sensing the twin cities' absence, the Amur then immediately resumed its snaking course around several smaller islands and, now joined from the Russian side by the similarly massive River Zeya, veered majesti-cally off northwards across its plain.

Consistent with the widely held Chinese assumption that I was from 'the Soviet Union', I elected to take one of the Russian-operated ves-sels that depart for Blagoveshchensk when full. This flexibility con-trasted with the stricter controls on much less numerous (two per day) Chinese-owned craft making the same crossing, a fact reflecting the imbalance in permissiveness with which each side treats the other. Similarly, while Russians may cross to Heihe for five days of visa-free binge shopping, Chinese entry into Russia has to occur in more organ-ised groups.

Amid the good-natured jostling on deck, I found enough space to stand astride my backpack as Russians in sunglasses and bright T-shirts sought to accommodate their bulging bundles of commercial loot, boxed prams, bulky electronics and lumpy bottles of Harbin beer held together with thick sticky tape. As everyone grinned in the post-pluvial warmth of the afternoon sun, a Russian tricolour fluttered from a rail above us next to an orange life belt that bore the stencilled legend 'Amur 2010, Khabarovsk'. Whether these cheerful trippers were excited to be returning home, proud of their recent purchases or merely slightly drunk was unclear, but it mattered little as much energetic chatter filled the quick fifteen-minute ride.

Russian passport control was more ponderous. The youthful border guard on the Chinese side had let me go relatively speedily after posing a series of non-sequitur questions—was I married? did I support Manchester United?—in Chinese and then all over again in nervous English. But getting into Blagoveshchensk was a laboured affair for everyone. Joining one of several long queues, I watched as each Russian returnee entered a pen next to a low window and was shut in as a clanging cream-coloured metal gate locked behind them. None had spent more than a few days out of the country, but despite the lack of mystery around what they might have been up to in Heihe, all were obliged to stand momentarily exposed to the brooding Russian state as passports were leafed through, sidelong glances were exchanged between border guards, and computer keyboards were studiously clacked. Groups travelling together had all dispatched one emissary to each queue, but with desperately slow progress across the board making it impossible to divine which was fastest, there was much shouting, beckoning and swapping of bags to meet import weight limits before it came to my turn. Eventually, however, I reached the front, and, after my documents had changed hands four or five times and I had been told to sit beside an air conditioning unit to fill in a form given to me by an official in a wide-brimmed hat, I re-entered Russia.

* * *

Heihe and Blagoveshchensk—'Blago' to locals—have each mirrored the other as outposts of empire and faith. The latter's religiously inflected appellation—'city of the annunciation'—even resisted a Soviet orgy of atheistic renaming, and both cities have been frontline bellwethers of political turmoil on their respective sides. At the dawn of the twentieth century, events surrounding an anti-foreign uprising in northern China by a group known to Europeans as the 'Boxers' (Yihetuan or 'Righteous and Harmonious Fists' in Chinese) broke the uneasy peace that had followed Russia's Amur expansion. Responding to these and other territorial impingements into China, the Boxers sparked brutal Russian counter-measures in Blago, and in July 1900 most of the city's Chinese population was driven into the river by

Cossack forces. Amid 'yellow peril' paranoia, up to 5,000 are thought to have perished.[7] Several decades later, an inverted Chinese strain of xenophobia during Mao's Cultural Revolution, so devastating to Enhe's Russians, saw Heihe serve as the site from which uncomprehending Blago residents were bombarded through loudspeakers with propaganda against Soviet 'revisionism'. But in the twenty-first century, earlier spells of expansionist or revolutionary cross-border violence have given way to a more peaceable and interdependent relationship. Without this, my own passage over the Amur would have been more difficult. Given the prevalence of restricted zones around the likes of Zabaikalsk and Olochi, Blago is also a Russian rarity in being an open and accessible town directly on the border. This made it an intriguing place to begin the next Russia-based leg of my journey.

Travelling through the Russian Far East, I would temporarily leave most of my temporally displaced travel companions, as Qu Qiubai, Hu Yuzhi, Sergei Tretyakov and Ethel Alec-Tweedie would only rejoin me when I re-entered Manchuria at the Sino-Russian border's easternmost point. Chekhov and Boris Pilnyak, who stayed on Russian soil throughout their Sakhalin- and Japan-bound journeys, would remain with me, even if the former's commentary was at times in questionable taste. Blagoveshchensk, where, Chekhov noted, 'all anyone is talking about is gold', was one of the playwright's favourite stops, and not for entirely sophisticated reasons. Writing in June 1890 to his friend Alexei Suvorin, he reported that 'the Japanese start at Blagoveshchensk—by which I mean Japanese women, diminutive brunettes with big, strange hairstyles'. Ever the urbane sophisticate, Chekhov then proceeded to offer a lurid treatise on the appeal of Japanese prostitutes, describing their 'artful coquetry', which made him 'feel as though [he] was taking part in an exhibition of high-level riding skill'. Whether Suvorin welcomed these cultural insights is unclear, but set beside the eloquent descriptions of local scenery that Chekhov was exaltedly writing to his family at the same time, these salacious letters perhaps reveal what he had really meant when vaunting the Amur's 'freedom'.[8]

Chinese people appeared earlier in the playwright's journey than the Japanese, though they initially left him with few impressions other than seeming 'extremely polite'. But contemplating China at large, Chekhov was sure that this politeness concealed sinister designs. 'The Chinese will undoubtedly take the Amur back off us,' he reported from Blagoveshchensk, 'although it won't be us who give it to them, but someone else—possibly the British who are ruling and building fortresses all across China'.[9] Yet in Blago today it is hard to imagine such a prophecy ever seeming plausible, for the city's non-Chineseness is one of its most remarkable features. Used to conditions over the river where even the most 'Russian' aspects of life in Manzhouli, Shiwei or Heihe take unequivocally Chinese form, I found the return to Russian East Asia startling. It was relaxing to become an invisible foreigner again amid a local population that—much more so than in Yakutia or other areas of inner Siberia—is overwhelmingly Slavic. But whilst I was already familiar with these demographics having lived in Vladivostok, I still wondered despite myself what these Russians with their profusion of blond, brown and red hair were doing here.

Lyuba, a melancholic but solicitous *babushka* who showed me around Blagoveshchensk's Regional Museum, had long been wrestling with a more personally existential version of the same question. As we padded around the marble floors of the grand nineteenth-century building, dodging an energetic group of Heihe primary school children on a tour, she provided a self-reflective commentary on the exhibits documenting Blago's early history.

'Sometimes I wonder what General Muravyov thought he was doing bringing us here in the first place,' she sighed wearily as I examined cabinets of curling letters and military orders, only to be distracted by four neckerchiefed pupils wrestling vigorously for a seat on the hall's only bench. 'Was it just so that we'd have to buy expensive plane tickets to Moscow and eat Chinese fruit and vegetables all the time?' she continued. Lyuba's grandparents had originally come to the Far East from the fertile Black Earth region on the Russo-Ukrainian border, and perhaps this was why products of the soil were foremost in her mind. Trying to lighten the mood, I suggested that Muravyov, whose erect statue stands proudly on Blagoveshchensk's riverbank facing Heihe, probably wasn't thinking much about airfares in the 1850s. But her grim smile was brief. We moved into the next room and stepped further back in time as a mammoth oil painting loomed above us.

'This is the Battle of Albazin,' Lyuba said with a languidness suggesting that merely contemplating Russia's four centuries of eastward exploration exhausted her. The picture was a seething mass of strug-gling limbs and weapons, and the pointed pinnacles of a blazing wooden stockade illuminated a menacing sky as moustachioed Cossacks raised swords at approaching ranks of pike-wielding Qing infantrymen. Albazin may have been chalked up in the late seventeenth century as a Chinese victory, but here it was presented simply as a momentary setback in Russia's inexorably heroic push eastward.

'We generally avoid this particular painting with Chinese tourists,' said Lyuba as one of her colleagues, a local student who spoke excel-lent Chinese, attempted to marshal the whooping school group past us into the next room. 'The Chinese seem to think that Blagoveshchensk belongs to them. But I don't understand why!'

When Russia's Beijing embassy opened an account on Chinese microblogging website Weibo in March 2013, it was indeed immedi-ately deluged by comments demanding that 'Chinese territory' along the Amur be restored. In a telling indication of the divorce of Chinese nationalism from love for the Communist Party that Weixie had attested to in Enhe, these statements from impassioned netizens also sarcastically suggested that Russia retract the plague of Communism with which it had infected China whilst it was at it.[10]

'It makes no sense,' Lyuba continued. 'I mean, we used to have Alaska, and we're not asking for that back!' I thought about mentioning Crimea, but decided to stay on topic. Yet Lyuba's concerns about pos-sible Chinese hopes to 'reclaim' the Amur were, despite echoing Chekhov, rooted in comparably contemporary events.

'The problem is our own government hasn't taken care of us,' she lamented. 'And it's because they haven't developed things here that the Chinese can't be stopped—they're taking over.' Despite Blago's undeniable Russian appearance, Lyuba saw an insidious threat in the local branches of the large shopping centre I had visited in Heihe. 'There are all these Huafus here now!' she told me, 'Big Huafu, Little Huafu, Celestial Huafu. When will it stop? Things were much better under the union.'

Throughout Russia's easternmost reaches, I would be hearing simi-lar concerns over Moscow's neglect and domination by outside forces, accompanied by a telling focus on commercial matters. Confronted by China's growing presence, older far easterners unsurprisingly recall bygone Soviet days as a halcyon age; more so than anywhere except the Arctic north, this was a region deeply reliant on the pre-1991 socialist order. Land grants and exile had brought some migrants here under tsarism, but for all Lyuba's complaints it was not really Muravyov but the Soviet system that most rapidly populated the east via salary incentives and industrial subsidies. As I had already witnessed in Tynda, the withdrawal of these and the traumatic arrival of market forces has seen hundreds of thousands depart eastern Russia since the chaotic 1990s, convincing many of the superiority of Soviet ways. The concurrent arrival of China as a local player has only reinforced these feelings in some quarters.

Yet this is a complex dynamic, for the 'foreign' presence sometimes seen as a threat has also injected much-needed vigour into borderland life. Since the Soviet collapse and concomitant severing of supply lines, locations like Blago have relied heavily on Chinese goods, and on outlets like the Huafu empire. Even Moscow's recent attempts to reinvigorate the region through domestic *grands projets* such as a new Eastern Cosmodrome outside Blagoveshchensk (designed eventually to replace Baikonur, Russia's current space port in Kazakhstan) have done little for the consumer economy.[11] It is unsurprising therefore that Chinese business continues to step in to fill the gap, and indeed, without it Russians would likely have much more to complain about than they already do. China's proximity makes the Russian Far East a more appealing place to live, and all urban centres here have in fact seen a steady increase in population over the last decade, bucking regional and national trends.

Moreover, as I had seen in Heihe, local cross-border reliance is in fact becoming increasingly symbiotic. Russian shoppers like those on the Amur ferry have underwritten Heihe's development for two decades, but as shown by the Heihe children in the museum, Chinese visitors coming the other way are now also an increasingly vital part of Blago's consumer landscape, especially with the rouble weakened. South of the Amur, there is growing taste for Russian goods including foodstuffs and natural products, which are deemed safer than their health scare-dogged Chinese equivalents. The increase in enthusiasm for these foreign delicacies has been so rapid as to create curious distortions during their adoption: Russian *medovik*, for example, a layered honey and cream cake, has somehow acquired the name *tilamisu*—tiramisu—in north-east China, despite having little in common with that dessert aside from deliciousness.

Much of Blago's appeal to Chinese visitors lies in the fact that its perpendicular streets offer 'European' vistas that would not look out of place in Berlin, Prague or Budapest. Wooden cottages with carved eaves and net curtains like those I had admired in Chita slouch comfortably behind rows of ivy-clad trees, while grander tsarist edifices in brick and stone proudly stamp pastel-painted imperial solidity on to street corners. Parades of cornicing and steeply sloping Parisian-style roofs alternate with Habsburg-esque imposture. As I explored the town, cyclists and rollerbladers sped past the brick spire of the old Polish Catholic church, the only religious building to have survived early Soviet demolitions and, as part of a wider Orthodox revival, now converted to serve the Russian patriarch. Yet as Lyuba had promised, Blagoveshchensk's Huafus were there too, with the main branch resembling many of the architecturally eclectic buildings that populate Chinese skylines. A long glass-ceilinged arcade lay within a futuristic-looking tower of pale blue glass topped by a lop-sided gold cone. This neatly inverted the stylings of Heihe's Huafu, which had been housed in a bulbous brown and burgundy pseudo-European construction complete with Doric columns. Everywhere were hints at a mirrored meeting of worlds, and near Blago's Huafu a Chinese café named Panda sat beside the Taras Bulba Slavic Restaurant, named after the classic novel by Nikolai Gogol.

On a warm summer evening such as it was, however, few locals were squirrelled away inside shopping centres or stuffy cafés, and I followed groups of local *flâneurs* down to the openness of the riverside. Blagoveshchensk's Amur promenade has been subject in recent years to a burst of reconstruction gripping much of the city centre, and traces of the old Soviet concrete embankment showed that the renovated shoreline had moved several dozen yards closer to China. Whether this indicated rapprochement was unclear, but notwithstanding the signs of interdependency between the cities, Blago's riverside furniture was less conciliatory a spectacle than Heihe's had been. Standing on a pedestal, a bronze statue of a stern young Russian rifleman with a guard dog looked across the Amur, while downstream a small Soviet gunship sat perched atop an angled platform, its prow pointed high into the air as though about to launch itself towards the opposite bank. Here were signs of a desire to guard against the Chinese takeover so feared by Lyuba.

Nevertheless, around these militaristic monuments the mood that evening was of summertime revelry. As local boys leapt off some steps into the river, shouting and laughing as they hit the water and thrashing wildly in the current below, three Chinese workers nearby discussed the possibility of taking a dip. After each had tested the others' willingness, it became apparent that none of them actually knew how to swim. Later, shifts changed on a riverfront building site and a few loose bands of Chinese migrant cement-pourers and brick-stackers filed out of a gap in a corrugated metal barrier. With newspaper cones of roast sunflower seeds bought using wordless hand-signals from an elderly Russian lady, they approached the railings to look across the river. As the group played at pretending to hoik each other over the edge into the water, a Chinese couple—out of place amid the exclusively male company of the workers—sat on the marble edge of a nearby flowerbed.

'They're looking at our Chinese moon,' the husband said pointing at some of the workers who were admiring the celestial body suspended over the Heihe side. Hearing him, the workers awkwardly looked over their shoulders before turning back to their hushed conversation. Small Chinese cruise boats puttered past in the gathering twilight, the passengers on board crowding to the near side, their cameras flashing as they strained for glimpses of the nineteenth-century naval buildings and triumphal arch that sit a little back from Blagoveshchensk's main promenade.

'What the hell are they taking pictures of?' asked a Russian man grumpily standing in front of the reconstructed arch, originally an 1891 monument to the visit of the future Tsar Nicholas II during his grand Asian tour.

'You!' his wife replied teasingly, trying to cheer him up.

At 10 p.m., the illuminations on Heihe's waterside buildings started to flicker on. The manager of the small hotel I was staying at had joked that one of the best things about living in Blagoveshchensk was being able to look across at Heihe at night, and as neon lines gathered in vertical rows, abstract graphics bounced up and down forty-storey apartment blocks and pointed spires thrust glowing red orbs up into the night, the sight was certainly an impressive one. Over in Heihe, it was still only 8 p.m.—China's unity under a single time zone (until the mid-twentieth century it had five) has strange effects when rubbing alongside Russia's eleven-hour span—and so gazing over the river on a Blagoveshchensk evening means looking both ahead to a neon-age Chinese future, and back in time two hours. Little spoilt by a lank-haired Russian guitarist incongruously crooning acoustic Nirvana and Deep Purple songs, the atmosphere on that warm evening was idyllic, a convivial gathering of Russian and Chinese neighbours who, even if they saw different things and lived on different timescales, nevertheless looked in parallel lines.

* * *

For further insight into Chinese lives in Blago, I got in touch by WeChat with Zhe from the Skovorodino–Nerchinsk train, and we agreed to meet for lunch at a Soviet-style cafeteria in the centre of town. Following his paternal visit to the shores of Lake Baikal, or so I thought, Zhe was now back in the city where he was finishing up his master's degree and was in search of work. We discussed this subject as we queued with our plastic trays, selecting mayonnaise-laden salads from refrigerated cabinets and asking surly *babushki* to slop sauce on our *kotlety* and buckwheat. With good Russian and a reliable network of Chinese contacts, Zhe was confident of being able to set up in business, but as we settled at a table, conversation moved on to other topics. It soon transpired that, small talk over, we both had confessions to make regarding our first meeting on the train. Mine came first.

As we had rolled through the land of Genghis Khan under the leer of the shirtless Russian drunks down the corridor, I had not wanted to complicate matters and so had allowed Zhe to assume I was Russian. It hadn't been an explicitly spoken lie, but when he asked where I began my journey to the Far East and I replied Moscow, it was evident from the ensuing discussion that he assumed my home must lie somewhere in the orbit of the towering Kremlin walls. In Blago, I clarified.

'So you're English?' he asked slightly incredulous, a clump of may-onnaise-covered peas hovering in mid-air on his near-weightless Soviet-remnant aluminium fork.

I answered in the affirmative, mumbling something about not wanting my foreign identity to become a source of curiosity to our neighbours on the train. I was getting tired, I told Zhe, of conversation that usually ran along the lines of: 'England! Manchester! [In Russian, 'Manchester' mostly means 'Manchester United'.] Are you from Manchester? London?' No, Nottingham. 'Robin Hood!' And then, wistfully, 'Ah, cloudy Albion …' 'Are you a spy?' No. 'Ah, but you are studying us so you can spy on us?' No. 'Do you like Manchester?' They're ok. 'Are you sure you're not a spy?' Yes.

'Right!' exclaimed Zhe, with unanticipated empathy. 'It's true, Russians can treat foreigners strangely and they're especially racist to the Chinese. Actually I have something to tell you too: that wasn't my dad on the train at all, it was a boss I sometimes do some work for. And we weren't going to visit Lake Baikal, we were on a business trip to meet people in Irkutsk.'

Zhe grinned, pleased to be able to set the record straight and tickled by the fact that my act of dissemblance had actually contributed to his own. 'I didn't tell the truth because I thought if the Russians on the train—like you—found out that that guy was a wealthy businessman, then they might try to rob him.'

Any disingenuousness I felt was thus neatly counterbalanced by being considered a potential thief, so we decided to call it quits. Yet while my identity-concealment was induced by a desire to avoid circular conversations, fear of being robbed was of course another matter altogether. I told Zhe I was sorry he felt that way about Russians. He had been in Blagoveshchensk six years, and it seemed unfortunate that his abiding response was fear of having things stolen.

'Yes, sadly you have to be careful here,' he continued, leaning across the table. This time a slice of *bliny* was dripping condensed milk down his fork. 'But it's not all one way, and I do have some good friends from Russia. The problem is that the situation is bad on both sides. Basically, the Chinese deceive the Russians in business and then the Russians beat up the Chinese in return. It's kind of a cycle.'

This summary offered further, albeit grim, evidence of Heihe and Blagoveshchensk's give-and-take relationship. In Blago's Victory Square, I had even met an elderly Russian souvenir-seller who, mirroring vendors on Heihe's main streets, had learnt enough Chinese—'Do you want this? It's cheap!'—to peddle sets of Soviet coinage and fridge magnets to visiting tourists. Zhe and I spoke for a while longer about the contours of this sometimes mutually exploitative Sino-Russian dynamic, as well as our future plans; despite his trepidation, he was hoping to stay here as long as possible, he said. His cross-border contacts gave him a competitive edge he didn't have in China, and maybe he would even meet a Russian wife, a sure-fire way of gaining status back home.

But if Zhe was staying put, I was set to move on, and so, having promised to keep in touch on more transparent terms this time, I returned to my hotel. As I packed, moody black thunder clouds were rolling in again, and by the time I was in a taxi to the railway station, many of the city's roads were already under inches of slopping brown water. As we passed along the riverside, I saw that the Heihe bank was still bathing in piercing pre-storm sunlight. There was much that brought these two cities together, but rain god Yu Shi seemed to be intervening to point out that striking differences still remained.

Russian Far East metropolises like Blagoveshchensk have mostly halted their 1990s population slides by relying not only on supplies of Chinese goods but also on the emptying of the surrounding countryside. 'Ghost villages' (possibly as many of 20,000 of them) are dotted all across Russia's horizonless taiga and tundra,[12] but the Far East has witnessed a faster pace of rural evacuation than most of the country. As a result, trains like the one I was boarding along the Trans-Siberian's easternmost stretch have become like ships between remote islands of habitation, plying vast empty seas that turn seasonally from green to white. Leaving Blago behind, I forged a northward passage up a branch line along the Amur-tributary River Zeya back to the main Trans-Siberian artery.

At Belogorsk, where a dazzling silver Lenin stands pointing on the platform in front of a lurid turquoise station, a rotund middle-aged man boarded and entered the compartment that I was already sharing with a mother in her forties and her young son. As Qu, Hu and Tretyakov discovered a century ago, conversation ignites much more easily in the close intimacy of sleeper compartments than in Russia's other public places, and as the train-ship gathered speed again, isolated comments coalesced into hushed conversation between the new arrival and the others. The boy was upset, and since waving a teary goodbye through the window to his father back in Blagoveshchensk—departures in this land of weeklong journeys between diffuse towns portend long absences—had been looking morosely at the floor.

'Do you want to look out of the window?' his mother asked, motioning to the tree-specked plains that stretched into the gathering dusk. The boy shook his head.

'What is there to look at anyway?' the Belogorsk man sighed thoughtfully. 'No people. Nothing. Just land, so much land …' He blew on the surface of the black lemon tea that had just been brought to him by a carriage attendant. Gripping the tall glass by its metal base, he took a sip and adjusted his posture. 'But like Peter the Great said,' he went on, 'it's hard to give up territory once you've got it.' Silence fell, each of us in thought, the quietness of the continental vastness punctured only by occasional slurps of tea. After a while, the man spoke again.

'They planted the soya late this year,' he said as we passed some rare cultivated fields. This drew the mother's interest.

'When I went to Beidaihe all there was all around was corn,' she responded, referring to a Chinese seaside resort popular with both Far Eastern Russians and the Chinese Communist Party leadership. Conversation then turned to the different ways in which the Chinese and Russians cultivate their respective sides of the Amur, with a conclusion being reached that the 'Asians' south of the border make better use of their land. I began to wonder whether these people had themselves been planted here especially for my interest, for as on previous occasions my very presence, even when—as now—I said little, seemed to make China–Russia affairs crop up in conversation. But it seemed more probable that, as wherever humans live near one another, what the neighbours are up to was never far from people's minds here.

Sleep took us all at an early hour. Restrictions on alcohol-consumption aboard Russian trains have tightened in recent years, and so with no conspiratorial transition to shared drinking of the kind I had experienced many times previously on the Trans-Sib, the man and I heaved ourselves aloft to our upper bunks as the mother and her son settled down below. Gentle swaying lulled us dreamward as we slid over the verdant ocean.

* * *

The early bedtime did little to alleviate my half-asleep befuddlement as I disembarked early at Birobidzhan, the next city of any significant size on this eastward stretch of railway. The capital of Russia's 'Jewish Autonomous Region' had a dull and muffled feel in the foggy pre-dawn. At the railway station with its bilingual sign in Russian and Hebrew-script Yiddish, overhead lights cast a spooky aquatic glow on to the grey brick platform. In front of the station, a grand marble fountain featuring a robust oversized menorah lay still, a metaphor both for my antisocially early arrival and for the silent mourning of one of the Russian Far East's many diminished settlements (Image 8).

Birobidzhan is newer still than the Russian Far East's mostly mid-nineteenth-century conurbations, and arose at the confluence of the Amur-bound Bira and Bidzhan rivers during the 1930s. A decade and a half before the establishment of Israel, the Jewish Autonomous Region was founded, depending on whom you ask, either as a haven from anti-Semitism elsewhere or as a distant location to which Stalin could banish the Soviet Jewish population. In its early years, Birobidzhan attracted settlers not only from Russia but also Europe and the Americas, marking a significant reversal in Jewish fortunes in the Russian Far East. An 1860 law following the annexation of the Khabarovsk and Primorsky territories had banned Jews from coming within 100 versts (around 66 miles) of the Chinese border amid racist paranoia that they would monopolise control over the region's newly discovered gold.[13] But with the creation of the new region thousands moved here, and by the late 1940s around a quarter of its 120,000-strong population was Jewish. Yet if Birobidzhan initially represented a beacon of positivity, the project soon came to be dogged by the familiar ravages of climatic harshness, bureaucratic incompetence and at best ambivalent official support that characterised many Russian or Soviet colonial ventures in East Asia. What this promised land promised actually turned out mainly to be harsh mountains and flat plains oscillating between frozen waste and mosquito-infested swamp according to the season, and as late Stalinism became increasingly anti-Semitic, many Birobidzhan residents departed back west again after only a few years. As exit from the Soviet Union became possible for some from the 1960s, more left for less insect-ridden alternative homes in the United States and Israel. These numbers increased dramatically as travel restrictions were eased further under Mikhail Gorbachev in the 1980s, and today under 0.5 per cent of the regional population of around 175,000 is Jewish.

The station's menorah and Yiddish signage showed nevertheless that the imprint of the Jewish presence remains patchily evident. Both the USSR and the PRC furnished the spaces inhabited by their minorities in mirrored ways, blending 'ethnic' iconography with the architectural styles of the day to symbolise the autonomy supposedly granted to once-oppressed imperial populations. Birobidzhan's 'Jewish' elements were thus not so different from the wooden 'Russian' houses of northern Inner Mongolia. There being little else to do at this blisteringly early hour, I set off from the station in search of other such symbols.

As I walked down Oktyabrskaya Street following some vague directions muttered by the somnolent station warden, the 'Jewish' gloss on the town seemed to run about as deep as the flimsy wooden cladding on Enhe's buildings. The place was largely a Soviet space, the cinema and cultural centre glowering in the gloom were majestic monuments to florid socialist classicism, and the Philharmonia a white marble hulk of a building that jutted in confident modernist directions, resembling its equivalent in Hamhung, North Korea. In the neat square between the concert hall and telegraph building, which was topped by more Yiddish lettering, a gaggle of slurring students was loitering outside a closing bar. A good-natured evening had turned acrimonious with the Tuesday sunrise, and as a lank-haired youth in a red T-shirt yelled about Lenin and Stalin and was restrained by his panicked girlfriend, their harsh shouts sounded all the more jarring as they bounced off the socialist façades around them. Down an avenue named in honour of the sixtieth jubilee of the USSR, Lenin himself stood impressively among some low pine trees, one hand in the pocket of his long coat, his face raised as if squinting off towards the misty banks of the River Bira.

About as evident as any residual Jewish traces was the local Chinese presence, and in a square bearing a monument to Ukrainian Yiddish writer Sholem-Aleichem, a giant gold coach just arrived from China was parked outside the nearby Central Hotel. Originating in Jiamusi, an old Manchu settlement in eastern Heilongjiang, the coach had crossed the Amur by ferry from Tongjiang to Nizhneleninskoe in the south of the Jewish Autonomous Region. These summer ferries are replaced in winter by a metal pontoon bridge laid on the frozen river, although a 2013 Sino-Russian agreement mandated the construction of a permanent bridge nearby. Work started on the Chinese half almost immediately and was complete within two years, but as of 2018 reciprocal efforts from the Russian side are yet to commence in earnest. Unconvincing assurances were made in 2016 by the evocatively named Russian firm 'Rubikon' that their work would be finished within two years,[14] but in proportion to the imbalance in populations at either end of the project—Tongjiang has 160,000 people while Nizhneleninskoe is a decrepit settlement of just 215 souls—the Chinese half-bridge still simply juts out into mid-river. Should they feel minded to do so, Nizhneleninskoe's 215 residents may gaze out over the Amur at a cheerful red banner on the end of the bridge reading 'Chinese China–Russia Bridge Administration'.

My crepuscular wanderings had made me hungry, and so I entered the Central Hotel's 'Vostok' restaurant in search of breakfast. Inside, a small drama was unfolding as a Chinese guest struggled with buffet etiquette, studiously ignored by Russian waitresses who were grimly replenishing small piles of sliced black bread and diverse dairy products on a trestle table. As he tried to communicate that he was staying at the hotel and wanted to eat, another sullen staff member walked over.

'ARE YOU A GUEST?' she bluntly repeated several times in Russian, somehow failing to guess what he might want as he helplessly gestured at the piles of *bliny* and pots of jam.

I helped clarify things, ate a prodigious number of deliciously fresh *syrniki*—flat miniature cakes of a slightly sweet substance somewhere between cottage cheese and real cheese—and then continued my perambulation around town. The city gradually awoke as I walked, the mist clearing and the air thickening with heat under a blotchy grey-white sky. On a street named after Stalinist henchman Feliks Dzerzhinsky, I noticed a restaurant celebrating Birobidzhan's friendship with its Chinese sister city Hegang and, next door, an office for delegates from Hegang styled like a garish Daoist temple guarded by white stone lions. But mirroring the drowsy stupor inside my own head that the heavy Vostok breakfast had exacerbated, these showed few signs of life. I continued on towards a cluster of buildings that since 2004 has sought to maintain something of Birobidzhan's Jewish past.

At the Freid Centre of Jewish Culture on Sholem-Aleichem Street, an elderly man shuffled me disinterestedly into a room containing many brown sofas and cabinets of trophies won by local Jewish sportspeople and musicians. The synagogue next door, he told me, had just been fumigated and was not safe to enter. But he said I could look at the trophies, whose stylised engravings displayed Cyrillic letters made to look like Hebrew and celebrated gala performances attended by Jewish participants from across Russia and the former Soviet republics.

'There aren't many of us left now,' said another of the centre's organisers, having entered silently through a side door. 'But we still have our singing groups and coordinate with other Jewish societies in Khabarovsk and Vladivostok.' She pointed herself out on a photo depicting the elderly ladies who formed the local musical ensemble. Though jovial enough, the group hardly resembled the vanguard of a Jewish revival. There was, she said, little hope that much would be left after they were gone. I browsed for a short while longer, but the staff appeared keen to deal with the fumigated synagogue, so I moved on.

Birobidzhan seemed adrift in the vast taiga ocean, lost between a quickly snuffed-out twentieth-century idealism and, as suggested by the slowness of Russian bridge construction, a paralysed uncertainty over links to China in the twenty-first. On Komsomolskaya Street, an ice cream-seller who was eating one of her own ice creams gave me a frown whose thunderousness pierced even my sleep-deprived mind. It was time to leave already, it seemed, and so I went to the bus station to find transport onward to Khabarovsk, passing the 'Samarkand' restaurant and a small amusement park named 'Ararat', dead echoes of a lost Soviet East, on the way.

* * *

The three-hour minibus ride to Khabarovsk had me languidly oscillating between bursts of uncomfortable sleep and conscience-stricken jolts awake as I checked to see if anybody had noticed me gormlessly dribbling on myself. This fitful rest meant that on arrival I could greet my host Ilya, a friend of a friend and also an IT consultant, Lord of the Rings enthusiast and medieval re-enactor, with renewed buoyancy. I was also eager to see what had changed since my last trip to Khabarovsk, proud bearer of the title of 'coldest city in the world with a population of over half a million'. This was the first place since Moscow that I had visited before and I had remembered liking it.

Thanks to its 'capital' status and only modestly kleptocratic government, for much of the 1990s and 2000s Khabarovsk was a more appealing place to live than its distant neighbours Blagoveshchensk or Vladivostok. The city's grand main street, named after treaty-negotiating land-grabber Nikolai Muravyov-Amursky—again speaking of Russia's conquistador attitude to its colonial east—boasts neoclassical, art deco and *style moderne* buildings leading down to a tiered Amur embankment with Narnia-esque lampposts. Today, these building ensembles house a dignified parade of Russian, European and Japanese restaurants, small coffee shops, bakeries and majestic hotels. Chekhov found similarly graceful surroundings here in the early summer of 1890. Khabarovsk was his last major stop before he plied the wild final stretch of the Amur towards its estuary at Nikolaevsk and, ever-lyrical about the mighty river, the doctor-playwright wrote wistfully to a friend to recommend the area: 'spend some time in Khabarovsk, on the Amur,' he enthused. 'There you'll see so much that is novel and surprising that you'll remember it to the end of your days ...'[15]

Outside the centre, Khabarovsk's post-Chekhov districts become steadily more concrete and Soviet as they radiate away from the river, and thoroughfares are correspondingly named after an eclectic blend of socialist grandees from Marx to Kalinin. In a key position opposite China's north-easternmost corner, to which I myself would later bend my route, the city has been a strategic hub for successive Russian and Soviet empires, and its wider region is still home to indigenous groups whose fates have been mirrored by those of separated brethren over in China. Ilya, although only thirty years old, would be a source of much reminiscence about these layered legacies.

'You'll probably find there are more immigrants here than when you last came,' he said matter-of-factly as we stopped to buy fruit from an Uzbek greengrocer on our way up the hill to his flat. It was nearing 8 p.m., and Ilya was impressed that the man was still working. 'But I don't mean that in a bad way. That guy, he's fine,' he added, nodding back to the fruit-seller. 'He's there when I set off for work in the morning and look, he's still there now. And his prices are good.'

As we entered his home, I asked whether there had been friction around the new arrivals. Xenophobic attacks on migrants from the former Soviet Union and East Asia have been a grim feature of life in Russian cities for much of the post-1990s age.

'Look, we generally think about it this way here,' Ilya said earnestly as he ushered me inside. 'The people from the plains—the Uzbeks, the Chinese—we have no problem with them. They come here to work. It's the mountain people—the Georgians and the Armenians—they're the ones we have issues with.' Ilya was unable to explain precisely what it was about a high-altitude background that would make people cause trouble, but checking online later I discovered that a similarly deterministic mountain/plains distinction is made by the German philosopher Hegel in his work *Philosophy of History*. Just as British society remains freighted with the imperial detritus of its Victorian inheritance, so a trove of abstruse nineteenth-century ideas like Hegel's, having mutated and meandered through the writings of Marx and Lenin, became lodged in Soviet and thus post-Soviet common sense. It was striking to be confronted by an example of this here on the edge of China, but more socialist intellectual sympathies emerged as Ilya voiced his positivity about Khabarovsk's neighbours.

'Lots of people here are concerned about some sort of Chinese invasion,' he said, 'Russians are suspicious because they don't understand them. But not me. I don't speak Chinese of course, but I was born in the Soviet Union so I'm an atheist like the Chinese. To be honest I admire what they're doing. Maybe if they got more involved over here it wouldn't be such a bad thing. I mean, if we could learn how to work and do Communism properly like them then we'd really be able to get things done.' I recalled the unfinished bridges near Birobidzhan, Blagoveshchensk and Yakutsk.

That Ilya channelled his admiration for the Chinese through positive references to Soviet Communism may in part have been related to his ownership of a spacious and convenient Khrushchev-era apartment in central Khabarovsk. Originally allocated under Soviet incentive schemes to his grandfather, a prominent geologist who early in his career had travelled 4,000 miles from Belarus to work in the Far East, the flat had followed a curious path of hybrid ownership. Initially awarded on professional merit, the place had then defied top-down redistributive logics to follow decidedly un-Marxist lines of family inheritance. With the collapse of the Soviet system, it had, like many other such assets, again transformed by becoming valuable private property. In a convoluted way, therefore, Ilya had done very well out of the Soviet system.

As well as the apartment, Ilya had inherited his geologist grandfather's passion for the surrounding wilderness of hills, forests and scarps, and frequently made long excursions to wander the breathtaking remoteness of the Khabarovsk region or canoe down its roaring mountain rivers. As we sat in his snug kitchen, the windows thrown open to usher a summer breeze through this neat repository of Soviet aluminium teapots and floral crockery, Ilya also related his local pride to broader geopolitics.

'It's not that people like me especially love the Chinese,' he clarified. 'But what we really hate is those clowns from Moscow turning up and telling us what to do. They're the ones who most fear the Chinese, so it's almost more of an enemy's enemy type situation.'

I nodded, recalling Lyuba's Moscow-directed barbs back in Blagoveshchensk and mentioning to Ilya that I had heard similar disdain for the capital expressed in other Soviet-era Far Eastern kitchens. 'Yes! This is classic kitchen table politics,' he said, grinning. 'All that's missing is a bottle of vodka and some *zakuski*!' But, like many younger educated Russians, Ilya did not drink. The disastrous social consequences of the country's longstanding attachment to the bottle had provided a powerful negative lesson to him and his friends. Besides, healthy outdoor pursuits served as more than adequate replacements for long nights sunk in alcoholic delirium. I was in any case glad of the chance for some rest, so we retired early.

Strolling down one of the city's boulevards the next day, Ilya explained more about the host of other new lifestyle choices that serve as an alternative to alcohol. 'Trade with China has made all kinds of things possible,' he enthused. 'Like being a vegetarian for instance. You can't grow anything much here, except down south towards Vladivostok where it's a bit warmer. But Chinese fruit and vegetables coming over the border means there's now more choice than ever, and vegetarianism is very popular now.' As we walked, rollerbladers and cyclists whipped past us. 'All this is from China too,' he commented. 'I remember when rollerblades first appeared after the border opened, now they're everywhere.'

As in Blagoveshchensk, the collapse of Soviet supply-lines in the early 1990s had seen China, then well on the way to emergence as a manufacturing behemoth, become a vital source of even Khabarovsk's most basic goods. Hard currency was as scarce as new clothes or household items, and so these were often bartered for things that Russians were able to get their hands on, including timber and scrap metal.[16] This was another example of how this eastern stretch of Russia had grown used to interdependence with China.

But if this reliance had worried Lyuba back at Blagoveshchensk's Museum, the younger and generally cheerier Ilya triangulated his view of China very differently in reference to the Soviet past. Lyuba proudly remembered socialist times first-hand as a mostly China-free period, and so the presence in her midst of Chinese commerce only served as a reminder of the painful end of the mighty union. But Ilya, who had been born too late to have more than fleeting memories of the collapse, saw cross-border exchange as beneficial and China as an example of what could have been, had Soviet socialism reformed successfully. His fierce pride in and enjoyment of the vast wild spaces that are so central to Russia's self-image did not translate into an exclusivist nationalism. He and Lyuba were both aggrieved at the neglect eastern Russia had suffered from the centre in recent decades. But, bearing a transnational version of his grandfather's spirit of eastern opportunity, Ilya less nostalgically saw China's proximity as part of a grand new world of possibility. He had himself crossed the border many times, taking goods over and buying things with the proceeds.

'There are three Russian things the Chinese love,' he said sagely. I half expected him to say something reductive about women, recalling a common boast among Russian men about the pulchritude of 'their' female compatriots. But as usual, Ilya was more interesting. 'Black bread, chocolate, and condensed milk,' he said. 'They can't get enough of the stuff. You can get anything in Fuyuan for a few 70-rouble tins of milk! Can you believe it?'

Boats to the border town of Fuyuan leave from piers below the end of Muravyov-Amursky Street, and although I would be heading to that condensed-milk-thirsty town on a more circuitous route, I went down for a look one evening. In front of booths offering tours to north-east China, locals padded past in bare feet and swimwear towards a stretch of Amur beach, while on neighbouring piers Khabarovsk's celebrated disco boats were warming up for that night's cruises. As at Blagoveshchensk, traffic to Fuyuan is far from one-way in these days of cheaper roubles, and by the riverside four crop-haired Chinese travellers were reclining in the seats of their rented people-carrier awaiting the next boat, soothing themselves with apricot ice creams after a raucous two days of mid-week male-bonding.

Several symbols of Russia's relationship with other 'Easts' were also in evidence on the riverbank, and one café offering Uzbek *samsy*, *manty* and *lagman* and Tatar *cheburek* was named 'Oriental Flavour', odd given that the 'oriental' places referred to were thousands of miles to the west. Indeed, Khabarovsk's geographical, political and social setting is confounding in other ways too, for despite being a border town lying on the Amur, the city does not face China directly. Visible across the mile-wide mass of solemnly turgid brown-and-grey waters were low-lying hills with capes of tufted cloud, yet these were not shrouded visions of the mysterious Middle Kingdom, but still Russian territory. South-west of Khabarovsk, as I would be seeing more clearly from the other side, another border river—the Ussuri—meets the Amur and several island fragments disrupt water flows and sightlines alike. Before crossing into China to clarify these muddled international borders, however, I would learn of still other kinds of blurred boundaries from some of Khabarovsk territory's indigenous inhabitants.

* * *

The mid-river island immediately visible from Khabarovsk's Amur embankment is divided between Russia and China, where it is respectively known as Bolshoi Ussuriisky and Heixiazi Island. This divide, and the divisiveness of borders in general, were particular causes of concern for Leonid, an ethnic Nanai campaigner, Khabarovsk political activist, writer, officiator at shamanic rituals, self-identifying Jurchen, Manchu, Russian Orthodox believer, and head of an NGO representing the native minority populations of the Far East. In keeping with the solidarity often shared among Russia's non-Russian ethnicities, regardless of how far apart they live, Dmitri from back in Yakutsk had put me in touch with Leonid. After a brief phone call, I met him and some of his fellow-Nanai campaigners on Khabarovsk's Komsomolskaya Square.

135

Solemnly greeting me *bachigoapu*—'hello' in Nanai, a Tungusic language related to Manchu—Leonid got straight down to business. 'I want to establish a joint Sino-Russian Hezhe–Nanai ethno-tourism park on Bolshoi Ussuriisky Island,' he told me, gesturing at the fragment of mid-Amur territory visible from the square. His preoccupation with this ambitious project reflected the longstanding perspective of local indigenous groups who have seen North East Asia's mighty continental rivers not as edges hemming in populations tied to Moscow or Beijing, but as centres of their world. Before either Russians or Chinese settled here in significant numbers, indigenous peoples such as the Ulchi and Oroqen hunted in the forests here, or like the Nanai subsisted mostly on fishing. The rivers Amur, Ussuri and Sungari were thus givers of biological life, economic livelihood and a shamanic worldview that imbued these natural surrounds with great spiritual power. But for a century the Nanai have been growing steadily estranged from their historic riverine lives. Split into a Russified group north of Khabarovsk and a Sinicised community to the south in China, they are known over the border as the Hezhe. On the divided island, Leonid wanted to reunify these two constituencies.

'Basically it comes down to land, we need some of our land back,' he said as we settled on a bench in front of the slender blue-domed Cathedral of the Dormition of the Mother of God. 'The Russians behave like occupiers here, and we're not happy.' Offering evidence of the invidious 150-year-old coloniser presence on Nanai territory, Leonid pointed at the cathedral, a building reconstructed in an Orthodox religious revival underway since the end of Soviet times: 'Look at that thing. They can just build whatever they want, but when it comes to decisions affecting us and our culture, or my plans for a park, they don't even consult us. Our way of life here has been destroyed systematically over the years. Most of us who live in the city don't speak the language anymore, hardly anyone fishes, and these days our young people only care about buying a Japanese car with air-con and driving round like idiots.'

The rebuilt cathedral was indeed an evocative symbol of the changes afoot in Khabarovsk, not only following the Soviet collapse but ever since the city's 1858 foundation. Before this, the ancestors of today's Nanai/Hezhe—then derogatorily labelled 'Fishskin Tatars' given their use of that material to make clothing—lived relatively secluded from either Chinese or Russian imperial influence. Occasional contact included visits by scouts or cartographers, but mostly indigenous groups interacted among themselves in regional networks of trade and exchange that extended across North East Asia to today's Sakhalin, Hokkaido and eventually Alaska.

Among the first European observers of the Nanai/Hezhe was a group of early 1700s French Jesuit missionaries dispatched by the Manchu Qing court to map the region. Aside from recording aspects of their animistic beliefs and traditions, the missionaries also reported that some southerly Chinese-influenced communities raised pigs. Most fascinatingly to the missionaries, these animals were fed almost exclusively on fish, a practice that rendered the meat 'unfit for consumption' in the view of these Gallic *gourmands*.[17]

But from the mid-nineteenth century, sporadic interest from Beijing gave way to the mass arrival of settlers from across both the Russian and Chinese empires as the Qing hit crisis point and the Russians annexed swathes of East Asia through which I had been travelling. Now more pressing questions than what to feed pigs faced the Nanai/Hezhe. Colonial efforts to 'civilise' these 'natives' began with demands of loyalty to the Manchu emperor from one side and a Russian Orthodox god from the other. These were followed in the twentieth century by vigorous 'modernisation' campaigns as socialism took hold in Russia, and later in China. Early Soviet ethnologists wondered whether seemingly hierarchy-free peoples like the Nanai might already be practising a kind of 'primitive communism' and could therefore take a shortcut to the egalitarian utopia that was the logical end-point of Marxist history. But soon enough condescending imperialist ideas regained primacy in both the USSR and PRC, and backward-seeming indigenous semi-nomads were forcefully encouraged to settle en masse into permanent villages.[18] Seasonal trips up- and downriver and intimate knowledge of land and water were replaced by fixed registration in collectivised fishing 'brigades', and industrialised exploitation of the local environment that ravaged forests and fish stocks on both sides of the border.[19]

Leonid explained to me that many of Russia's 12,000 Nanai today inhabit a chain of Siberian-style wooden villages strung north of

Khabarovsk along the middle and lower Amur where it flows solely across Russian territory. Having fared as badly as anywhere in the region since Soviet times, these mostly depopulated settlements are today wracked by social ills including alcoholism, unemployment, drug addiction and premature mortality as they struggle to subsist on seasonal fishing. Even fresh water itself, for centuries the lifeblood of Nanai existence, is unavailable in these plumbing-free villages. Since the river is too dirty, water must be brought—and paid for—by tanker truck every few weeks.

How had it come to this, I wondered. What was it that made the Russians disregard Nanai interests?

'They think if they give us too many rights then we'll get together with the Chinese and the other indigenous groups and drive them out,' Leonid replied. 'But the worst of it is that this paranoia is basically unfounded. What they don't seem to realise is that it's much easier for Nanai to talk to Russians than to the Chinese.' This explanation, echoing what I had heard from Dmitri back in Yakutsk, attested to the inevitable inter-community familiarity engendered by colonialism. The colonised usually know their colonisers much better than vice versa.

'Besides,' he continued, 'it's not like things are better for our Hezhe brothers over the border. The Chinese have destroyed our culture there too. If anything it's worse there because the Han haven't forgiven the Manchus for ruling over them as the Qing dynasty and so they punish all Tungusic people. Us and the Manchus—we used to be known as the Jurchen and we harassed and ruled over the Chinese for centuries!'

Leonid had come to our meeting wearing an extravagant blue robe whose stitching and cut, he confided, were actually Manchu rather than Nanai in style. Emblazoned with the Chinese character for 'dragon' (龍), the robe would make further appearances during my stay as I accompanied him to functions and media events where he advanced his cause for the ethno-park. We also attended a performance of the local native theatre troupe he ran, named 'Buri' after the original Nanai name for the confluence where Khabarovsk was later founded. Indeed, in Chinese the city is still sometimes called 'Boli' after Buri's Manchu equivalent, although the official name is the more cumbersome 'Habaluofusike', a Sinicisation of 'Khabarovsk'.

But back in the square, conversation shifted to another of Leonid's causes, the need to have the Nanai inscribed into the Khabarovsk city constitution as a locally indigenous group. Decades of supposed 'civili-sation' had not helped the Russian state recognise that indigenous peoples are still indigenous in urban areas.

'The thing is,' one of Leonid's co-campaigners said, 'that it's really in their interests to give us rights. We've told them, when this is all effectively Chinese territory in twenty years' time and we're over-whelmed by immigrants from Uzbekistan and the Caucasus'—here mountains/plains distinctions seemed irrelevant—'then the Russians will be outnumbered and will wish they had the kind of mechanism for defending minority rights that we're asking for!'

Leonid took up the conversation again. 'I've been saying to those goats for a decade,' he said, referring to contacts in the local legisla-ture, '"You want to know what it feels like to be Nanai? Just wait until you're swamped by Chinese and Central Asian guest workers." They laughed at me then. But they're not laughing now.'

We left our bench and walked down Muravyov-Amursky Street. As Leonid explained which parts of the perfidious government were housed in which buildings—Indigenous Affairs, astonishingly part of the Ministry for Management of Natural Resources, lay down an unas-suming side-street—our conversation continued to oscillate between giddy idealism and hard-nosed realism about where the Nanai's best prospects lay. Leonid's historical reveries of once-mighty Jurchens repeatedly came up short against reflections that, however recent the Slavic arrival here, ordinary Nanai and Russians, for better or worse, do inhabit a common post-Soviet reality. But he still had plenty of complaints about being lorded over by detached Moscow elites, which, while echoing Ilya's, were sharpened by the presence of ethnic antago-nism. And China was, as ever, a complicated presence in all this. Although mirroring Russia's destruction of Nanai/Hezhe ways, the country to the south was for Leonid also a canvas on which to project utopian ideas of ethnic reunification.

As I would later see for myself, the Chinese Hezhe in fact enjoy a much higher material standard of living, even if, as Leonid noted, they are arguably still more Sinicised than the Nanai are Russianised. His awareness of this was unusual, for with few resources for travel, many Nanai are not especially familiar with Hezhe realities. Like the Shiwei Russians, the post-Soviet era's permeable borders and greater mobility does not guarantee that kin separated in times past will actually see or have anything to do with one another. Some reciprocal Nanai–Hezhe visits have occurred on a limited scale since the early 1990s, but a few tearful meetings between elderly individuals who now share only a few snatches of common language have always been led by ethnic Han Chinese or Russian organisers, and have often had trade rather than cultural concerns as their primary motive. Nevertheless, Leonid's optimism in the face of this remained dogged, and was if anything paradoxically fuelled by governmental intransigence. As we parted at the end of my time in Khabarovsk, he welcomed my return: 'Come to the ethno-park when it opens! If the island project is realised, then who knows, the Nanai and Hezhe could be liberated and reunited like East and West Germany!' he said cheerfully and walked away swishing his robe dramatically.

* * *

Leonid's quixotic ambitions for cross-border tourism on native terms drew on distinctly Cold War precedents, but in the indigenous lands along the Russian Amur several sites are emerging as tourist destinations because of deeper regional histories, including Chinese ones. On Khabarovsk's outskirts, a modest building of great interest to Chinese visitors once served as a prison-home to the last Qing Emperor Puyi. Having ruled two states, adopted Western fashions, been imprisoned in the USSR, applied to join the Soviet Communist Party, and returned to China to work as a gardener, Puyi led a life embodying the region's many early mid-twentieth-century cataclysms, and I would be seeing more of him when I later visited the north-eastern Chinese city of Changchun. But first there was another head of state, one who founded rather than concluded a dynasty, and other Chinese pasts to look for in Khabarovsk region.

Downriver, nestled amid the blighted Nanai villages I had discussed with Leonid, is the settlement of Vyatskoe, site of a secret 1940s base for the Soviet Red Army's Chinese- and Korean-dominated 88th International Brigade, birthplace of Kim Jong Il, and today also a developing destination on the Chinese tourist itinerary. Reached after an hour's drive north of Khabarovsk on the potholed highway to Komsomolsk, Vyatskoe has never been a glamorous place. Hearing of my planned excursion there, Ilya had wryly mentioned that the place is unflatteringly nicknamed 'Blyadskoe' by locals, a play on a very rude Russian word. But I was not discouraged from boarding the Komsomolsk bus, requesting permission to jump off at the relevant turning, and then walking from the highway down a newly tarmacked road through the trees. Vyatskoe itself is perched above a picturesque inlet where a branch of the Amur snakes around a small wooded islet, and on a spot overlooking this I walked between slowly rotting Soviet-era holiday cabins looking for signs of life. A pavilion daubed in faded paint celebrating Vyatskoe's 150th anniversary in 2009 looked like it was itself a century and a half old, and a leisure complex for employees of the Khabarovsk Metal Construction Plant appeared to be taking a long break of its own. But traces of the less peaceful era of the 88th Brigade were also in evidence.

After several minutes scouring the buildings around the holiday cabins for signs of life, I encountered Olga who came out of her house ducking under a low washing line and shooing away the pair of geese who roamed her small yard. It was rare, she said, to meet a traveller from so far away, but less surprising to hear about my motive.

'More and more people come to our little village these days looking for the 88th Brigade history,' she reflected. 'It's basically just Chinese people though. This summer we've had lots of groups, sometimes up to forty people.' I was lucky to have met Olga, for she had been in contact with Chinese visitors since even before the latest flurry of activity. She thus had a privileged perspective on recent developments.

'Some veterans groups have been coming here for years,' she continued, pointing as we walked through the village to a plaque dated April 2005 on the side of a large wooden building. The sign read, 'We will always remember what happened here' in Russian and Chinese, yet it emerged that the version of what was being remembered was not so straightforwardly translated across borders.

Vyatskoe assumed a role as a military camp when north-east Chinese and Korean liberation fighters, forced to retreat from Japanese conquest of their own lands, moved into the Soviet Far East in the early 1940s, making the most of the woods that today still provide continuous tree cover along much of the Manchuria–Russia border. Here they would receive Soviet training in a location that was strategically close

141

to the Chinese and Korean frontiers, but also remote enough to be beyond Japan's reach. Olga led me to where the village met the forest, unlocking two diminutive but newly constructed cabins housing memorabilia from this time. Gathered through both official and unofficial international channels from the families of Chinese veterans, local history enthusiasts, and the descendants of local residents on the Russian side, the modest collection of blurry photos and yellowed letters offered a fading portrait of Vyatskoe's martial past. Among the largest contributors is the family of Mikhail Uza, a half-Chinese, half-Nanai intelligence agent who served here alongside the 88th Brigade's most famous soldier, and commander of its First Battalion, the first North Korean president Kim Il Sung.

On one side of one of the cabins were several rarely seen photos of the future DPRK leader during his time in the village, a sojourn recollected by Kim himself in his auto-hagiography *With the Century*. But while official North Korean history acknowledges this period in the life of the country's 'Great Leader' and eternal president, its account diverges from that documented by Russian evidence. Kim's time in Vyatskoe is made to sound much shorter than it was, a discrepancy with especial significance where the birth of his son-and-heir Jong Il is concerned. The Pyongyang-authorised history maintains that Kim Il Sung left the USSR in 1941 to return, via Manchuria, to a secret guerrilla camp at the foot of the sacred Korean peak Mount Paektu, an evocative setting where Kim Jong Il was supposedly born in 1942. But, as inconveniently meticulous Soviet records attest, Kim-the-elder in fact remained on the banks of the Amur for four further years, and his son was born in 1941 in Vyatskoe where he acquired the Russian nickname 'Yura'. The Kims in fact only left the USSR for Korea in August 1945 as Red Army forces, the 88th Brigade among them, swept over far eastern Soviet borders to liberate Manchuria and Korea from Japanese occupation at the end of World War II.

Unsurprisingly given its challenge to the DPRK foundation myth, there has been no North Korean involvement in or even acknowledgement of the increasing local and Chinese interest in commemorating Vyatskoe's past, despite invitations to collaborate.[20] As I explored the rest of the village with Olga, it was also evident that first-hand recollections of that fateful time when the Kims were neighbours are grow-

ing increasingly obscure. On a slope at the opposite end of the settlement from the cabins, a local man named Vladimir who, born in 1942,
reported having faint memories of those times, conceded that no one
with strong connections was around anymore.

'The last of the women who knew them has passed on now,' he said
laconically. Female life expectancy has long exceeded its male counterpart in Russia, so women often remember most. Near Vladimir's
wooden house, a large empty plot of thick knee-high grass marked the
site of the home once inhabited by the Kims.

'And that place burned to the ground a few years back,' Vladimir
added, 'quite a while ago now. I woke up one night and saw a great light
outside, and when I came out in the morning the whole place was
gone, the remains still smouldering ...'

Yet if Korean traces were disappearing amid amnesia and ruin,
Chinese versions of 88th Brigade history were resurgent, and not only
in the form of Olga's tour groups. The new track I had walked down to
Vyatskoe from the highway, its smoothness defying the old Russian
adage that the country's main problems are 'idiots and roads' (*duraki i
dorogi*), was a clue to this, and I headed back towards it to investigate.
The new surface had been laid to allow Chinese trucks easier access to
a large plinth where I found teams of Uzbek and Chinese workers
pouring concrete and shifting loads of faux marble slabs through the
surrounding trees. The men's housing, prefabricated cabins like those
of Yakutsk's Chinese market traders, stood nearby, and work proceeded
mostly in silence. A building plan pinned to a noticeboard nearby stated
that the monument being erected would comprise a 50-foot high metal
spike behind a sculpture of three hands gripping rifles and a Chinese
sword, all emerging from an ornate golden globe. The project, the
placard continued, was dedicated to the 'united anti-Japanese forces'
of the 88th Brigade, and would also eventually include a full reconstruction of the camp and a formal graveyard to the Chinese guerrillas
who died while training here.

'We don't know much about the history ourselves,' said one of the
Chinese workers, an employee of the Beijing-based Ruiyang Land-
scaping Company that was undertaking construction. But evidently
someone did, and the scale of the endeavour spoke of backing from
both sides. Indeed, the Vyatskoe memorial follows a steady stream of

commemorations in the wake of the seventieth anniversary of the end of World War II, a milestone that saw symmetrical visits by Presidents Xi and Putin to Moscow and Beijing as guests of honour at each other's 2015 military parades. For Moscow, this offered a useful opportunity to trumpet its purportedly strengthening relationship with China as relations cooled with the West over the Ukraine crisis. From its side, Beijing has been working hard to harmonise its record of World War II with 'global' (essentially Western and Russian) narratives. Hence 1930s–40s battles on Chinese soil that were once presented primarily as chapters in China's Communist-led liberation from colonialism now form part of a worldwide 'anti-Fascist struggle'. Having long ago learnt the harsh lesson of exclusion from the post-World War I Versailles peace conference, China's latest assertion of a role mirroring Russia's in World War II is also a claim to a more prominent place in the contemporary global order that emerged from that conflict.

Yet developments by the Amur offered telling indications of the limits to such harmonisation efforts, and to Sino-Russian rapprochement in a wider international context. For all its apparent Sinophile vigour, Russia-backed commemoration of the 88th Brigade must tread lightly around the sensitive North Korean dimension to this history, not least because Moscow's desire to have a seat at every global negotiating table, and its shared border with the DPRK, means it continues to cultivate relations with Pyongyang. In Vyatskoe, all the residents I spoke to knew of the birth of Kim Jong Il here and were amused that North Korea failed to acknowledge it. Indeed, the hubbub of monument construction had only enhanced the currency of the Kims as a local topic of conversation. But while wry grins and sardonic comments must remain local so as not to become a sticking-point in Russo-North Korean relations, in the borderlands 'local' very often also means international, particularly as ever more Chinese enthusiasts make the regional pilgrimage to mark their ancestors' heroism on foreign soil.

* * *

Before departing on the Trans-Siberian's very last southward flourish, I visited Khabarovsk's Regional Museum, where many of the themes I had heard discussed throughout the Russian Far East were summed up on walls and behind glass. Immediately inside the recently expanded building's new wing was a vast map of the Amur River basin. Covering both Russian and Chinese sides of the watershed, this topographical projection was free of the state borders that offer torment and entice-ment in equal measure to Leonid, Ilya, Zhe, Lyuba, regional history buffs, Birobidzhan bridge-builders and tourists moving in both direc-tions. The museum even boasted several glass tanks in which live Amur fish flopped around, trapped behind invisible boundaries as local chil-dren tapped on the glass.

In an upstairs room, another map, this one covering all Eurasia, offered still more poignant testament to border troubles. Here the disintegration of the USSR was represented by bright white lighting that shone from behind the map piercing the gaps between new post-Soviet states. This vivid image showed how, with the empire cast asun-der, old Russia's West became new Europe's East, and 'Oriental' 'Stans fell into China's western ambit. A brand-new exhibition hall on an upper floor focused on the history of the Orthodox Church, whose jubilant reaction to the Soviet collapse had been a source of scorn to Leonid. Pro-Chinese atheist Ilya had similarly referred to Orthodoxy as 'just another Leninist opiate'. Rebirth out of Soviet stricture had permitted the church to make a wider return to East Asia, and as som-bre music played in the background, grainy photographs documented past and present Orthodox missionary activities in Tokyo and Beijing. I would be exploring traces of these when I eventually made it to the Chinese capital.

Between here and Beijing, however, lay Manchuria, and one final Russian outpost. My previous visits to Khabarovsk had occurred during a year I spent living in Vladivostok as an undergraduate student, and, although this had been a difficult time in many ways, it seemed a shame not to return there now it was so near. Closeness being relative in eastern Russia, getting to Vladivostok still involved a twelve-hour over-night train, the evocatively named 'Ocean' express, aboard which I shared a compartment with a taciturn Chinese man from Jilin province and a girl and her grandmother on their annual trip to a Primorsky sanatorium. As if in farewell to Khabarovsk's once and present role as a bastion of eastern Orthodoxy, a blonde woman wearing a white Adidas tracksuit bustled into the compartment just before departure and wordlessly placed a selection of small icons on the lace tablecloth. Nonplussed, we looked at one another and so, equally wordlessly, the icons were gathered up again and the tracksuit bustled out.

Vladivostok, which means 'rule the east', is known to those who feel affection for it as 'Vladik', but I was not sure quite whether I fitted into this category. My first return since living in the city was made not without reservations, for my year of Chinese language study there had been a rollercoaster of fascination and heartbreak. Initially, time had seemed to race by with the novelty of distance and the distracting complexities of getting established in an alien system and language. But soon life had seemed to slide into a languid sadness, days had drifted listlessly by, and as winter marshalled its arsenal of freezing shards progress through the first term at the Far Eastern National University's Oriental Institute had seemed to grind to a halt. Winds whipped neglected tower blocks, water pipes froze, the Sea of Japan froze, I froze. Winter holiday visits to South Korea and China and a move out of the student dormitory had rubbed momentary salve into my growing familiarity with *toska*, a deeply Russian form of existential angst, and I was comforted by the feeling that I was learning much about Russia, China and myself. But a romance with another foreign student—an American perhaps negotiating her own *toska*—somehow brought out the worst in me and then only revealed itself to me as love when it was already too late, leaving stark, remorseful memories of that time. As the train rolled out of Khabarovsk down track that had first opened in 1897, before the Trans-Sib was complete, the *Ocean*'s locomotive thus also seemed to be dragging with it plenty of mental freight from a more recent past.

Beyond the affairs of my young heart, much of what had been difficult about life in Vladivostok in 2007–8 was associated with the state of the built city. Vladik's tsarist-era buildings originally bore the ornate bombast of a thriving and cosmopolitan port. By the 1880s, only two decades after the city's foundation, its population was over a third Chinese and also boasted significant numbers of Koreans, Japanese, Europeans and Americans.[21] But 130 years later, and twenty years after socialism collapsed, these edifices had lain grim and crumbling, streets were largely devoid of road markings or traffic lights, and in winter pavements were rarely cleared of ice. Danger and desolation conspired and inevitably depressed. But I had perhaps seen Vladivostok at its lowest ebb, for—people had told me—a flurry of reconstruction around the city's hosting of the 2012 Summit of the Asia-Pacific Economic Cooperation forum had since transformed the place. It might not be the 'megapolis' I had heard it dubbed by one drinking companion along the way, but the changes did at least include two new enormous bridges, and given the lethargic pace of construction elsewhere in the Russian Far East this had to mean something.

The day I spent in Vladivostok was a fog-shrouded one, but the changes that were visible did indeed appear staggering. I left my bags at a small hostel—there used to be no hostels catering for no travellers—and boarded the luminous yellow number 15 bus, which wound through town over both bridges. The first of these, linking the shores of the city's Golden Horn Bay, a curious 'orientally' named body of water also referred to as the 'Eastern Bosporus', was almost completely shrouded in mist. One of the bridge's pylons sprouted out of lumpy concrete at the end of Pushkin Street where I had lived in the second half of my previous sojourn, and as its tips disappeared into the impenetrable closeness of the sky I began to feel a still greater sense of mystery and uncertainty than I had arrived with. The bus crossed to the Churkin peninsula, scorned locally as home to most of the city's thugs, and moved on to the second, longer bridge. This links the city to the offshore Russky ('Russian') Island, and since the island offers few attractions aside from the new campus of Far Eastern Federal University (the relocated and upgraded Far Eastern National University I had attended), it has been dubbed a 'bridge to nowhere' built merely to enrich Putin and other Moscow-based cronies.

Arriving at the gates of the transplanted university, I felt increasingly lost in the fog and drained by hot days and long journeys. In two 1932 letters sent en route to a second stay in Japan, Boris Pilnyak described sensing something similar, writing from outside Vladivostok: 'Trains, trains, trains, the train, the taiga ... in west Siberia it was hot, now I'm freezing.' Several days later from the city itself he added, 'I'm so confused by the mixed up times, I can't fall asleep before six or seven in the morning (twelve in Moscow), so I sleep all day.'[22]

Peering myself through seasons and across time, I looked briefly at the campus and then returned to town to continue touring old haunts as the opaque air pushed me closer to my memories. On hilly Aleutskaya Street (named after the same people as Alaska's island chain), I could not tell whether it was fatigue or emotion that was causing the tightness in my chest. Some Korean students clustered outside the door of the dormitory building where I had once lived, talking in hushed tones. But I did not approach them; what would I say except a bland 'I was here'?

On the peak of the city's most famous hill, Eagle's Nest, a wedding party grimly sipped champagne and hollered to each other as it began to rain, attempting to enjoy the vistaless backdrop under a cross-bearing statue of the alphabet-inventing Slavic Saints Cyril and Methodius. Weddings being a one-day affair, this was their only chance for photographs overlooking the bay. These snapshots would be just as featureless as those of the Chinese tourists who, on a similarly tight schedule, were also huddled nearby.

Down below in the city centre, newly paved streets boasted newly installed traffic lights, and I visited a new bar named after Mumiy Troll, a rock band who are Vladivostok's most famous musical export. Ilya Lagutenko, the band's lead singer, had studied Chinese at the university's Oriental Institute two decades before I had, and so this made for a strange kind of disembodied reunion. Towards evening, the skies cleared a little and a parade of distant barges became visible off the beachside promenade. I ate some chewy cubes of barbecued lamb *shashlik* dipped in sweet and watery ketchup. Vladivostok bears finality as its birthmark, and as far as Russia was concerned, this was the end of the line for me. My visa was expiring even if my difficult memories, now diluted like the ketchup, were not, and it was time to return from the frontiers of recollection to more tangible borders to the west.

6

THE GREAT NORTHERN WILDERNESS

MANCHURIAN AMUR

The approach to the Chinese frontier at Pogranichny, whose name—
meaning 'by the border'—points to one of the landscape's unambiguously human-imposed features, is more gradual than at Zabaikalsk or
Blagoveshchensk. The bus across hours of wild countryside was made
still slower because the road through the town of Ussuriisk was under
repair, touched by tentacles of improvement reaching out from
Vladivostok into the surrounding province. As rickety yellow construction vehicles laid asphalt amid spouts of black smoke, we lurched
left and right to avoid unfinished sections of paving. There being no
analogue to Mr Ren reeling off foreign vocabulary next to me, everything was calm on board. This was the public bus up to the border
rather than the chartered vehicles that convey most Russian shoppers
and traders all the way into China, and so the seats were half-empty.
Passing Snegovaya ('snowy'), we actually shed passengers as listless
young conscripts disembarked to trudge across fields to a nearby border guard garrison. No one spoke, a few pairs of earphones hissed,
and everything cocooned within the upholstered brown interior of the
bus seemed muted by the vast stillness of the surrounding hills.
Scrubby slopes and thickets would continue to roll westward from
here through Manchuria to Mongolia, forming a Eurasian landscape

that, as Mr Bian had noted in Shiwei, remains remarkably consistent despite its varied inhabitants.

But the mirrored differences between most states are exaggerated at borders, and parochial Pogranichny had many counterparts to Blagoveshchensk's austere nationalistic furniture. 'By the border' were symbols of the Russian Far East's by-now-familiar air of guardedness. A rotund Lenin, his flat cap scrunched up tightly in his right fist, over-looked the cracked tarmac and shallow puddles of a sad main square whose only glimmer of life was a newly installed playground. Under a rainbow banner reading 'Pogranichny, we love you!' a few local children were larking on the swings, slide and roundabout. But any love the town received was of the nostalgic variety, and behind Lenin an overgrown park displayed a solemn row of Soviet-era graves to fallen border guards. Cement headstones repainted in striking silver were moulded into busts, military pennants, figures bent in mourning and squat obelisks. Flecks of crimson picked out eternal flames and diminutive Soviet stars, and one metal plaque celebrated the 'unbending courage' of Red Army soldiers who fell fighting Japan's 1920s–30s incursions into the young USSR. The Russian term meaning 'courage'—*muzhestvo*—is cognate with the word for 'man'—*muzhchina*—and this militarised gallery conveyed a steely frontier masculinity. At a nearby grocers, I bought a vanilla ice cream made by the popular retro brand 'CCCP', and ate it as I wandered back from this array of territorial inscriptions to the bus station.

As was by now routine, my nationality was an immediate source of consternation at the border. Russian and British passports are (for now) both red, and so for officials sitting low down in dingy booths, the realisation that the next person in line—me—was not like the others came as a last-minute shock. Even when my non-Russianness had been ascertained, discerning the meaning of the jumble of words 'United Kingdom of Great Britain and Northern Ireland' was challenging even for English-speakers. Oksana, as her name badge identified her, was evidently not an English-speaker, although it seemed impossible that her grumpiness that afternoon stemmed solely from linguistic difficulties. Frowning thickly, she pored over my passport with a funerary seriousness, flicking back and forth between irrelevant visas and stamps, perhaps wondering as Lyuba had back in Blagoveshchensk what the point of long-distance travel was. I could only stand, stranded once again between civilisations, looking back apologetically at the Chinese tourists and traders who were waiting to follow me through this officious gauntlet. But just as time seemed to be dissolving into an eternally stagnant Soviet present, there were three bangs. Three exit stamps in three places and a frown onward. I gratefully shuffled past Oksana, rejoining members of the Heilongjiang tour group with whom I would be sharing my bus ride onward.

Mr Wang, a timber trader who had been travelling to and fro between China and Russia since the 1990s, was sick of the whole business. 'All this makes you think they don't want us to come to their country at all,' he despaired. 'China welcomes foreign business, but Russia makes things so hard, it's like they just don't care.'

As we climbed back aboard and the bus rumbled across the no-man's-land between the Russian and Chinese border posts, I asked why he thought this might be. 'This part of Russia is big and has hardly any people,' he explained. 'They don't care about foreign business and they don't care about this part of the country. Look,' he pointed out of the window at a slope of tangled bushes, which, topped by rusting radio masts, were receding behind us. 'There's nothing here. All this would be cultivated in China, here the land is just empty.'

On the Chinese side, there was more bustle, a feeling enhanced by the excitement many members of the Heilongjiang group were evidently feeling at the prospect of returning home. The border guards at Suifenhe were as confused by my presence as I was amused by their broken sign that solemnly read 'CHIN IMMIGRATION INSPECTION'. But theirs was curiosity rather than hostility, and I was processed quickly, glad that this would be the last of my three border crossings.

* * *

In Suifenhe, I settled on a hotel called Sisters run by a woman called Nadya, a local with a carefully chosen Slavic name, a facility for the Russian language, and a capacity for fierceness befitting the frontier. Such straightforwardness is held across China to be a hallmark of the north-eastern character. Standing imperiously in the middle of the lobby when I arrived, Nadya was trying as politely as possible, yet in a no-nonsense fashion, to attend to the seemingly limitless needs of a corpulent Russian man with no shirt on. As he and several female companions heaved boxes of recently purchased Chinese merchandise into a storeroom, she shooed them along, little amused by the regular breaks they took to suck on green bottles of local Xuehua beer.

Having executed that task and finally able to turn to me, Nadya explained that the hotel's name was a reference to the fact that her sister Ira had set up shop at the other end of the old China Eastern Railway in Manzhouli. 'We're a kind of north-eastern dynasty,' she added gaily, ushering me into the lift where a garish poster covering one wall advertised nightly performances at the hotel restaurant by a possibly Chinese or Russian person calling himself 'DJ Sergey'. A Russian woman got in with me, and I asked if she had attended one of these cross-cultural soirées.

'Of course,' she said indignantly, 'you have to cheer yourself up somehow.'

It is a sign of the routineness of Russian shopping trips to Suifenhe, or indeed Manzhouli or Heihe, that they are now viewed with jadedness by some. But there still remain many for whom the chance to escape the tedium of home brings a frisson of excitement. Perhaps in anticipation of the pulsating techno proffered by DJ Sergey, a gang of Russian men spent much of my stay at Sisters running up and down our shared corridor hammering on each other's doors and taunting one another with offers of a *kunya*. A Russified version of the Chinese word *guniang* meaning 'girl' as unknown to most Russians outside the Far East as the word *lieba* (bread) to non-northeastern Chinese, *kunya* refers to local women whose services generally extend beyond the traditional Chinese massages they advertise. For some male Russian travellers at least, crossing the border to Suifenhe means entering a new zone of foreign permissiveness.

But whatever the diversions offered to a foreign clientele, Suifenhe mirrors Pogranichny's Russianness in remaining thoroughly Chinese. If the latter asserts its national belonging in defiantly military terms, the former exudes a blend of commercial boisterousness and confounding cultural bricolage that are unmistakable characteristics of modern China. Shops along Suifenhe's bustling Longxugou Pedestrian Street blurted out recorded messages in both Chinese and Russian, often incomprehensibly distorted in both languages, saccharine Mando-pop drifted across the town's central square, and local cafés offered bubble tea and experimental concoctions that included cups of iced instant coffee mixed with red wine.

As I made my way through this incoherent but invigorating synaesthetic soup, I was beckoned over by Maxim, a local electronics dealer. Not discouraged on learning that I was a Western tourist rather than a potential Russian shopper, he proceeded to offer an account of local life that was itself a work of fantastical nationalistic impressionism. Originally from Changsha on China's distant central plains, Maxim had left school at fourteen and had been engaging in audacious ventures of exchange and barter in Suifenhe ever since. But despite being here for over ten years, he remained vexed by local business practices.

'I just don't understand Russians,' he said as we stepped inside his compact wire-draped shop to shelter from a brief summer shower. 'You can know them for a year and be getting on really well, going out for drinks and everything. But then you upset them just once and they'll never speak to you again! I've had this kind of situation with several people.'

I asked whether the fall-outs had their origins in trade dealings. 'Quite possibly, yes,' replied Maxim. 'And ok, maybe I cheated them a tiny bit once or twice, sold them phone chargers over market rate. But not enough to deserve what happened next! Now they just ignore me. My old friends even still come to this part of town when they visit Suifenhe, but they'll just walk straight past my shop, wave, and go and buy from somebody else. It's embarrassing!'

To Maxim, who held firm to the Chinese belief that doing business with someone ideally meant forging a relationship beyond mere economics, this was wholly confusing. 'Russians are very direct,' he continued. 'They know what they want and just go for it. Normally Chinese people when they're out shopping like to walk around a bit first, talk to sellers, cultivate feelings with them.'

I asked if that was the same everywhere in the country, in Changsha as much as up here. 'Definitely these things are important in Changsha,' he said, 'but actually north-eastern Chinese are quite like Russians in some ways. They're much more direct than us southerners. I think it's because of the historical relationship here,' he continued, segueing into history, which turned out to be his favourite subject.

'You see, when Mao Zedong liberated China from the Japanese in 1945, Stalin helped him,' he said. Even if it wasn't exactly Mao who had defeated the Empire of the Rising Sun, Suifenhe had indeed been a crossing point when Soviet troops, along with Vyatskoe's Chinese and Korean guerrilla-exiles, entered Manchuria at the end of World War II. But from here Maxim's narrative veered off into more fanciful territory. 'And because of Stalin's help, Chairman Mao returned Khabarovsk, Vladivostok and Ussuriisk to Russia,' he said, undeterred by my doubtful looks: by the 1940s, all these locations had been thoroughly Soviet.

'China used to be huge!' he went on, 'Timur, a Mongol during the Qing dynasty, ate up all of Asia, just like Germany ate up all of Europe! This was a great empire.'

Now confused over whether imperialist predation was supposed to be bad (Japanese or Russian) or good (Chinese), I tried to think of something to say in response. But I need not have worried, as this haphazard blend of several centuries of Inner Asian history soon collapsed under the weight of its own conjecture, and Maxim returned to more geographically and temporally immediate concerns. 'Anyway,' he said, 'north-easterners hate the Japanese. I mean, I hate them too, but people here *really* hate them. If it hadn't been for them, and the Civil War, there'd be two billion of us by now. They're so horrible, I wouldn't talk to a Japanese person if I ever met one.'

But he was talking to me, I pointed out, and from a Chinese point of view had the British seizure of Hong Kong and many other concessions not been just as detestable as the Japanese invasions of northern China?

'Ah, but the British were fighting against the Qing who were Manchus,' Maxim explained. 'What the Japanese did was against the Han.' I felt more confused. For Maxim, the need to distinguish between today's friends and enemies demanded that European colonialism in the south of a Manchu-ruled empire seem less egregious than Japanese invasion of the Manchus' own north-eastern homeland. As I would be discovering as I explored deeper into Manchuria, Japanese soldiers had indeed committed unspeakable acts here during the 1930s and '40s. But I was reasonably confident that the British mid-nineteenth-century sale of opium to Han Chinese at the point of a gun was also pretty bad.

It seemed unlikely that I would manage to wade through this morass of layered resentments. Many previous conversations across China had convinced me of the complications of parsing unreckoned-with history defined largely by patriotic priorities in a hyper-internationalised present. In selectively forgetting according to contemporary needs, China is far from unique, even if the state's formidable censorship skills make its efforts in this regard more effective than those in Russia and indeed the UK. For Maxim and many others, Japan's colonisation of parts of China is far more pressing a bone of contention than Britain's longer and deeper incursions into China. Geography too plays a role here. Japan remains an East Asian regional rival and counter-party in fiery territorial arguments over rocks like the Diaoyu/Senkaku Islands. But Hong Kong's return to Chinese rule in 1997 and Britain's, albeit reluctant, retreat into its rightful role as a small country on the other side of the world have mostly seen the clouds of justifiable anger dissipate like sickly sweet opium smoke.

In any case, Maxim had by now moved on from global affairs to vaunting the wisdom of China's rulers, and wanted to discuss the differences between the queen and the Chinese Communist Party. But I felt it was time to move on and made my excuses. 'No problem, stop by again!' he said jauntily. Wishing to avoid leaving him with the feelings of abandonment caused by his former Russian friends, I departed with a confident 'ok!' There was much to see in Suifenhe beyond the commercial bustle.

* * *

As in Manzhouli at the other end of the 1897–1903 Russian-built CER, an old Russia still lurks in Suifenhe's shadows, though here it takes more varied form. Tumbledown colonial brick houses resembling Manzhouli's lie near the train tracks that still run through the heart of town, slumping beneath the incongruous pseudo-Slavic domes of Suifenhe's skyscrapers. But if these dwellings are ignored, there is plentiful evidence of history's preference for preserving grandeur over the fabric of everyday life. Some larger buildings, such as the former Russian and Japanese consulates (Image 9), remain more or less intact, while others have undergone curious enhancements. The Orthodox St Nicholas' church now bears a 15-foot-high plastic red cross above its doorway, and its onion-domed tower displays a square clock resembling a 1980s Seiko watch face. The town's quaint 1898 art nouveau railway station has been supplemented by a bland concrete portico featuring the logo of the Chinese national railway company, as well as bold façade-obscuring banners trumpeting Suifenhe's desire to 'build a golden bridge to the Asia-Pacific'.

These modifications may reflect local efforts to reclaim these arte-facts of a foreign past for China, as the history of the CER has at times been as traumatic as the Japanese colonial experience I had discussed with Maxim. As I picked my way along the railway line from the station past the ruined trackside houses, my eye was caught by a marble plaque attesting to this. Affixed to a bridge, whose low archways today strain to span a modern four-lane highway, the plaque explained that this was 'The First Bridge in the Far East', the easternmost of the CER's origi-nal bridges. Its text went on to offer a succinct description of how, having grabbed vast tracts of Chinese land via its Engels-condemned 1858 and 1860 treaties, St Petersburg had switched its approach to exploiting Qing enfeeblement into the railway sphere.

Tsarist Russia's keenness on knitting the empire together with iron rails had by the last decades of the nineteenth century come to focus on linking the distant east to the rest of the country. During an 1890–1 tour of Asia, the then-future Tsar Nicholas II had visited eastern Russian cities en route to Japan (where someone tried to kill him), and in Vladivostok had attended a ground-breaking ceremony for the Trans-Siberian Railway. This enormous project would be started from both ends simultaneously. But with Chinese Manchuria still jutting out into the space between Vladik and Chita, railway-boosters back in St Petersburg realised that a route across Qing territory would be much shorter and avoid several challenging bridges (including over the Amur) than one entirely on Russian land.[1] Following the tried-and-tested methods of European powers carving out bits of China, there-fore, plans were hatched to secure the necessary territorial concessions from Beijing.

The May 1896 attendance of Chinese imperial envoy Li Hongzhang at Nicholas II's coronation—at which the new monarch was also pre-sented with the Japanese Emperor Meiji's ivory eagle, which I had seen back in Moscow—seemed the ideal moment for this, and so the hap-less Li suddenly found himself dragged into treaty negotiations on the sidelines of the enthronement. 'Persuaded' by influential figures such as the rabidly pro-railway Finance Minister Sergei Witte, and in slightly

Image 1: Izmailovo Market, seen across the old Cherkizon wasteland (Chapter 1)

Image 2: Approaching Neryungri (Chapter 2)

Image 3: 'Genghis Khan's country' (Chapter 3)

Image 4: Zabaikalsk railway station with the 'national gate' into China in the background (Chapter 4)

Image 5: Central Manzhouli (Chapter 4)

Image 6: Manzhouli tourist church and giant Russian doll (Chapter 4)

Image 7: Heihe's drenched Amur riverbank with shadows of Blagoveshchensk in the background; stone pillar reads 'Sino-Russian border' (Chapter 5)

Image 8: Railway station and menorah fountain at Birobidzhan, capital of Russia's 'Jewish Autonomous Region' (Chapter 5)

Image 9: Former colonial Japanese consulate building, Suifenhe (Chapter 6)

Image 10: Fishermen near Fuyuan, with Russian hills across the Ussuri River (Chapter 6)

Image 11: New Synagogue, Harbin (Chapter 7)

Image 12: St Sophia's Cathedral, Harbin (Chapter 7)

Image 13: Old Russian house, Sun Island, Harbin (Chapter 7)

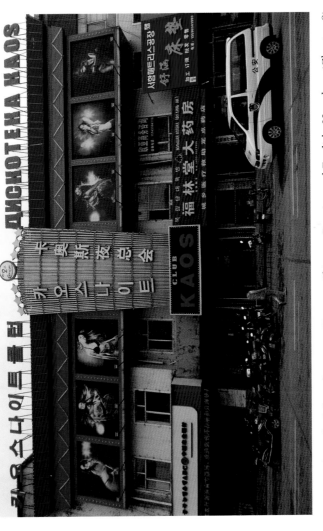

Image 14: 'Kaos' Club with signs in Korean, Chinese, Russian and English, Hunchun (Chapter 8)

Image 15: Three-way Sino-Russo-Korean photo spot, Fangchuan near Hunchun (Chapter 8)

Image 16: Soviet aviator monument, Changchun (Chapter 8)

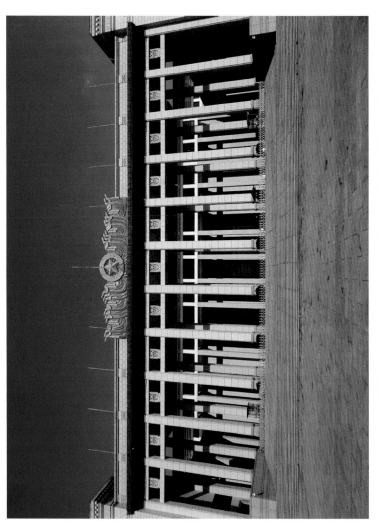

Image 17: The Sino-Stalinist National Museum, Beijing (Chapter 9)

obscure circumstances, the Qing representative signed the Li–Lobanov Pact, known in China as the 'Secret Sino-Russian Treaty'. According to the Suifenhe plaque, negotiating techniques applied by the Russian side included 'intimidation and bribery', and indeed Li—who may also have been drunk throughout—reportedly benefited to the tune of 3 million roubles for his acquiescence.

Neither the Qing nor the Romanovs had much more than twenty years remaining as rulers of their respective empires. But with Russia still flailing around for primacy in North Asia, work began soon afterwards on tracks across a band of Heilongjiang and Jilin provinces. By 1903, the link between Vladivostok and the western stretch of Trans-Siberian was complete, while a line running solely on Russian territory (with a huge, still-impressive bridge over the Amur at Khabarovsk) would not be completed until 1916, just a year before Nicholas II was dethroned. Departing momentarily from its decrying of Romanov perfidy and Qing weakness, the Suifenhe plaque noted soberly that the completed CER extended an impressive and precise 2,489.2 kilometres.

The early history of these 2,489.2 kilometres was more akin to that of a separate sovereign state than the joint Sino-Russian venture that its founding contract claimed it to be. Officially managed by a new China Eastern Railway Company and financed by the Russo-Chinese Bank, the project—like the entire Trans-Siberian—was often run like a personal fiefdom by Finance Minister Witte. Having gained prominence as a railroader supplying troops and equipment during Russia's 1877–8 war with Ottoman Turkey, Witte displayed the hubristic gusto needed by someone laying tracks stretching a quarter of the way around the world. Any allusions to 'China' in the names of the CER's guiding institutions were thus quickly rendered symbolic, especially after the Qing official supposedly heading the CER company was summarily executed in 1900, not to be replaced. As it fended off the Russian Foreign and War Ministries' efforts to play a role, Witte's Finance Ministry saw itself to be executing a project of social as well as infrastructural engineering, bringing Russian civilisation to the Manchurian taiga. This eerie foreshadowing of another, much later, Russian railway in East Asia—the USSR's northerly BAM—both revealed how much of twentieth-century socialism's technophilia was inherited from nineteenth-century progressivism (in China as much as in Russia) and offered evidence of the recurrent nature of Russia's struggles with destiny and identity in the east. Like the BAM a century later, the CER and Trans-Siberian were the last infrastructural megaprojects of a doomed empire, the imperial centre's final attempts to map *fin de siècle* ambition on to distant and misunderstood terrain.

Also like the Soviet Union, the Russian Empire's demise was hastened by a blundering Asian military misadventure, though in this case defeat brought about near-immediate loss of sections of the symbolic railway. The 1904–5 Russo-Japanese War ended much more quickly than Brezhnev's tortuous 1980s Afghan campaigns, and Russia's capitulation fed into the air of crisis and revolt that culminated back in St Petersburg in the revolutions of 1905 and, more portentously, 1917. Tsar Nicholas II and his government had much to answer for after the war, the first defeat of a European power by an Asian one since the Mongols' thirteenth-century rampage across Siberia. Martial embarrassments included the tragi-comic deployment to the conflict of Russia's Baltic Fleet, which sailed halfway around the world only to be sunk immediately. The humiliation culminated as southern stretches of the recently completed CER were ceded to Japanese control.

This would not be a permanent settlement, for as I would see later in the Sino-Russo-Japanese railway hubs of Harbin and Changchun, Manchurian tumult saw the line change hands many times between White Russian, Sino-Soviet, Japanese, purely Soviet, and Chinese Communist superintendence over the first half of the twentieth century. But compared to those bigger and better-known towns, Suifenhe has a distinctly Russian past that seemed somehow more intriguing given its ongoing status as a place of frontier contact. Traces of the first Russian arrivals felt almost completely detached from today's domed tower blocks, subterranean shopping arcades and DJ Sergey. Again as in Manzhouli, China has asserted unequivocal sovereignty, symbolic and political, over Suifenhe and monuments to its changing fortunes.

Many colonial CER-era constructions have new occupants, the Japanese and Russian consulate buildings respectively housing a language school and a gloomy art gallery (displaying, during my visit, an exhibition by local Russian and Chinese painters). With geopolitical priorities having shifted long ago, no foreign ministry today would consider opening diplomatic offices in this ramshackle border town of

100,000 people. Other repurposings are subtler, but equally expressive of decisive Sinification: the old Russian school is now a dilapidated local nursery, while in a curious twist the abovementioned St Nicholas' Church now serves as a house of worship not for Orthodox Christianity, which is not an officially recognised religion in the PRC, but for official Chinese state Protestantism. A short distance from the railway station stand the elegant former offices of the CER administration. This edifice, known simply as the 'Big White Building', was once a key port of call for early Chinese revolutionaries travelling to Russia for meetings or political sanctuary. Even the PRC's first foreign minister-to-be Zhou Enlai snuck through its doors during the 1920s. But in a very different age such caution would no longer be required: the building's grand art nouveau rooms, once workspace for Witte's imperial pen-pushers, now serve as a comfortable hotel for Chinese Communist Party officials. Convinced by all this that I was now definitively in north-east China, I was keen to move on.

* * *

From Suifenhe, I would be leaving the border farther behind than on my first Inner Mongolian incursion into China. Commensurately, locations where Sino-Russian experiences were mirrored through direct cross-border contact and interdependency would transition to places where the mirrorlands' reflections would take on deeper forms. Farther into Manchuria, local experiences of imperial and socialist pasts have resembled very closely those I had already explored in Siberia and the Russian Far East.

The terraces flanking the road to the city of Jiamusi, origin point of the golden coach I had seen back in Birobidzhan, were sown thickly with corn and potatoes. Routes into and out of Suifenhe boasted billboards depicting Presidents Vladimir Putin and Xi Jinping jovially shaking hands, but other visual evidence of Russian influence dissolved quickly as I headed north by bus. Initially, single-storey rural houses with terracotta roofs, and the occasional power station, crouched between steep green hillsides, but this was not to last. China's far north-east, the face of the rooster to which maps of the country are often compared, has been dubbed the 'Great Northern Wilderness' (*Bei da huang*) by the notionally civilised imperial centre. Few hills or trees blemish its huge surface. This sparsely inhabited flatness was once mostly swamp and plain similar, Sergei Tretyakov observed, to the steppe of Russia's Black Sea coast and quite unlike the 'pine-covered hills with their Mongolian, Chinese or Japanese contours' around Chita.[2] But a new Russian echo came to the wilderness in the 1950s and '60s amid a headlong Maoist campaign to reclaim the area as productive farmland for the industrialised agriculture of the new socialist state. As well as reprising Russian cultivationist aspirations on the other side of the Amur from the 1850s, this drive directly aped Soviet agricultural initiatives unfolding at much the same time under Khrushchev's 'Virgin Lands' campaign, an ultimately ill-fated effort to increase farm yields in Central Asia from 1953.

Indeed, northern Manchuria, also known to some as 'China's Siberia', shares much with Russia's remote imperial edges. Commonality also runs deeper than today's border-hopping Russian shoppers or movement in the other direction by Chinese workers or tourists. Neighbouring populations separated by the border have been subject to strikingly parallel fates in each of their respective polities. In Romanov and Qing days, similarities resulted from the perhaps grimly inevitable consequences of living in huge 'civilisation'-dispensing land empires, while under Sino-Soviet socialism fates were often shared because of direct inter-state influence. Throughout recent centuries, Manchuria and eastern Russia have alike been loci of exile and sites for projecting dreams of imperial destiny. Relatedly, they have been homes to indigenous groups subject to cognate processes of incorporation by states that have seen them merely as parts of the 'wild' landscape they inhabit.

Soviet mass agricultural campaigns, primarily collectivisation under Stalin, had attracted Chinese admiration even before the Chinese Communist Party took power in Beijing in 1949 and moved into the Great Northern Wilderness. Writing in 1935 at a time when the worst excesses of collectivisation—including the horrific Holodomor famine in Ukraine—remained mostly obscured under layers of propaganda, Esperanto scholar and Siberian voyager Hu Yuzhi expressed awe at what the Soviets were attempting. Describing the state of Russian production, internal debates over collectivisation between Stalin and others, and the mechanisation process and creation of *sovkhozy* (state farms) and *kolkhozy* (collectives), Hu wrote in his travelogue:

Although few in China are paying much attention to this, I personally consider it to be the Bolsheviks' most daring feat since the October Revolution, their most vigorous assault on capitalism ... the gradual destruction of the wealthy peasantry is the clearest expression of the victory of the socialist line. And although collectivisation is not yet complete, such an audacious attempt is already something worthy of our attention.[3]

This inspiring Stalinist exemplar, and a borrowed talent for concealing the terrible human cost of mass agricultural reform, would come to underlie the Beijing authorities' own land reclamation operations in the far north-east. Like Soviet collectivisation, which, as Hu observed, had represented a vital step in consolidating the Bolshevik revolution, the Great Northern Wilderness campaign was part of Mao's efforts to reaffirm the CCP's grip on power. Both mobilisations were intended to forcibly disseminate revolutionary consciousness and exert greater central control over populations beyond the Chinese or Soviet Communist Parties' loyal vanguards. In China, it seemed to be the urban youth who needed this more than anyone.

The manpower required to reclaim the Manchurian swamps was thus drawn from participants in another Maoist campaign, the Down to the Countryside Movement (1960s–70s). This mobilisation and its precursors saw members of China's urban 'educated youth' (*zhishi qingnian* or *zhiqing*) dispatched as 'volunteers' to less developed parts of the country. In ideological terms, this was meant both to offer uplift to rural areas and, foreshadowing Brezhnev-era thinking about languid late Soviet participants in the BAM project, force politically unreliable youngsters to learn from their earthier rural contemporaries. Mao's had after all been a much more peasant-oriented analogue of the Bolshevik revolution.

Rusticating city-dwellers also dovetailed with pragmatic challenges facing the young PRC after two of Mao's earliest and bloodiest social and economic experiments. The first of these, the Great Leap Forward (1958–61), had ravaged the countryside, and refugees fleeing famine there had in turn brought serious overcrowding and hardship to the cities. As the pendulum swung the other way, therefore, it became vital to relieve pressure on urban centres, and so late 1950s efforts to move people out were repackaged and expanded from the 1960s as Down to the Countryside. The second of Mao's disasters, the Cultural Revolution, also had threatening consequences, one of which turned out to be the formation of thousands of brigades of young and anti-establishment 'Red Guards' across the country. As these foot-soldiers of the Chairman became iconoclastic mobs unable to attend schools or universities, which were all closed, they came to seem like ideal candidates for the mutual re-education experience that time in the villages would notionally bring.

In all, a total of 17 million urban youths were thus 'sent down' across the country, and while many did not make it far beyond the immediate surrounds of their hometowns, those who came to northern Manchuria generally hailed from the country's eastern metropolises around Shanghai. Mao had proclaimed in 1955 that 'the countryside is a wide expanse of heaven and earth where we can flourish',[4] a statement whose spatial component certainly applied to the vast terrain I was now crossing between Suifenhe and Jiamusi. But flourishing was less assured, and Down to the Countryside ultimately resulted in millions of dislocated young Chinese being denied educations and fulfilling careers. Thus while there is undoubted nostalgia for this era of rural camaraderie, and recognition that migration to the Great Northern Wilderness likely rescued many from starvation back in the blighted cities, complex emotions persist among members of this 'lost generation'.

Yet unlike those killed and beaten during the Cultural Revolution, most of whom remain as voiceless as Stalin's victims are becoming in Putin's Russia, the *zhiqing* are not entirely forgotten. Victims of Mao's campaigns are not all treated equally by today's more prosperous present. Jiamusi has a riverside square named in honour of the *zhiqing*, and, having arrived as evening fell, I made my way down there. All across the tiled and colonnaded space, troupes of middle-aged dancers were indulging in China's love for coordinated 'square dancing' (*guangchang wu*), and as they twisted their bodies, hands and necks in time, rhythmically sentimental songs blared through loudspeakers perched on the paving. As I reached the plaza's centre, the cacophonous soundtracks of competing dance groups blurred into a frantic stew of jarring rhythms, producing a kind of accidental frontier dubstep.

A statue in the middle of Zhiqing Square towered over the bobbing and dipping dancers, offering a powerful statement of the

Promethean effort to subordinate nature to man's will that had brought their parents here. Muscular in bulging bronze, a shirtless youth wrestled a rushing bull under a brightly illuminated curve of metal bearing the simple legend '1968', the year a million 'sent down youth' began to arrive in Jiamusi before fanning out to reclaim the northern lands. Lower down, a plaque explained that the monument was erected to commemorate their sacrifices for 2008's fortieth anniversary of this. But halfway through, the inscription shifted away from the contentious subject of how best to remember this Mao-instigated hardship, and settled on more comfortable territory, praising the decision of the local CCP Committee to develop the apparently 12,953-square-metre space. Soviet or Chinese, Communist parties have long preferred the technocratic comfort of facts and figures to reckoning with less tractable aspects of human life. The impulse to reform human nature, born in revolutionary Moscow, is usually expressed in such non-human terms.

From here, I continued along the riverbank where evening strollers were paddling in the shallows of the bloated Sungari River—Songhua in Chinese—which flows through Jiamusi. Red candle-buoyed lanterns drifted up like miniature hot air balloons into the night sky to mingle with the music of karaoke singers. Under the yellow neon of a riverfront apartment building, a guitar-strumming student in a Union Jack T-shirt and canvas shoulder bag was earnestly crooning heartfelt pop songs to a few giggling young couples. Farther upstream in a wooden pagoda, a cluster of older people with a banner advertising them as the 'Riverside Singing Troupe' had attracted a more mature crowd. Accompanied by keyboard, electric drums, saxophone and a grinning man waving an artificial rose in each hand like a kind of socialist Bez, this band of fifty-somethings was in full swing as I approached.

The audience was rapt, nodding and swaying along to Cultural Revolution-era odes to Mao Zedong and the Motherland, a canon known as 'Red Songs' for their politicised provenance. Four tunes in, a woman who appeared to be the group's matriarch switched gears and began to rap in waves of staccato resembling the popular comedic form *xiangsheng*, or crosstalk. 'Mao Zedong is really great!' went one line early on in her solo, making me wonder if this was a reinterpretation of an old classic. But as subsequent verses continued to advance through time, it became clear this was no hoary sixties favourite. 'Deng Xiaoping made Reform and Opening Up!' the beat continued.

'Jiang Zemin wasn't bad either! Hong Kong returned in '97!' the rapping woman gripped the microphone in her right hand, nodding in time to the rhythm. It seemed I was witnessing a full run-through of Communist Party history.

'Then there were the 2008 Olympics!' The narrative had outgrown mere praise for the Party and was now charting China's more general recent rise to global prominence. The performer surveyed the audience's rapt faces. 'Hu Jintao, Wen Jiabao, you did a lot to help the poor!' her hagiography resumed, but it then took a more ambivalent turn.

'But the wealth gap is still too big! How will you deal with this?' Under her wreath of curly hair, the woman's face took on a vexed look, possibly brought about by the difficulty of fitting this social commentary to the beat. Furrowed brows also rippled around among the assembled listeners as the relentless clacking rhythm continued to emanate from the drum machine. But things got on course again for a patriotic finale. 'Uncle Xi is in charge now, China is a great power, the little Japanese people must give us back the Diaoyu Islands!' she concluded to thunderous applause. This had been a feat both musical and historiographical, and everyone was justifiably impressed.

'Let's get those Japanese bastards!' someone shouted from the audience, attracting approving laughs as the crowd dispersed. Maxim had not been wrong when he suggested such attitudes were prevalent up here.

* * *

If the River Sungari was the focal point for cross-generational sociality in Jiamusi that evening, then this was only the latest sign of its long-standing importance to life on these fluvial flats. Like Siberia, Manchuria has long relied on great North Asian waterways as arteries pumping economic and spiritual lifeblood into it, especially in pre-railway days. I would soon be heading to Harbin, the greatest city on the Sungari, but first I doubled back on myself from Jiamusi, heading north again to the Amur—the Chinese side this time—and thus crossing more of the Great Northern Wilderness. The stuffy coach to Tongjiang rolled over boundless flatlands pricked with corn stalks and wind turbines. Although their distant edges were invisible, we were actually passing between huge fields belonging to farms with evocative names like Qianshao—'outpost'—semi-private agricultural conglomerates that have replaced the state-run operations founded by the young urban volunteers of decades past. Today, it is not socialist campaigns that determine what is grown where, but nationwide and global markets for soya, dairy, and the north-east's coveted rice, which, uniquely, is grown during the short cultivation season falling between winters.[5]

Market rather than socialist economic forces also govern today's Sino-Russian exchanges, and after several horizonless hours I arrived at one of the very first places where such post-socialist trade began. Tongjiang opened up as a cross-border entrepôt during the late 1980s, soon after Sino-Soviet relations began to emerge from several decades of deep freeze. Even Ilya Lagutenko, Sinologist lead singer of Mumiy Troll whose bar I had visited in Vladivostok, came to the city as part of a 1989 youth delegation. While Tongjiang has since given way to Suifenhe, Heihe and Manzhouli as a shopping destination, it today hopes to remain relevant by serving as origin point of the bridge that currently juts halfway towards Birobidzhan.

Even more so than usual in this region, the riverside seemed a good starting point for the brief stop I would be making here. Blagoveshchensk, Birobidzhan, Fuyuan and Khabarovsk are all located at confluences, but Tongjiang advertises this fact in its very name, which comprises the characters for 'together' (tong—同) and 'river' (jiang—江), in reference to the meeting here of the Sungari and Amur. On arrival, I walked westward down an arrow-straight road out of town past the gaudy blue pyramids and giant golden cross of a warehouse-like new church. The sun was setting redly somewhere beyond the end of the road, and cyclists and mopeds carrying whole families of three passed me on my way. As in Blagoveshchensk and Khabarovsk, locals here make the most of balmy summer evenings by the riverside, the movement of the water with each spring thaw seeming to ease the flow of interpersonal interactions.

Next to the small Tongjiang docks, couples sat beneath the silhouettes of darkened cranes, fishermen waded the shallows between the shoreline and a file of decrepit barges, and a gaggle of dockworkers heaved chains into a pile next to a rusty pier. With human activity made smaller and quieter by the openness of land, water and sky all around, intimate conversation was hushed, and even the thumps and hoots of an employees' basketball match underway in front of the grey marble customs house seemed muted in the creeping dusk. From a concrete track along an embankment, Tongjiang's skyline of radio masts and boxlike half-finished skyscrapers huddled under a storm cloud. Pinkened by the setting sun and reflected in the swampy pools near where I was standing, the cloud made it look as though an atom bomb of rose petals had detonated over the city.

I surveyed the calming scene for a while and then turned back towards town, passing on my way a family who, assuming I would not understand, took to speculating about my identity.

'American,' said the mother decisively. Her husband and daughter looked doubtful, but offered no alternative theories. Seeking my attention, and in strange incongruity with her guess at my origins, the mother hailed me with a lusty cry of 'Tovarishch!', 'comrade' in Russian. Judging by her likely age, she would have grown up at a time when Russian rather than English was the first foreign language learnt in Chinese schools, and much the most helpful tongue in which to address people looking like me. But I was tired and tovarishched-out, and so left them to their strolling. Much of my fatigue, like Boris Pilnyak's in 1932, resulted from not yet having adjusted to time shifts. In summer, Khabarovsk and Vladivostok are three hours ahead of the single time zone covering China. The crossing from Pogranichny to Suifenhe had thus made for a significant temporal leap in exchange for little spatial displacement, and so by early evening I was feeling the effects of my journeyings.

The next morning, however, the time difference proved an advantage as Tongjiang, like fishing communities the world over, was up early even by China's crack-of-dawn standards. To judge by the din outside my window that woke me, the whole town was already in vigorous motion around 5 a.m., and as I pulled myself out of bed and peered out of the window, cohorts of uniformed workers from the cosmetics store opposite were already engaged in coordinated dips, crouches and pirouettes, performing a clocking-on routine common to many such Chinese workplaces. As loudspeakers outside other shops began their full-throated announcements of the day's deals, I decided to make a start myself and strolled out to find a hearty northern breakfast in the form of *youtiao*, greasy dough sticks, and *doufunao*, a jelly-like slab of tofu in a salty gravy whose name literally means 'tofu brain'. Towards a different section of the Sungari riverbank from that I had visited the previous evening, men and women squatting on stools were untangling nets on the pavement as serious-looking wholesalers in baseball caps and sunglasses eyed up the morning's catch. It was not a particularly impressive one, and most onlookers seemed nonplussed as stubby silver slivers twitched on tarpaulins and lither, longer fish were sliced open and strung up on wooden racks. But I had in any case determined to head that day to nearby sites of more momentous fishy activity.

* * *

For northern Manchuria's indigenous Hezhe people, fish reveal yet again how riverside life here has mirrored that over the Amur in Russia. Originally a single group with the Nanai whom I had visited to the north-east around Khabarovsk, the Hezhe have seen their own pescatarian culture and economy upended by experiences under the Chinese Empire. Just as the Nanai lived downriver long before Russians arrived, so the Hezhe were catching the forefathers of today's river produce well before Han Chinese settlers or the Beijing-based state were a significant presence here. Speaking dialects of the same Tungusic language and travelling with relative freedom up and down the Sungari, Amur and Ussuri before waves of Sino-Russian colonisation from the 1850s, the Nanai and Hezhe only have separate names today because of their respective incorporation by mirror states over the twentieth century.

While some southerly Hezhe communities had been involved with the Qing dynasty earlier, and were even incorporated into the Manchu military 'banner' armies stationed throughout the empire, much their most decisive and systematic incorporation has occurred since the mid-twentieth century under the CCP. As well as borrowing Soviet ideas about mass agricultural reform, the Chinese Communists also adopted wholesale a Stalinist system for classifying ethnic groups, and following their 1949 accession to power launched a vast campaign to 'discover' and classify all the old Qing Empire's peoples. Consequently, the Hezhe went from being distant and little-known inhabitants of the frontier to one of the People's Republic's fifty-five official minority 'nationalities', or *minzu*. As such, and like the Nanai under the Soviet Union, this notionally entitled them to certain forms of ethnic autonomy following socialist principles of national self-determination. But for much of the time since the idealistic 1950s, *minzu* policy has had a divide-and-rule character, with groups like the Hezhe treated as 'backward' natives who must be dragooned unsympathetically into modern ways by the Han majority. As Leonid had noted, Russia has treated 'its' Nanai in much the same way.

China's Han majority themselves officially count as an ethnic group, but are, like Soviet Russians, rarely discussed in terms of having any particular 'ethnic' characteristics. 'Real' *minzu*, on the other hand, are often expected in an apparently trivialising fashion to perform their identities by singing, dancing or dressing up in colourful clothes. Everywhere, from the PRC's annual parliamentary sessions' gaudily dressed 'minority delegates', to the yearly China Central Television New Year Gala's minority-themed songs and skits, state occasions are replete with performances of what it means to be a minority, staged largely for Han consumption. The situation is of course more complex than these crassly Orientalising examples suggest, for as in Russia the fact that generations of *minzu* have grown up with such performances as the primary means of expressing ethnic identity has encouraged many to adapt tactically to this. Many today purposefully and often sarcastically buy into state-promoted versions of ethnicity in order to get ahead in the PRC system. I would be seeing examples of this among the Hezhe.

Whatever the successful reappropriations by some, however, Sino-Soviet ethnicity policies can, and very often have, turned sinister. Back in mid-1930s Soviet Moscow, Hu Yuzhi observed an elementary form of the Stalinist nationalities system in action at a cultural soirée show-casing the music and dance of the Crimean Tatars and several Caucasian peoples, all clad in rich ethnic costume.[6] Yet less than a decade later, Stalin would violently deport the Tatars from Crimea to Central Asia, showing how exoticisation at the imperial centre could very quickly turn to demonisation. A capricious state may be as willing to abuse you as put you on a pedestal. Treatment of imperial minority peoples as a kind of internal 'Orient' in fact dates to well before the Communist age in both Russia and China.[7] But south of the Amur, the ways in which the PRC-era iteration of this practice had intensified through borrowing from its Soviet precursor quickly became obvious as I entered the Hezhe lands.

I began in a Tongjiang park that boasted both the aqueous name Sanjiangkou—'mouth of three rivers'—and, according to the publicity, 'the only Hezhe museum in the country'. After a small Hezhe display at Jiamusi's museum with some blurred photos of rotund men wrestling and a model of a child poking a large fish in the eye with a stick, the Hezhe Museum did not disappoint. Here was a vivid exegesis of the Chinese ethnic classification system, offering selective emphasis on Hezhe 'culture' (songs and dances), 'economy' (hunting and fishing) and 'religion' (animism and shamanism).

Numbering between 4,000 and 5,000, the Hezhe are among China's least numerous minorities with a population around a third that of the Russian Nanai. For comparison, other official *minzu* include the Tibetans (7.5 million), Uyghurs (10 million) and Manchus (10.4 million). Yet with official messaging declaring all *minzu* to be equal despite these enormous discrepancies, each must be portrayed as having contributed proportionately to the making of the Chinese state, past and present. The museum's history section thus offered a moving account of the Hezhe's loyal service first as subjects of the Qing Empire, then defenders of the realm against tsarist Russian aggression and Japanese Fascism, and finally proud bearers of the banner of Communist rule.

A delicate line was trodden throughout between vaunting the PRC's ethnic diversity and stressing its national unity. Within an inseparable and eternal Chinese 'ancestral land' (*zuguo*), I read, the Hezhe had shown a love of freedom (for China against scurrilous foreign threats) and a commitment to (Chinese-style) democracy. Such had been their unbending loyalty, a statistical table explained, that the 1930s–40s Japanese occupation of Manchuria had sought to punish them by wiping them out entirely, reducing Hezhe numbers to only around 300 souls. How such a small population had battled global Fascism was not explained in detail, and in fact historical sources elsewhere show that, for understandably pragmatic reasons, Hezhe and Nanai fought on all sides—Russian, Japanese, Chinese—during North East Asia's twentieth-century conflicts.[8] Many were also slow to become officially 'Chinese', and one visiting ethnologist-adventurer observed in 1930s

Tongjiang (then known by the Hezhe name Lahasusu) that those inhabiting mid-Amur islands cared little which country they were in and simply minded their own business.[9]

Yet for the museum's purposes, the Hezhe had been valiant and single-minded subjects who, after the foreign scourges had been evicted, were finally rewarded once China was under CCP rule. The upstairs galleries told this story first by emphasising the charming but unsophisticatedly miserable nature of past Hezhe lives. Placards suggested that the old fish- and deerskin clothes displayed in cabinets may have been warm, and shamanistic worship of animals and plants fun, but these were not really ways of going about things in the long run. 'Since almost dying out as a *minzu*,' one information board explained, 'and under the leadership of the Chinese Communist Party, the Hezhe have seen staggering development in all areas, and their political standing has constantly increased. Again and again they have made historic leaps. They have flourished, progressed economically, developed in education, their culture has prospered and the sight of people living a happy life can be observed everywhere.'

True to the CCP's explicit 'civilisational' mission, promoted more globally and powerfully than ever in the Xi Jinping era, this Hezhe story hove unerringly to the Marxist conception of history that still prevails in museums and classrooms across China. Movement through time was to be measured in terms of material 'progress' and politico-economic evolution: even very early Hezhe fishing implements were, for example, described as tools permitting the 'acceleration of economic development' in the north-east. Yet, this was also a nationalistic story about China, and despite the Hezhe and their ancestors having lived for centuries at a great distance from centres of imperial power—especially during eras when Beijing was not the capital—their history was periodised according to whichever dynasty controlled the country's main Central Plains region at the time. Only cursory mention was made of the kindred Russian Nanai, and there was no explanation of how most of this ethnic group had ended up north of the Amur despite their apparent predilection for fighting off tsarist aggressors.

Yet so much for the past. Aside from the museum's vague claims concerning Hezhe flourishing in the era of 'Socialism with Chinese Characteristics', I had heard little about contemporary Hezhe lives beyond Leonid's lamentations over their Sinicisation back in Khabarovsk. Since he had never actually met any of his Chinese confreres, these claims probably needed verification.

I left the museum and approached a girl who was sitting at the reception desk playing the agriculturally themed hit game Happy Farm on her mobile phone. 'Yes, I'm Hezhe,' she said, frowning at my question. She seemed surprised that anybody cared.

Did she speak the language?

'No.'

Were there many Hezhe around here?

'Go and look at the museum.'

Did other Hezhe in China still speak the language?

This time she did not even deign to speak and just gestured emphatically towards the galleries.

I told her I had already looked at the museum and wanted to talk to an actual person. She shrugged.

Perhaps her virtual farm risked going the way of Khrushchev's Virgin Lands if she kept talking to me, but I suspected that her reluctance to chat at least partly stemmed from a sense that in China *minzu* affairs belong in museums, or on TV. Behind glass display cases, authoritative and correct versions of ethnic identity could be preserved, safely placed there by the correct authorities. Incidentally, the museum had portrayed these authorities as a deeply caring bunch, offering a photo gallery on the top floor documenting the 'loving care' (*qinqie guanhuai*) shown by local Han officials as they attended the performance of a Hezhe 'fish dance' and inspected a Tongjiang school. Earlier conversations with Nanai had suggested to me that similar official attitudes had prevailed in the USSR, but Leonid's forthright desire to explain Nanai affairs to me directly rather than pointing me to Nanai-themed museum exhibits had suggested a rather different approach in today's Russia. But I had not lost hope of finding more vivid examples of Hezhe life, and so I left Sanjiangkou to look further afield.

Better luck materialised by chance while I was browsing a small row of shops selling miscellaneous Russian trinkets back towards the centre of Tongjiang. Here I got talking to Mr Wang, a stocky middle-aged Han man with thinning hair, a tanned face and a flamboyant leopard print shirt, who claimed to know some people who could help me. 'You're looking for Hezhe?' he asked loudly (his default mode), grinning to display a mouthful of gold teeth. The latter were trophies of his career in distant Shanghai's Lujiazui financial hub. 'I'm from Jiejinkou,' he said, naming a small village downriver from Tongjiang, 'so I know loads. Officials and everything. God those guys can really drink. Wait, let me make a few calls.'

There followed a succession of brief exchanges between Mr Wang and his purportedly high-level contacts back in Jiejinkou. Most conversations—both ends were audible since he preferred to keep his phone on loudspeaker mode despite it being pressed up against his face—proceeded as follows:

'Hey bro [*gemen'r*].'

'Ah?'

'It's me.'

'Ah.'

'Listen, I have a foreign friend, he's looking for Hezhe. Are you Hezhe?'

'No.'

'Ah, ah. Ok bye.'

'Ah.'

Mr Wang's calls revealed that, despite his assumptions, neither the head of the village nor the local Communist Party secretary, nor his two remaining Jiejinkou schoolmates were Hezhe. As in Russia's Nanai areas, the national imperial majority evidently had little sense of what minority identity actually was, or who might have it. But these fruitless efforts did not discourage Mr Wang. He was planning to head to Jiejinkou that afternoon anyway, he said, and, evidently now on a mission to play his part in China's widespread culture of hospitality towards foreigners, offered to give me a lift.

A couple of hours later, we were off, rumbling in his very shiny Hyundai along the concrete riverside road. As we passed through settlements evocatively named First Village, Second Village and Third Village, Mr Wang commented on various features of the local landscape. The deafening Mando-pop he was playing through the stereo made him difficult to hear, but I was able to gather that he was explaining the difference between the bare Russian hills to our left and the Chinese ones up ahead that had wind turbines on them. Patterns of land use do indeed set adjacent areas of Russian and Chinese territory apart along this stretch of the Amur, and it was also clear that much more agriculture was occurring here on the southern riverbank than on the otherwise identical Russian side.

Hezhe engagement in this cultivation of corn and other hardy crops suited to the short northern growing season is one of several indications of their assimilation to Chinese ways of life, even if many still inhabit traditional riverside fishing areas. Yet some also practise the old ways, even if today much of this is a response to the demands of Han tourism. After we had barrelled into dusty Jiejinkou, Mr Wang said he had some business to attend to and pointed me towards a house inhabited by someone he thought still made traditional Hezhe fish skin clothing. Less interested in the ways of ordinary folk than in hobnobbing with his local grandee friends, he made his excuses and we parted ways, each voicing non-committal assurances to perhaps see each other again later.

I approached the concrete home at the end of the village, which was indeed something of an improvised tailor's shop. Responding to my knocks on the door was a smiling and hospitable Ms You, the house's owner and, it turned out, a superb seamstress. In a room to the left of her front door, we settled on her *kang*, a raised area of flooring common to northern Chinese rural houses, which, when draped in blankets and heated from below by flues linked to the stove, makes a cosy sleeping and sitting place in winter. There being no need for insulation now, however, hers was covered by a simple floral cloth. On the other side of the room was an antique sewing machine on a table, while built-in cupboards down one wall stored her tailoring kit and examples of her painstaking work. Opening one of these, Ms You brought down a selection of extraordinary near-iridescent jackets, trousers and waistcoats, each made entirely from the skins of chum salmon or pike, intricately stitched with knotted pieces of twine as buttons and clasps.

'Lots of people wore these sorts of things in the old days,' said Ms You, adding that, now in her mid-fifties, she could remember her father owning an old suit that had belonged to his own father. 'But you shouldn't imagine that this was some amazing Hezhe technology,' she said, departing from the Tongjiang museum's narrative of indigenous innovation. 'Really it was just that we didn't have any better clothes.'

When did Hezhe fashions begin to change, I asked. The answer was closer to the official line concerning Hezhe uplift by the central Han Chinese state. 'Only when the Chinese brought us better things to wear,' said Ms You simply.

Further conversation suggested that Ms You felt that being a Chinese *minzu* had brought many other benefits. As well as the sturdy house she and her family lived in—provided under a campaign to make Jiejinkou an attractive destination for 'ethnic tourism' and far superior to any Nanai dwelling downriver—recent developments had brought unprecedented work opportunities. Having learnt the craft of fish skin tailoring from her mother, she was now able to extend the reach of her expertise far beyond her family, and beyond Jiejinkou, Heilongjiang province and even China. The labour-intensive garments she and a few others in the village produced were very popular in museums worldwide, she said, and her works had been exported to Switzerland, the United States and Canada and elsewhere in China, often selling for over $1,000 a piece. In light of this, Ms You noted, it mattered little that she was engaged in a slightly 'fake' novelty version of traditional Hezhe culture. She took pride in the fact that her activities had made her a representative for her people, and the walls of her room were adorned with group photos from trips to Beijing, Shanghai, Harbin and elsewhere where she had been a delegate at *minzu* congresses and meetings. Ms You appreciated that 'being Hezhe' in this way had allowed her to engage in a very old practice for very new reasons: like her mother before her, she was now teaching her daughter how to make fish skin clothes to sell on global markets.

Lunchtime in the You household afforded more indications of how Hezhe today seek to make the most of their position in China, acting as much more than passive recipients of the condescending state attitudes propounded in their museum. Invited after chatting with Ms You to share a meal with her son and nephews, I joined them around a table in a concrete-floored kitchen across a corridor from the room with the *kang*. The younger men had recently returned from a fishing trip and, tired from their exertions, initially sat in silence. The only sounds were the clacking of chopsticks and occasional slurping as they helped themselves from dishes of cooked and raw fish, rice, pickled cabbage and assorted offal. This was a far more Chinese-inflected meal than anything the Sovietised Nanai would enjoy.

But things became more animated as Yougang, one of the nephews, pulled an anonymous looking plastic bottle of local 56 per cent alcohol *baijiu* from under a sink behind him. Unlike the truck-delivered water of the Russian Nanai villages, Jiejinkou's houses have had running water for years, and the taps over this sink were fully plumbed in. As he decanted the liquor into chipped floral rice bowls, the thirty-nine-year-old fisherman began to talk, asking where I was from and what on earth I might be doing in their village. Hearing that I was interested in the history of the Hezhe and the border-river that lay only a few hundred feet away, Yougang gave me a short run-down of Hezhe culture as he saw it, placing anticipated emphasis on the importance of fish ('if you only eat fish, you never get ill,' he declared) and Hezhe bravery under Japan's occupation of Manchuria. But as the rapidly draining *baijiu* restored the energies of the brothers and cousins, conversation became more vigorous and moved away from these orthodox themes.

Some aspects of contemporary border life were proving bothersome to Yougang and the others, most significantly the increasingly fierce Sino-Russian competition for fish along this stretch of river. The Russians were too lazy to fish properly, they complained, and so failed to make the most of the apparently abundant stocks on 'their' side of the Amur, even as those in Jiejinkou struggled. Quite how it was that fast-swimming fish showed enough national consciousness to stick to one side of the river or the other was unclear, but belief that this was the case had evidently provoked arguments between boats: as the brothers confided darkly, several recent incidents had seen Russian patrol craft clashing with Chinese fishermen deemed to have crossed the demarcation line along the Amur's fastest-flowing channel.

Although our conversation remained on fish-related and other themes close to Hezhe hearts, such discussion departed from specifically indigenous affairs to acquire a stronger patriotic China/Russia flavour. Yougang's and the others' explanations of what was happening on the Amur increasingly opened with the expression 'we Chinese people …', and their status as citizens of the PRC clearly mattered most in their dealings with Russia, regardless of their distant Nanai relatives. For these Hezhe, continuing their riverine way of life was reliant on a pragmatic allegiance to the Chinese state. Here, then, was a vivid mirroring of the recognition of inescapable 'Russianness' that had been voiced by my Sakha and Nanai friends: centuries after expanding into these North East Asian lands, both old empires now exerted similar force over the region's native peoples. The fate of once-united groups divided by this process made this clearest of all.

As the *baijiu* and the meal came to an end, Yougang offered to give me a lift back into the village centre in his Chinese-made four-by-four. We walked out, continuing the discussion of both Sino-Russian and Hezhe-Han relations. When he was younger, Yougang told me, he had spent three years working on building sites in the Jewish Autonomous Region around Birobidzhan. Whatever the intensity of fish-related arguments here in Jiejinkou, he generally had a positive view of people from 'the Soviet Union'.

'Those Soviets can drink a lot of alcohol,' he said in an approving echo of Mr Wang's earlier statement about the Hezhe. This was per-haps the main local metric for judging a person's, or at least a man's, character. 'And Russians are good people,' he continued. 'But I can't deny I did have problems there. Normally it was with the police—they always want bribes, and they really bully Chinese people.' With attacks or acts of extortion targeting people of 'Asian' appearance in Russia, China's relative safeness is perennially cited as one of its major advan-tages, by local Chinese and border-crossing Russians alike. 'Basically there are lots of mafia in Russia,' continued Yougang before adding mischievously, 'whereas in China we only have one mafia. It's called the Communist Party.'

As we lurched slowly down the hill through the village, some of the activity of this national ruling 'mafia' was strikingly visible. Like the Russian stylings of Enhe and Shiwei, Jiejinkou's houses and other build-ings have been clad in tan-coloured wooden planks to give them a more ethnic feel. Many of them are also decorated with lurid murals depict-ing improbable aquatic scenes. On one roadside home, a great Poseidon-like figure reared up out of crashing waves brandishing a trident, while clouds of brightly coloured fish, dolphins and whales wheeled around the windows and doorway of the local government offices. As we passed a headache-inducingly vivid depiction of a bearded Caucasian-looking giant placing a group of tiny people into the mouth of an enormous moustachioed catfish, I asked Yougang what these were all about. He broke into laughter.

'We have no idea what those are,' he said. 'One day some party leaders from Harbin turned up and said they were here to make the village beautiful. They started painting and when we asked what all these pictures were, they said, "This is your history! These are Hezhe legends!" But we didn't have a clue what they were talking about.'

Other acts of munificence from the provincial government included the village's metal lampposts, spindly poles in abstract human form carrying solar panels aloft like dainty cocktail trays. As posters on the roadside explained, all this had been brought about to promote the 'urbanisation' of Jiejinkou and the creation of a 'beautiful and happy new Hezhe village'.

Yougang's salty cynicism about these measures to render his home settlement correctly ethnic seemed to justify the comparison between Russians and north-eastern Chinese made by Maxim the Suifenhe vendor: sarcasm about local 'mafias' and the like were in my experience much more redolent of attitudes north of the Amur than those encountered deeper into China. But there was further nuance to Yougang's views, for it turned out as we continued downhill that for over a decade he himself had been a member of the very Communist Party he mocked. This, he told me, meant that he still had many friends in high places, including soldiers in the local border defence garrison.

'Up there,' he pointed ahead at the barracks building and watchtower visible through the trees. Symbolically, this outpost of the Chinese state sits atop vertiginous rocks overlooking the river above a traditional Hezhe angling spot known as the 'Fishing Platform'.

'Let's go up!' he said. I sceptically consented, beginning to wonder whether taking a car ride through a village with a drunken fisherman and former Party member had been a good idea. 'We definitely should,' he persuaded me confidently, 'my friends up there will be really happy to see us!'

Despite my doubts, our lunch of assorted fish, unidentifiable entrails and *baijiu* had left me in too somnolent a state to put up much resistance, and so we careered up the hill. Leaping out of the car, entering the barracks and climbing the stairs, Yougang dashed ahead whooping gleefully, as I vainly attempted to suppress my blundering inebriated fug.

The local commander of the Shenyang Border Defence Division appeared very surprised by the Hezhe man and his thoroughly non-

Chinese-looking companion who suddenly burst into his second-floor office. But as quickly as we had entered we were gone again, continuing through a back door and climbing higher up the hill behind the building. Luckily, someone who did actually know Yougang was manning the sentry post at the top, and he and I chatted briefly as each of us tried to work out who the other was. Should I really have been there?, we were both almost certainly wondering. However, the insuppressible Yougang was unburdened by such security or legality concerns, and swept his arm out over the view that had opened out before us. The Amur's stately silver waters, the brilliantly green Russian hills opposite and the ultramarine sky overhead combined to make this an extraordinarily beautiful scene. From our perch between giant land empires with such different attitudes to border security—I would never have got anywhere near a garrison like this in Russia—no national or state boundaries were visible. And with the only audible sound being birdsong from the nearby forest, it felt for a moment as though we had leapt back to an age when Hezhe and Nanai could cross the waterway below as freely as I had been welcomed into their worlds.

* * *

While certainly my most arresting Amur vista, this would not be my last, for there was one final node of northern Sino-Russian contact to visit before returning into Manchuria proper. The riverbank became much messier east of Jiejinkou as the Great Northern Wilderness reasserted itself at the threshold of man's control. Recent rains had made the Amur teem on to the floodplain, and pools swirled disconcertingly close to the road to Fuyuan, which sits perched on the very edge of human certainty. Thrusting out into the confluence of the Amur and Ussuri rivers, the town lies concealed behind scattered bluffs and false islands from nearby Khabarovsk, whose riverside park had offered views and boats towards where I now was. A breezy, modestly sized place, Fuyuan had a few streets of shops catering for the groups of Russian tourists who come to shop for clothes, toys and foreign diversion of the kind sought all along this Asian frontier.

After a restful night in a hotel west of the town centre with a pleasing view across the Amur, I set out to complete this leg of my journey with an exploration of what is both China's most north-easterly and its most easterly point. I did not have to wait long to understand that, despite its marginal location, Fuyuan has been as entangled as anywhere in the twists of Chinese and Sino-Russian history that have gripped the rest of Manchuria. Getting breakfast in a small shop near my hotel, I was approached by Mr Li, a seventy-year-old local who wanted help reaching a bottle of Sprite on a high shelf, and as we fell into conversation it soon became clear that his biography echoed much of the region's dramatic recent decades.

Before retiring, Mr Li had plied both the rivers that meet here, taking his modest fishing boat to the nearby confluence where, if you know the waters, bounteous catches can be secured where currents drive shoals into dense defensive clusters. He had learnt to read the rivers as a teenager, having made the arduous journey from starving Jiangsu Province to the wilderness with his father. His mother had not been strong enough to undertake the escape, and so the pair, refugees rather than volunteers, had arrived in Fuyuan to start anew in 1959. Here was testament to how Maoist disasters made this necessary well before the official start of 'Down to the Countryside'.

'The Great Leap Forward was worst in 1958, but the cities were still famished the next year so we had to leave,' said Mr Li, displaying surprising candour about an event that remains little discussed in China, suppressed as political censorship conspires with the pain of remembrance. Competing for atrocious scale with the worst of Stalinist collectivisation, the Great Leap Forward's disastrous industrial and agricultural drives caused around 36 million famine deaths.[10] 'There wasn't enough to eat, but at least father and I managed to get here,' Mr Li added laconically. Fearing the worst, I did not enquire about the fate of his mother.

Like many arrivals on these reclaimed lands, Mr Li senior had taken up farming, encouraging his son to follow a path that would also guarantee a reliable food source. But as Yougang too had found, fishing here offered more than just sustenance, for plying rivers that were also international borders meant direct contact with Russians. At first, this was an interesting diversion, for the 1950s and early '60s were a time when Sino-Soviet relations basked in the glow of official socialist 'friendship'.

'When I first started working we got on very well,' Mr Li said. 'We'd even meet mid-river and tie our boats together sometimes to have a bit of a drink.' During the halcyon days of the alliance, the Soviet Union was affectionately known in China as *laodage*—'elder brother', praise indeed in a country that, despite Mao's best efforts to destroy traditional relationships, still deeply values kin connections. But as sometimes occurs between siblings, affection mutated into an equally intense hatred when relations soured.

'But in '63 and '64 things suddenly got worse,' Mr Li went on with what I was coming to realise was his typical understatement. This 'getting worse' had seen Maoist propaganda blasted at Blagoveshchensk, a short war fought over an island in the very Ussuri river where Mr Li fished and, as I would be later learning in Beijing, a vast network of nuclear shelters constructed under the Chinese capital. But for Mr Li there had been very personal consequences too. 'After the relationship with the Soviets soured we couldn't talk to them anymore,' he said. 'We'd still be fishing side-by-side on the river, but all we were allowed to do was look at them. I was so sad, and lonely without my Russian friends. But those were the rules.'

Like the Cultural Revolution, the 1960s–80s Sino-Soviet Split remains an under-examined period on both sides, and a particularly inconvenient historical blip in an age of vaunted bonhomie between Presidents Putin and Xi. Chinese frontier-dwellers also have their own pragmatic reasons to forget, for as elsewhere, positive ties with Moscow and the opening up of border areas have brought new opportunities through the arrival of Russian and domestic visitors alike. Keen to show me evidence of the new Chinese interest in the area around Fuyuan, Mr Li introduced me to a tour guide friend of his who offered to take me to some of the local sights.

Mr Liu (this corner of the country seemed dominated by all the most common Chinese surnames) was more animated than his older companion and excitedly listed the attractions we would be visiting. Most of these were on Heixiazi Island, the earthy mid-Amur protrusion close to Khabarovsk, which, known in Russian as Bolshoi Ussuriisky, was where Leonid hoped one day to build his Nanai–Hezhe ethno-park. In stark contrast to that frustrated situation, Chinese tourism here was booming in part because of its geopolitical novelty: decades of territorial discord meant that until 2008 the island was completely off-limits from both the Russian and Chinese sides. But a resolution concluded that year defined each country's access to the waterways around Heixiazi and split the island between Russia and China. Khabarovsk was thus comfortable feeling somewhat insulated from a direct foreign presence, but Chinese river craft could still happily navigate along the Amur's main channel passing to the island's north. Most crucially for locals in Fuyuan, 'border tourists' of the kind I had met in Shiwei and Manzhouli could now come flocking. As Mr Liu excitedly explained, the island's many attractions now included, in various states of construction, a towering suspension bridge, a giant pagoda and a silver monument of some fish. There was also a brick Orthodox church on the Russian side that could be peered at from near the borderline.

Leaving Fuyuan along a road flanked by several dog meat restaurants and fishing tackle shops, we headed out of town towards the bridge. Mr Liu's car was a rattling black Hongqi (Red flag), a socialist-era Chinese brand made in the north-eastern city of Changchun. Having dropped markedly in prestige since it was usurped in the late twentieth century by black Audis as the vehicle of choice for the CCP leadership, the company has since been making a comeback in the more nationalistic Xi Jinping era.[11] Mr Liu's Hongqi was an original, however, and, like thousands of Soviet Ladas and Volgas over the border, was holding up well. As the road entered an area of flooded marshland, Mr Liu adopted a bolt-upright posture befitting this fadedly grand vehicle.

Until the last decade, when the arrival of travellers made tour-guiding a viable option, Mr Liu had been a farmer, an arduous job he had been happy to give up as he aged. Recently, he had expanded his portfolio of services beyond the seats of his Hongqi to offer informal (and incidentally illegal) boat trips along the Amur in a friend's fishing craft, during which he followed a looping course around Heixiazi Island and along Khabarovsk's riverfront. 'I know the Russian Far East is backward compared to the rest of the country,' he said, explaining the appeal of these excursions. 'But for us Chinese, Khabarovsk is very advanced, a civilised European city. We think it's great.'

That travelling to this distant corner of the country afforded Chinese tourists a glimpse of something 'European' hinted at a situation that would come into clearer focus on the next stage of my journey. Here in China's farthest eastern reaches, the Russian presence has brought certain visions of 'Europe' very close, and thus shaped Chinese people's understandings of what that western continent might be like. Being directly adjacent to or, in the case of Harbin, to which I would head next, actually inside China, these Europes are a mirror-image of the Asias lodged deep inside Russia. They consequently offer a revealing lens through which to examine the Middle Kingdom's mirrored approach to its immediate neighbours, and to the 'West' at large.

But back in Asia we soon reached the police checkpoint before the bridge over to Heixiazi. Mr Liu got out of the car to ask a policeman if we could enter the car park from which special tourist buses cross to the island. Visits to Heixiazi were evidently still regulated, despite the tourist 'opening' of recent years, but the officer saw no problem, and we continued on a short distance, next pulling up in front of a desk run by the China International Travel Service. Here, however, the effects of regulation became more evident.

'No no no!' a young employee in a green travel company T-shirt shouted in English, his face erupting in horror as Mr Liu and I got out of the car and approached him. 'No foreigners!'

Stooping under the picnic table umbrella where the agent was sitting, we remonstrated with him for a while. I was not a Russian secretly hoping to infiltrate the Chinese side of the island, we explained, but just a normal British tourist, in as much as that was a normal thing here. The employee's shock subsided a little, and his initial officiousness dissolved into questions about English football. But as I sought to steer conversation away from Wayne Rooney's hair transplant and back on to my hopes of getting to the island, it became clear that this was not a negotiable position. People higher up would not allow it, the green-T-shirted man said, adding 'very sorry', again in English.

It was not the fault of anyone present that these were the rules, and indeed if anything my exclusion was much more normal a state of affairs than the near-slapstick levels of permissiveness I had seen elsewhere in China's Russian borderlands. But for a while I forgot that this was what one would expect at the frontier of two authoritarian bureaucracies and, frustrated by what seemed a wasted journey, had a bit of a strop. Like a sulking child, I offered only monosyllables to Mr Liu as he turned the car around, but I could not sustain this for long and soon enough his indomitable exuberance and entreaties not to be annoyed reinvigorated me. As we bumped back along the road, he was again in full tour-guide mode.

'Wusuli village is the smallest village in the world!' he enthused as we passed a single house by the roadside. 'It only has one household!' How this made it a village was unclear, for such a classificatory compromise seemed to leave open the possibility that it might as well be named 'the world's smallest city' or 'Africa's tastiest pumpkin'. But I did not argue, as Mr Liu seemed far too cheery to merit such pointless pickiness. Furthermore, he then explained, he had actually been keeping another attraction up his sleeve in case the island did not work out.

Sun Square, so named to honour the rising heavenly body that strikes this part of the Chinese world before any other, lay a short distance farther east. In summer, when the distortions of China's single time zone are especially evident, tourists are here as early as two or three in the morning to see the first dawn to hit Chinese soil. But at any time of day the square's towering statue of the Chinese character *dong* meaning 'east', surrounded by stalls selling the usual Russo-Soviet chocolates and trinkets, is an impressive sight. I did a slow circuit of the expanse of paving that juts out directly into the Amur–Ussuri river confluence. On the square's eastern edge, sporadic groups of domestic tourists were squinting at a few cloud-shrouded Russian villages across the Ussuri. A short distance farther on, some fishermen, youthful successors to Mr Li, were using the plaza's conveniently flat surface to untangle their nets (Image 10). It was, as in so many other places in northern Heilongjiang, a surprising blend of traditional and very new activities at China's edge. The diverse spectrum of humanity, the sweep of forested hills on the Russian bank, and the seething expanse of lapping brown water at this merging of continental rivers together proved sufficiently awe-inspiring to banish any of my lingering churlishness.

7

HARBIN

EURASIAN ATLANTIS

So far, I had not boarded a train during this second spell in China, as no line runs west to east along the country's far northern fringe. Just over the border, Russia's Trans-Siberian does move this way, pumping modest vitality into the most habitable strip of the country's eastern reaches. Like Canadians, or pulp in a neglected carton of orange juice, Russians have mostly settled to the bottom of the space they exist in, and so the Trans-Sib rarely strays more than 60 miles from the Chinese border. But the scale of relative habitability resets when you cross into China and so, with flows of power, money and people running southward to less frigid regional and national centres, railways do not trace the country's edges but poke in spokes towards the tips of this jutting Manchurian limb. I was myself now heading for the heart of the body-politic via a city that owes its very existence to railways. And so, having exited the wilderness back through Jiamusi, I took the train to Harbin.

High-speed lines now crisscross China's north-east as they do much of the rest of the country, but I went the old way, settling on the firm green benches of the diesel-powered stopping service. This was 'hard seat' class, the second most humble accommodation offered on Chinese trains (in a vestige of socialist fairness, standing tickets can still be bought for most routes, even those lasting up to two days), yet my fellow passengers were drawn from a wide spectrum of socioeconomic backgrounds. Next to me was an office-worker in his mid-twenties whose attention was divided between a Tang dynasty-era costume drama playing on his Lenovo laptop and photos of his young son posing on a recent trip to Beijing, which he flicked through on his mobile phone. Opposite us, obscured from the on-screen action of sage ninth-century kings in wild headdresses earnestly discussing matters of state, a woman and her daughter sat amid a growing mound of vegetable peel. The mother, most of her body lost in a loose black robe, had a face burnished with good humour, and smiled as she sliced cucumber, tomato and another vegetable that probably belonged somewhere, I was unsure where, in the broad Chinese family of *gua*, which includes every imaginable melon, pumpkin and gourd.

As the pair munched contentedly on these simple farmland snacks, the daughter eyed up the array of iPhones, iPads and e-readers dotted about the carriage. 'When can I have a mobile phone?' she asked her mother, adding pleadingly, 'over 90 per cent of American children have one!' This confidence in statistics was impressive—she cannot have been more than eight years old.

'So we have to do everything America does, do we?' the mother chided her gently in response, her tone suggesting this was not the first time they had discussed the subject. Surprisingly, this answer appeared to work, and even if the girl preferred the idea of playing on Angry Birds to eating raw cucumber, she did not pursue the issue.

Across the aisle from us, a university politics teacher was on the long journey back to Taiyuan in Shanxi province to see her family, and the little girl's mention of the United States had sparked her interest in me. Was I myself from that land of cellular phone-endowed children, she wanted to know.

I answered in the negative, although often in this part of the world—on either side of the border—I had long ago realised that the United States and UK were not readily distinguished. The lecturer and I then got talking about international affairs at large, as well as the personal matters it is somehow so easy to discuss on trains. I asked whether her students studied Western political ideas as well as Chinese ones.

'For our undergrads it's mostly Marx and Engels,' she said, 'they don't study many Western things in detail.'

This echoed a view that I had heard previously while studying history in the north-western town of Urumqi: despite in many regards having been consummate European aristocrats, the fathers of Communism were not really considered 'Western' in China. Here was the mirror at work again. These bearded intellectuals likely seem less associated with 'the West' because their ideas mostly arrived in China via Russia. At the precise point in time when leftist thought was being brought east by Boris Pilnyak and Sergei Tretyakov and gaining traction among the likes of Hu Yuzhi and Qu Qiubai (with whom I would soon be reunited), Russia was increasingly defining itself in opposition to capitalist Euro-America. As the socialist versus non-socialist divide was mapped on to Russia's older civilisational Asia/Europe debates, the socialism that reached China thus seemed of blurry national provenance. Further complicating matters, Communism was then also an avowedly internationalist doctrine.

'In England they love Marx too, by the way,' the teacher told me with authority.

Many people are interested in him, I agreed, adding that I had seen his tomb in Highgate Cemetery.

'Indeed,' she shook her head wistfully. 'He was in exile in London, the poor man.' Was London 'Europe's Siberia', I wondered to myself. But the teacher seemed to have considered Marx's time in England more of a holiday. 'The English are gentlemen, they treated him well,' she reflected, echoing a Chinese stereotype about genteel Englishness that usually accompanies parallel statements about the romantic French and the hardworking Germans.

As we continued our dialectal engagement at slightly crossed-purposes, a storm was brewing outside the train. The tempestuous air exacerbated the already close atmosphere in our crowded carriage, and windows were opened wherever possible, only to be slammed shut again at great speed as sudden bursts of rain would unexpectedly come pelting into the faces of those seated nearest them. We stopped often, and each halt brought about a grand dance of elbowing musical chairs as people getting off were immediately supplanted by those with standing tickets who had been loitering in the aisle waiting for a chance to sit.

The blissful relief this provided was, however, usually short-lived, as new passengers with reservations would immediately shove their sweaty way on board and demand that these opportunists relinquish their seats again. Couples or families had had to buy tickets scattered throughout the carriage, and so negotiations and trade-offs ensued as great chains of movement were proposed in tones that teetered perpetually on the brink of acrimony: 'No! If you swap with that girl there then my wife can sit here and then if I move this man's sack of potatoes and get that kid to sit on his mum's knee then maybe we can sit across the aisle from each other and share our instant noodles and sunflower seeds that way?'

Usually things broke down somewhere along the chain, with someone insisting on keeping their window seat despite the regular rain-spattering and opening and closing duties it brought with it. Others seemed to refuse merely because, in a world already dogged by uncertainty, the one thing they were sure of was their allocated seat and they were sticking with it.

Around me the company remained mostly stable, although at the Harbin satellite town of Suihua we were joined by a student with a fashionable Beijing-style haircut, shaved sides topped by a loose swish of longer hair. Plumping himself opposite the man with the laptop, he very quickly became visibly annoyed at the villagerish ways of the vegetable-peeling lady and her daughter next to him. As the pile of cucumber ends and gourd rinds grew ever larger on the narrow table they shared, his efforts to appear urbanely aloof were undermined by the venomous squints he repeatedly shot sideways. Enduring near-constant shoving by elbows or hips, he seemed increasingly desperate to reach the sophisticated comforts of the big city ahead.

Harbin may not quite be on the scale of China's truly vast metropolises whose populations reach 20 or 30 million, but it is by no means a sparsely inhabited outpost. Significantly, the city's 10 million-plus population greatly exceeds the 6.7 million who inhabit the entire Russian Far East, a region the size of Europe (if the European part of Russia is discounted). Little wonder then that our student neighbour made a great show of his relief when we arrived, for we were in a place where his haircut would get the attention it deserved. Harbin's cosmopolitan spirit has been there since its foundation, as mirroring Russia's Asia this city has always presented a kaleidoscopic projection of Europe in China.

One reason for many outsiders to come to Harbin these days is the city's winter Ice Festival, which, despite temperatures reaching $-30°C$, draws tens of thousands of mostly domestic visitors to gaze at vast frozen igloo-palaces illuminated in gaudy neon. Enormous Russian-style buildings, including mock-ups of St Basil's cathedral or the Kremlin, are erected from colossal blocks of ice, forming a vivid spectacle that contrasts starkly to north-eastern China's otherwise rather sootily austere image. Since the region's colonisation by Russia and Japan early in the twentieth century, and continuing through the Mao years, Manchuria has been home to vast industrial complexes churning out steel, automobiles and other machinery. But many of these have struggled to modernise following the post-Mao end to the socialist command economy, and, mired in financial sclerosis, the north-east has sought a new direction. The Ice Festival today is thus far larger in scale than at any time since its mid-1960s foundation. But if all this winter bustle is a novelty to locals who remember greyer times, much of this represents a reincarnation of an older vibrancy to Harbin life. From the beginning, this place had all the colour and crowds one would expect from a unique Eurasian extrusion into China.

Harbin arose, as cities often did in this region, in part because of a river. Over 200 miles upstream from Jiamusi where I had strolled its music-bathed banks, the Sungari is still a significant obstacle here to anyone crossing the Northern Wilderness, and at the turn of the twentieth century it was Russian builders of the China Eastern Railway who were traversing the flats. More or less equidistant between Manzhouli and Suifenhe—the railway's points of exit/entry into China where I had seen numerous traces of its heyday—the necessary bridge over the Sungari seemed a suitable site to locate the CER's administrative centre. The spot was already somewhat familiar to the Russians since an 1895 steamer expedition had travelled along the Amur from Khabarovsk to Lahasusu (now Tongjiang), and then up the Sungari to seek Manchu trading outposts.[1] The aim had been to source food, for as already observed, Russia's promised North Asian 'breadbasket' had been a great agricultural disappointment. Slavic settlers, particularly their growing military contingent, had come to rely for sustenance on the very country they had hoped their far eastern gambit would allow them to dominate.

Cartographic work during the excruciatingly slow boat trip had identified a site known as 'Harbin'—meaning 'a place for drying fishing nets' in Manchu—as a suitable point where the CER and Sungari could intersect. At the time, a village with a neighbouring distillery and a small incense factory was located here, although local Russian and Chinese histories differ over which of these was more important in influencing the choice of site. Chinese sources soberly emphasise the significance of the latter, which still gives its name to the old Xiangfang (incense factory) quarter of Harbin.[2] But upholding a precedent laid down when Qing emissary Li Hongzhang was plied with vodka and persuaded to approve the CER in 1896, alcohol undoubtedly played a prominent role the town's early history.

As well as being the halfway point on the main CER line between Chita's Mongolian steppe and Vladivostok's Pacific coast, Harbin also became the node of a second branch line. Southbound trains would travel from here down to Dalny (a Russian name meaning 'distant', which has transmuted, via Japanese, to today's Dalian) and a warm-water Russian naval base annexed from China at Port Arthur (now Lüshunkou). With its crossroads role thus cemented, the town began to grow rapidly. During and after the CER's headlong 1898–1903 construction, thousands of both Russian and Chinese migrants arrived here. While many of the first Russians were soldiers guarding the railway, early Chinese came as labourers whose low wages and seemingly superior adaptability to tough conditions made them pre-ferred employees to lay the rails. Imperially minded Russians would later lament that this Chinese influx put Russians in an immediate minority, fating Harbin to return to Beijing's control from the begin-ning.[3] But this was far from assumed in the early years, and more than enough of both groups lived here to give this ramshackle out-post a certain cosmopolitanism. Diversity was at times a source of discord, not altogether surprising in a place that by 1902 was col-lectively consuming 1,000 buckets of vodka per day (though possibly not directly from the bucket), and fights broke out between these mostly male settler communities.

Arriving in 1926, the politically pugnacious Boris Pilnyak entered into the spirit of things, writing to a friend in March that year:

> You'll have to forgive me for saying it, but Harbin's cognacs and vodkas are even better than Moscow's! Someone's going to have to take them away from me at some point, as the morning after is always full of remorse and regret that you can't go back and change past actions ...[4]

Yet despite these modest beginnings, heavy drinking, routine brawls and frontier surroundings,[5] all of which at first seemed to reconfirm Russia's historic predilection for ill-fated blunders into inhospitable eastern locations, Harbin succeeded. Decades before Mao enthused about Manchuria's potential as a location for Chinese national flourishing, the city and its surrounds became an arena for the enactment of a Russian frontier destiny. Though St Petersburg's disastrous defeat in the 1904–5 Russo-Japanese War deprived it of the just-finished branch line to Port Arthur, this conversely also ushered in an era when Harbin could boom as a centre for soybean and lumber production strategically located between Russia, China and Japan. Traders in these and other goods swelled the part of the urban population not directly associated with the railway, numbers that increased further in the 1920s and '30s as a vast eastward exodus of Russians came here escaping the 1917 Bolshevik Revolution and Civil War. Many of these 'Whites' had the aristocratic tastes expected of tsarist loyalists, so their arrival caused Harbin's cultural life to effloresce as newspapers were founded, theatrical and concert performances staged, and the town's Russian school network expanded. The city became a place where nobles, generals and traders hiding out from Bolshevik persecution could continue a kind of Russian imperial existence that was fast disappearing farther north. For a few decades, this isolated population staved off extinction, much like the mammoths of Wrangel Island who—perched in the Bering Strait away from predators—outlived their continental cousins by several millennia. By the early 1920s, Harbin was the largest Russian settlement beyond Soviet borders, home to over 100,000 exiles. Local Russians became a unique pseudo-ethnic group—the Kharbintsy, or 'people of Harbin'—a label that would echo throughout Asia and beyond down to the present.

Under the influence of the new arrivals, the town's urban fabric was transformed, and a feast of art nouveau, and later art decoratif and art deco buildings arose under the guidance of architects such as Vladimir Planson and Aleksei Levteev. Already well regarded from projects in Khabarovsk, Vladivostok, Port Arthur, Dalny and other waypoints on Russia's eastward march, such figures could explore new modes of architectural expression here on the frontier. Unlike the wooden Cossack stockades built at sites like Yakutsk during the first defensive phases of the Asian adventure, nineteenth- and twentieth-century Russian towns in Asia were assertively spacious. Open public squares, wide avenues and solid buildings sought to reflect the permanence of the civilisational mission. Harbin became a kind of gallery of architectural innovation and, as I would see, many monuments of the age still stand proud today.[6] This grand and bustling Manchurian city thus in some ways resembled British, French, German or other colonial 'treaty ports' on Chinese soil from the same period. But unlike in Shanghai, Canton, Hong Kong or elsewhere, the Europeans who arrived here came not by sea, but overland on rivers and rails. This—together with Russia's historic cataclysms and exoduses—permitted Harbin to grow into the largest foreign settlement in all China,[7] and continental North East Asia's most significant trading hub.

For Russian and international actors alike, this was a convenient place to which operations could be shifted from the Russian Far East after the business-unfriendly Bolsheviks took over. Firms such as the Japanese Matsuura trading house, already established in Vladivostok, moved in quickly to cater to Harbin's new settlers[8] alongside numerous émigré Russian, British, French, German and American companies and banks. Owing to its unique political position and the presence of these commercial interests, Harbin also came to have consular representations from twenty different nations. Passing through in 1925 after her gruelling Trans-Siberian journey, Ethel Alec-Tweedie was received by the British consul whose hospitality allowed her to 'rid myself of the dirt and dust and demoralization and barbarism of Russia', a project apparently requiring two baths and an entire cake of soap.[9]

In the twenty-first century, some of the heritage of this cleansing frontier metropolis with its artistic, musical, theatrical, sporting and educational pursuits, its Chinese and Russian towns, salons, grand halls, broad boulevards and modern institutions, is recalled with similar nostalgia on both sides of the border. One recent Russian history of Harbin, entitled *A Russian Atlantis*, describes with misty-eyed longing the old lives in this 'great cultural centre' that have long been 'washed away by the river of time'.[10] Despite the very land-based nature of the Harbin project, author Nikolai Kradin employs a maritime metaphor, telling us that this was 'a unique island' of creative and cultural life, drawing particular attention to the work of the abovementioned architects and railway engineers, and the city's pluralistic religious landscape. A Chinese publication, *A Grand View of Old Harbin*, echoes this nostalgic sentiment, introducing its collection of historical photographs of the city as 'tokens left behind by a past age', which can 'make a lost time appear once again in the present'.[11] Both volumes see Harbin's first decades as a unique blossoming, which, having appeared quickly out of nothing, eventually wilted again under the mists rising off the Sungari.

Yet such broad-brush nostalgia is about as much as the two sides have in common, as each sees the city's past through later-tempered nationalistic lenses. Significant divergence emerges over the fact that, even if Harbin was unlike other European treaty ports in seeing civilisations meet as terrestrial neighbours rather than across vast oceans, the transition here between Russia to the north and inner China to the south was not a particularly smooth one. From Russian perspectives, Harbin seemed a melting-pot that 'brought East and West face-to-face, creating a new opportunity for a peaceful and fruitful synthesis'.[12] This was 'a new place to think' beyond Russia proper, which thus also made an 'inestimable' contribution to Chinese modernity.[13] Yet although Chinese sources agree on the CER's 'Eurasian' role and the 'European-style architectural ensembles' and 'modern industry' that appeared here,[14] crucially this was not a modernity that China itself had chosen. At root, Harbin was still a Chinese place 'full of foreigners', and whatever their notional 'contribution' this was a situation wherein China was a decidedly inferior partner.[15] 'Synthesis' was occurring largely on foreign terms in 'a Russian colony where Chinese people felt vexed because everything was in Russian'.[16]

For all his Russophilia, these were very much Qu Qiubai's impressions as he arrived in Harbin on his way north by train in 1920. At this point, the post-revolutionary exodus of Russian Whites was in full flow, and Qu made contact with an old Russian friend, incidentally a relative of Leo Tolstoy's, who had recently arrived in the city. Over a cup of Russian tea, the friend and his sister sought to prepare Qu for his onward journey, explaining the cultural peculiarities of Russia, describing differences between Western European and Russian traditions and between Orthodoxy and other Christianities. But for all their sincere efforts, Qu realised that his companions knew little of the seething and rapidly changing pit of revolutionary chaos that was the Far Eastern

Republic and their Bolshevising homeland. The pair longed to visit Moscow to see how things were there, but said that they could not now get permission from the Soviet government to cross the border.

'It's easier for foreigners like you to get in,' they told him. Little spoke more clearly of the turmoil enveloping both countries than the fact that Sino-Soviet borders remained porous to some outsiders, but were closed to Russians unwelcome in the new country lying on the other side. Yet these foggy frontiers were also at play right there in Harbin itself.

Learning that they were unable to return, Qu asked how his companions felt about their new home in China. 'China?' they asked incredulously. 'But we are not in China. Do you really think Harbin is China?'

Taken aback, Qu responded politely, but later reflected on how minimal Russian contact with Chinese culture really was in the city.[17] Those Russians who did seek more direct experiences seem to have been swashbuckling types like Boris Pilnyak. As drunk on new experiences as he was on cognacs and vodkas, Pilnyak voiced the inverse impression of that which awaited Qu at the Foreign Ministry canteen in Moscow, writing breathlessly in 1926: 'What an unbelievable delight it is to eat Chinese food—we've eaten worms, miniature dragons, and eggs green to the point of transparency which they bury for several years before eating …' Yet even this culturally omnivorous writer was left complaining at the unfitness of rickshaws for carrying a Russian frame. I could see that this might have been an issue if one were as stuffed with Chinese food as I had been back in Skovorodino.[18]

But while the myopia of some émigré Russians was one thing—to this day, ignorance of the host culture seems to remain a point of principle among privileged expatriates the world over—the extent to which Harbin's Russianness had colonised the minds of local Chinese residents was still astonishing to some. Heading back to his lodgings one evening, Qu stepped out into the blissfully quiet but also blisteringly cold night, and hailed a horse-drawn cab, telling the Chinese driver the Chinese address of his guesthouse. The driver looked at him in baffled incomprehension. 'Aren't you from around here?' he asked. 'How is it that a Chinese person in Harbin all of a sudden doesn't know his own address in Russian?!'

Overcoming his shock, Qu explained that he was indeed not from Harbin and described where his accommodation was situated. He later learnt that any Chinese here who could not use Russian simply called the streets 'first', 'second', 'third'. Confronted by this and other confounding aspects of Chinese existence in this 'Russian' city, Qu became increasingly bitter, his emotions reflecting the place's own broader ambivalence.

As people, languages and cultures from the two mirrored empires jostled side by side in this cauldron of international adventurers, exiles and businessmen, Harbin thus truly resembled the 'island' described by historian Kradin. 'White' Harbin was strikingly out of step both with the Soviet state it had fled, and with the China all around it. Yet this would not last forever: even Wrangel Island's surviving mammoths eventually succumbed to extinction, and the city I was now arriving in was nothing if not Chinese. My time here would help me better understand why this was.

* * *

With nary a Kharbinets nor a horse-drawn cart to be found, many Harbin residents now get around in red-and-yellow VW taxis, which, in a peculiarity shared by other north-eastern cities, drivers seek to stuff with as many passengers going in vaguely similar directions as possible. From my hotel, named Luxiya in internationalist imitation of the Japanese pronunciation of 'Russia', I set out in one such vehicle towards Zhongyang, or 'Central', Avenue. Once the pivot of the old Russian city when it bore the telling name Kitaiskaya, or 'Chinese', Street, this was the heart of Harbin's Pristan district and home to the city's major banks and fashionable department stores.[19] Elegant tsarist architecture designed by Planson and Levteev still flanks this pedestrian thoroughfare, as it did then.

Wending his way down Kitaiskaya in 1920, Qu Qiubai peered at displays of Japanese products in shop windows, astonished at the price of everything. Passing Chinese newspaper vendors hawking Russian publications, he spoke to Chinese beggars who complained that the power-grab in Russia by the 'poor people's party' (a Chinese name for the Bolsheviks) had given them new competitors as hundreds of Russian vagrants now roamed Harbin's streets.[20] Why does this Chinese city have a street called 'Chinese' street?, Qu wondered on his way to a rendezvous on the Sungari riverfront with a former classmate from

Shanghai. And why were the local Chinese here in such thrall to their Russian overlords who, he noted slyly, were after all hardly the best kind of Europeans?

'The Chinese don't notice the piles of piss and shit here,' Qu despaired, 'all they see is the grandness of the great big Russian shopping arcades. But our people need to get a grip! At the moment, we're not even a match for the Russians, whom the rest of Europe mocks for their wildness and barbarity.'[21]

Three years later, the barbarians of the poor people's party were making their presence felt even more strongly, for as Sergei Tretyakov noted when he visited, Harbin was now 'sleeping a deep commercial sleep'. Although 'stuffed full of goods', the city was unable to export most of its wares north since the new Soviet government had halted foreign trade. In this buyer's market where suits and boots could be picked up for a song, the Russian Kharbintsy were, Tretyakov added, 'nourishing themselves on rumour' about everything from the fate of Lenin's corpse to starvation in old Russia and an impending pogrom to be carried out by the local Chinese. A loyal Bolshevik and committed rationalist, Tretyakov scornfully dismissed anything that seemed to denigrate the new state of which he was an emissary.[22]

Today, in a much less Russian age, Kitaiskaya's transition to Zhongyang has paradoxically made the street more 'Chinese' than ever, as it is the central pedestrianised hub for most of Harbin's domestic touristic and revived commercial activity. As I followed the thoroughfare north towards the Sungari, the summer cobbles were thronged with shoppers. Admiring the Russian façades, repainted in gaudier tones than their original pastel shades, the promeneurs licked milk and chocolate flavoured ice lollies, dairy products being integral to the 'European' atmosphere that Chinese tourists come here to sample. Inside the elegant shops were many of the same novelty wares I had seen in Manzhouli, Heihe and Suifenhe—a department store named after the European Russian city of Tver advertised inelegantly painted *matrioshka* dolls at a 40 per cent discount. Indeed, in some places such items seemed even more concentrated than in the borderland towns farther north, for without competition for space with cheap car parts and mobile phones (as a larger inland centre, Harbin has whole separate districts for these things and is less of a destination for cross-border shuttle traders), wallets embossed with images of Lenin and Stalin, and chocolates of questionable origin had the place to themselves. Befitting the city's old-world grandeur, shopfront signage was also of better quality than in those smaller towns, even as it still advertised the Russian pseudonyms such as 'Vika' or 'Ivan' that local entrepreneurs had adopted to catch the attention of passers-by.

These emporia with their mostly Chinese-manufactured pseudo-Russian goods fittingly reflect Harbin's pre-eminently Chinese present. But along Zhongyang Avenue and its perpendicular side streets, which still bear the 'first', 'second', 'third' labels mentioned by Qu, spectral mementos of the older city remain concealed amid the error-prone neon Cyrillic and layers of slightly too thick garish paint on corniced frontages. One such ghost signalled its presence several times as I walked, communicating via red-and-white shop signs featuring a beaming moustachioed baker with a big nose and bow-tie, and a cryptic motto in English: 'Inherit Century'. This is the logo of 'Churin Food', the hand-me-down successor to a Russian Far Eastern institution and a company whose fate is a metonym for Harbin's entire history.

Founded as a trading house in the Siberian city of Irkutsk in the 1850s, Ivan Yakovlevich Churin's business initially supplied foodstuffs to Count Muravyov's expeditions down the Amur, later riding the wave of Russia's eastward expansion to establish branches in Blagoveshchensk, Khabarovsk and Vladivostok. Construction of the CER brought Churin & Co. into Manchuria where it added stores in Harbin and Port Arthur. Like many firms whose successful operations in their country of origin were snuffed out by the Bolshevik Revolution, Churin lived on in north-east China, contributing to the time-capsule of pre-revolutionary life persisting in Harbin after 1917. Indeed, just beyond the reach of the new Moscow government the company throve, and despite the uncertainties of occupation by Japan's Manchurian 'puppet' Manchukuo state after 1932, another eight branches were opened throughout the region in the 1930s and early '40s. Relations with the Soviet authorities were problematic at first, particularly over assets still held in Russian banks. But by the 1930s the company had had its formal ownership transferred to the local Harbin branch of the British-run Hong Kong and Shanghai Banking Corporation (now HSBC), which fended off nationalisation efforts by the Japanese authorities and held on to

Churin & Co. until 1947. At this point, the company fell briefly into Soviet hands when the Red Army swept into Manchuria following the end of World War II. But with a fraternal Communist regime governing China after 1949, the Russians again transferred the company, like the entire CER, to the new Chinese government in 1953. Run by the PRC state for much of the second half of the twentieth century, Churin managed to weather the Cultural Revolution and anti-Russian animus of the Sino-Soviet Split. Re-privatised more recently and pronounced 'Qiulin', the company has survived to sell its baked goods and wildly popular sausages to Harbin's Chinese tourists 160 years after its foundation.[23]

As though celebrating this enduring presence, the lights behind Zhongyang Avenue's Churin signs were flickering on with the street's Victorian streetlamps as the summer evening languidly drew in. High on the demure façade of the pilastered 'Modern' Hotel, a Russian man appeared on a balcony with a microphone and began to croon 1970s Soviet sentimental classics to a jauntily plodding backing track, before accelerating into a racy version of Stas Mikhailov's 2004 hit *Bez tebya* (Without you). The central section of the avenue ground to a halt as Chinese tour groups and backpackers stopped dead to crane their necks and smartphone cameras upwards at this living specimen of the foreign culture they had come to Harbin to taste. As some impromptu dancing nervously started on the paving, I was reminded of the heady atmosphere around the bonfire back in Shiwei. In both places, it seemed, the growing numbers of Chinese tourists exploring the world, including 'foreign' corners of their own land, were increasingly finding chances to engage in a spontaneity not usually possible in their daily lives. As it happens, Russians' purported carefreeness and general love of revelry—from cognacs to eating green eggs—are often spoken of admiringly by north-eastern Chinese. Whether they knew it or not, therefore, these Harbin visitors were perhaps engaging in a new kind of international cultural rapprochement more genuine than that of the city's early days.

* * *

After the raucous commerce of Zhongyang Avenue, I needed some peace, and so the next day sought the spatial and temporal refuge of Harbin's New Synagogue, which lies just outside the thrusting heart of touristic Harbin (Image 11). Where worlds collide, a short walk can make all the difference, and even before I had fully entered the building's solemn colonnaded interior I already felt secluded. Built in the 1920s, the sturdy terracotta-toned 'New' Synagogue is only new by comparison with the 1909 'Old' one, whose delicate layer cake of red-and-white stripes lies around a mile away. Both buildings once catered for the Russian Jews who figured prominently in many areas of life across the empire, even numbering among the original CER soldiery deployed to Harbin in the late 1890s.[24]

Like most new arrivals, Jewish Kharbintsy settled in quickly, and within a few years the Old Synagogue already supported a school, ritual bathhouse and library. Yet if these institutions' air of permanence was consistent with much of young Harbin, those who frequented them had a more urgent need than most to lay down solid roots. In the eastern Russian Empire, Jews were marginalised by a segregation regime stricter than anything regulating Chinese migration. Even as Russian eastward migration had proceeded apace after the mid-nineteenth century's territorial annexations, one of St Petersburg's regular anti-Semitic turns had seen an 1899 law passed that banned Jewish settlement anywhere east of the Urals. Those treading the Harbin synagogues' chessboard flagstones could not, therefore, unlike many Kharbintsy, simply ride the rails or Sungari back up over the border if things got tough. Yet driven by this need to survive on the Manchurian plain, Jewish-run businesses flourished here from the earliest years, and, with a population that showed a much more favourable male/female balance than either Russians or Chinese, the community gained a stability and a political voice unthinkable back in Russia proper: over a quarter of the representatives on Harbin's 1908 municipal council were Jewish. Such was the rare space of exception provided here, that several decades later, Harbin accommodated thousands of European Jews fleeing the Nazis and, as in Shanghai far to the south, the synagogues thus became a wartime home to an ever more diverse worshipping population.

This history of refuge, and that of Jewish Harbin as a whole, is today narrated at the New Synagogue, whose well-funded exhibitions largely tell the story of a Chinese, rather than an émigré city. I was admitted by a local man of few words who pointed me straight to the upper gallery. Immediately before me was an idyllic picture of this 'paradise in far east', as one definite article-eschewing English caption put it. On a screen of grey marble tiles a gleaming backlit world map was criss-crossed with plotted lines, routes of escape from Khabarovsk, Vladivostok, St Petersburg, Moscow, Odessa and even Berlin and Vienna, all converging on Harbin. Facing persecution in all these locations, Jewish Kharbintsy made community support and mutual assistance central pillars of their new lives, and between the gallery's evocatively arranged collections of old German pianos and wooden Russian furniture were photographs of Jewish-run homes for the elderly, soup kitchens for the poor and relief groups for those afflicted by the periodic flooding of the fickle Sungari. A charitable organisation with the Hebrew appellation Gemilus Chesed (Acts of loving kindness) supported the many left dispossessed by the social and economic tumult that was always a feature of frontier life.[25]

The exhibition also incorporated Harbin's Jewish history into a grander story about China in the world, stressing in particular the country's capacious hospitality towards foreign guests: 'they encountered no anti-Semitism among the Chinese, such as is prevalent in other lands', one caption read. By contrast, it was implied that Harbin's other main populations were less welcoming: one local Jewish pharmacy owner named Gofman, it was noted, was 'kidnapped by Russian bandits at the instigation of Japanese gendarmes' during the 1930s. Harbin's openness towards Jewish arrivals may have been a characteristic preceding the period when the city came under Chinese control (governance was either Russian or joint Russian–Japanese until the late 1940s), but the local authorities had nevertheless made great efforts to leverage this past as a means of reaching out to the wider world. The synagogue's exhibition also included a large gallery of famous Jewish figures with little or no link to the city, with displays profiling Albert Einstein, Karl Marx, Emile Durkheim and Franz Kafka. Also here were Russian-language writers Isaac Babel and Shalom Aleichem whose statue I had seen in Birobidzhan, that other site of short-lived Jewish refuge over the border.

Another series of black-and-white photographs under glowing red Stars of David depicted Harbin's Jewish-mediated international connections, including visits by local officials to Russia and Israel. On one image of a 2007 delegation to Birobidzhan, I thought I spied the lady from the Freid Centre who had told me about the Yiddish singing groups there. In pride of place were pictures of a trip to Harbin by former Israeli Prime Minister Ehud Olmert, whose father grew up in the city and whose grandfather is buried in the old Jewish cemetery in its eastern suburbs. The subtle but consistent message was that Harbin was always an unequivocally Chinese place, open, as China has been since the 1980s, to all the world. Any perspectives that, like those of Qu Qiubai's friends, might have suggested a more complex inheritance, or the involuntary origins of this internationalism, were understandably absent. But however obvious these caveats—and nationalism's arbitrary omissions are never difficult to skewer—I could not help feeling that the smug tone in which this story was told was at least partly justified. At least where the twentieth-century periods under discussion here were concerned, Europe and Russia's claustrophobically murderous politics hardly offered a preferable model. Nor indeed did the upheavals and home-grown totalitarian excesses later visited on Harbin by China under Mao. Celebrating this legacy, in however flawed a fashion, thus seemed worthwhile.

In fact, Jewish success here formed only part of a wider atmosphere of religious toleration in pre-1949 Harbin. In the face of official Soviet atheism, religion was a cornerstone of Russian émigré lives. Military chaplains had been among the earliest non-soldier and non-worker residents of the rising town and at first had handled most local Christian affairs. But by the 1940s Harbin had over twenty Orthodox churches,[26] now administered by the Russian Ecclesiastical Mission in Beijing. This body, whose presence in China dated all the way back to the seventeenth-century Sino-Russian encounters on the Amur, was the oldest official Russian representation in China of any kind, and secured its operations in the Chinese capital—on the very plot today occupied by the Russian embassy—under the 1689 Treaty of Nerchinsk. But for all this institutionalisation, and in a further sign of Harbin's pluralism, many early Christian arrivals actually had little to do with official imperial Orthodoxy, since Russian settlement policy preferred to dispatch those considered religious deviants to the CER zone. Whether or not these were the people consuming the vast quantities of vodka that swilled around the fledgling town, prevailing official sentiment held that anyone stubborn enough to reject the religious mainstream would likely make a suitably hardy settler.[27] And so as in the case of the town's Jews and later its White refugees, those with an at-best-precarious place back in Russia saw moving to China's northern fringes as a viable means of escaping 'through the looking glass'.

From the 1920s, Harbin's shiny mirrorland world began to show new fragility as the strain of inter-imperial competition over Manchuria ratcheted ever tighter. Russia's early Soviet authorities, despite vocally decrying colonialism in their propaganda, retained their imperial fore-bears' firm grip on the CER. Defending it against attempted seizure by local Chinese warlord Zhang Xueliang in 1929, they also spread leftist agitation along the rails to harass Harbin's religious and commercial 'White' bubble. Not for the last time would Soviet imperialism be justified on the basis that it was actually a means to spread revolution. But after Japan's 1931 invasion of Manchuria and establishment of the Manchukuo state the following year, Moscow was forced to sell the railway line to the 'puppet' government in 1935. Harbin's new Tokyo-backed authorities put fresh pressure on both Chinese and Russian resi-dents of all political stripes, even managing to recruit some local Russians into their colonial army. Slav members of the 'Asano' brigade thus featured among those fighting against the Soviet forces who, fol-lowing Japan's 1945 defeat in World War II, streamed in and resumed their place as Manchuria's primary foreign exploiters. This included gaining control once again of the CER.[28]

Renewed Soviet interest in the region in turn allowed the Chinese Communist Party to use Manchuria as a bulwark to defeat their Civil War rivals, the nationalist Guomindang (executors in 1935 of Qu Qiubai, who greeted death singing the *Internationale*), a feat they achieved in 1949. With the Communists thus in power over their newly founded PRC, the Soviet authorities finally consented in 1952 to trans-fer the CER to full Chinese control for the first time in its history. Yet if this act closed north-eastern China's most intense era of inter-impe-rial competition, the foundation of Communist China was only the start of the Harbin international community's most devastating period. Not even the preceding decades' dealings with ideologically diverse Russian, Japanese and Chinese overlords could prepare the Kharbintsy for the xenophobic and anti-religious ravages of China's Cultural Revolution, exacerbated by the concurrent anti-Russianism of the

Sino-Soviet Split. And so from the 1950s–60s onwards most fled, once again forced to seek refuge, but this time dispersing even farther afield to the United States, Israel, Australia and beyond.

In light of this, the New Synagogue's evocations of bygone Jewish life appeared all the more ghostly. They were also an unusually explicit link to one of Harbin's old religious communities, for if Churin & Co.'s story reflects the fate of much local commerce in this whirlwind of history, then the obscured pasts of the city's other religious buildings speak of similar transformations in local society and demographics. Leaving the synagogue and making my way down tree-lined alleys where locals at flimsy tables were cooling off with skewered kebabs, Korean-style cold noodles and Harbin Beer, I passed the former Jewish Middle School, an arresting building in the style of a Saracen's palace standing quietly deserted in the urban summer haze. Faded stickers in the windows suggested that the place had recently served as a school for local ethnic Korean Chinese, a notable minority across much of north-east China. I would soon be heading to their main regional home along the North Korean border, and exploring more of the Japanese history of Manchuria that brought some of them as far north as Harbin and the Russian frontier. Like Jewish Kharbintsy, they had been exploited victims and revolutionaries, but also business owners and law-enforcers, within a larger colonial enterprise.

Tokyo's 1930s–40s colonial project in Manchuria was notionally a joint Japanese, Korean, Chinese, Manchu and Mongol endeavour, but this diversity paled in comparison to Russia's imperial tangle of peoples and faiths. As well as Jews and Orthodox Christians, early settlers in Harbin included Muslim traders belonging to the Tatar ethnic group, yet another constituency in Russia's internal 'East'. A short walk beyond the Jewish school, I came upon the elegant early twentieth-century Tatar Mosque, an institution that offered the trader community services in both their own Turkic language and Arabic.[29] The mosque building, no longer operational, now stands in the shadow of a six-storey block of 1980s apartment buildings daubed with murals of Chinese Communist hero Lei Feng. Its marble steps today serve as a favoured spot for local couples to shoot wedding photos. These photo sessions, a near-universal ritual for modern Chinese city-dwellers, are usually staged on a different day from the ceremony itself and involve donning Western-style suits and voluptuous white dresses and standing before as 'European'-looking a backdrop as possible. That a former mosque now hosts Chinese couples mimicking the sartorial stylings of Western Christian weddings seems to encapsulate the extraordinary patchwork multiplicity of Harbin's history. But it also shows how much richness is subsumed under the generically 'European' visions of that history that predominate among many of the city's present-day residents. Central to this is the most iconic of Harbin's monuments to past times: St Sophia's Cathedral, a towering block of Byzantine brickwork that stands in a square surrounded by tiled Chinese skyscrapers (Image 12). Simply called 'Sufiya' by locals, as though in reference to a familiar friend, the ornate reddish-brown building, topped with a bulbous green dome, has hosted no services for decades, serving since 1997 as a museum of Harbin history.

* * *

Kharbintsy lives were not all persecution or worship, however, and particularly for those with means exile offered a chance to recreate some of the leisure activities they had enjoyed back home. In the midst of the Sungari's snaking channels, a bar of land known as Sun Island emerged as a primary relaxation and recreation site, with *dachas* for those who could afford them and summer river beaches for those yet to make their fortunes. The island is today one of the Harbin Ice Festival's key venues, but in summer serves as a kind of Russia-oriented theme park for Chinese tourists to get an alternative 'European' experience away from Zhongyang Avenue's commercial surroundings. Chinese visions of Europeanness conjured up here—more elaborate than anything I had yet seen along the border—blend exoticising and ambivalent histories in a manner comparable with Russia's approach to Asia.

From the riverside embankment of Harbin's Stalin Park (nothing in Russia has Stalin's name any more), crimson cable cars to Sun Island jerk out of a 2000s-vintage white lump of a building resembling a Disneyland castle. With a pod all to myself, I was hoisted steeply upwards, soaring over the Friendship Hotel, which, located on Friendship Street, is a brutalist 1950s Sino-Stalinist palace built to mark the short-lived PRC–USSR alliance. As the commercial areas of old Pristan receded, occasional groups of tourists passed in cars coming the other way, offering waves that I returned. Their expressions suggested confusion at what a solitary Russian might be doing crossing the Sungari like this. The towering pylons supporting the cables cast dark shadows that dwarfed the ferries on the muddy river far below, and, having passed the ride's zenith, I swooped over a roped-off section of river full of splashing children in armbands and landed on the island.

The park at whose entrance I now stood was advertised as 'China's largest base for performing Russian customs', 'China's largest Russian fine dining centre' and 'China's largest centre for creating Russian oil paintings', a trio of claims somewhat incongruously illustrated on towering billboards by a photograph of five nearly naked European-looking women. Although these figures in string tights were presumably meant to appear Russian as they gestured towards the park's centrepiece, a fenced-off enclosure named the 'Russian Village', their bikinis were confoundingly decorated with American flags. This, it turned out, was merely a hint at the incoherent bricolage of national symbols that was to come.

At the entrance to the Russian Village, I was handed a miniature imitation passport by a grimacing Russian man dressed in military fatigues. He said nothing as I passed through the gate, and the crowd of Chinese tourists thrusting to get in behind me combined with his surliness to discourage me from attempting conversation. Immediately inside the entrance was a field of waist-high figurines in moulded concrete, including a man with a blue beret playing the accordion, a rotund peasant lady with an enormous nose holding a loaf of bread on a dish, and a caricature of a shirtless Native American firing a bow and arrow. Truly this was the world of the 'foreign'. Emanating tinnily through speakers suspended on artificially rustic wooden telegraph poles was a Russian music mix whose diversity provided a rich sonic backdrop, from shrill Slavic folksongs to lilting *chanson* and contemporary hip-hop. It was unclear whether Vladimir Vysotsky's guttural growl, the marijuana-themed expletives of Guf or the witty self-mockery of Noize MC was most obscure to the tourists thronging the place.

Along a cracked cement pathway between scrubby patches of grass was another array of squat concrete figures, this time five shabby *matrioshka* dolls depicting a seemingly arbitrary selection of Russian and Soviet leaders. Putin was largest, followed by Yeltsin, then Gorbachev, then an especially faded and crumbling doll that vaguely resembled a kind of zombie Brezhnev, and finally Lenin, the smallest of the crew. If the absence of Chernenko and Andropov was unsurprising, quite what happened to Khrushchev and Stalin was an intriguing question. But their omission did admittedly chime conveniently with how historically problematic each leader had been for China, even if one still has a Harbin park named after him.

In any case, none of my fellow-tourists were much interested in the dolls as the main draw was proving to be several *dachas*, which, though moved or modified to fit the layout of the park, nevertheless preserve something of Russian-era Sun Island. In one of these wooden buildings nestling tastefully between some trees, I happened upon a small exhibition describing the early 2000s construction of the park and the attention and 'loving care' local Communist Party leaders had shown the project. Another building housed a studio where local artists were producing the 'Russian' artwork I had seen advertised outside, but most intriguing of all was a house painted in yellow and green, which was labelled 'Russian Home in 1950' in Russian and '1950 Soviet Home' in Chinese. I followed a group of parasol-wielding Cantonese-speaking families into the building past two metal statues of Greek warriors that flanked the garden path (Image 13).

Despite its label, the *dacha* sought less to mimic any precise aspect of bygone Russian domestic life than it did to offer a treasure trove of items from throughout Harbin's international history. As now seemed normal, this was supplemented by a few obtuse elements from the present, including a large Carlsberg beer tap mounted on a wooden bar that confronted visitors right inside the front door.

Sitting on a stool behind the bar was Ira, a transplant from Vladivostok in her mid-thirties who was looking on with resignation at the much-too-large group of people now crammed into the house's single main room. Did all Soviet dwellings of the 1950s have Carlsberg on tap, I asked her.

'Obviously not,' she said, her mouth creasing into a grim smile as she asked some tourists not to fiddle with a wall-mounted hunting rifle next to a bilingual Chinese and Russian 'Do Not Touch' notice. 'That thing is in here because the Chinese think that we Russians just sit getting drunk with our feet up all day,' she said bluntly.

Ira was well versed in received Chinese wisdom concerning Russian habits, as she was both married to a local and had worked in Harbin for several years as a translator and import/export consultant. Yet for all that she evidently resented insinuations that she and her people were alcoholics, she said she was also happy to be out of Russia and did not miss Vladivostok, despite its recent renovations.

'They've ruined the place with their stupid bridges,' she said with the same brand of far easterner venom that Ilya had shown for the Moscow overlords back in Khabarovsk. 'Sure traffic is supposed to be better now, but ordinary people are left cowering in the shadow of those horrible things. And the city is still too expensive and dangerous to walk around in at night. It's terrible.'

By contrast, Ira was more settled with life in Harbin. 'I have two kids now, so I'm not going anywhere!' she joked. 'And even if it's a bit annoying dealing with these people every day, work at the Russian Village is alright. At least it keeps me in one place, whereas being a translator I had to travel about all the time.'

Yet the work was evidently not of the most serene variety, and as we chatted Ira repeatedly had to break off the conversation to shout admonishments at over-enthusiastic tourists who were fingering the exhibits. She also requested that I keep swaying left and right to screen her from people attempting to take photos of her. The exotic sight of a real blonde Russian in a real Russian house was proving irresistible to some visitors. Having myself been bothered on occasion by amateur photographers at Chinese tourist sites, I wondered how deep her sense of being an 'other' in this former Russian city ran. Did she think her husband viewed her in such exotic terms?

'No, not really,' she replied, 'I guess you could say he prefers a sort of American or international lifestyle. It would be too hard for us to be together if he was really totally Chinese.'

Were the Chinese so different from the Russians, then?

'There are lots of big differences, of course,' she said. 'They have a totally different worldview, traditions, habits. But there are also differences between how they see us and how we see them. When it comes to us Russians, their minds have really been changed because they keep rewriting their own history. This really influences how they think about us.'

Ira's main issue was that the Russian contribution to the development of Harbin was being underplayed. She felt that recent emphasis on past humiliation by foreign powers, a particular keystone of the national conversation under Xi Jinping, had put Russian residents of today's Harbin in a difficult position. But in fact, trouble had started well before this. Even when the park was being built, she said, this negative attitude towards Russians had been obvious from how the old owners of the Sun Island houses were treated. These people had not been Russians—those 'original' owners were of course long gone—but Chinese people who had acquired the homes here sometime between the 1950s and 2000s. According to Ira, they had been summarily evicted and poorly compensated to make way for the park: any trace of the Russian past was apparently fair game for government seizure, further indicating to her that the Communists were trying to control history.

'It was a land-grab, pure and simple,' she said, 'people were just told that they had to get out because the government needed to "develop" the place. Sometimes an old man still turns up here,' she added quietly. 'He still feels like the house belongs to him, even if he can't use it. So he comes to check up on it.'

Here in a sense was a sign of the complicated ways in which Russianness, Europeanness, or foreignness in general lurk in modern Harbin. To many Russian and some Chinese eyes, Sun Island's traces of early twentieth-century émigré leisure are an evocative reminder of a romantic bygone age. Yet while key to attracting domestic tourists, the very existence of these colonial remnants on Chinese soil reminds those who curate it of a difficult legacy of foreign encroachment. Dealing with this is made still more problematic because north-eastern China's orientation towards Russia has undergone so many violent pendulum swings over the past century—from imperial adversary to Soviet inspiration, anti-Japanese liberator, socialist blood-brother, 'revisionist' enemy, post-Soviet trade partner and, most recently, authoritarian 'friend'. It would be foolhardy for any leisure-focused tourist attraction to try to grapple with such hideously complex material. This may be why, at Ira's *dacha* as elsewhere, Sun Island favours an indiscriminate approach to 'Russian' and 'European' affairs, subsuming complexity under a paraphernalia of concrete *matrioshki*, Greek warrior statues and Stars and Stripes bikinis. And for all the stifling of history and memory around this circus-like Russian Village, Ira admitted that not everything here was badly done.

'The thing with the beer tap is too much,' she mused, 'but it is true that too many of our young people drink excessively. And there's real history here on the island which the Chinese have helped to preserve.' She gestured around the room. 'Like that fridge for example—it's over 100 years old.' She ushered me into a corner and opened the heavy door of an upright metal box. This solid pre-electricity appliance seemed a fitting symbol of the resilience with which the often hard-pressed Kharbintsy had carved out lives for themselves here, leaving a legacy that endured despite the ravages of history.

Another reason today's Harbin both vaunts and struggles with its 'European' past is that lives for local Chinese settlers in the colonial city were hardly easier, and were in many cases much harder, than those of Russian migrants. But perhaps most central of all to this ambivalence is the fact that much Kharbintsy history only unfolded precisely because this was neither Europe nor China. As Russian Whites extended pre-revolutionary lives here post-1917, and the local Jewish population carved out a niche away from Russian oppression and the camps of World War II, being distinct from European Russia and Europe in general was a pillar of Harbin's identity. Yet as Qu Qiubai had observed, for much of its past the city was not really Chinese either, its main avenue 'Kitaiskaya' gesturing to China as a remote externality comparable to those invoked by the city's Amurskaya, Mongolskaya or Kievskaya streets. This non-European and non-Chinese status, mirroring the not-quite-Asian but not-quite-Russian character of Russia's East had not engendered an idealised cultural synthesis. Many of Harbin's past residents had nevertheless been suspended somewhere between the vast lands to the north and south, and in a curious way Ira seemed the same. While more than happy to have left Vladivostok's disinterested government and unsafe streets, she did not feel ready for a fully 'Chinese' life either. Perhaps the Kharbintsy did live on after all.

* * *

Before leaving, and to bring myself right up to the present, I caught up with a group of Harbin residents I had encountered earlier in my stay and who, appropriately, occupied various points on the blurry local–foreign continuum. I was initially introduced to their diverse company—they comprised a Manchu, an American and a Russian descendant of actual Kharbintsy—by Dave, an affable Australian fellow-guest at the Luxiya Hotel. Visiting Harbin on a backpacking trip around China, Dave had only moved to the Luxiya because of a somewhat odd Couchsurfing experience. 'She just wanted me to sit at home with her and drink tea all the time,' he said of his middle-aged Chinese former host. 'That started right away—I'd just arrived and was raring to see the city, but we had to sit there for hours doing nothing.'

Having eventually escaped this familiar mismatch between near-suffocating Chinese hospitality and the awkwardness of a Western guest desperate to leave but unable to do so out of politeness, Dave was now keen to sample Harbin's nightlife. He had met one of the group we were heading to see during the Beijing leg of his trip. 'I've only spoken to these guys a bit so I'm not making any promises,' he said. But I had nothing planned, and had had enough of solitary Dostoyevskian musing on the nature of the human soul and identity, so I happily accepted his invitation to tag along.

We found the group at one of central Harbin's open-sided beer tents where locals and tourists alike spend raucous summer evenings drinking the city's favourite beverage, Harbin Beer. Made in a brewery founded in 1900 by a Polish German man named Jan Wróblewski to supply thirsty CER workers, the beer has followed as tumultuous a proprietorial trajectory as the Churin foodstuffs company: from Polish German origins, it passed through Russian, Czech, Chinese, Soviet and PRC state hands during the twentieth century before eventually being privatised and ultimately acquired by alcohol behemoth Anheuser-Busch in 2004.

Among those quaffing Harbin in the tent that evening was Amanda, Dave's main point of contact, a Princeton PhD student in Chinese history, and the primary social instigator that evening. But her enthusiasm for many things, particularly if beer was involved, did not extend to all aspects of Harbin life. This was in part because she had recently had her handbag slashed by a thief who had nimbly extracted her passport through the resultant slit. She had only bumped into Dave in Beijing because she was there getting a new one from the US embassy.

'Yes, I'll be ready to leave,' Amanda sighed as we talked. 'But I've enjoyed it here and there's plenty to learn, personally I've found out a lot about Russia.'

Among other novelties, Amanda's discoveries in China's north-east had included the existence of non-Slavic Russians. 'Right, right!' she said when I mentioned I had recently come down from Siberia. 'I had no idea about all the people who live there. But I was speaking to this Asian-looking guy here once, and when he said "I am from Russia" it literally blew my mind!'

Though unsure of the literalness of this reaction, I found it a common one. As Yakutsk and Khabarovsk friends had made clear, the voices of Sakha, Nanai and dozens of other non-Russian peoples from the vast old empire are rarely heard within Russia itself, let alone in New Jersey.

Sitting next to Amanda was George (his English moniker), who belonged to another largely neglected North Asian people, though a China-based one. Ethnically Manchu, a recent computer science graduate and enthusiastic amateur English-learner, George came from old Harbin stock, at least on his father's side. 'My mum's actually Han Chinese,' he said, 'but my dad is Manchu and so they chose to register me as Manchu too.'

By his paternal line and his administrative status, therefore, George was a descendent of Manchuria's native inhabitants, historical speakers of the language in which Harbin is named, and co-members of the broader Tungusic family of peoples that includes the Hezhe/Nanai and Evenk. Manchu identity carries vastly less weight in today's China than it did when Harbin was founded, for then the Manchus still ruled all China as the 1644-founded Qing dynasty. By contrast, for most of the time since the 1911 overthrow of that imperial line, and especially following its partial resurrection by the Japanese in the 1932–45 Manchukuo state, Manchu-ness has been a problematised and systematically suppressed category. The next leg of my journey would offer more evidence of how this had come about. The erosion of Manchu identity is today symbolically reflected in the fact that 'Manchu' is often abbreviated simply to 'Man' in common PRC parlance.

Yet as George's case showed, even if China's post-imperial rulers, both Nationalist and Communist, once sought to erase a sense of difference among this people who previously dominated the majority

Han, the less extreme post-Mao age has seen something of a Manchu revival. Unlike previous generations, George's parents were keen to classify their son as Manchu in the 1980s without fear of sanction. In doing so, they followed a pattern common among many borderland dwellers in mixed marriages, for like the multi-ethnic Soviet empire before it, the PRC has afforded various symbolic benefits to (implicitly culturally inferior) non-Han minorities.

'Yes, I think we get five extra points on the university entrance exam,' George said, making me recall the conversation I had had with Langjuan in Labudaling about her pleasing *gaokao* score. She had been right to be glad, for the exam is a gruelling ordeal for most. Indeed, many Han citizens of the PRC therefore resent this apparent favouritism towards minorities in an ever-more-competitive educational environment.

Did George think the system was fair, I wondered. 'Favouritism' hardly seems like the best characterisation of Beijing's minority policies given Uyghur or Tibetan experiences, but some see the bonus points as especially misplaced in the case of the Manchus who have become almost indistinguishable from the Han. 'I don't know,' he said philosophically. 'But you do what you can to get ahead in China. It is true though that Manchu identity is pretty hard to put your finger on. After the Qing and the Manchukuo thing, the Han didn't want us to be separate so they forced us to assimilate.'

After the tumultuous twentieth century, fewer than 100 people out of a population of over 10 million are today thought to speak any Manchu language, but assimilation processes in fact began well before this. The 1689 Qing–Russia Treaty of Nerchinsk may have had a Manchu and no Chinese version, but ruling the mostly non-Manchu Chinese Empire for two-and-a-half centuries demanded bilingual administration and coaxed many Manchus towards Sinicisation. Indeed, already from the 1660s official policies were encouraging Manchus to use the language of the Han majority, with such success that a century later Qing emperors had reversed course and were chiding their subordinates for ignorance of the ancestral tongue.[30]

In light of these historic shifts, it is unsurprising that Manchu identity seems inscrutable even to those who officially belong to the group, and George was mostly at a loss to explain the particularities of 'his' people. 'Er, we traditionally don't eat dog meat like the Chinese or

Koreans do,' he ventured uncertainly. 'And actually I think we can possibly even have more than one kid, or I mean we could before they started allowing lots of people to do that,' he added. 'I'd quite like that,' he went on. 'Only-children have a hard time understanding how others feel.' George's struggles with his Manchu-ness appeared bound up with the broader difficulty of knowing oneself in a changing China.

After several hours in the nocturnal buzz of the beer tent, we moved on to Box Club, a minimally decorated local dive bar whose walls were covered with snaking trails of scrawled graffiti. Here I finally had a chance to talk to Andrei, a diminutive Russian with a lank mop of brown hair who had come to Harbin from Nakhodka east of Vladivostok. His great-grandfather, he told me, had been among the original Kharbintsy, but, after being driven out of China during the Cultural Revolution, his grandparents had made their peace with the Soviet government and returned to Russia. Andrei's life in Harbin was thus an act of long-delayed return, but in only the latest reflection of the city's multitudinous transformations, his existence here was now reliant on work as an English teacher at a local nursery school.

'I pretend to be Canadian at work so they give me more money,' he told me slyly, referencing a widespread trick whereby white people from non-English-speaking countries dissemble to conform to the native-speaker-mania of Chinese educational establishments. Many feel comfortable doing so given that there is often no reason why native speakers of English make better pedagogues than non-natives. If anything, a teacher who has learnt English as a second language may have more empathy with the learning experiences of his or her students.

But whatever its deceptions, the employment situation of Andrei, who like many thousands of Russians before him had spilled out of the Russian Far East to make a new life in neighbouring Manchuria, was as clear a sign as any of Harbin's Chinese present. It is possible to learn Russian in a few high schools in this old Russian city, but by and large opportunities for foreigners are now determined by China's impetus to equip its youngsters for an Anglophone future, rather than any Russia-focused nostalgia.

'My whole life is in English basically,' said Andrei. 'It's got to the point where I don't even really like hanging out with Russians.' Our present company—Amanda, George, Dave and some other English-speakers we had joined at Box—reflected this. Like many Russians, Andrei also reserved a special cynicism for his homeland, and when I mentioned that I had in fact visited Nakhodka several years previously while living in Vladivostok, he was astonished.

'What on earth did you want to go there for?' he asked. I told him I had travelled with a Chinese friend to have a look at the massive cargo port there. Nakhodka forms the freight terminus of the Trans-Siberian, and its towers of shipping containers and timber ready for transport beyond Russia's Pacific shore were a sort of monumental tourist attraction in themselves.

But mention of Russia, the Chinese, and the port seemed to send Andrei into a reflective frame of mind. He had not forfeited all sense of national pride and evidently felt aggrieved at the state of Sino-Russian relations. 'The Chinese don't care about or appreciate us at all,' he said. 'They're not interested in us as a country or people—for them we're just a pile of resources they want to exploit.' Growing up in the shadow of Nakhodka's dockside cranes had perhaps reinforced Andrei's awareness of the emptying out of a land already largely evacuated of humans.

His now somewhat morose frame of mind mulched into the considerable inebriation he had brought with him to the bar, where several hefty bottles of Japanese Kirin beer had followed the Harbin down his throat. I felt at least partly responsible for bringing on this newly ponderous mood but, hardly clear-minded myself, decided to exit the conversation as it veered off into incoherence. I told him I should return to prepare for my departure the following day.

'Sure, sure. Pop by again if you need anything,' Andrei slurred, managing a grin as I stood up to go. 'Do you get the reference by the way?' he then asked with a wink. 'Pop by again if you need anything.'

I said I didn't.

'Do you know that Russian cartoon, actually it might be Ukrainian, *Once Upon a Time There Was a Dog*? It's a line from that cartoon—"pop by again if you need anything".'

I admitted that I had no idea what he was talking about, and so, apparently distressed by this gap in my knowledge of eastern Slavic fairy tales, the bleary-eyed Andrei stood up unsteadily and proceeded to recount, loudly and in Russian, the relevant part of the story to everyone sitting in our corner of the bar. This entailed re-enacting a conversation between a wolf and the cartoon's eponymous dog, a performance whose raucousness and exuberance were matched only by the confusion of those looking on. Leering maniacally and providing a soundtrack of impressively realistic howls, barks and yelps as his hair covered his eyes, Andrei staggered and danced around, ending with a bow and another recitation of the famous line: *zakhodi, esli chto!*

Had Andrei's great-grandfather attempted an equivalent Russian-specific cultural reference a hundred years ago in whatever the early twentieth-century version of Box Club was, it is very likely that many onlookers would have understood. But in today's Harbin both the allusion and the language it was delivered in were lost on the audience who mostly looked around at one another as if to ask what had just happened. Yet Andrei was satisfied, feeling he had done justice to this childhood favourite of his.

'There you go then, now you know,' he said, adding for good measure, 'it's much better than any of that Disney crap.' I did indeed now know, and I was also glad that behind an officially 'Canadian' Potemkin identity, Russian cultural sympathies still lay concealed.

* * *

Leaving Harbin as I had arrived, by train, meant a return to the city's austere grey behemoth of a railway station, an eight-storey tombstone in the town's newer Chinese centre. The original Harbin station, a bulbous *style moderne* confection whose grave the new terminus marks, long ago went the same way as anyone who would have appreciated Andrei's performance. Today, many more people ride the Russian-initiated trans-Manchurian route than ever used to take the old CER, and so the station was rebuilt decades ago to expand capacity. But like so much here, the practical measure of dismantling an old building had deep symbolic resonance, reinforcing the decisive severance of the modern Chinese city from its Russian past. In this case, the amputation seems almost literal, for the first Harbin station was stylistically modelled on that which lies thousands of miles away at the other end of the line, Moscow's Kursk railway station where Hu Yuzhi, Mrs Alec-Tweedie, and anyone bound for China boarded eastbound trains. While not a universal practice, the placing of architecturally similar stations at either end of new lines was an occasional feature of Russia's golden age of railway-laying: long-distance mimesis thus still today character-ises St Petersburg's Moscow station and Moscow's Leningradsky station (which still has its Soviet-era name), as well as the Yaroslavsky and Vladivostok stations at the nodes of that other great trans-continental route, the Trans-Siberian. But while these spatial bonds persist, Harbin's link to Moscow is gone, and the trains still plying the old trans-Manchurian route now do so on an unequivocally Chinese time-table. Accordingly, I consulted the China Railways website, booked my online tickets for the next stage, and left for another corner of Manchuria where the mirrorings of Russian pasts and presents are only one part of the international picture.

8

SOUTHERN MANCHURIA

ISLANDS OF THE IN-BETWEEN

'You should go to Changbaishan,' Andrei had mumbled wistfully as our conversation in Harbin had meandered towards my next destination. 'When I first saw the summit, I felt I could happily die there.'

He was alluding to a sacred mountain whose foothills I would now indeed be approaching, although I would not on this occasion be climbing to the top. Poking pristine 2,700 metres above the troublesome nations far below, the peak is known in Korean as Paektusan and has long been venerated as a place of ancestral origin by both Koreans to the south and Manchus to the north. Its wooded slopes disgorge the two rivers that have marked the Sino-Korean (and thus today the Sino-North Korean) border since the eighteenth century, a line that bisects the azure volcanic crater lake gleaming at its summit. Changbaishan's overlapping spiritual significance to multiple peoples, including, it seemed, Andrei, and its rugged frontier surroundings made it a fitting emblem for the southern Manchurian lands to which I was bound. Here Chinese, Russian, Manchu, Korean and Japanese worlds have all collided, a concatenation of cultures that has served only to throw Sino-Russian reflections into sharper relief.

Bridging old and new, I boarded my first Chinese bullet train of the journey clutching a Russian-style 'Churin Foods' sausage. Since 2015, strands of the world's largest high-speed railway network—over 17,000 miles of it by mid-2018—have reached right into Manchuria's south-easternmost corner, but to get there a change in the old Manchu river port of Jilin was required first. Having somehow caught a cold in Harbin despite the oppressive heat, I spent the ride there ripping through the surrounding north-eastern farmland in a 200-mph semi-slumber, arriving delirious with a blocked nose and a swimming head. Managing a final farewell to the Sungari in this city where Kim Il Sung once attended high school, I had a stroll along the riverbank, and enjoyed a dusk meal of donkey meat dumplings in the lengthening ochre shadows of the local Confucius Temple. Then, aboard another white bullet, I glided south-eastward among rolling wooded hills, passing Changbaishan to the south on the way.

The final stages of the ride to Hunchun offered fleeting snapshots of North Korea's Onsong County over the River Tumen as we zipped in and out of the railway's neatly burrowed tunnels. Unlike the thickly forested slopes here on the Chinese side, the Korean riverbank comprised treeless scarps scarred by the small farmland plots locals had hewn into this vertiginous land during the DPRK's 1990s–2000s famine. Below this, ribbons of smoke slowly unfurled from the chimneys of decrepit single-storey villages, a stark contrast to the rail-side development zones, tractor-equipped farmhouses and home satellite dishes (mostly for local Chinese Koreans to watch South Korean television) here in China. As so often on the China–Russia border, it was clear which of the old red allies had navigated a more prosperous path out of high socialism. Indeed, Hunchun sits sandwiched between two countries, Russia and North Korea, where slick facilities such as the train from which I soon disembarked are conspicuously absent.

The town's rail terminus with its quad-lingual Chinese, Russian, Korean and English signage further underscored the Middle Kingdom's claim to be the central player in this corner of North East Asia, even if conversations in Hunchun would reveal the potential for history to undermine this aspiration. Like many of China's airport-like high-speed stations, it lay somewhat out of the centre, and the shiny yellow-and-green bus that took me into town initially rolled across farmland. Clattering trucks and cranes showed, however, that Hunchun, recipient of tens of billions of dollars in central government investment since the 2010s, has every intention of swallowing much of this terrain.

At the River Tumen Business Hotel, Russian shoppers recently arrived from the ramshackle southern tip of neighbouring Primorsky province (informally 'Primorye') lounged in the lobby. Many from Vladivostok and southward have come to prefer Hunchun to other border destinations like Suifenhe. Massive investment in the town has lent it a well-kept feel, and has drawn in a wide array of traders, tour guides, private hospitals and dentists to serve a Russian clientele. Many Primorye residents now come here for all their medical needs, which can be met much more cheaply and quickly than back home. Although lacking Manzhouli's mimicry-obsessed megalomania, Hunchun's centre also offers some pseudo-European architecture—including a bulbous green-and-yellow mock-tsarist post office. But these are interspersed with buildings that sympathetically incorporate local Korean elements. The latter is a common feature in towns across Yanbian Korean Autonomous Prefecture, at whose eastern end Hunchun lies, which is official home to north-east China's ethnic Koreans, known in Korean as Chosonjok. Most concentrated in Jilin province, although today spread all over China, and today numbering over 2 million, Chosonjok mostly speak both Chinese and Korean. Their dialect of the latter is at root closer to that spoken in neighbouring DPRK's North Hamgyong province, yet reflecting the many ways in which Koreas meet here, it is increasingly influenced by the smoother, English-infused South Korean variety. The only significant minority group in China to be wealthier on average than the majority Han, the Chosonjok occupy a unique position in their autonomous borderland home, created for them in 1952 as a reward for their resistance to Japan's 1931–45 occupation of north-east China and their support for the Chinese Communists.

Before being named 'Yanbian', this area around Hunchun was for decades known as 'Kando' in Korean ('Jiandao' in Chinese), whose characters—間島—mean something like 'in-between island'. The Koreans who first settled here—and in neighbouring areas of Russia—were refugees, poor farmers crossing the sluggish Tumen to escape successive disasters, from famine in the 1870s to Japan's colonisation of the Korean Peninsula from 1905. For these migrants, the area had exactly the interstitial quality that the name implied, for, like Harbin to the Russians, Kando was not Korea but nor, as a remote outpost of the crumbling Qing Empire, was it fully China. The segment of my journey that began in Hunchun would take in several other such in-between locations.

By order of Hunchun's local government, which is made up of both Han Chinese and Chosonjok representatives reflecting the roughly 50/50 split in local population, all signage must be in Chinese, Russian and Korean, languages with three entirely different scripts. A fourth is frequently added to this mix when English also appears (Image 14). The town's businesses cater to everyone from Han and Korean locals to Russian tourists and patients, North Korean businesspeople, and visitors from other parts of China who come to savour the triple-borderland ambiance. Now hooked on the confounding semiotic allure of quasi-Russian souvenirs, and keen to sample their North Korean equivalent, I first headed to a shop targeting a domestic traveller clientele.

The place did not disappoint, as in addition to offering a variety of typo-ridden cans of fake Baltika beer, the emporium's glass cabinets also displayed collectable folders of printed-in-China DPRK banknotes and fake pin badges bearing the faces of Kim Il Sung and Kim Jong Il, among other exotic wares. As I browsed, I was approached by Mr Pak, a retired Chosonjok police officer who, some small talk about the hot weather revealed, was in the shop mainly to benefit from the air conditioning. Following our meteorological foreplay, Mr Pak broached more serious matters and explained that this early August day was actually special for him for several reasons.

'Today is my seventieth birthday,' he declared solemnly.

I congratulated him, and remarked—sincerely—that he seemed very spritely for someone so senior. This impression was reinforced by the black plasticky net vest and shorts he was wearing. 'Thank you,' Mr Pak replied, 'but there are more reasons why today is significant: today in 1945 the Soviets came through Manchuria to help us fight the Japanese!' I had not until then realised that it was the 9th, but this was indeed the anniversary of that event that tied together many locations I had visited, from Vyatskoe to Harbin. 'Where are you from anyway? The Soviet Union?' he asked.

England, I replied, adding in an attempt to curry favour that we had fought on the same side as the Soviets against the Japanese.

'Yes, but you sold opium to China!' Mr Pak retorted mischievously in an echo of comments I had heard back in Shiwei. There was no malice in his voice, but the Han store attendant who was evidently familiar with Mr Pak and his antics began to look wary.

'It wasn't actually him!' she correctly pointed out, likely hoping to avert the outbreak of an international incident in her fragile hall of glass cabinets.

'I know, I know,' said Mr Pak.

But since the subject of ethnicity and nationality had now been established, I tried to steer the conversation towards Korean-related matters, asking which Korea he preferred. Unsurprisingly, this proved no less contentious.

'We Chosonjok are all one people with the North Koreans, of course,' Mr Pak said. 'Actually all this land around here and to the north used to be ours. This part of China was the Koguryo kingdom, and even if the Chinese say we turned up after them it was the Chinese who got here later. From all the way down in Shandong!' Historical disputes persist over this region's Koguryo past (37 BCE–668 CE) and 'whose' history—Korea's or China's—it was a part of. Unlike protests over Russia's mid-nineteenth-century annexations of Qing land, which are mostly limited to demotic trolling, online and off, long-vanished Sino-Korean boundaries remain a matter of official dispute among East Asian states that have been neighbours for longer.

Had Mr Pak been to North Korea?, I asked him.

'Yes, many times before I retired,' he said. 'It was easy then, all you needed was a little letter of introduction from your work unit and you could go anywhere. Pyongyang is a great city.' China and North Korea to this day remain one another's sole treaty allies, and until a recent cooling in relations the River Tumen has long been a highly porous divide.

How about the South?

'Yes, I've been there too, I flew from Yanji,' Mr Pak replied sounding less positive. This plane journey, which I had taken myself, today involves a rather absurd loop skirting around North Korean airspace, although this was not the reason for Mr Pak's change in tone. 'South Korea is just America's little pet dog,' he explained.

The peace-broker store attendant was again looking uneasy, and so I refrained from pursuing the matter further, or facetiously asking whether or not—given Hunchun's large number of popular dog restaurants—being a dog was such a bad thing. Besides, Mr Pak's was a common sentiment, and from older PRC citizens in particular I had often heard praise for the traditional Cold War-era relationship with the North Koreans, as well as that with the Soviets. On one occasion travelling between Pyongyang and Beijing by train, I had encountered a Han Chinese father, and veteran of the 1979 Sino-Vietnamese border war, who was taking his son to the DPRK to teach him about socialism. Many who were raised on an ideological diet of Marxist internationalism still stress that, whatever North Korea's problems in the present—and they acknowledge there are many, perhaps solvable through Chinese-style reforms—solidarity with a brother country must be remembered.

Yet however strongly held, such views are largely those of a demographically declining cohort whose offspring have a quite different outlook. Indeed, Mr Pak's own children, like those of many Chosonjok, had dispersed throughout the metropolitan centres of China, and some of his grandchildren had taken a step further and gone to study in Seoul, capital of the notional 'dog' nation. But one did not have to travel hundreds of miles to meet them in order to observe such generational divergences, for younger Chosonjok who have remained in Hunchun also care much less for the erstwhile socialist brother. Having wished Mr Pak happy birthday again, I made my way to a nearby coffee shop, one of dozens in the town decorated in the style of South Korea's ubiquitous and ever-changing cafés. Here, befitting the surroundings, very different perspectives predominated.

The young owner, Ji-ok, walked over and we got talking. In vivid contrast to Mr Pak's acrylic vest, she was wearing jeans, a checked dress shirt and thick black-rimmed glasses. Fashion, like coffee, flows effortlessly into Yanbian from South Korea, brought by the hundreds of thousands of Chosonjok who since the 1990s have spent years living and working below the 38th parallel. 'South Korea is much more developed than the North so everyone wants to go there,' confirmed Ji-ok. 'We love the food and the drink and the clothes, the music, the coffee culture and TV shows are just so cool!'

Yanbian is indeed full not only of cosy cafés but also intimate neighbourhood watering holes, craft beer bars, and stylish restaurants serving pizza, Thai food and burgers. This is extraordinary in a Chinese context, for none of Yanbian's urban centres has a population over

400,000 and yet all feel much more cosmopolitan than places even five times their size elsewhere in China.

Ji-ok took a seat on the leather sofa opposite me, as smooth K-Pop hits played quietly in the background. Like everyone her age, she said, she cared very little for the country just over the Tumen. 'The North is so backward,' she said bluntly, using the South Korean word *Bukhan*, which differs from the North's own label for itself, *Choson*. 'They're poor and mean and don't have anything to offer us. To be honest, these days nobody really thinks about them at all.'

What about Rason, I asked, mentioning a North Korean development zone that lies just over the border from Hunchun. With considerable Chinese supervision and investment, the town has made a certain amount of fitful economic progress during the 2000s. Until international sanctions cut off the supply in 2017, Rason has also been the source of Hunchun's seafood, giving the latter landlocked town a considerable reputation among Chinese tourists who load up here on coveted spider crabs, hairy crabs, clams and mussels.

'Rason's terrible,' said Ji-ok. 'They're trying to do what China did in Shenzhen in the 1980s, to develop and open up like we did. But it's much worse than that. Still really backward.'

This refrain about backwardness was almost the only view about the DPRK that it was possible to extract from younger Yanbian Chosonjok, even when I asked specifically about the shared history Mr Pak had reminisced about. As in the former Soviet space, socialism and its complicated aftermath have created a deep rift in inter-generational worldviews. These bifurcated perspectives draw attention to the unusual position the Chosonjok occupy today in having two foreign countries to look to as a source of 'Koreanness'. China's minorities fall broadly into two groups, one for whom, like the Hezhe, Manchus, Tibetans or Uyghurs, no independent state exists in their name. The second, however, may, like the Russians, Mongols or Kazakhs, look beyond China's borders for a country that serves as a repository of their national culture and language. Yanbian's Koreans are spoilt for choice, with each Korea exerting different pulls, whether nostalgic or pragmatic, political or economic, on different age-groups.

During much of Yanbian's socialist past, choosing perfidiously capitalist South Korea was understandably entirely out of the question. Yet perversely, expressing loyalty to, or even mere interest in, North Korea could at times be just as problematic. Other conversations with older Hunchun residents revealed that the 1950s–60s era of shared socialism that followed the tumult of Japanese occupation, the Chinese Civil War and the Korean War had only brought temporary calm to Yanbian. The treaties of socialist 'friendship' signed at this time between the Soviet Union, North Korea and China embraced the region's low brick backwater towns on three sides. But during the 1960s the Sino-Korean relationship broke down just as the Sino-Soviet one did as Beijing and Pyongyang leaders diverged. Quickly casting aside the Soviet and Chinese support that had been pivotal to his accession to power, Kim Il Sung set about developing his own personality cult to rival Mao's, raising fears among the Chinese authorities that Yanbian's Koreans would prefer the former as an emancipatory sun-god. With radical Maoism reaching its own high point and as Yanbian accordingly received its own 'sent down' Shanghai Han youths like those working the Great Northern Wilderness, the borderlands became a dangerous place to be. As in ethnically Russian Enhe and Shiwei, the xenophobia of the Cultural Revolution meant links to friends and relatives over the Tumen, which many Chosonjok had, became highly stigmatised.

For Chinese Koreans, this proved a painfully ironic turn. Many local families had only recently shown utmost loyalty to China, having lost sons in the 3-million-strong Chinese 'Volunteer' forces who from October 1950 joined the Northern side in the Korean War. Participation in this conflict, which Mao had only reluctantly agreed to join after Stalin promised him loans worth $300 million and the dispatch of technical advisors to the fledgling PRC,[1] initially meant that surviving Chosonjok parents and siblings were considered 'martyr families'. Mao's own eldest son Anying had perished in this roiling early Cold War cauldron, and so sacrificing offspring to this cause carried a deep symbolism. But all this changed when the Cultural Revolution made any connection to the neighbouring state, including battle records, highly toxic.

Facing persecution amid suspicion of loyalty to Kim Il Sung's 'Korean revisionists' to the south, many Chosonjok were thus forced to destroy all evidence of past or present connections to their ancestral peninsula, burning letters from loved ones and discarding mementos.

Some even retraced their forebears' footsteps by fleeing 'back' to North Korea. If this now seems an extraordinary act given subsequent developments, it was then considered a viable option amid both the hostile climate in China and the speed of the DPRK's post-war recovery. Aided by Soviet subsidy, inherited Japanese industry and tight socio-political cohesion, this East Asian 'people's democracy' looked in the 1960s–70s to be the more promising Korea.[2] If discovered trying to defect over the Tumen, one most likely faced execution, but to some the risk still seemed worthwhile.

Today, sardonic Chinese views hold that the only good to come out of the mid-century revolutionary storm that engulfed Yanbian was the death of Mao Anying. Much the most capable and ambitious of the Chairman's several ignored children, Anying had been dispatched to Moscow in 1936 aged just fourteen. There he studied at the Stasova International Children's Home (or 'Interdom'), acquiring the Russian name Serezha and gaining considerably greater literacy in Russian than in Chinese (in which he had received little education).[3] Progressing to the Soviet capital's Frunze Military Academy, he then received training that would equip him to serve in Korea as Russian translator to the Chinese Volunteer Army's commander Peng Dehuai.[4] It was whilst working in this capacity that he perished, and his 1950 interment in a DPRK military cemetery thus, some dryly suggest, possibly rescued China from having a North Korea-style Mao dynasty ruling over it for decades. In a sense therefore it may be thanks to the US Air Force bomber that killed him that the post-Mao era brought the possibility of release and opening to Yanbian and China as a whole.

After Mao, the Chosonjok in particular benefited from the reforms enacted by Mao's non-kindred successor Deng Xiaoping. Their success at first had an important Sino-Russian dimension. As elsewhere on the China–Russia border, the converging currents of Deng's new domestic policies and thawing Sino-Soviet ties from the late 1980s saw a rapid increase in international commercial opportunities in Yanbian. Cross-border trade with neighbouring areas of Russia began to thrive, driven in part by new relationships among Yanbian Koreans and their long-lost cousins in Russia. This latter group, known as the Koryo saram or 'Koryo people' in reference to an old name for Korea, were descendants of the same Koreans who had fled across the Tumen from the

1870s but ended up in tsarist territory. Whatever the grimness of the comparison, many had endured arguably still greater trauma than the Chosonjok in the decades since their separation. In 1937, accusations that the Koryo saram were Japanese spies had seen most deported by Stalin from the Soviet Far East to Central Asia, an ordeal during which thousands perished.[5] Ensuing decades saw them struggling to forge new lives in the steppe, mountains and deserts of Kazakhstan, Uzbekistan and Tajikistan, where they were in many cases remarkably successful in rising to prominent roles in Soviet politics and industry.[6]

But by the 1990s significant numbers of Koryo saram had elected to return to their grandparents' homes in Primorye in the more liberal Gorbachev era. Younger people now only spoke Russian, but senior community members could connect with their Yanbian neighbours in Korean. Their Koreanness-mediated Sino-Russian networks thus in turn helped form supply chains in everything from consumer goods to timber, scrap metal, concrete and leather, which Chinese firms hungrily bought up from the now-collapsing Soviet industrial base.

Fatefully, the increasingly mobile reform era, which also saw Nanai reconnect with Hezhe, Blagoveshchensk shoppers cross the Amur to Heihe, Chinese workers travel deep into Russia to Yakutsk and Moscow, and Manzhouli transform from remote rail junction to tourism hub, was rung in by rock anthems performed by both Chinese and Russian Koreans. Beijing-based Chosonjok musician Cui Jian's 1986 hit 'Yi Wu Suo You' (Nothing to my name) captured the ever-growing sense of identity crisis and stasis sweeping through young urban China in the late 1980s. Three years after its release, the song became an anthem for the 1989 Tiananmen Square protesters, among whom Cui appeared in person on several occasions, although the man dubbed the 'father of Chinese rock' has mostly escaped the persecution and exile visited on the movement's student leaders in the decades since. From the Russian side of the border, late Russian rock icon and Koryo saram singer Viktor Tsoi occupies a very similar position to Cui, with whom he extraordinarily even shares his surname—Tsoi simply being the Cyrillic counterpart to *pinyin* Cui (Choi in Korean itself). Tsoi led the 1980s band Kino and, like Cui, produced music reflecting myriad late Soviet discontents. These struck a chord with the *perestroika* generation. Perhaps his most famous work, the 1986 song 'Peremen' (Changes), which is delivered like all his output in a languid vocal style not unlike that of Joy Division's Ian Curtis, was adopted as a protest anthem mirroring 'Nothing to My Name'. Somehow, then, it was Russia and China's Korean minorities who, with all their experience of the violence and sacrifice of socialist state-building, were most in touch with the post-socialist Zeitgeist.

Yet contact with Russia-based traders was far from the only international wave cresting over Yanbian in the 1990s as new hope and tragedy from the Korean Peninsula swept through the region in equal measure. The very same Soviet breakup that permitted Chosonjok–Koryo saram contact also severed North Korea's main economic lifeline and, as the effects of poor planning and bad harvests were compounded, near-complete economic collapse followed.[7] This brought about a devastating famine comparable in its effects to that which had driven the original Chosonjok cross-Tumen migrations in the 1870s. Starving refugees were forced to escape to Yanbian seeking food, sometimes finding shelter in sympathetic Chosonjok homes around Hunchun and elsewhere where their language, culture and experience of socialist extremes were well known. The shallow and languidly flowing Tumen, already easily forded on foot, was made still more crossable as North Korean law and order broke down and hungry border guards came to rely on bribes from refugees simply to remain alive.

Yet as North Koreans arrived, increasing numbers of Chosonjok were leaving. In 1992, only two years before the onset of famine in the DPRK, Beijing had normalised relations with Seoul, accelerating an exodus from the forested hills, cornfields and rice paddies of Yanbian to the burgeoning skyscrapers, neon and cosmopolitan glitz of South Korea. Even before a streamlined visa regime was introduced to allow Chosonjok 'compatriots' to 'return' to the South (to which few in reality had any kind of historical connection), thousands were already finding illegal ways to migrate, assisted by often exploitative intermediaries. Exorbitant fees charged by these middlemen, as well as other costs, meant that in the early days most families could only afford to send one representative. Strings of attachment were therefore stretched as a husband or wife working in Seoul, Daegu or Busan sent most of their earnings back to a spouse assigned to manage the money by investing in property or business.

Work was easy to find, and although to this day many of the 800,000 Chosonjok now in the South are employed in low-prestige jobs as waiters, cooks, cleaners or masseuses, these positions are nevertheless much better paid than even more respectable professions back in China. Despite facing long hours, irregular schedules, and difficulties fitting in to a South Korean society that often disdains them as not 'real' Koreans, many Chosonjok readily succumb to the allure of South Korean culture and fashion. As evident at Ji-ok's café in Hunchun, the remittances sent back to stay-behind partners have been channelled into Yanbian's ubiquitous eateries, coffee shops and nightclubs. Today, therefore, no overseas travel is required for young Chosonjok couples to enjoy an evening of deafening K-Pop, or home-baked cookies, over-priced desiccated cheesecakes and great squidgy cubes of honey-bread consumed with impossibly small forks while ignoring one another and fiddling on mobile phones. Small rustic-effect restaurants offer *makgeolli*, a milky, sweet and mildly alcoholic rice-based drink, alongside Americanised Korean favourites, from *bulgogi* rice-burgers to delicious sweetcorn cocooned in a layer of cloying plasticky cheese on a hot iron plate. Out on Yanbian's streets, the mimesis takes more monumental form as real estate developments mimic South Korean residential complexes and large pastel-shade tower blocks bear bold compound names and numbers high up on their outside walls. Yet for all this (South) Koreanisation, the Chosonjok exodus has continued, matched and indeed vastly exceeded by an influx of Han Chinese from elsewhere in economically straitened Manchuria. This has made Yanbian a paradoxical place, for the same processes that have given the prefecture's urban spaces a more Seoul-like appearance have also made its population proportionately much less Korean.

* * *

Another badge of Yanbian's post-socialist transformations, especially evident as I explored Hunchun, has been the recent emergence of its dual borders as tourist destinations in themselves. While the boundary with Russia remains a mostly calm—if heavily policed—area, this development seems most extraordinary because the North Korean border remains a source of constant tension and periodic alarm. From the seizure by DPRK authorities of two American journalists filming along the River Tumen in 2009[8] to the defection of a North Korean soldier who crossed into China in January 2015 and killed four villagers near the town of Helong,[9] the area remains prone to unpredictable incidents. Yet this has done little to impede the elevation to must-see status of several local border posts including Fangchuan, a site southeast of Hunchun. Here at the tip of a tapering ribbon of Chinese territory, China, Russia and North Korea all converge, a fact vocally advertised by a clamouring squad of taxi drivers who greet every arrival at Hunchun's rail and bus terminals advertising trips down to this destination. It is second only in its appeal to Paektusan, they say. After arguing for a while over price, I took up one such offer.

Mr Teng drove a shiny new green VW taxi, yet another artefact of Hunchun's recent good fortune. A Han Chinese former farmer who was more dismissive about North Korea than anyone I had yet met, the fifty-two-year-old Mr Teng had parents who had come to Yanbian in the 1960s from northern China's Shandong province, forced north by food shortages, like so many Manchurian arrivals over time. As someone born and raised in Hunchun, he presented himself as an authority on most local and regional matters, relishing the chance to offer categorical commentary on everything from Kim Jong Un's hairstyle to the relative merits of women from different countries. Discussion of North Korea began as he told me about a trip he had made a few years previously to Rason, the nearby DPRK special economic zone dismissed by Ji-ok. Like many, he had been there to visit a local casino catering to travellers from China where gambling is illegal.

'North Korea is awful,' Mr Teng spat. 'They confiscated my mobile phone and wouldn't let me have it back until the end of the trip! And they tell you what you can and can't take pictures of.' All tourists visiting the DPRK are subject to restrictions, but reports of bad behaviour by Chinese visitors mean citizens of the supposedly fraternal nation have been receiving even stricter treatment in recent years.

'The place is still a feudal society,' he continued bitterly. 'Their leaders can come to China or go to Germany or wherever, but the ordinary people can't go anywhere. I met a North Korean here once. He was wearing a white shirt and baggy trousers and had badges of Kim Il Sung and Kim Jong Il. Most of them have terrible clothes and not enough to eat. How is it that a country spending so much on its army and missiles can't even feed its people?'

At least it was better than the 2000s, I ventured, mentioning the famine.

'Yes true, it is a bit better now,' he conceded. 'Before, loads of them fled over here but now there aren't so many. That's because China's helping them to develop though. We give them a lot.'

Was this a good thing?

'Good or bad, our government only donates food and coal and things out of fear,' he resumed indignantly. 'They just do it because Korea is so vicious and treats China badly. We know if we don't give them anything then they'll get angry and try to hurt China. And now they have nuclear missiles we don't know what Fatty Kim the Third will do.' Mr Teng's use of the common Chinese nickname for Kim Jong Un—Jin San Pang—made clear where he stood on this particular statesman.

As Mr Teng fulminated, the road wound along next to the serpentine Tumen, China becoming ever narrower, Russia and North Korea drawing closer on either side. The two would eventually meet, putting a 10-mile gap between Fangchuan and Chinese access to the Sea of Japan, a quirk of the 1860 Qing–Russia Treaty of Peking that has vexed generations of Chinese governments ever since. Still more frustrating these days is the fact that neither Russia nor the DPRK seem to be making very good use of the land immediately over the borders from Fangchuan. As I had seen previously on a visit made while living in Vladivostok, the Russia–North Korea rail crossing at Khasan/Tumangang is a crumbling monument to Moscow's long-disconnected life-support for the Kim dynasty. Khasan's broad sidings and cavernous tiled railway station now usher through but one Moscow–Pyongyang train per week, the desolate town serving as a temporary halt for Russians heading to Rason, where the Russian Railways company has laid a track. There are also North Korean work teams coming the other way. From forestry projects in the Russian Far East (some ironically close to Kim Jong Il's obfuscated birthplace at Vyatskoe) to construction sites that reportedly included 2018 World Cup stadia,[10] between 45,000 and 50,000 North Korean workers are thought to be spread, archipelago-like, across Russia today.[11]

We were nearing the tourist complex at Fangchuan, and Mr Teng swerved to a halt in a large car park. From here, we continued by shuttle-bus to the looming fortified pagoda in thunderous grey stone from which, slogans promised, we would be able to take in 'three countries at a single glance'. The building was about to close for the evening so we bustled in and whizzed in a spacious lift up to its pinnacle. From the outside gallery at the top, the surrounding atmosphere was perfectly still. As the sun sank upstream, the sulky Tumen meandered its way between China and North Korea past Tumangang Workers' District on the opposite bank. We peered over the battlements as blue-and-grey evening clouds rolled in, backlit by fading pink patches of dusky brightness (Image 15). The Chinese sentry post monitoring the Russian border below also looked deserted. Evidently not anticipating an invasion any time soon—a reasonable expectation since the last border trouble here was a 1938 battle with the Japanese at Zhanggufeng—the local PLA detachment was perhaps taking a break. Downriver towards the coast, the 1959-built Russia–Korea Friendship Bridge interrupted the placid flow of the Tumen as it dissolved into sky. Beyond that, the Sea of Japan stretched as a blue-grey band along the horizon, its inaccessibility seeming less a product of geopolitics and more to do with its distant position hanging in an otherworldly haze.

'Let me take a picture of you,' Mr Teng broke the silence. 'I'm a great photographer.' I handed over my camera and he keenly rotated the device several times in such a way, it later turned out, as to eschew the top of my head from most shots. We stayed a while longer, but as the hillscape sank further into darkness, it seemed time to leave this cul-de-sac international crossroads.

Driving back to Hunchun, we picked up another passenger just as darkness finally enveloped the Tumen. He was a Chosonjok farmer ('can you hear his funny accent?' Mr Teng asked blithely right in front of the man) and was on his way into Hunchun to visit his cousin in hospital. As we rumbled along the road, passing a section known as 'China's narrowest point' and occasionally veering off the main track to jolt through muddy villages in order to avoid speed cameras, I asked how the farmer, who had spent time sojourning in South Korea, felt about the country that now lay darkly invisible just across the river to our left.

'We probably have relatives there,' he said. 'But we don't know them now. We don't really have anything to do with the place, to be honest, even though my ancestors came from there a century ago.' Between Mr Pak and Ji-ok in age, the farmer attested to how, as for the Shiwei Russians or the Hezhe/Nanai, the hardening of boundaries under strong national regimes had been pretty successful in estranging once-kindred populations over the twentieth century. Whether because of Maoist campaigns, or China's more recent impatience with Pyongyang (whose nuclear tests have caused small earthquakes in Yanbian), ever fewer Chosonjok spend any time thinking about the DPRK.

As was already clear, sentimentality was an equally alien notion to the Han Mr Teng, whose detachment from North Korea apparently also extended to local Chosonjok. He had little to say about these people among whom he had spent his entire life, aside from accent-related comments and the observation that 'their' women were very attractive. We dropped off the farmer, and Mr Teng's mind turned to what I might be doing that evening.

'Do you want me to find you a nice Korean girl?' he suggested. 'One in her twenties will cost you 200 yuan, but it's much cheaper if you go for thirties or forties.' Hunchun may be more orderly than Manzhouli or Suifenhe, but it remains a borderland location with its fair share of liminal vices. Mr Teng's offer, betraying a remarkably exoticising view of people whom he spoke to on a daily basis, was meant as a hospitable gesture, but I declined. I had, I felt, gained plenty of insight into local relations without requiring such distasteful intimacy.

* * *

Hunchun had been my last stop directly on the Russia–China border and the end-point of the frontier's vast arc from Mongolia in the north-west to Korea in the south-east. I was now bound inland again. A brief stop in the sleepy town of Tumen with its road and railway crossings to the North Korean settlement of Namyang afforded more opportunities to reflect on the North/South balancing act of Yanbian's 'in-between' Chosonjok. Rectangular 1980s apartment blocks give Tumen a distinctly Soviet feel, and, as the location of a business park employing North Korean factory workers and possibly a detention centre for DPRK escapees, it is on the frontline of China's quandary over how best to deal with its difficult neighbour. Here, Chinese efforts to accost refugees face competition from South Korean organisations, notably evangelical churches, who hope to help defectors move to South Korea. A cynic might suggest that their aims also include the supplanting of the Kimist myth about a divine father and son ruling over heaven and earth with an eerily similar alternative story.

On the lush riverbank, with the DPRK just a few murky yards away, a trilingual Korean, Chinese and English sign warned readers against engaging in 'Smuggling, drug trafficking, fish catching etc. that will endanger the security and order of the boundary'. Lower down it added: 'No shouting and photographing at Korea', although it was hard to imagine how this would be policed given the distraction provided by the tour companies raucously running short river cruises nearby. As at Fangchuan, border tourism is booming in Tumen, and in a riverfront coffee shop where I found a cooling and incongruous iced mocha, posters advertised trips across the river to North Korea itself, from half-day walks around Namyang to full four-night excursions into the nearby mountains. Tellingly, the posters placed particular emphasis on the opportunity trippers would have to 'feel the natural conditions and human sentiments of mysterious North Korea', further suggesting the increasingly exotic terms in which Chinese people are seeing a country once considered as close, in words made famous by Mao Zedong (though not coined by him), as 'lips and teeth'. [12]

Although periodically closed when cross-border tensions rise, Tumen's bridge over to Namyang is also an attraction, one I was initially uncertain about visiting given the proximity of uniformed border guards and beaming portraits of Kim Il Sung and Kim Jong Il on a building on the other side. But I need not have worried. Like seemingly sensitive stretches of the Sino-Russian border, this was a highly permissive fault line.

'You're here to tour the border?' asked an enthusiastic attendant in a tracksuit and tourist agency lanyard, leaping up from his chair.

Was I allowed?

'Of course! Go up there first,' he pointed to the gateway that arched over the road to Namyang. 'Then come back down and I'll take you on to the bridge.'

A cracked spiral stairway led me to a viewing platform on the gate's crosspiece from which one could peer—through military-style binoculars on tripods no less—at Namyang's propaganda banners and fatigued buildings. The archway I was standing on was decorated with the golden calligraphy of former Chinese President Jiang Zemin, showing that China was hardly immune to the veneration of leadership seen in more fanatical form over the border. But through the binoculars North Korea was made to seem a distant and, yes, a deeply mysterious place.

This message continued down below as I was chivvied on to the bridge by the guide, who turned out also to be from Shandong province, alongside a cluster of Chinese tourists and an accompanying border guard. Between some abstract modernist lampposts around halfway across, a pair of red-and-yellow lines indicated the border, which was labelled in Chinese and Korean writing on the road. This, the guide's patter suggested, was the point of no return, a rift between worlds. Having made appropriately awed noises and taken a few photographs, we then returned towards the Chinese bank.

'Where you from?' the border guard asked in unexpected English as we walked back.

I told him.

'Aha, England!' he replied jubilantly. 'London! Beckham! Rooney! Manchester! ... Arshavin!' he then added anachronistically.

But even if this man's Premier League knowledge was not entirely up to date, such friendliness seemed consistent with Tumen's self-image as 'The north-east's golden port and charming border town', a status it proclaimed on red-and-white banners along most of its streets. Other messages added that it was a 'Model Area for International Cooperation', demonstrating that touristic mystification proceeded hand in hand with local efforts to promote DPRK-ward ties as part of a normal inter-state relationship. If Western views often hold that North Korea is a non-place, a 'hermit kingdom' of conspiracy and charade beyond conventional understanding, China's, and indeed Russia's, Korean populations and longstanding socialist ties make for a potentially less hysterical relationship. But Tumen had offered plentiful evidence that everyday Chinese attitudes since Mao may have morphed into something 'in between' empathy and exoticisation.

* * *

If neighbouring North Korea now seems increasingly strange and distant from the Chinese centre, however, this in some ways only feeds into much older visions of Manchuria and its frontiers as a wild and exotic land. In Yanji, Yanbian's prefectural capital to which I continued from Tumen by bus, my only real plan was to visit the Yanbian Museum. But the town's 'Exhibition Centre for Ethnic Products' proved too great a draw, and shed light on the allure held by this part of the world long before socialism.

Up to the late nineteenth century, when it was still dominated by the Manchus and other non-Han indigenous groups, Manchuria mainly figured in Chinese minds as a vast trove of natural products treasured across the empire. From fungi to ginseng, deer horn to sea cucumbers, a great ecological bounty was harvested, often illegally, from the region's forests and—before China lost sea access to Russia—its coastline. Indeed, the still-used Qing-era name for the cove where Vladivostok is now located is Haishenwai, meaning 'sea cucumber cliffs'. Chinese kelp-collectors remained a significant part of the Russian city's population right up to the 1930s, exporting the slippery commodity down the coast to Shanghai.[13] Such goods, many of them featuring in traditional medicinal pharmacopeias, remain popular among tourists to the Yanbian–DPRK–Russia triangle today. Demand is such that in a telling case of economic expansionism, trade in endangered sea cucumbers has become a lifeline for derelict post-Soviet settlements east of Hunchun as locals gather the seafloor-lurking echinoderms for sale over the Chinese border.

Consequently, Yanji's Exhibition Centre for Ethnic Products was just as revealing of the town's current position as the Starbucks and Uniqlo that, underwritten by its astonishing Korea-derived prosperity, opened here in 2017. As I entered, a saleswoman who sheepishly admitted to being Han Chinese—since the 1990s, Chosonjok invariably prefer the better paid South Korean version of such roles—urged me to buy some ginseng, which, she said, came from Paektusan itself.

'It increases strength!' she enthused. 'You just cut it up, steep it in some strong liquor like *baijiu* and then drink it.' This sounded like a powerful cocktail: commonly referred to as 'Chinese vodka', *baijiu* is usually at least 50 per cent alcohol and comes in a range catering to every conceivable budget and social status, from the alcoholic's favourite Erguotou—available in hipflask-sized green bottles for around 8 RMB ($1)—to Maotai, favoured banquet beverage of high officials and big businessmen. The drink has played as iconic a role in north-east China's heavy-drinking past and present as its better-known Russian counterpart.

I gave a doubtful look and moved on down the supermarket-style aisles of imported South Korean confectionary and seasoning, she filing attentively behind me. In a freezer, a selection of frozen and shrink-wrapped items was pressed anonymously up against the frosting inside the lid.

'Look!' she said, sliding back the glass and fishing out a furry ice-encrusted deer horn attached to a sheet of cardboard with 'Product of Yanbian' printed on it in Korean, Chinese and English. 'This increases strength too!' I was beginning to see that 'strength' actually meant something rather specific the way she was using it. Tonics derived from horns of all kinds, including those of rhinos and deer, and the tusks of narwhal and elephants, are meant to cure various diseases in traditional Chinese and Korean medicines, but are also popularly believed to enhance sexual prowess. This, apparently, was the implication of what I was being told in the Exhibition Centre for Ethnic Products, a fact that became still clearer as the attendant rooted around in the freezer again and extracted a vacuum-packed foot-long deer penis.

'You slice it up and steep it in alcohol,' she began again, 'it increases ...'

I felt I had got the idea by now so told her I could probably do without this particular local treasure. Unlike the various remedial properties ascribed to horns, deer penis is more unambiguously seen as an aphrodisiac and cure for impotence. But I had little idea how I would keep this large frosted member long enough to give it to anyone who might appreciate it, so I decided it was time to move on. There was still the museum to see, and it would probably be better without the encumbrance of frigid slices of mammalian anatomy.

'Would you like to see pictures of some Russians I saw?' the sales-women offered, bounding eagerly after me as I headed for the door. 'I have them on my phone!' Despite the region's multicultural identity, it seemed the sight of 'real' foreigners here was as exotic to her as the shop produce was to me. I examined the blurry pictures of confused-looking Russians for a few polite minutes.

Outside again, and at only my usual level of 'strength,' I boarded a diminutive city bus. Along a rattling route commentated on by alternate Korean and Chinese stop announcements, this took me to the Yanbian Korean Autonomous Prefecture Museum, one of several grand local buildings with a bold Korean-style curled roof. The ground-floor gallery showed photographs of national leaders visiting Yanbian on local inspection tours—Xi Jinping even dropped by in 2015. This conveyed much the same image of distant dignitaries swooping in to grace the borderlands and dish out orders that my Khabarovsk friends had complained about in reference to Moscow. The idea that remote, and often ethnically minoritarian, edge spaces need regular attention from the imperial centre has long been a feature of politics on both sides of the border, from the Qing emperors' imperial tours of Manchuria to Tsar Nicholas II's pre-enthronement voyage to Blagoveshchensk and Vladivostok.

The museum's 'History and Development' section offered a more bemusing blend of messages, from pictures of weeping mothers on busy railway platforms seeing their sons off to the Korean War, to a nearby display that celebrated the 2011 arrival in Yanbian of AB Inbev's Budweiser factory. Little seemed to capture the topsy-turvy nature of the post-Cold War order better than this juxtaposition of the bloody conflict known in Chinese as the 'War to Assist Korea and Resist American Aggression' and the vaunting of the '300,000 tonnes of beer!' that could now purportedly be produced here by an American-owned factory. Yanbian, the display explained, was a rapidly internationalising place, a fact illustrated by further pictures of glum Russian shoppers poking at goods in Hunchun, and an intriguing gallery documenting a visit from the South Korean branch of the Harley Davidson fan club. They seemed to have had a lovely visit roaring up and down the region's picturesque mountain roads. But if these displays, together with photographs of Chosonjok officials taking Chinese lessons and police officers cracking down on gamblers in local internet cafés, initially appeared incoherent, there was an overarching message to be gleaned. Slogans dotted around the walls left visitors in no doubt that the region's development, ethnic unity, law and order, and strong connection to the centre, were all benefits that existed only thanks to the Chinese Communist Party.

Upstairs, the gallery dedicated to the culture of local ethnic groups initially appeared to have fewer ideological undertones. Local Manchus made a brief cameo appearance, but most attention was understandably focused on Yanbian's titular and notionally 'autonomous' Chosonjok. As I made my way round the extensive and thoughtfully assembled displays on local Korean festival wares, dress, cuisine, language and music, I encountered a tour group from Vladivostok and their guide, who spoke accented but very fluent Russian.

'Koreans came to Yanbian in the Qing period, although some people say it was earlier,' she was explaining. Mr Pak had been one of these 'people' with his mention of the fifth- and sixth-century Koguryo Kingdom, though the Russians seemed unfussed either way. Tales of epic trans-continental journeying, as well as historical arguments over who was where first, are ten-a-penny at this crossroads of worlds. The group moved on saying little, the guide having to quicken her high-heeled pace to keep up.

'This is a traditional Korean home!' she said in front of a floor-to-ceiling recreation of a rural Chosonjok living room, complete with a family of waxy dead-eyed figurines. The Russians stopped, suddenly interested in the curly roofed wooden house with its yard of simple tools and plasticky corn sprouts. Perhaps this fantasy 'Asian' homestead resonated more than run-of-the-mill migration stories. Indeed, despite having long lived in the midst of 'eastern' peoples—Chinese, Koreans, Japanese—many Russian far easterners share Mr Teng's remarkable unawareness of the history and culture of their immediate neighbours.

Yet for all that this display offered a mostly depoliticised account of local mores, it was perhaps inevitable that the role of the Chinese Communist Party in guaranteeing this idyllic lifestyle for its Korean subjects would rear its head sooner or later. As in other minority-focused museums, many of the placards accompanying the exhibits suggested that it was mostly thanks to Communist nurturing that the Chosonjok had successfully reached their present happy state by 'opposing imperialism, feudalism and bureaucratic capitalism, and fighting valiantly against the Japanese'. The story here spoke slightly less of absolute dependence than those often told for smaller minorities like the Hezhe. Such a narrative would ring even hollower here than usual among these prosperous and confident Chinese Koreans who enjoy plentiful freedoms to explore their Korean identity and yet nevertheless harbour little interest in the 'separatism' Beijing fears elsewhere on its fringes. But official propaganda rarely leaves anything to chance, and their status as an unequivocally 'Chinese' and CCP-allied minority was not to be doubted, whatever their other in-betweennesses.

* * *

The demand of China's national unity discourse that every minority be shown to have made its contribution to booting out foreign imperialists can lead to some curious narrative contortions, particularly in parts of the country where the major external aggressor throughout history has been the Chinese state itself.[14] The early USSR faced many of the same challenges in accounting for how former imperial subjects like the Yakuts or Nanai had somehow 'chosen' to join the union, although World War II—the Great Patriotic War—later proved very helpful in buttressing narratives of common struggle. The PRC's various ethnic groups have never fought a war together, but in Manchuria, there is at least a clear historical enemy—Japan—whom many Chosonjok, and some Hezhe, can plausibly be said to have opposed. The presence of the Manchus, who for so long *were* the Chinese state, and Russia's chimerical role in history as both inspiration and outside threat, pose thornier problems and add to the sense that this is a region stuck in the interstices. But in very broad terms, the legacy of the Japan-backed Manchukuo state (1932–45), which I would be moving on to explore, is one that many can decry together.

From the late nineteenth to the mid-twentieth centuries, the whole space encompassing north-east China, the Russian Far East and the Korean Peninsula fell under Tokyo's imperial ambit. Japanese occupations of Korea (1905–45), Primorsky province (1918–22) and Manchuria (1931–45) each met varying levels of resistance, from urban heroism like militant An Jung-geun's 1909 assassination in Harbin of Korean Resident-General Ito Hirobumi,[15] to guerrilla battles deep in the dense woods of Kando/Yanbian.[16] Indeed, it was a fierce Japanese military response to the latter form of resistance that drove Kim Il Sung and his partisan comrades over Soviet borders to their hideout at Vyatskoe in 1940.

Being a militarised technocratic operation, Japan's short-lived empire greatly preferred operating in rational cities to hacking through unruly forests (home terrain for both Kim's and Mao's liberation armies), and it was to Manchukuo's grandest conurbation that I was bound next. The capital of the 'puppet' state, Changchun was known under the Japanese as Shinkyo ('new capital', Xinjing in Chinese), the administrative centre of a polity whose existence had driven a host of other regional transformations, including the transplantation of Koreans all the way north to Heilongjiang. But the city also has an earlier and mostly forgotten Russian past, and I would first be looking for fragments of this. Again forgoing the new high-speed lines, I took the slower overnight train out of Yanbian, so legibly placed between China, Russia and the Koreas. Changchun's deeper-buried legacy of Russo-Japanese and other in-betweennesses would require more detective work to root out.

Russia's brief spell as the most important outsider presence in Changchun coincided with the city's emergence as a stop on the China Eastern Railway's southward branch line from Harbin to Port Arthur. Having lost control in 1905 of this warm-water port, a harbour of a kind that has driven Russian expansion from the imperial Pacific push to Crimea in 2013, tsarist forces retreated, leaving a string of quaint railway stations and pastel-coloured mansions all the way down to Port Arthur. As Lüshunkou, this is now a Chinese naval base. The Theodore Roosevelt-brokered peace that concluded the Russo-Japanese War handed these and the southern stretch of the China Eastern Railway (as well as an essentially free hand in Korea) to Japan. From then until 1931, Changchun thus became the uneasy junction where Russian and Japanese railway imperialisms met, with two separate stations allowing for the required change in gauge between the newly rebranded Japanese South Manchuria Railway and the broader Russian CER.

Passing through Manchuria in 1920, Qu Qiubai marvelled despairingly at this aggressive internationalism, lamenting the fact that his journey from Beijing had involved riding the railways of three different countries—China, Japan and Russia. China seemed miserably at the mercy of foreign powers, and Qu's arrival in Changchun brought the first real sense that he was approaching the northern country. Here he had his first face-to-face encounter with a 'real Russian man', a dishevelled cart driver with long straggly hair.[17] Both here and later in Harbin, Qu observed first-hand that Russia's terrestrial imperialism had brought all manner of people overflowing southward from the tsar's realm, not only colonial governors or aristocratic generals but much less privileged figures who, as the foot-soldiers of expansion, now competed for scarce resources with China's own poor.

My own first destination was Changchun's gritty Kuancheng district, the area north of the centre where Japanese and Russian dominions once met. Getting there on foot involved several arduous and sweaty attempts to skirt around road-widening and flyover-stretching projects whose vehicles were raising thick clouds of dust liable to blanket any already-obscure tsarist relics. Places undergoing industrial or urban revolution are never prime spots for pedestrians, and as so often in early twenty-first-century Chinese cities, detours were necessary over piles of rubble, around stacks of obstructive iron struts, and across barren expanses of freshly levelled concrete strewn with litter.

Having navigated this, the first rewarding traces of times past came in the form of two dark circular water towers looming near Changchun's West Square. These would once have stood next to the Russian railway, but are now stranded because of rerouting. Stylistically eclectic, the first was a sturdy lump of grey concrete overshadowing a police station car park, and the second a more delicate reservoir with dangling sinuous ladders, its slender iron supports bedded in a roundabout of impenetrable hedges.

Still more splendid in its isolation was the former Railway Workers Club, a grand two-storey yellow building farther to the north. I stopped outside to wipe the dust from my face and get a better look at the white cornicing skirting around the colonnaded doorway, its conical tower on one corner, and helter-skelter pillars leading up to narrow arched windows.

'They've replaced all those windows since the Russian times,' said an elderly man who had appeared at my side, seemingly out of nowhere.

I said I thought that made sense. The building is now a hospital for employees of Changchun Auto Factory, and while there was less one could do about the impractically narrow entryway, presumably more modern windows provided better insulation.

'Maybe,' he replied enigmatically. 'But it looks worse now.' Given the combination of pervasive dilapidation and violent renewal in evidence throughout Kuancheng, I was pleased to hear someone express even a vague interest in older architecture. I asked whether there were any more Russian buildings among the area's 1970s apartment blocks, once spaciously laid out for an era of mass socialist housing but by all appearances left to crumble in recent years.

'That way,' he pointed. 'There's a school inside a school.'

I thanked him and, not entirely sure what he meant, crossed the road to follow his directions down an alleyway. After several false turns and doublings-back, the building loomed up suddenly and I saw what he was talking about. Through the gateway into a massive recently built primary school, a long low stone building was visible. This was the old Russian school for the children of Kuancheng's CER workers. 'It's just used for storage now,' a guard informed me when I asked if he knew anything about the building.

But even if the presence of the factory-sized school engulfing its Russian-constructed predecessor had preserved some spatial memory of old Kuancheng, it remained a largely unacknowledged legacy. A bright red-and-yellow poster that hung on one end of the Russian building read, 'Etch history on to your mind,' continuing 'do not forget our national humiliation, vigorously promote Chinese culture'. History here evidently had other priorities, though in some ways this seemed an effective kind of anti-imperialist revenge: a low, sad building, long ago erected by invaders who had caused this 'humiliation' now displayed a warning to avoid such mishaps in future.

Nearby, and in a still worse state of repair, were two once-elegant Russian residences whose intricately carved wooden gables had been almost entirely swallowed up by a mass of low improvised brick dwellings. Smoke rose from one of the house's many chimneys, but decades of mass-occupancy and rickety extensions had so altered the layout of the building that I could not even be sure how I might find the front door, let alone enter. Around the corner, however, the old two-storey Russian telegraph office had been turned into a tidy little museum, and after gently throwing a few small stones at a ground floor window I managed to lure out the attendant who half-heartedly explained the stories behind the grainy photographs that were attached to the walls inside. The small exhibition had nothing to do with Russia, instead depicting the activities of Changchun's early twentieth-century Chinese revolutionaries and especially its telegraph workers. This was a highly localised reminder of how anti-foreign resistance in China was often aided by the very communications infrastructure—from telegraph to rail—that the foreigners had themselves installed across the country. These technologies fostered a sense of connectedness by which common cause could be made, and organisational instructions disseminated as they had been from here in Kuancheng.

* * *

Before the telegraph workers and others greeted their 1940s liberation, however, Changchun still had to endure the full Japanese invasion of Manchuria and the accompanying seizure of the entire Russian CER, which put an end to the meeting of worlds at Kuancheng. The fact that apportionment of Manchurian territory revolved around control over stretches of railway reflected the centrality of these iron roads to both Tokyo's and St Petersburg's imperial projects. This impression was further reinforced when Japan's September 1931 intervention in China's north-east was, to the world's passive dismay, justified via a false flag attack on tracks at Mukden (now Shenyang). But beginning during the joint Russo-Japanese period and accelerating after Manchukuo was founded, urban space also became a key arena where Japan sought to stamp its spatial authority on the modern imperial realm. Beyond Kuancheng's scattered remnants, Changchun's layout still serves as a chart of its non-Chinese past.

For one thing, West Square with its water towers and other 'squares' in the city are not square at all, although this is only really a problem in English since the Chinese / Japanese word translated as 'square'— *guangchang / hiroba*—makes no commitments to shape and simply means 'wide place'. But distinct from the many squares laid across China in the socialist age, Changchun's wide places, like those of other Japanese-designed cities such as Shenyang and Dalian, are generally large rotaries, circular suns from which straight avenues radiate out, reconverging in new combinations at new rotaries. Along the city's broad spoke-like avenues, grand Japanese imperial buildings still lurk behind rows of trees and up stately driveways. The curly points of green tiled roofs sit atop solid rectangular colonnades, speaking of the delicate balance of refinement and dominance that the edifices of Shinkyo sought to communicate.

As I paced the hot dry pavements in search of these buildings, the enduring colonial impression left on the city was marked by the fact that some still retain their original use: opposite Changchun's railway station, the quaint *style moderne* Chunyi Hotel has, since its 1910 founding as part of Manchuria's Japanese-run Yamato Hotel chain, continually fulfilled the same hospitable role. In 1924, Sergei Tretyakov stayed here on his way to Beijing, spending a night between the Russian and Japanese railways. Caught between worlds and witnessing a harbinger of the Anglicisation of international communication embodied by Andrei in Harbin, the writer found himself in the odd position of only being able to order dinner in English from the Japanese hotel staff. But this situation did at least give Tretyakov an excuse for a humorous aside as he fantasised about a Russian diner seeming to shout 'twerp' at a waiter when all he was doing was asking for some 'ham' (*kham* corresponding roughly to 'twerp' or 'lout' in Russian).[18] In-between spaces are often funny ones.

Most of Changchun's Shinkyo-era buildings have, however, been thoroughly reappropriated: the vast former Manchukuo State Council is now the headquarters of Jilin University Medical School, the arched eaves of the old Transport Department now a local college of public health. Perhaps most aptly, a Japanese colonial mansion south of the centre today houses a care home for retired Communist Party cadres, one set of unaccountable overlords having given way to another, veteran members of China's 'only mafia' as Yougang had put it back in Jiejinkou.

Exempt in a kind of placid isolation from the sweeping changes afoot across much of the rest of Changchun is arguably the city's most significant Japanese-era remnant, the former Manchukuo Imperial Palace. Now lying east of the city's bizarrist office block-style railway station amid a clutter of uneven alleys, eighties apartment buildings and small shops selling scrap metal, tools and cheap household goods, this was once home to the Kangde Emperor. This man's biography speaks like few others of the extraordinary Chinese, Russian, Manchu and Japanese political jumble out of which the Manchukuo colonial project emerged. Kangde had, in a previous incarnation, been the Qing Emperor Xuantong ruling over all China. However, unlike his dynastic forebears who were known mainly by such 'reign names', it was by his given name, Puyi, as well as his English moniker 'Henry', that he became recognised the world over.

Puyi was born in 1906 into the ruling Manchu Aisin Gioro clan, 'Gioro' indicating the lineage's origins in a Heilongjiang location and historic Hezhe fishing site now known as Yilan. His short 1908–12 career as twelfth, and last, Qing emperor offered him little chance to inhabit the role, not least because he was only six when forced to abdicate. This act, carried out for him by his dowager Longyu, followed cataclysmic events far to the south-west of both Beijing and his ancestral Manchuria. A 1911 military revolt in Wuchang on the River Yangtze spelt the beginning of the end for the Qing, as protests by groups angry at their handling of foreign-run railways in China (like the Russian CER) fed into a wider climate of discontent. This sparked nationwide uprisings against the ineffectual, ponytailed, eunuch-dominated and colonially subjugated Manchu authorities. Mirroring the stuttering demise of the Russian Romanovs who, at much the same time, were collapsing in stages following revolutions in 1905, February and October 1917, the emperor and a depleted entourage of courtiers were initially permitted to stay on in Beijing's Forbidden City for a time. Meanwhile, a fractious and ramshackle republic whose distant and transplanted descendant still exists on Taiwan, attempted to take shape outside its walls from 1912. Following a brief 1917 attempt at imperial restoration, however, Feng Yuxiang, the warlord who had taken charge of the Chinese capital, made it clear by 1924 that Puyi's time was up.

At this point, the former Emperor's international horizons began to expand dramatically as he and the Empress Wanrong found refuge in the Japanese concession in the city of Tianjin, a short way to Beijing's east. While here, they happened to be visited in 1925 by Trans-Siberian adventurer Ethel Alec-Tweedie who, ever sympathetic to the sufferings of the hyper-elite in societies seeking a better deal, was appalled at their plight. Since Puyi had employed a Scottish tutor for his last five years in the Forbidden City, an imperial diplomat named Reginald Johnston, they were able to converse in English. But Alec-Tweedie's description suggests their exchange nevertheless retained the high stiltedness of aristocracy. The encounter mainly left her cursing warlord Feng as 'a Russian pawn', expressing outrage that the royal couple had left the palace 'in a second-class railway carriage with one servant', and bemoaning the lack of even 'a single piece of bric-à-brac' in their new home.[19]

But Puyi and Wanrong's seven years in Tianjin were not wholly monotonous, and as their confidence grew they began to appear more frequently in the salons, dancehalls and eateries of this vibrant jazz-age colonial town. Among Puyi's favourite venues was a restaurant called Kiessling's, which, although run by Germans, lay in a mostly Russian quarter of Tianjin. After 1917, many of the very same White Russian fugitives who had swelled Harbin's 1920s population continued south to other Chinese cities with significant foreign concessions, and Tianjin was thus something of an émigré hub. Puyi's evenings in 'Russia town', as it was known, where he would regularly enjoy meals of Russian sausage, bayberry juice and ice cream for dessert, would later prove fateful. This was his first round of contact with a country that would subsequently have a determinant influence over his entire existence.[20]

As well as the Russians, several influential Japanese statesmen and other intriguers also numbered among those with whom Puyi liaised during this period of revelry and hardship in Tianjin. Following the invasion of north-east China in 1931, these operators offered to install him as head of their atavistic Manchurian empire. Puyi was drawn to the idea, and both parties concurred that this would be a potential foothold from which the whole Chinese realm might eventually be reclaimed. The once-and-future-emperor and his new Japanese 'friends' of course silently held different views over who would actually rule China under such circumstances. And so in 1932 Kangde was enthroned and moved to Shinkyo, his own preference that the capital be in the old Manchu centre of Mukden having been roundly ignored. The building complex where he would—it turned out—unhappily reside for the next thirteen years lay on the edge of Kuancheng and had previously been the offices of the Russian-era Salt Tax Administration. This place, sometimes occasionally still referred to as the 'Salt Palace', is now officially and affectionlessly known as the 'Illegitimate Manchukuo Imperial Palace Museum'.

I had evidently approached the museum from the wrong side, and was therefore obliged to squeeze along several impenetrably narrow lanes thronged with hawkers, kebab sellers and their indecisive clients. Electric tricycles stacked with improbably high piles of polystyrene and cardboard boxes of rice cookers and beauty products wove along the firmer edges of a crumbling road surface. Stumbling around these obstacles, I tried at all times to keep the palace's low but sturdy outer fortifications in sight and, eventually managing to escape the alleys, emerged into a more peaceful area. Here the din of vendors ebbed away to be replaced by the clack of mahjong tiles. Around the museum entrance, elderly players sat in the shade of willows lost in tactical reflection and girded by dense clumps of onlookers. Relieved, I bought my ticket, which promisingly displayed a boast that the palace was rated an AAAAA-level scenic attraction by the PRC's national tourist board, and walked in.

The first of the complex's modest, temple-like wooden pavilions housed a rogues' gallery of 'Traitors and people who fraternised with the Japanese': problematically for today's tales of ethnic unity and shared struggle, Puyi was certainly not alone among former Qing staff and subjects who welcomed Japan's offer of a nostalgic quasi-return to imperial days. The multitudinous crimes of this anti-hagiography of Manchu, Mongol and Han villains were laid out here in sober terms. Little embellishment or blustering outrage appeared to be deemed necessary, and indeed to a population of museum visitors primed by the CCP's 'patriotic education' curriculum, the merest suggestion of pro-Japaneseness is often sufficient to raise hackles. Yet the tales of treachery told in the gallery—including accounts of people who had served Russian, Japanese and Chinese warlord masters in the first decades of the twentieth century—also shed indirect light on to the very real struggles that many in north-east China faced during this era of violent political upheaval. I for one could not be sure how I would have chosen friends and enemies when surrounded by competing Russian, Chinese, Manchu, Korean and Japanese agendas. Nobody, including the Communists themselves, knew then that the CCP would eventually ride resurgent to claim almost all the old Qing imperial lands and then demand retrospective fealty. For as long as it existed, moreover, Manchukuo appeared much more solid than the frail 'puppet' it is now usually labelled.

Puyi sat at the heart of this quandary over loyalties, and although some kin and intimate advisors remained by his side for stretches of his career, even the relative calm of his spell as Shinkyo's Manchu emperor was troubled by unstable allegiances. The strain of faded imperial existence saw Puyi and Wanrong, who had already endured so much, become irreconcilably estranged, and although continuing to play her part as empress, she succumbed to opium addiction in her unhappy entrapment.

Puyi meanwhile was busy being a ceremonial monarch, and the next section of the museum—entitled 'Emperor for the Second Time'—displayed photographs of his attendance at various theatrical Manchukuo rites. His queue and some the robes he wore while performing puppet authority hung in a display case.

'They're not real,' an attendant informed me apathetically without being prompted. Having become accustomed to the myriad fabulations and reconstructions used to narrate history in the contemporary PRC, I was not unduly concerned.

Entering the next section, I came to a display labelled 'The War Criminal', which attested to how brief Manchuria's 1930s–40s *Pax Iaponica* had been. Just over a decade into its existence, Manchukuo collapsed rapidly with Japan's wartime defeat. As Soviet forces invaded in August 1945 to drive the Kwantung Army out of north-east China and the Korea Army out of Korea, Puyi's existence resumed its erstwhile course of violent peripeteias, unravelling again towards yet another gripping chapter of Eurasian embroilment. Curiously, the USSR had actually been one of only a handful of countries worldwide to recognise Manchukuo as a state, a decision made by Moscow in the hope of averting a Japanese attack in the Soviet Far East. As the Red Army bore the brunt of the Wehrmacht's advance in European Russia, worries over Tokyo's intentions—already high enough to have triggered the 1937 deportation of Primorye's Koreans—seemed more urgent. The August 1945 liberation of Manchuria, which involved over 1.5 million Soviet troops and was as rape- and pillage-filled as the Red Army's rampage through Eastern Europe, was a release of this tension.

Already aware that their number had been called following the 6 August atomic bombing of Hiroshima, the Manchukuo authorities moved on 9 August—the day of the Soviet invasion and the bombing of Nagasaki—to spirit Puyi from Shinkyo back to Japan. In the uncertain security environment of the disintegrating state, Puyi and some of his aides, but not the long-ignored Empress Wanrong, were first moved down to the Korean borderlands of Kando. After a week lying low in a small village whose name, Dalizigou (big chestnut ditch), offers some indication of how fit for an emperor it was (Mrs Alec-Tweedie would certainly not have approved), the group moved on to Tonghua and then by air to Shenyang. From here, it was hoped, they would fly on to Pyongyang and then Tokyo, but as soon as they touched down in Shenyang it became clear that this would not be an option.

As Puyi himself later wrote, 'we had just landed in Shenyang and were waiting to change onto the next plane. But we hadn't been waiting long and I suddenly saw through the window a great squadron of aeroplanes appear in the sky …' This was the Soviet Air Force, and as the planes landed one by one, Russian troops disembarked and confiscated the Japanese soldiers' weapons. 'That evening,' Puyi continued, 'the Soviet general took us to a temporary field hospital where we spent one night, and the next day from Tongliao we were flown to the USSR.'[21] The twice-enthroned emperor, who may perhaps have evacuated faster if his wish to have the Manchukuo capital in Mukden/Shenyang had been granted, was taken to a detention centre outside Chita. Wanrong fared far worse. Attempting as part of a separate group to flee overland through Kando to Korea, the empress and her entourage were also arrested, although this time by Chinese forces. Held in a prison in Yanji and deprived of the opium on which she had come to depend, she died a miserable withdrawal death there in June 1946.[22]

By this time, and still ignorant of Wanrong's fate, Puyi had been moved from Chita to Khabarovsk, first spending a short spell in a camp close to the centre of town and then being moved to a modest two-storey house on its outskirts. For the past several years, growing numbers of Chinese tourists visiting Khabarovsk have been taken to a grand building on Dikopoltseva Street, which, some wily tour guides have claimed, was his 'imperial palace'. But while this was the rough site of the temporary camp that first accommodated the emperor, the supposed 'palace' is, to the great mirth of locals, in fact just as fake as the Manchukuo museum's robes. This university building dates from considerably later than the 1940s. However, from 2018 plans have been hatched to renovate the actual house outside town where he subsequently spent almost four years. Whether or not it matters to tourists, this will be a more authentic historical attraction.[23]

Bearing the unique distinction of being former leader of two now-non-existent countries, Puyi entered Khabarovsk mere months after the departure of a future leader of a country that did not yet exist.

Kim Il Sung, who had spent the preceding five years downriver in Vyatskoe, had recently accompanied the Soviets south on their rampaging liberation tour that continued to his native Korea. But while records of Kim's time in the Russian Far East are, as I had seen, patchy at best, Puyi later wrote extensively about his sojourn there. Among the observations he makes in his memoirs is the fact that, even if he did not inhabit an 'imperial palace', he was treated comparatively well in the USSR. The train car that took him on the eastern stretch of the Trans-Siberian from Chita to Khabarovsk (then a four-day journey) was filthy, but after arrival he had his own room, was well fed and was spared many of the cleaning, farming and logging duties that other prisoners, mostly Japanese Kwantung Army generals, were subject to. He was also not short of company, for alongside him in captivity were his brother Pujie and two cousins, Runqi and Wan Jiaxi, the latter of whom especially enjoyed his time in Chita where he fell in love with a female Russian staff member at their detention facility. Yet Puyi generally forbade such liaisons and sought to live a quiet life, devoting his time to reading Buddhist texts, playing mahjong and making sketches, many of which are on display at today's Palace Museum in Changchun. Reality nevertheless periodically intervened, and as guests of the Soviets, all the captive Aisin Gioros were obliged to engage in courses of Marxist–Leninist theory and the history of the Soviet Communist Party. Puyi's sojourn was also interrupted in August 1946 when he and his Russian translator Georgy Permyakov travelled to Tokyo to attend the International Military Tribunal for the Far East. There he mostly succeeded in portraying himself as a victim of Japanese coercion and was permitted to return to his mahjong and sketchbooks in Khabarovsk within a few weeks.

Meanwhile, the Soviet intervention in Manchuria had helped the Chinese Communists gain control there since Puyi had left. By 1949, the region had proved to be the bulwark from which the CCP could defeat their Nationalist Civil War foes and gain control over the whole country, in precisely the way Puyi had hoped he would be able to when he took the Manchukuo throne.[24] Learning of this development, and knowing he was unlikely to be looked on favourably by the vehemently anti-Qing Communists, Puyi panicked and in July that year wrote a letter to Stalin requesting permission to remain in the Soviet Union.

Well versed in Chinese imperial, Western colonial, and now Soviet socialist etiquette, his was a deeply flattering entreaty:

'First in Chita and then in Khabarovsk,' he wrote,

> I have always received every courtesy from the Soviet Army and have felt comfortable and at peace. During this time I have come to read all kinds of Soviet literature, and for the first time in my forty years have had the chance to study your [Stalin's] works *Concerning Questions of Leninism* and the *History of the Communist Party of the Soviet Union (Bolsheviks)*. From my perspective I truly see that the Soviet Union really is the most democratic and advanced country in the world, and it is the saviour and mainstay for all the world's toiling peoples and oppressed nations.[25]

Once the figurehead and embodiment of two regimes that Communists sought to overthrow, Puyi was now sounding a great deal like them, and even applied to join CPSU himself. Yet this application, and his request to stay, were both declined. Don't worry, his Soviet captors told him, turning his apparent political epiphany against him. They would never have sent him back to a China ruled by the perfidious Nationalist Chiang Kai-shek, but now the CCP was in charge he had nothing to be concerned about, particularly since he apparently now liked Communism so much. 'This is Mao Zedong's China,' everything will be fine, they said.

So in 1950 Puyi returned to the reimagined land of his birth to 'face the music', as one of the sporadic English captions in Changchun's museum put it. Sensing the chance for a PR coup to reassure the at-best-sceptical capitalist world of their benign intentions, the CCP authorities received Puyi and immediately entered him into a programme of re-education and rehabilitation. Yet another identity was thus fashioned for him as an ordinary Chinese citizen. This move was labelled a 'glorious achievement' by PRC Foreign Minister Zhou Enlai, who along with Mao Zedong appeared greatly to enjoy the turning of tables that this represented. The section of Changchun's museum dealing with Puyi's later years included a backlit photograph of the bushy-eyebrowed Zhou lolling lugubriously in an armchair while the more erect Puyi sat opposite. Nearby was another image depicting the former Son of Heaven sharing an apparently riotously funny joke with Mao. In the final extraordinary turn of an extraordinary Manchu life, Puyi would spend the rest of his days as a resident gardener at the

Chinese Academy of Sciences' Institute of Botany. This role afforded him the chance for one final fleeting Russian encounter, a late 1950s meeting with representatives of the Sino-Soviet Friendship Association, bookending a curiously consistent narrative thread running throughout his tumultuous career.[26] But by the time Puyi passed away in 1967, the Sino-Soviet Friendship had also expired.

* * *

On their bloody emancipatory way through Changchun/Shinkyo in 1945, a squad of Soviet Red Army soldiers had stopped at the Manchukuo palace to pose for a few souvenir photographs on Puyi's imperial throne,[27] a fitting christening for Manchuria's emerging roles first as a CCP stronghold and then as a model region for the socialist PRC. Relying—much as the nascent North Korea would—on leftover Japanese factories and Soviet help in modernising them (at least those that were not spirited back to the USSR), north-east China became the post-1949 home to a host of industrial megaprojects, which, since Stalin's 1930s transformation of Magnitogorsk, had been the cathedrals of state socialism. Changchun itself was the site for new iron and steel projects and the vast First Automotive Works, which to this day produces the Hongqi cars like Mr Liu's back in Fuyuan. Given the CCP's need to communicate the new, if rather Soviet, world order it was founding on the ruins of Qing and Republican Chinas, culture was also a strategic industry. The Changchun Film Studio, which arose from the Japanese-run Manchukuo Film Association, would spend the ensuing decades producing lively and heavily ideological movies—using propaganda techniques pioneered and honed in the USSR—and thus helping to make socialist China live in the minds of the masses.

If the Soviet imprint on Changchun thus came to be embodied in the naves of huge factories and workers' dormitories, and the spires of chimneys towering over the city, it at times also assumed more explicitly spiritual form. From the former palace I returned southward to the centre of the city where, in the middle of the non-quadratic People's Square, a secular shrine pierced the sky out of a grove of pine trees. This was Changchun's memorial to the Soviet pilots who supported the 1945 ground invasion, a monument like many others that today lie scattered throughout Manchuria, often being recent Russian-funded reconstructions of versions destroyed during the Sino-

Soviet Spilt. Most stand in out-of-the-way locations in 'martyrs parks' (as at Tongjiang and Jiamusi), on riverside or seaside promenades (Fuyuan and Lüshunkou) or even isolated in bus station car parks (Suifenhe). But this pillar in this old Japanese capital was unusually prominent, a bold celebration of the spirit of Sino-Soviet fraternity that swept through post-liberation Manchuria. Below a five-pronged red star and a dreamy carving of a Soviet bomber soaring through puffy clouds were the Cyrillic-etched names of fallen sergeants Veselov, Petushkov, Plotnikov, and a Chinese inscription reading: 'The Soviet military martyrs will never be forgotten.' The Russian was more effusive: 'Eternal glory to the heroes who fell in battles for the honour and victory of the Soviet Union' it stated in a grave serif font above some extinct incense sticks (Image 16).

However, just as Sino-Soviet Changchun succeeded Manchukuo Shinkyo, which succeeded Russo-Japanese Changchun, the city is now well on the way to yet another, twenty-first-century incarnation. At People's Square, the demands of urban development left little room for the past, and while the incense suggested tranquil reflection, this was shrouded by the billowing dust out of which the Soviet spike now peered. The digging of a metro stop directly underneath the square was proceeding apace, and as I approached I got talking to a man in a loose-fitting red T-shirt who had been fixing his earth-moving truck by the monument's plinth.

Mr Kou was from neighbouring Liaoning, the third of the Manchurian provinces that lies closer to 'inner China' than Heilongjiang or Jilin. A veteran of other subterranean endeavours, he had worked previously on the Beijing Metro, a project fitfully started in the 1950s–60s when thousands of Chinese students were dispatched to Moscow to study that city's grand subway. The network had only really taken shape between 2000 and 2013, however, as fifteen new lines were dug under the Chinese capital.

I asked Mr Kou how he found the work. 'Conditions are bad,' he said. 'Only 3000 RMB per month and you're underground all the time.'

Were they planning to dismantle the aviator monument, I asked, not a farfetched suggestion given how concrete and metal tides have swept away the old in cities across China.

'No way!' he said indignantly. 'Look at it, it's important. What is it anyway?'

I tried to explain, but both of us were distracted from the seven-decades-removed heroics of Soviet airmen by some deafening drilling that had just started a few feet away. 'We don't study that history anyway,' Mr Kou shouted. 'China's village education isn't so good. We're still developing, like this metro. China needs another twenty years to develop and finish its metro systems.'

Mr Kou's knowledge of his role in China's progress seemed, along with a need simply to survive, an important part of how he endured his dark and dirty job. As with Mr Zhao way back in Moscow, stoical devotion to an unknown future is a trait widely attested among developing China's population, but here dedication to grand narratives and grand projects of modernisation also seemed a poignantly Soviet ideal. I wished him all the best.

If Changchun was in many places bursting out of the seams of both its Manchukuo-era street plan and its more recent socialist past, there still remained a few serene spots that had weathered the maelstrom of shifting regimes. At one of these, I sought some repose before leaving the city, and north-east China, for good.

The Banruo Buddhist Temple dates back to 1922 during the Russo-Japanese era and, although reconstructed and moved during the Manchukuo redesign of the city, today still provides a haven of gentle constancy amid unsettling urban metamorphosis. As I walked slowly through its succession of courtyards with their pine trees, neat flower-beds and iron incense tripods, I was beckoned over by Zhengqiu, a monk wearing a chocolate-coloured habit. He ushered me into a side hall by the main shrine and we started talking. It turned out that Zhengqiu, who had been at the temple for the past ten years, had himself come seeking peace.

'I used to be a businessman,' he said. 'Biscuits. Very successful. I didn't want for anything. But when I was twenty-seven, a close friend—another businessman—died, and I started to wonder what it was all for. I'd studied Buddhism a little before that, but then I went backpacking to Tibet and witnessed a sky burial. I came back and decided to enter the temple.'

What did his mother and father think, I asked. This seemed a radical career change for someone establishing himself financially, usually a key parental priority.

'They opposed it, especially my mother. They understand little of religion. But sometimes you have to make sacrifices for a calling. My mother disowned me, even formally passed me to my elder brother's care.'

We walked out again into the quiet courtyard and I asked more about activities at Banruo. Zhengqiu told me it was the main active centre of Buddhist learning for the whole of north-east China. 'Buddhism used to be less popular, but now it's coming back. I think this is because even though the country is developing fast, we still have to attend to the spiritual side. All of us have a soul, and we have to care for our elders, and our children.'

I asked if there particular problems with modern Chinese society that Buddhism could help solve. 'The progress of the country is great, and development is important,' he said. Of course I fully support the Communist Party, it does nothing wrong. Its direction and education are both correct. But it can't provide us with everything. The Buddha didn't attain enlightenment as a gift given to him, he reached it by his own efforts. Everyone has a soul that must be cultivated, I learnt that after going to Tibet.'

Zhengqiu's was the view of many who seek to balance religious and political life in today's China, although he was attempting a separation of domains that the CCP itself is not always comfortable maintaining. Banruo, like other temples, churches and mosques across the country, runs only with party supervision.

I thanked Zhengqiu for his wisdom, a philosophy capacious enough to reconcile spirituality, family division and atheistic state Communism. His was a remarkable tranquillity. '*Amitabha*,' he said in farewell. 'Buddha be praised.'

Less peaceful than the atmosphere inside the temple was the ragtag collection of people loitering outside its cinnabar walls. Shading himself under a large Sprite-logo umbrella possibly purloined from a row of nearby restaurants, a fortune teller sat on a low stool, feet resting on a crumpled laminated map of the eight trigrams. He beckoned me over. Was he a Buddhist?, I enquired.

'No, no! This is Daoism!' he replied indignantly. 'Buddhism came from the west, from India, Daoism is a real Chinese religion!'

After some protestations that my fortune did not need telling, then some haggling after I had partially relented, I sat down, realising after all that I was not too concerned whether or not he was a 'real' fortune-teller. As Marx or Lenin would likely have assured me, invented prophecies held equal weight whether coming from a charlatan or a sage.

'You have soft hands like woman, you will be rich,' the man began, squinting at the furrows on my palm. 'Yes, rich. All these lines are long.' I pointed out that I did have relatively big hands. Could this be why the lines were long?

He nodded, seeming to ignore me. 'You should marry late, someone older than you are, of the year of the pig or the dog. Or possibly someone younger, a horse. You will have more than one profession. And you will be rich.'

I asked why it was all so positive, were no ills to befall me ever? And if they were, ought he not to mention them so I could be on the lookout?

'Er, you are good at getting things done.' He poked at my nose, looking uncomfortable. 'But you are stubborn.' I was unsure whether this was a general comment on my character or a critique of my current behaviour.

A friend of the fortune-teller then approached wielding an iPad and asking a question that usually causes me problems: 'Which zodiac animal are you?'

I was born just before Spring Festival, I told him, so I thought I was probably a cow rather than the tiger that fills eleven months of my solar birth year. Yet I had also heard that the parade of twelve half-drowned beasts now submits to Julian logic and changes on 1 January instead.

'No no, you are a cow,' confirmed the friend, twiddling the pixelated wheels on his Chinese lunar calendar app.

I said I had always feared as much.

'Was your paternal grandfather married twice by any chance?' he ventured. The haphazard questioning and use of apps was reducing my already modest confidence in the efficacy of this session, and so I shifted conversation from the celestial to the profane. Where were these men from, I wanted to know.

Despite his enthusiasm for a 'real Chinese religion', my original soothsayer turned out to have a more complicated background. He was, he told me, a Mongol from back in Inner Mongolia where I had been weeks previously. 'My wife and I speak Mongolian at home,' he said proudly.

But aren't Mongolians Buddhists not Daoists? I asked.

'Yes, but some believe in the eight trigrams like me,' he replied, adding reassuringly, 'I studied it myself.' A small crowd had now formed around us, and as I handed the man the Mao Zedong-bearing banknote amounting to the agreed fee, a woman in a leopard-print top remonstrated with me.

'Only ten *yuan*!' she exclaimed with incredulity. 'He told you such good things! You should give him more.' It was all settled in advance, I explained, but contracts, even verbal ones, clearly violated the flexible spirit of having your palm read by a mock-Daoist Mongol outside a Buddhist temple. The woman leant over to the fortune-teller. 'You're right, he does have the character of a woman,' she said in a stage whisper thoroughly audible to both me and the assembled throng.

I was unsure exactly what she meant, but my non-womanliness was at least partially, and unwelcomely, reaffirmed as I departed the temple down a side-alley of shops selling jade lions, incense sticks and ritual beads. 'Hello,' said a middle-aged woman in English, walking out of a suspicious-looking barber shop and grabbing my forearm.

'Hello,' I replied, a bit surprised.

The woman made a sleeping gesture, head tilted over joined palms, and then pointed at the barbershop. I asked if she was tired.

'One hundred, let's go,' she persisted, unamused.

Living up to the prophecy, I stubbornly declined. Besides any moral objections, I was in any case now poised to leave the erstwhile 'new capital' of Japan's in-between empire and head to China's 'northern capital'. Beijing is more than merely 'northern' in name and geography, for its entire historical identity has been crafted by peoples from China's northerly Manchu, Mongol and indeed Russo-Soviet fringes. The influence of the last of these has made it a mirror-capital for Moscow, where my journey had begun.

9

BEIJING

REVOLUTIONARY CITY OF THE STEPPE KHANS

Like its Russian counterpart, the political centre of the Chinese world lies far from its geographical heart. On another train from Changchun, I followed the same south-westward trajectory taken by the Manchu invaders who founded China's last imperial dynasty in 1644. Beijing, while outside the north-eastern Manchu homeland, is part of the same mirrorland world, and the Qing foundation here was not the first time the city had fallen to northern conquerors. Before the Han Chinese Ming dynasty, whom the Manchus defeated, had been the Yuan, who were Mongols. Indeed, central Beijing owes much of its still-intact layout to these earlier northerners who from the 1260s rebuilt the city under Genghis Khan's grandson Kublai.

Back then, the place known as Khanbaliq—'City of the Khan'—or Dadu (great capital), did lie relatively close to the centre of Kublai's realm, which stretched from China's southern coast all the way north into what would later become Russian Siberia. But the Ming takeover in 1368 and the resulting loss of the far northern territories left the capital stuck out in the north-eastern corner of the country. This effect was further magnified under the Qing who, although reincorporating Manchuria into the empire, also vastly expanded its territorial reach westward into Inner Asia, giving Beijing a deep hinterland of mountains and deserts that it struggles to control to this day. The Orwellian measures the Chinese Communist Party now deploys in Xinjiang and Tibet demonstrate the difficulty of ruling from such a geographical and cultural distance, but in this the Chinese capital's experience is far from unique. Moscow too remains isolated from the eastern and southern domains where it historically first met China, and in places its grip over these remains contingent. From the vast haemorrhaging of former-tsarist territories during the Soviet collapse to ongoing friction in the mountainous north Caucasus, the capital that Russians call simply their 'centre' is also still trying to consolidate past conquests.

Given their mirrored histories of cyclical dynasties and outside invasions, both Russia and China also share experience of switching capitals under different governments. Debates over moving each bloated empire's seat of power closer to the geographical heartlands have continued, albeit inconclusively, into modern times. Proposals to relocate Russia's capital to the Trans-Siberian centre of Novosibirsk (previously Novonikolaevsk) emerged in 1907, gaining further traction when from 1942 the city assumed many capital-resembling functions as Russian industrial, administrative and even creative and artistic activities decamped eastward under pressure from the Wehrmacht.[1] Other eastern cities including Ekaterinburg and Krasnoyarsk have also been mooted periodically as alternative centres,[2] but the rapid dismissal of a 2012 Siberian proposal by Defence Minister Sergei Shoigu, himself from the former Qing territory of Tuva, revealed the negative attitude most Muscovites have towards the idea.[3] China has still fresher memories of shifting capitals, as during the fractured twentieth century Nanjing, Guangzhou, Wuhan, Chongqing and Chengdu all served as administrative hubs for one regime or other. In the past two decades, Beijing's water shortages, unbreathable air and car-clogged streets have sparked rumours about decamping to the more central but otherwise emphatically anonymous Xinyang in Henan province.[4] But official measures have only gone as far as banishing some government offices to Beijing's slightly less gridlocked, if no less polluted, exurbs.

Whatever their remove from Eurasian hinterlands, however, both Moscow and Beijing are places that have conversely been shaped by their ties to these territories. I had already observed how Russia's arduous trek east had rendered the capital a distinctly Asian place, and

Beijing too has long been not only a northern outpost for China (its name means 'northern capital') but also a southern bridgehead for those coming down from the regions I had been exploring. From its historical population of Manchus and Mongols, to the addition of words and sounds (including a growling Tungusic 'r') from their languages to the local Chinese dialect,[5] the steppe has swept through this city in ways that go beyond its climate of dust storms and harsh winters. However, of equal importance to modern Beijing, and to my upcoming explorations as my train rolled quietly in, was the influence of still another group of northerners. Like the Manchus and their Qing realm, this people is today mostly identified with a place that exists only as ghostly traces, spatial, cultural and political. But their home was also a huge empire whose impression on northern China was such that a European-looking English person journeying in the borderlands may still be mistaken for one of them. They were the Soviets.

The Beijing Railway Station into which I was arriving was one of the capital's more obvious monuments to the last great northern invasion. On pre-Soviet Chinese trains you entered Beijing, as Sergei Tretyakov did in 1924, on a looping route around the south of the city that ended at a very different station on the south-eastern corner of Tiananmen Square. Echoing Qu's account of his arrival in Moscow only two years earlier, Tretyakov described his gradual penetration into the heart of the capital:

> [First come] the outer walls of Beijing which envelop the city in a square, so wide that gardens are planted on top of them ... then behind them the Temple of Heaven sticking its tip up into the Beijing sky, which is blue like the clothes of the Chinese. Behind the temple a steely skin of radio masts, and visible above the city are a chimney and the upper floors of the Hotel de Pékin. Then comes the inner wall with its enormous six-storey barracks on each corner, and its blue-gold, delicately constructed and many-tiered gatehouses. And then, Beijing station.[6]

As I would be seeing, much of what Tretyakov witnessed (including, eventually, Beijing's blue sky itself) would transform radically by processes set in motion by the Moscow-sponsored 1949 foundation of the PRC. Among the primary agents of this transformation were Tretyakov's successors, legions of Soviet political, economic and industrial specialists who came to China to assist in constructing the new socialist state, and those who eagerly followed their advice. The Chinese built their own new country, and ultimately Moscow would have liked to control events south of the Amur more than it did. But much early work on reshaping China was inspired, as Qu and others had been since the 1920s, by a northern exemplar.

The experts' arrival was not wholly unprecedented, for in a sign of earlier Soviet indifference to who ruled China—as long as they were under Moscow's tutelage—some had been dispatched during the earlier Republican period.[7] But the socialist-era deployment from 1953 was far larger, and by 1960 up to 12,000 representatives of the 'Soviet elder brother'—as the northerly neighbour came to be known—were scattered across the country. As well as being instrumental in building up the PRC's state apparatus, which still operates largely intact today, these specialists played a more literally constructive role. In Beijing, Soviet advice and design principles guided a radical reimagining of urban space. Perhaps most emblematic of this were the 'Ten Great Buildings', monumental new public edifices erected to mark socialist China's tenth anniversary in 1959. In addition to Beijing Railway Station, this eclectic constellation of giant modernist works included the city's Military Museum, Workers' Stadium, Ethnic Culture Palace, the Great Hall of the People, National Museum and others, all but one of which (the redesigned Huaqiao Hotel) remain almost unaltered today.[8]

The Chinese architects who designed these buildings had diverse backgrounds and, having trained during the country's age of European and American semi-colonialism, were influenced by numerous styles and traditions. But with an entirely new Sovietised architectural education system introduced from 1952,[9] all practitioners, however established, were exhorted to retool in order to follow the early Soviet dictum that creative work be 'national in form, socialist in content'.[10] Official directives instructed that staples of classical Chinese architecture, such as the 'big roofs' (da wuding) of Beijing's Forbidden City, be jettisoned as all projects would be infused with political meaning. State socialism imposed still further, less explicit strictures on the planners' work because of the massive economic damage being inflicted on China at the time by Mao's Great Leap Forward. In these straitened circumstances, the Ten Great Buildings were essentially the only large-scale projects with sufficient resources to proceed in the late 1950s, and material scarcity permitted neither 'waste' nor extensive use of modernist concrete.[11]

Yet if the febrile ideological climate generated immense pressure to produce designs that were both politically correct and highly functional, these were also not the hyper-strict socialist realist days of the early USSR. In the event, the winners of the Zhou Enlai-supervised design competition, from Japanese-educated Zhao Dongri and Shen Qi's art deco-infused Great Hall of the People to Yang Tingbao and Chen Dengao's eclectic Railway Station, offered a synthesis of many styles. Navigating between austere formalism, fussy Western and Russian neoclassicism and Chinese yellow glass tiling, architects also found that settling on expressive modes that were adequately 'national in form'—i.e. Chinese—paradoxically meant jettisoning more obviously 'Soviet' elements: only the Beijing Municipal Planning Department-designed Military Museum ended up looking like it could have been lifted straight from Moscow. The PRC's decennial would in any case also turn out to fall during the autumn period of the Sino-Soviet alliance, so it was perhaps appropriate that Beijing's new builders strayed somewhat from their advisors' dogmatism.

Most iconic among the 1959 buildings are the Great Hall of the People and the National Museum, which, flanking Tiananmen Square's western and eastern sides, lie at the heart of the Soviet-inflected capital. More correctly rectilinear than Changchun's roundabout squares, and designed with the Chinese masses rather than Japanese invaders in mind, Tiananmen is not a particularly warm heart for the city. But it was here that I came soon after arriving in Beijing. As I approached on foot, the vast off-white surface stretched away from me, a far larger space than Red Square's already-massive black expanse. This was the perfect blank canvas on which to project the progressivist future of a new revolutionary state. Yet like its Russian equivalent, Tiananmen—which assumed its present form as part of the 1959 anniversary projects—also shows how new political orders feel compelled to piggyback on older authority. As in Moscow, in Beijing the seat of the *ancien régime* lies on one side of the main plaza, offering a faded glow of imperial light for socialist and post-socialist governments to bathe in. Here the counterpart to Red Square's Kremlin walls is the imperial palace, whose Gate of Heavenly Peace—which gives the square its name—lies distant across the wide expanse of grey Laizhou granite.[12]

The scale and openness of Tiananmen, whose 1950s remodelling required the removal of several miles of wall and one of the old city gates, were intended precisely to contrast with the fusty and restrictive Qing Forbidden City. But since then China's Communist dynasty has slouched into its own mid-imperial repose, shrinking away from its increasingly wealthy population and terrorist responses from its brutally ruled dominions. The area around Tiananmen Square is therefore now a jumble of security zones and narrow corridors between barriers, discouraging encroachment from the plebeian hordes. Negotiating my way through, I picked a path down the eastern side of the square heading for the National Museum, which houses the 2003-amalgamated Museum of the Chinese Revolution and Museum of Chinese History. On this summer Sunday, a long queue of visitors snaked excitedly nearby, the hubbub of regional dialects dwarfed by the enormous building whose design, according to one contemporary Chinese architectural study, represents 'political will, national pride, and the great victory achieved by the power of the masses' (Image 17).[13] Below a towering colonnade ten pillars wide, the museum's doorway follows imperial British-trained architect Zhang Kaiji's design and, resembling the classical style of a Chinese memorial gateway, is certainly correctly 'national in form'. The long line moved quickly towards this, and I suddenly found myself directly under the red socialist flags and thunderous yellow starred boss perched high above. A view over the entire square opened out, and as Mao's Mausoleum shimmered in the heat haze, the Great Hall of the People faced the museum with its horizon-hugging 336-metre width. Though bearing the unmistakable badge of Stalinist neoclassicism, the museum and the Great Hall were planned to mirror one another in *yin–yang* complementarity across the square. The spaciousness and light of open exhibition would be matched with solidity and weight of national politics.[14]

The National Museum earns its place on the world's largest public plaza by being the biggest museum anywhere in terms of floor area. All its interior spaces are correspondingly cavernous. The ground floor is mainly occupied by a gallery of paintings depicting the history of post-1949 'New China' in the vivid oily swirls and gilt frames of, once again Soviet-inflected, European high art. An atmosphere of strained respect reigns here, and the guides who shout distortedly through loudspeakers at disinterested tour groups in almost every other Chinese museum are conspicuously absent. A sign even asks specifically that people keep their voices down. I began at the beginning with the pre-history of the PRC, the leftist and anti-imperial movements of the late nineteenth and early twentieth centuries that swept up many young idealists of the time, including the likes of my historical travel companion Qu Qiubai. While this process began before the 1911 collapse of the Qing, Russia's October Revolution provided new inspiration for oppositionist activity, and as the echoes of 1917 reverberated around the world, Chinese students rose up in revolt against the venal and neo-colonial authorities of the post-Qing Republic of China. Diverse acts of dissent, from open protest to subversive literature in vernacular rather than classical Chinese, coalesced in 1919 into the May the Fourth Movement, a swell of new thinking from which Qu himself emerged. All this was narrated in the museum through a series of paintings, many of them produced in the early 1950s as the freshly founded PRC carefully crafted its own pre-history. Near one of these a man was bending down to explain this period to his son, earnestly lambasting post-imperial China's first president Yuan Shikai, though without raising his voice above the mandated level.

However, whilst the era of mass discontent with Republican corruption is key to socialist China's origin story, it is also a troublesome one for today's Beijing. Given the continuing inclination of unaccountable CCP officials to indulge in their own venal abuses, the present-day authorities count successor movements to May the Fourth among their biggest fears. Consequently, at the museum, this awkward period recedes quickly into the past, giving way to much more voluminous treatment of what happened next. A short distance along the gallery's crimson walls was a series of pictures of Mao Zedong, whose revolutionary career saw him assuming every possible pose and position, stooping to talk to farmers and miners, standing looking philosophical on a cliff-edge and sitting solemnly in his office holding a cigarette. Finally he stood waiting contemplatively on the Tiananmen tribune, flanked by fellow-revolutionaries Lin Biao and Zhou Enlai, preparing to announce the founding of the People's Republic to the square below. The air of reverence that was meant to surround these images was not everywhere maintained, and near one painting a teenager was pretending to offer a high-five to the Chairman's outstretched palm as his friend took a photo.

These paintings ushered us into the PRC age, and as a result the USSR now entered the picture more decisively, even as the approach to historical relations with that country was necessarily selective. High up next to a doorway, another small portrait of Mao showed him standing next to Stalin as a nearby caption briefly described the vital visit to Moscow made by the CCP leadership from December 1949 to February 1950. This trip was one of only two journeys Mao made outside China in his lifetime, the second also being a Soviet visit in 1957. As the placard noted, the first one was the occasion for the signing of the Sino-Soviet Friendship Treaty. Not communicated here was the fact that the journey itself turned out to be anything but friendly.

Being received in Moscow was, from the Chinese point of view, a crucial act of validation. Gaining approval from the leaders of the socialist world, whose support for China's indigenous Communist movement had been at best tepid for most of the preceding decades, would be critical for the new government's survival. Setting off with the intention of conveying birthday greetings to Stalin, something all global socialist citizens were encouraged to do, Mao travelled by train with fellow-CCP worthies including Zhou Enlai, crossing Manchuria to Manzhouli and then continuing through Siberia to the Soviet capital. When he arrived at Moscow's Yaroslavsky Railway Station—the very same terminus where Qu Qiubai had disembarked thirty years previously—he was met by Soviet politburo members Vyacheslav Molotov and Nikolai Bulganin. Disappointingly, and humiliatingly, Stalin was absent, and things seemed even less propitious when Molotov and Bulganin refused to share the food or drink that the Chairman had had set out aboard his train. Eschewing these necessary stages in the building of any firm Chinese relationship, the pair claimed that to accept would be a breach of protocol. They also declined to escort Mao to his accommodation.

Things got still worse once the Chinese delegation was settled in Moscow, as the programme of events to which they were invited seemed at best ill-conceived and at worst designed deliberately to offend them. In addition to a cheerless memorial to the death of Lenin at the Bolshoi Theatre on 21 January 1950, dreary entertainments included a performance of the 1927 Soviet ballet *The Red Poppy*. The first such work to be written and staged in the USSR following its foundation, the drama unfolds on the background of a then-still-imaginary Chinese socialist revolution, and as such may have seemed an ideal choice for the visitors. But much of the ballet's domestic popularity, it turned out, rested on its portrayal of the Soviets as heroic liberators of the Chinese, who correspondingly appeared as a benighted and hapless bunch of generic 'orientals' incapable of independent thought. 'Poppies' were also hardly a propitious symbol given China's colonial experiences. This stark reprise of the old Russian Empire's often-demeaning relationship with 'Asia', an attitude evident in everything from Qu Qiubai's 1920s Moscow conversations to contemporary Yakut or Nanai experiences, caused deep offence among those of Mao's delegates who attended. Much of the rest of the visit continued in this vein.[15]

Eventual meetings with Stalin proved to be an awkward parade of diplomatic jostling dogged by repeated miscommunications and apparent intransigence on the Soviet side. Among the negotiations' many problems was the fact that the Russians, tellingly, appeared to have little idea of precisely what they were talking about when it came to discussing key issues such as Sino-Soviet borders, the CER, and territorial concessions in Manchuria. Almost none had ever been anywhere near the borderlands, and consequently adopted a strategy that prioritised bluster and condescension to avoid accidently giving anything of substance away to their 'Asiatic' guests. China's rulers, whose imperial predecessors had for centuries been accustomed to receiving foreign tributary missions, were put in a frustratingly supplicatory position.

Yet somehow a treaty was signed on 14 February 1950. Russian and Chinese facsimiles of the document—no Latin or Manchu this time—appear in the museum alongside the credentials of the PRC's first Soviet ambassador, Wang Jiaxiang. Moscow renounced some (although not all) of its privileges in north-east China, handed over the China Eastern Railway and Puyi, and dispatched the advisors. Their tutelage would facilitate Changchun's industrialisation, agricultural mobilisation in the Great Northern Wilderness, the classification of the minority Hezhe, Koreans and Manchus, the construction of the Ten Great Buildings, and the drawing up of the PRC's first Five-Year Plan. This latter economic tool, long abandoned by Moscow in the era of oligarch capitalism, has been employed in China ever since, and 2015 saw the introduction of the thirteenth plan.

During the decade-long honeymoon that followed, Beijing made little publicly of Mao's humiliation in Moscow. This all changed during the 1960s–80s Sino-Soviet Split (more on which below), but today's bromance between Presidents Xi and Putin means the old friendship has come full circle: the 1950s era of superficially positive ties are useful once again. Artefacts of the Sino-Soviet alliance, such as the Mao–Stalin painting, now merely burnish the image of a China that, under Xi, is more confident than ever in its international relationships, from Belt and Road to bullishness over trade with the United States. The museum offered further evidence of the CCP's desire to present a robustly positive history of its foreign engagements. Below the surface, however, one exhibition that did this also served as a coded account of post-1949 China's more varied and ambivalent global fortunes.

Leaving the painted gallery of New China's new history, I continued to Hall No. 18 where a snaking corridor of brightly lit glass cabinets presents a chronological array of gifts from foreign leaders on state visits to China. Taken as a whole, the dazzling display generated a euphoric sense of the admiration and friendship felt by all foreigners towards the CCP, but a more nuanced story emerged as I examined who gave what when. Marking the early post-treaty alliance, many Soviet gifts from the 1950s came to Mao Zedong directly, addressing the Chairman as 'comrade' and including a traditional Slavic wood carving engraved with the Russian legend 'I want peace', a drinking horn from the Georgian Soviet Republic, and the Promethean image of a cast iron man taming a cast iron horse forged at the Urals Heavy Machinery Factory. In this era of socialism in Eastern Europe and leftist decolonising movements across Asia and Africa, China also frequently exchanged gifts with other members of the then-relatively unified fraternity of 'red' states. Porcelain came from Vietnam's Ho Chi Minh, ornaments from North Korea's Kim Il Sung, traditional artworks and precious stones were brought to Beijing by Tanzanian liberation leader Julius Nyerere, Guinean Ahmed Sékou Touré and Mobutu Sese Seko from DR Congo. A miniature golden wine barrel and carved wooden eagle were proffered by Hungary and Albania respectively. But as relations with the USSR cooled during the 1960s, offerings from the giant northern neighbour and its global protégés dwindled to a trickle. In 1964, a single vase from the politburo of the Romanian Workers' Party stood as a lonely last outlier of this short-lived period of camaraderie with the Eastern Bloc.

However, after a noticeable lull in almost all gifts coinciding with the introverted turmoil of the Cultural Revolution, new sources of generosity appeared as I continued round the exhibition. These spoke of hitherto unknown international ties. By the 1970s, products of Soviet industry were replaced by tentative offerings from capitalist countries, including a porcelain bird from Henry Kissinger and, in a possibly pointed reference to China's main regional rival, a coral bonsai tree from Richard Nixon. Such items became solider and more generous as confidence in renewed Sino-US ties grew, and soon enough even local representatives of the Illinois State Government felt emboldened enough to offer a stately, if also subtly critical, bust of Abraham Lincoln. Into the reformist era under Deng Xiaoping, China found its circle of Western friends expanding still further: the 1980s saw Margaret Thatcher offer an engraved silver plate and, in violation of traditional Chinese gifting practices, François Mitterrand gave a clock (the Chinese phrase *song zhong*, 'to give a clock', is homophonous with 'funeral ceremony').

Gifts from Beijing's few remaining socialist allies during the Sino-Soviet Split, Albania and North Korea among them, were a relatively consistent presence throughout. Kim Il Sung in particular, adept at playing off the two feuding Communist superpowers against one another, showered the Chinese leadership with tea sets, roughly hewn wooden ornaments of every imaginable shape, and even richly symbolic horse statues, the 'thousand li horse' or *chollima* being a symbol of the headlong charge towards socialist modernity that North Korea seemed for a while to be making.

At last, however, a modest lacquer dish shaped like a duck signalled a thaw in the Sino-Soviet relationship. Beginning with this item in 1984, a late Soviet flow of less ideologically pregnant gifts followed, before ending as abruptly as the union did with a small 1989 painting of the Kremlin given by Mikhail Gorbachev. Yet the breakup of the USSR meant that Beijing suddenly acquired a whole coterie of new

Eurasian suitors. In the 1990s, former Soviet foreign minister and now president of the independent state of Georgia Eduard Shevardnadze brought an enamel plate engraved with the English word 'Peking', while Kazakhstan's Nursultan Nazarbayev appeared to be vying with Tajikistan's Emomali Rahmon in a Central Asian strongman struggle over who could produce the most hideous vase. After the hesitancy evident in the diminutive late Soviet gifts, post-Soviet Russia too regained its erstwhile generosity: Boris Yeltsin betrayed his predilection for certain forms of recreation with a silver wine set, and a freshly anointed Vladimir Putin heralded Russia's new-found materialism with a collection of silver coins, an ornamental balalaika, and a dazzling lacquerwork panel depicting a young couple sitting on an old-fashioned *telega* cart. With its backdrop of onion domes, this latter piece looked from a distance to be a time-worn bucolic scene, but closer scrutiny revealed modern tractors working the field in front of the couple and skyscrapers lurking between the spires: here was a telling encapsulation of rugged Putinist neo-traditionalism.

Having thus arrived at the present, I next made my way upstairs to a part of the museum offering a less subtle interpretation of China's past and current place in the world. 'The Road of Rejuvenation', a permanent exhibition that opened in the north galleries in 2011, charts China's course from its 'century of humiliation' by foreign powers to the megapolis-constructing, spaceship-launching and economically assertive modern state it has now become. Thanks, of course, must go to the CCP. One particularly vivid section of the exhibition depicts territorial incursions made by scurrilous colonial aggressors from the mid-nineteenth century. A large map on one wall illuminated, one by one in pale blue, the bites taken out of Qing dynasty land, accompanied by a tabular breakdown of which area was ceded to whom, when, and by means of which 'unequal treaty'. That the Qing had themselves conquered many areas that, like Xinjiang and Tibet, were not previously 'China' was elided.

It was also here that Russia's imperial interactions with China emerged as starkly different from those of other European powers. While the likes of Macau (ceded to Portugal), Hong Kong (Britain), much of Shanghai (France), the Shandong Peninsula (Germany) and Manchuria (Japan) can today all be said to have been triumphantly reclaimed by a victorious post-dynastic Beijing, areas that changed hands with the 1858 and 1860 Treaties of Aigun and Peking remain not merely Russian colonies but parts of Russia proper. Friedrich Engels' pronouncements regarding the vastness of St Petersburg's gains—and China's losses—were certainly not ignored here, and great swathes of the regions I had crossed during my journey encompassing Vladivostok, Khabarovsk, Blagoveshchensk, Birobidzhan, the northern Nanai lands, and southern Yakutia all lit up with the others to denote territorial deprivation.

But no sooner was this suggestion of as-yet-unrighted historical Russian wrongs made than a very different vision of the northern neighbour appeared. As the Road of Rejuvenation wound into the twentieth century, a huge portrait of a bald and goateed Russian dominated one of the gallery walls. This painting of Lenin in Moscow, a reproduction of a famous work by socialist realist artist Vladimir Serov, has much in common with the portrait of Mao on Tiananmen I had seen downstairs. The Bolshevik leader stands elevated high above those he is leading to liberation, peasants, soldiers and sailors thrusting and thronging around him as someone grips a red flag that flies off the painting's edge, torn to tatters by long revolutionary struggle. Also like the later Mao on the old imperial gate, Lenin appears on a backdrop symbolising the old order, his hand stretches out into an eminently aristocratic white marble ballroom of Corinthian pilasters and blazing chandeliers. Here, then, in a museum at the heart of the Chinese capital, was a layered and ambivalent portrayal of Russia, which in a few short decades had transformed from oppressor to beacon of hope for those seeking emancipation. This Janus-like role played by one empire to the other illustrated yet again the mirrored relationship between the pair for, indeed, Beijing's shifting views of Russia have reflected not only revolutions happening over there but also contradictions and debates unfolding deep within the modern Chinese state itself.

* * *

The transformative impulse of Lenin's revolution had travelled across Eurasia just as I had and, as the museum showed, had gathered sufficient momentum by the 1940s to remould China into the modern Leninist state it remains today. The shared symbologies of the Lenin and Mao paintings—old and new, leader and led—made this appear a seamless process whereby a political code from one rejuvenated empire could be transferred smoothly to another. Yet the changes brought to China by Mao, who in fact assumed the combined roles of Lenin, Stalin and revered historical emperors who reunified China after fragmentation, challenged Chinese people as never before. All were exhorted to undergo difficult transformations that were as much personal as they were national. The Soviet project had itself been an incitement to reform humanity, its philosophers imagining a new *Homo Sovieticus* with elevated levels of strength, self-mastery and consciousness befitting the revolutionary order. But the Chinese version of these debates had a different tone, for they built on older questions over how a person could be both 'Chinese' and 'modern' at all. Such dilemmas had been acute in China ever since the country's late imperial collision with expansionist European powers, Romanov Russia among them.

Before even beginning his journey to Moscow, Qu Qiubai found himself in the eye of this storm over identity. Less than a decade after the Qing collapse and with Mao Zedong still working as a history teacher in his native Hunan province, Qu arrived in Beijing in early 1920 to prepare for his departure. Like Mao, his former-classmate at Peking University's Marxist seminars, Qu at the time saw Marxism merely as one among several appealing political traditions. His search for a way to understand China's confrontation with modernity remained eclectic. But what was certain was that China's changes were affecting his own relationships. As he hurried to gather his belongings from the four years he had spent studying in the Chinese capital, his cousin offered to assist him while they discussed his imminent journey. This was a much less fond farewell than it might have been, for, Qu noted:

> Although my cousin was just trying to help me out according to the rules of 'old-style familial duty', my own 'new-age free spiritedness' ended up spoiling my mood: I just couldn't let myself be a prisoner to his 'old' ways, and I struggled to put up with his contrarian views. He didn't want me to go to Russia, thought I was running right into trouble and even to my own death ... and yet he didn't say anything, and just told me that after I got to Russia I should study hard and not waste the opportunity.[16]

China's post-imperial condition was generating new intimate dilemmas for Qu. Contradictions now existed between recognisably 'Chinese' values, such as obligations to family and tactfully suppressing your true feelings, and the demands of the new 'modern' order, such as engaging with the wider world by travelling there. Nevertheless, his Russian-language diploma would have been wasted otherwise, and Qu set off regardless, his cousin's exhortation to 'study hard'—a tradition where Leninist and Chinese priorities collided—ringing in his ears. Qu needed no encouragement, for the potential of the new Soviet socialist system to tackle China's, and perhaps humanity's, deepest problems seemed extraordinary. As the twenty-one-year-old writer reflected on leaving Beijing, 'behind every person's struggle to put food on the table lurks the shadow of global economics—it's as though a gigantic ghost is hovering overhead, writing a minus-sign in front of all their positive figures'.[17] Moscow, he hoped, would offer a new calculus.

I had already explored much of what Qu saw and did in Moscow and on the trans-Manchurian and trans-Siberian journey that took him there. But the clearest indication of the impressions left on him by those experiences came after he returned to China. Back in Shanghai in 1923, he joined the newly formed Chinese Communist Party. Co-founded by Mao, the party had held its first national congress two years previously, a bilingual Chinese/Russian programme for which I had seen on display in the National Museum.

While Moscow blew hot and cold in its support during the CCP's early years, the 1920s saw no lack of leftist agitation in China, something all too evident to another of my historical travel companions, Ethel Alec-Tweedie. Finally ending her trans-Siberian odyssey in Beijing in the summer of 1925, she disembarked and almost as her foot touched the platform became appalled at the number of workers' strikes occurring across the city. Pro-Soviet messaging seemed to saturate the local media. Alarmed like much of the global aristocracy (as well they might have been) at this trend, Alec-Tweedie decided that the whole thing had been 'brought about to amuse Russia, who had her tongue in her cheek and a very big wink in one eye'. 'The wonderful success of Russia,' she mused, 'filled the Press daily ... and promised China the same millennium of bliss, and poor China believed the well-distributed lies, and sank lower and lower into the abyss.'[18]

If Alec-Tweedie's tone once again betrayed the expert cynicism of privilege, she was correct in identifying the millenarian aspect of the Soviet message. The new revolutionary age appeared to many redolent of the Christian day of judgement when those who—perhaps like Alec-Tweedie herself—presided over Qu's rigged 'global economy' would finally be brought to account. It may have taken another quarter-century for the reckoning to occur, and when it did it may have been a violent orgy of starvation, misdirected murder and indiscriminate hatred. But the ball Lenin had set in motion rolled on nonetheless. Encapsulating this momentum in a 19 January 1930 poem entitled 'Go forward China!', revolutionary Chinese poet Yin Fu, whose 'We Are the Young Bolsheviks' was mentioned back in Moscow, wrote:

> Go forward China,
> The modern world
> Is one great mass of waving banners and flags,
> It is your historic destiny:
> A giant hand is unfurling the flag: You
> Must go forward China!
>
> The world in the 1930s,
> Is a new one,
> Our time
> Is flooding towards us in great waves,
> Ours may not be the cause of the rebellion in the Pacific,
> Nor the flags and banners flying in the Urals;
> But every last piece of grit is calling out to you;
> China, go forward, China![19]

The road from the storming of St Petersburg's Winter Palace to Mao's Tiananmen proclamation was rough, both for everyday Chinese people wrestling with new identities, and for Uncle Joe's humiliated visitors in Moscow. Yet today it is China's socialist system, not Russia's, that remains intact and has brought economic opportunity and relative material security to hundreds of millions. Yin Fu was right when he suggested that China's 'historic destiny' represented a somewhat hazy reflection of that lying ahead of the Ural mountain toilers.

* * *

Over the past six decades, China's version of socialism has indeed as often been defined by its opposition to Soviet–Russian ways of doing things as it has by the inspiration taken from them. South-east of the National Museum and adjacent to Beijing's Dashilar district, a once-derelict but now kitschily restored market area that over the centuries has accommodated everyone from Manchu nobles to prostitutes and opium-smokers, lie traces of the less fraternal period that followed the Stalin–Mao 'Friendship'. The ill omens haunting Mao in Moscow took several years to come true, but by the 1960s the longstanding strain underlying Sino-Soviet relations crawled into the open. Matters were not helped when in 1956 new Soviet leader Nikita Khrushchev denounced his predecessor Stalin, whom Mao revered despite his slights, at a secret session on the sidelines of the Soviet Communist Party's Twentieth Party Congress. What made this act particularly awkward was the fact that most of Khrushchev's venom was aimed at Stalin's personality cult precisely at a time when Mao, and indeed Kim Il Sung in Pyongyang, was laying the foundations for one of his own. This, and doctrinal differences over where global Communism was going, particularly Moscow's growing preference for coexistence with the West, eventually precipitated a complete breakdown in relations. The Kremlin began to be denounced as a den of invidious 'revisionists' wilfully distorting Marx's and Lenin's teachings as friendship turned to outright enmity. In 1960, all Soviet experts were withdrawn from China,[20] and by 1969 things were so bad that the two vast empires felt it necessary to fight a border war over a miniscule and otherwise unremarkable islet in the Ussuri River between Khabarovsk and Vladivostok. Outright nuclear conflict between the two socialist giants seemed so imminent that *New York Times* Moscow correspondent Harrison Salisbury felt compelled to pen a book entitled *War between Russia and China*.[21]

As I had heard along the way, Sino-Soviet border dwellers had experienced the split as a tangle of traumas bound up with the concurrent Cultural Revolution. Propaganda had blared from Heihe to Blagoveshchensk, Fuyuan fishermen had had to ignore their Soviet river-mates, and as all associations with 'foreign' things toxified amid cooked-up spy scares, the ethnic Russians of Enhe and the Koreans of Yanbian were persecuted for disloyalty. This introverted and shuttered time, among the darkest of several dark chapters of China's recent history, has no monuments or museums dedicated to it, a situation likely to continue for as long as the CCP remains in power. This may well mean that the tens of millions of still-living Chinese victims of Mao's cultish excesses never see their experiences adequately addressed by officialdom during their lifetimes. Moreover, as shown by Russia's discouragement of research into Stalinism, including the builders of Tynda's 'Little BAM', political relaxation is not a one-way street. Permissiveness can be rescinded again to silence inconvenient voices from the past.

In today's Beijing, the lack of explicit memorials to the turbulent events of the 1960s means such traces must be sought obliquely, discerned through absences as well as presences. Passing Dashilar's Starbucks, Quanjude Roast Duck shop and the anachronistically bulbous trams that have been 'reintroduced' to the area, I walked along Damochang Street, whose name—meaning 'Polishing Workshop Street'—reflects the historic presence of guilds of bronze- and stone-polishers in the area. A short distance along, amid sporadic restoration efforts underway in the surrounding alleys, a small white-tile building stood over the entrance to the 'Beijing Underground City' whose invisibility and inaccessibility captured well the paranoid age it inadvertently commemorates. This 'city' was constructed on Mao's orders in the aftermath of the 1969 Soviet border war and comprises a warren of subterranean tunnels, rooms and man-made caverns, which, in the event of Soviet nuclear attack, was intended to serve as a bomb shelter-cum-home for up to 40 per cent of Beijing's population.

As an engineering feat, the hand-hewn tunnels, which cover more than 33 square miles, are a legacy of the Maoist vogue for exploitative low-tech mass mobilisation. During its ten-year duration, the project drafted over 300,000 people, including schoolchildren, as 'volunteer' labour. Just as evocative of the age as these methods were the building materials used inside the hollowed-out space. The bricks needed to construct the hundreds of anti-air-raid structures, stores, restaurants, residences, wells, warehouses, factories and even a mushroom-cultivation farm were cannibalised from Beijing's ancient city walls, which, having stood in some form or other since the thirteenth-century days of Kublai Khan, were dismantled at great speed during the 1960s.[22] Before the Sino-Soviet Split, many involved in rebuilding the Chinese capital, including the Soviet-inspired town planners and architects responsible for the Ten Great Buildings, had advocated retaining the walls. But with the Soviet experts gone, such admittedly surprising nostalgia was banished, and the newly hostile era demanded that the grey-brown bricks of these massive fortifications be put to new, albeit still defensive, uses.

Until 2008, a section of the Underground City was accessible to visitors who could jump back into this dank and nervous past. But if the site's opening to tourists in the first place marked the onset of improved post-Soviet relations with Russia, their subsequent re-shuttering also marked the onset of a new historical era. As well as safety concerns in a more regulation-heavy China, the primary reason for the closure was the construction of two new subway lines. Part of Beijing's upgrade ahead of the Olympics, this led to the filling in of several old tunnels. The 2008 Games, seen by many both inside and outside China as the country's moment of arrival on the twenty-first-century global stage, was thus also a time to exhale and dispel memories of cowering underground from a menacing neighbour.

Walking down the dusty *hutong*, I almost missed the now-faded lettering in peeling red tape that marks the former tunnel entrance for tourists. Near a rusted iron doorway under an air conditioning outlet some elderly locals were sitting enjoying the sun, and I approached to ask about the subterranean world beneath us.

'It's dangerous down there, don't go in!' a grandpa with two teeth grinned at me. 'It was built to defend against the Soviet Union. But today that place is called Russia, and they can't hurt us now!' This man, evidently more terminologically up to date than some of his borderland compatriots, was no socialist nostalgic. I asked him and the others whether any of them had visited the Underground City.

'Yes, I have,' said a crop-haired granny in a black blouse cooling herself with a fan decorated with red butterflies. 'But there's nothing down there, it's extremely dull.' Based on this judgement, I thought, it seemed unlikely the place would be reopening any time soon, and further questioning revealed this was a singularly unsentimental group of pensioners who were much more interested in present-day China's successes.

'Look at this,' said the first grandpa, rising unsteadily to his feet and hobbling a few feet beyond the blocked tunnel entrance. He pointed his walking stick at a community billboard of a kind used by central government to communicate policies to the masses, from birth control regulations to bans on 'religious cults'. This one displayed a curiously apt set of posters charting China's recent economic and political rise, with one panel depicting the familiar image of Xi Jinping shaking hands with Vladimir Putin. On another, Chinese and Japanese GDP figures were represented by cartoon trees, with the former's 2011 outstripping of the latter shown by its wide verdant canopy, which now left its neighbour cowering bonsai-like in shadow.

Such imagery, alongside the Road of Rejuvenation's focus on China's foreign colonial experience, is expressive of the country's continuing official emphasis on comparison with other states, including its erstwhile exploiters, as it seeks validation in relative not absolute terms. In former times, Soviet socialism was the yardstick against which to measure oneself, and then, shortly afterwards, an errant philosophy to be repudiated and smashed. But now as I had been informed outside the Underground City, Russia is not really in a position to threaten China as it once did, and so other comparisons, notably Japan and the United States, are more germane. Once again, then, the legacy of contact and influence with the mirror-empire to the north lurked in subtle traces in the Chinese capital. The two remaining places I wished to explore would need less excavation.

* * *

By demolishing ancient walls, both to build the Underground City and expand Tiananmen Square, socialist Beijing succeeded in extirpating some of the traces of the ossified feudal order as Yin Fu's 'new age' dawned. But many of the positional logics of the old capital remained intact nonetheless. For one thing, the axis running down the middle of Tiananmen Square and thus the line of *yin–yang* reflection between the National Museum and Great Hall of the People is the same north–south pivot around which the entire dynastic city was organised centuries ago. This axis, which skewers the Drum and Bell Towers in the north, the centre of the Forbidden City in the middle, and Dashilar in the south, also determined the compass-point positioning of the Temples of Heaven, Earth, the Moon and Sun. The latter former sites of imperial ritual are all now tourist attractions or pleasant parks. Mao's Tiananmen Square mausoleum where the Chairman lies waxily entombed in Lenin-mirroring fashion also sits on this line, placing the first Communist emperor, like his Soviet forebear, at the symbolic heart of both capital and nation.

Elsewhere too, Beijing's modern population continues to follow trajectories plotted by thirteenth-century town planners. Like Moscow's Boulevard Ring, Beijing's Second Ring Road and Line 2 of the city's Metro both follow the precise path of the old city walls, and while the thudding boots of imperial guardsmen on the ramparts have now been replaced by millions of daily commutes at ground or underground levels, the ghostly appellations of the imperial city gates still haunt these journeys. Subway stops and traffic flyovers above them bear the names of Xizhimen (West straight gate), Andingmen (Stability gate), Chongwenmen (Gate of esteemed learning), Xuanwumen (Gate of promoting valour) and many others. During the Qing, the fortifications through which these gates permitted passage marked the division between the inner Manchu city, a privileged realm for the north-eastern conquistadors' military banner ranks, and the outer Han Chinese town. These were also spheres of distinct ethnically inflected gender identities, for while inside a kind of martial male 'valour', the *wu* of Xuanwumen, was habitually associated with the Manchus, outside was the domain of a more literary and scholarly archetypal Han masculinity, the *wen* of Chongwenmen. With the bannermen notionally preoccupied with polishing their arms and preparing for war, a tradition that decayed in the late Qing into a resentment-fuelling lifestyle of government-subsidised indolence, the inner city was mostly sustained by trade conducted outside it by Han merchants. Today, this same spatial divide remains crucial for demarcating new kinds of privilege, as the phrase 'within the second ring' provides an immediate indication of how central and convenient a place is, and a significant boost to real estate prices.

The mirrorland to the north also has its place in the vestigial logics of the imperial city, and in the old city walls' spectral shadows I next went looking for such traces. Tucked into the north-eastern corner of the old Manchu town near Dongzhimen (East straight gate) is Beijing's historically Russian quarter, whose origins predate even the first official Qing–Romanov contact of the seventeenth century. That collision of empires, equally out of their cartographic depth in the steppe around the River

Amur, had led not only to a Qing victory and the Treaty of Nerchinsk but also to several significant captures and Cossack defections to the Manchu side.[23] Following the pacification of the Albazin stockade, these prisoners and turncoats thus accompanied the Qing forces on their return to Khanbaliq-Beijing. Here they found a small existing population of earlier Russian arrivals who, generally coming from the fort at Yakutsk, had either accidentally wandered into China over blurred boundaries or deliberately fled the relentless toil, freezing winters, insipid mosquito-infested summers and threats from bears, tigers, wolves and understandably hostile natives that dogged Siberian expansion.

At the time, the authorities in Moscow, still failing to grasp quite who or what they were dealing with on their eastern frontier, gave up readily on the disappeared 'Albazinians', as they came to be known. Conversely, the hospitality the group received from Emperor Kangxi was unstinting, and everything from financial blandishments to homes, wives and official positions in the banner ranks was provided. Such treatment was consistent with how the Qing dealt with the various non-Manchu peoples they sought to win over, and like their fellow northerners the Mongols, the Russians were granted their own Beijing district, to which I was now heading. They were also allowed a place of worship, and the Chinese capital's first Russian Orthodox church, St Nicholas, was established here in 1683 in a former Buddhist prayer hall refitted with icons and other trinkets from the now-razed chapel at Albazin. With this institution at its heart, the Russian quarter took shape in its corner of the Manchu town, fittingly enough in an area that previously served as an entrepôt for processing Manchurian birchwood into bannermen bows: the link to the north was thus maintained.[24]

As the now-neighbouring empires groped towards greater familiarity with one another over subsequent decades, the Russian presence in Beijing became more formalised. In 1712, petitioning from St Petersburg led to the establishment of the Orthodox Ecclesiastical Mission, and interactions between the community it sustained and their Manchu hosts were further codified under the 1727 Treaty of Kyakhta, which also established new protocols for Sino-Russian trade. Uniquely for a European power, Russian relations with the Qing were managed in Beijing by the Lifan yuan, a government department whose competencies primarily included dealings with inner Asian people such as the Mongols, Tibetans and Uyghurs. Unlike the maritime Portuguese, Dutch, British or French who were dealt with through the more Foreign Ministry-like Zongli yamen, the Russians resembled the imperial fringe's Buddhist nomads and high-mountain horsemen in having arrived by land, and so were treated accordingly. Though culturally much closer to the other Europeans with their intermarried royals and epauletted counts, dukes and barons, the Russians retained their unique Eurasian relationship with China over centuries following their collision on the Amur. Three hundred years after the Albazinians' haphazard arrival, emissaries of Moscow remain in precisely the part of the city that they were granted by Kangxi.

Emerging from the labyrinthine Dongzhimen metro station, I picked my way around the edge of the huge Russian embassy compound at the junction of Andingmen East and Dongzhimen North Avenues. Russian traces were subtle at first, present initially only in the area's distinctly socialist appearance as side roads off Min An (People's Peace) Street in front of the embassy were lined by dreary rows of 1970s apartment buildings. The wall of one of them bore the Chinese legend: 'Once a Party member faces the flag he becomes a responsible member of his community'. But the surrounding streets also had more obvious Russian elements in the form of a popular restaurant named 'Traktir Pushkin' and a supermarket with the Cyrillic name 'Yura'. A bookshop on one corner displayed several Chinese-language books about Vladimir Putin. The president has something of a cult following in China as a no-nonsense 'real man', a figure boasting Manchu-esque *wu* masculinity proper to inner Beijing. New tomes about his leadership, charm and strength are published in China every year.

Other nearby buildings housed small Russian shops called 'Friendship' and 'Grandma's', whose shelves were stacked with imported Russian black bread, 'Napoleon' cakes, Alenka chocolate, condensed milk and an array of vodkas; there was no sign of the borderlands' spurious Chinese-made 'Lenin'- or 'Stalin'-branded beverages. Many of these items attested to a Russian fondness for confectionary, something that I share and perhaps the only culinary realm in which Russian fare is superior to Chinese. This Slavonic sweet tooth, it seems, has long left an imprint on Beijing. During her time here in 1925, Ethel Alec-Tweedie herself visited a popular cake shop and was told that most of its custom came from the Soviet embassy.

'Ye gods!' she exclaimed using one of her most beloved invocations, 'Russia and Siberia starving and the people in rags. And yet the only Legation to be extravagant enough to order cakes and sweets in large quantities was Russia ... Fact is stranger than fiction, eh?'[25]

In a comparably profligate present for much of Russia's elite, I continued down Min An Street beyond Grandma's towards the Russian embassy's Cultural Centre, a newly refurbished building whose billboards offered various connections back to earlier points on my journey. Next to the centre's sleek glass entryway was an explanation of Russia's 4 November 'Day of National Unity', which in 2005 replaced the annual commemoration of the October Revolution (a Soviet calendar switch from Julian to Gregorian had put the event in November, despite its name). The date chosen to celebrate National Unity derived, the information panel said, from a day in 1612 when Russian forces reclaimed the Kitai-gorod area of Moscow—where my journey had begun—from a Polish invasion. In this, they had purportedly shown 'the epitome of heroism and solidarity of all people regardless of origin, religion or position within society'. Chinese workers targeted by thugs in Russian cities—a common occurrence on Unity Day that has become an excuse for ultra-nationalist rallies—might wonder what happened to that spirit.

Nearby, a display of publicity photos sought to offer further confirmation to China that Russia too was a diverse but unified entity. The central image was of a blonde woman sitting on the banks of St Petersburg's River Neva. As she gazed sullenly out of the photo, her back was turned to the cruiser *Aurora*, the ship that fired the opening gunshots of the October Revolution. Subtler Chinese resonances than this gesture at Leninist times were present in pictures of the dramatic Altai mountains on Russia's borders with Xinjiang, Moscow State University's iconic Stalinist tower, which I had seen aped in Manzhouli, and a gallery of cheerful looking Russian minority peoples in national costumes redolent of a CCP propaganda poster. In more 'natural' settings, a Tuvan man aimed a bow and arrow outside a lamasery, and a group of unspecified individuals labelled simply 'a minority' squatted in an animal hide wigwam boiling something over a fire. My Nanai and Hezhe friends either side of the border would have recognised well this seemingly celebratory but also genericising treatment.

But while all this cultural spill-over outside the embassy walls attested to the brooding Russian presence nearby, getting closer to the source was unlikely. The embassy's security, seemingly reinforced by the ten lanes of traffic swooshing around the adjacent ring road, offered few hints of what was inside. A few rooftops did peek out above the solemn grey perimeter walls, most prominently an all-seeing rotunda atop the main embassy building. Also visible was the curling tip of the compound's Orthodox church, whose own history has been one of oscillating revelation and concealment. Originally erected in 1901, the Church of the Dormition of Theotokos the Most Holy replaced several Russian places of worship sacked during the Chinese anti-colonial Boxer Uprising. For much of the Soviet era, however, the embassy authorities used the old church as a garage, not wishing to let a good building go to waste whatever its associations with a now-dead god. Only in the Putin era were the oil stains and junk cleared out again as the building was reconverted and reconsecrated in October 2009 amid a new Russian cosiness between the sacred and (often very) profane.[26]

This experience of desecration and rehabilitation was in keeping with the Chinese history of the wider area around the embassy that I was now exploring, for this north-eastern part of old Beijing offers an unusual concentration of restored or reconstructed imperial relics. Many of these would have been well known to Beijing's modest mid-Qing Russian community of priests, Cossacks and scholars. To the west of the Russian compound are the diminutive Bolin Temple and the much grander and incense-clouded Lama Temple, where recorded messages warn passers-by not to approach fake fortune-tellers like the one I had consulted in Changchun. A little farther on, I neared the Guozijian, the old college where members of the imperial household and high officials were once educated. Here crowds of tourists raucously clustered, gathering for whirlwind assaults on this and the next-door Confucius Temple. During the Qing, Confucius witnessed plenty of venerable footfall here and, indeed, Puyi's own last ceremonial act before being unceremoniously ejected from Beijing in 1924 was a visit to the shrine of the bearded Shandong sage.

Strolling the alleys around the Guozijian and trying to imagine them through the eyes of the area's long-departed Slavic denizens, I meandered back towards the embassy. Down a leafy alley loud with chirping cicadas, the Tongjiao Temple nestled appealingly opposite a drycleaner's shop, and so I entered its high red walls, which were inscribed with the names of donors and daubed with the confessional 'I devote myself to Buddha' in 5-foot-high characters. The temple's tranquil sapling-planted courtyard with its prayer flags, potted plants and wash basins seemed a world away from the commotion of ring roads and metro stations I had just escaped. Here there was more space to reflect on the lives of the Albazinians and their descendants, whose corner of the old city had a remarkable religious cosmopolitanism with its places of Orthodox, Confucian and Buddhist worship.

For its part, Tongjiao originated as a temple for court eunuchs during the Ming dynasty, but by the Qing had become a nunnery, a status it retained well into the twentieth century when it became Beijing's primary such institution. Like the embassy's church-turned-garage, this however put it squarely in the crosshairs of state atheism, and so during the Cultural Revolution it was shut down. But again like the Russian Temple of the Dormition, and so many such sacred places across China, it has witnessed a post-1980s revival. I asked a temple steward dressed all in black what went on here now.

'Well we have nuns here again,' he said noncommittally in a thick Manchu-tinged Beijing accent.

How many?

'About twenty,' he thought.

Where were they?

'They just come in at festival time really. They work the rest of the time,' he said looking as though he greatly preferred sweeping the courtyard to speaking to nosy foreigners.

The only occasional presence of sutra-chanting devotees may disappoint tourists scouring the area for 'authenticity', but today's day-job-juggling nuns were only the latest indication of Tongjiao's many epochal transformations. This was the 'real' China much more than lives devoted solely to Buddhism would have been. As Zhengqiu had said in Changchun, the post-socialist return to religion is a pragmatic approach to spiritual emptiness after all.

The Buddhist, Confucian and Orthodox legacies clustered around Beijing's first Russian quarter, and their parallel fates under socialism, also showed how interactions between the mirror empires have often been mediated by faith in different forms. From the Catholics on each side negotiating the Treaty of Nerchinsk, to the Chinese capital's early Orthodox Mission, through to the religious fervour underlying both countries' unity in socialism, official ties have long revolved around questions of belief and devotion. Correspondingly, the Sino-Soviet schism was as fierce at times as that between Eastern Orthodoxy and Roman Catholicism—the reason Moscow could consider asserting 'Third Rome' status—1,000 years earlier. Acting in concert with the unique geographical relationship between the two places, faith has also provided a lens through which each side has observed the other, from Russian wanderings of Chinese leftists to studies of China by Russians inhabiting imperial Beijing.

Likely the most famous religious Russian resident of the Qing capital was a Chuvash monk and emissary to the Orthodox Mission Iakinf (Russian for 'Hyacinth'), Bichurin, author of an intimately detailed 1828 tome entitled *Description of Peking*. Covering everything from the construction of buildings to town planning, temples, monuments, monasteries, local banana gardens and the organisation of the military banners, the *Description* also discusses educational activities in the missionary compound, which was known as the 'Russian Hall' (Eluosi guan). This was where the children of Qing officials, three per year from each of the eight banners, were trained in Russian–Manchu translation, and, while Bichurin is uncomplimentary about the quality of instruction,[27] this institution contributed to an environment in which much knowledge was flowing back and forth. Bichurin himself is today considered a central figure in early Russian Sinology and was even lauded by the head of the Russian Orthodox Church Patriarch Kirill during a May 2013 visit to Beijing.[28]

Among the nuggets of information transmitted back to the Slavic heartlands by Bichurin's *Description* was information about the above-mentioned city walls, including florid elaboration on the entrance passages and tiered wooden crowns of its many gateways. These portals were, the monk shows, just as important for understanding the layout of the imperial capital as the metro stations and roundabouts named after them are today, and served as reference points for entire districts. It was towards one such gate-centred area—that around Chaoyangmen (Gate facing the Sun)—that my final walk in Beijing took me.

* * *

Moving eastward along what in Bichurin's time was a stone-paved road with two dough shops and the still-standing Yuan-era Daoist Dongyue Temple, I was fulfilling two goals. First, this route along the west–east crossbeam of the ancient city axis would take me through a Russian area of much newer vintage than the old Dongzhimen concession, namely Yabao Road, which is now home to most of the Chinese capital's day-to-day Sino-Russian interactions. Secondly, Yabao aptly runs between Chaoyangmen and the old imperial Altar of the Sun (Chaori tan), now the scenic Ritan Park. The latter seemed a fitting final destination for my entire journey since I had been moving throughout towards the light required to illuminate the many mirrored lives I had briefly entered. Culturally if not spatially, I had also been heading 'towards the rising sun' (*vstrech' solntsa*), a lyrical term used to describe the Russian movement into Asia.

Over a rusting footbridge, I first crossed the immense width of the Second Ring Road and descended the stairs alongside a now rarely used channel for pushing bicycles up and down. Yabao Road's name means 'elegant treasure', a politically correct whitewashing of the earlier '*Yaba hutong*'—'mute's alley' (after a possibly fictional local man)—but as I approached its ramshackle junction neither name seemed especially appropriate. Certainly not resembling a trove of elegant treasure, the place also rang with a din of shouted Chinese, Slavic and Turkic languages, and the blaring horns of cars struggling to navigate throngs of traders, three-wheeled pedal rickshaws and piles of boxes.

This was much more like the unmediated contact between populations I had seen up on the border than the officious atmosphere around the embassy, and the spectacle provided a reminder of precisely the high-paced, money-oriented lifestyle that might persuade one to become a Buddhist nun at Tongjiao Temple. Indeed, Yabao Road emerged as a centre of Sino-Russian and Sino-Central Asian (hence the Turkic languages) trade precisely as the newly religious post-Mao and post-Soviet era was beginning. In a 2012 song entitled 'Yabao Road', Beijing underground singer-songwriter Zhou Fengling muses on this connection, evoking symbols of Communist China in the reform era including 1980s cartoon characters Lan Bao'r and Lü Bao'r, Deng Xiaoping's Four Modernisations policy, and fresh fashions sweeping in from Hong Kong and Taiwan. Also central to the song's imagery is the notion of 'throwing yourself into the sea' (*xiahai*), a widely used label for entering the market- rather than the state-driven economy. Zhou describes his generation as like a tight-knit group riding the crest of a wave and thus resembles revolutionary poet Yin Fu writing of a different revolution eighty years earlier, characterising the new age as like a great cascade of water breaking over China.[29] And, while this time it was Deng's efforts to 'Reform and Open' the country rather than the collapse of the Qing dynasty or the Chinese Civil War that marked the transition, in both cases Russian arrivals heralded the changes that were afoot.

I began to walk down the road. '*IP karta, SIM karta nado?*'—need an IP card? Need a SIM card?—offered a tough-looking female Chinese vendor near the junction with Chaoyangmen South Street. I waved my hand in a movement that means 'hi' to Russians but corresponds to 'no' in East Asia. Many more such gestures proved helpful farther along Yabao Road as the pilots of the rickshaws, emblazoned with Russian advertisements for honey and Chinese advertisements for Russian lessons, insistently offered rides. Street-side signage displayed Russian and Chinese flags with the label 'KARGO' offering 'speed', 'reliability' and 'professionalism' on goods deliveries to all Russian cities. Shoving past me were broad Siberian men heaving bulging shopping bags, glamorous dyed-blonde girlfriends reeling off purchases loudly into mobile phones, and stern leather-jacketed traders from the Caucasus leading veiled wives and children through the crowds.

On the corner of an alley leading off the main thoroughfare, a Uyghur melon vendor was having an altercation with an Uzbek woman over slices of cantaloupe. Uzbek and Uyghur, closely related Central Asian languages, are Russified and Sinicised siblings, and are largely mutually intelligible. This did not help. 'We are both Muslims, are we not? I am giving you a fair price!' the thickset Uyghur man was bellowing as the woman complained at the thinness of the slices.

Next to the melon cart, Wuhe from Hebei province was standing trying to push flyers for a nearby massage parlour into the hands of the surly group of onlookers. '*Massazh nado?*'—need a massage?—he asked me.

Was he the masseur? I enquired in response.

'Sure! I know how to do it,' he said after briefly looking surprised at a 'Russian' addressing him in Chinese. 'I was in the military in Guangdong, but I hated all the army stuff and so I learnt how to be an acupuncturist instead. Then I went to Dubai and worked in a Chinese salon there. Now I'm back.'

Was business good?

'Things are better in winter,' he said. 'All the Russians come then to buy coats. But Russians also love massages. It's all legit, mind you! I have regular clients for bone treatment especially.' As in the borderlands, shopoholism was seemingly not the only ailment for which Russians sought salve here. 'The problem is,' he continued, 'the Russians are getting more cunning. Before they spent cash like crazy but with their financial crisis and they all haggle much harder now'.

Did he have any interest in going to Russia, I asked. Had Dubai given him a taste for travel?

'I'm not sure,' he said, his brow furrowing. 'I don't think I really have that many Russian contacts who could help me make the trip. Business competition is too intense here to make friends, it's every man for himself. I've been working here since 2008 but things never really let up. It's always so busy.'

Outdoor hawking like Wuhe's was one thing, but the real hub of Yabao Road's commercial activity, especially in winter when outside temperatures reach −20°C, are the bowels of its mammoth shopping centres. One boasts a cavernous inner atrium decorated with a trickling fountain and three imposing onion-domed gazebos, but most are tight warrens of corridors named 'Goya', 'Yabao Red Square' and 'Heavenly Yabao'. Mirror images of Moscow's distant Novocherkizovsky, or the neighbouring Huafu malls of Blagoveshchensk and Heihe, these exude an air of manufactured exclusivity very different from the more ramshackle furclad surrounds of Mr Zhao back in the Russian capital. Temperature-controlled boutiques with alluring names like 'Mykonos', 'Paradise' and, more confusingly, 'I love you' in Russian, lie concealed behind tinted glass walls and thick curtains. One, 'Alaska', perhaps even sought to appeal to atavistic Russian dreams of lost eastern territory, or at least hoped to imply that its coats were warm enough to be worn there. Once inside, it felt impossible to escape without a mink *shuba*, although I managed to do so.

In the basement of 'Heavenly Yabao', snatches of conversation like those heard in borderland towns could be caught down the corridors, the sound deadened by low ceilings and displays of dangling nightwear.

'Do you have this nighty in white?'

'I want green tea. No, GREEN!'

'No, no magnets! No magnets!'

'How much? *Dwo shchaw tchyen?*' another Russian customer made a token stab at Chinese, laden with thick sibilants. Chinese language competence among Yabao Road's Russians sometimes seemed better than in Manchuria, but rarely emerged with anything other than a strong accent. Slavic phonology tends to obscure Mandarin's subtler tonal distinctions.

On speaking to several shoppers, it emerged that their main concern was smooth shipping of their purchases back to Russia. An official anti-corruption drive and parallel tightening of import restrictions under Vladimir Putin has made people nervous about bringing luxury items like fur coats into the country. In the entranceway to the 'Goya' building, a large poster advertised trouble-free transport of mink, beaver, rabbit and lambswool garments to locations including Moscow, St Petersburg, Perm, Ekaterinburg, Vladivostok, Khabarovsk and Novosibirsk. A blonde Russian woman in a businesslike blue dress stood in a glass booth under the poster and I asked about its claims.

'Yes yes, it's all no problem,' she assured me. 'Everything is above-board, we have connections.' Why would connections be needed if things were above board, I wondered. My question was met with a grimace.

Before heading for the Sun Altar at the eastern end of Yabao Road, I first passed a temple of a different kind. 'Chocolate' nightclub is dedicated to the fervent leisure-time pursuits of the Russian and Central Asian clientele from the nearby shops. As I had learnt on previous visits, its hallowed interior boasts a jumbled aesthetic of gilt-framed European-style paintings attached to the ceiling at jaunty angles, and, at least in the mid-2010s, a dwarf bartender was employed to greet guests and appear on publicity shots alongside scantily clad Russian women. Nights there are filled with jaunty Russian techno-pop, shots of vodka and Armenian cognac, and a raucous atmosphere bordering on the menacing. But it was in any case much too early for any of that, so I moved on to Ritan Park a short distance farther on.

In imperial times, Iakinf Bichurin observed, this was the spot where the emperor came every two years to make sacrificial offerings to the sun, one of several calendrical processions the ruler performed along

Beijing's axes. As celestial bodies seasonally aligned—the sun ceremony occurred on the spring equinox—the emperor was borne magisterially between the palace at the centre of the city and the temples and the surrounding altars of the sun, moon, heaven and earth. In doing so, he reaffirmed his role as a being who hovered somewhere between the celestial and earthly components of Beijing's urban cosmology.

As in Bichurin's time, Ritan today retains its three western gates as well as one for each of the other compass points, and I passed under the West Heavenly Gate into the park. In imperial times, the altar was surrounded by various concentric walled compounds, but the Soviet-style urban re-imaginings of the 1950s had seen the park assume its present form as a much more open area suitable for accommodating a wider public. Now in the late summer dusk, middle-aged singers and dancers were clustered among the trees while retirees clacked chess pieces and mahjong tiles at low stone tables. I followed winding paths around a small pond, ducking under low-hanging willow branches and glimpsing pavilions atop jagged rocky promontories. Venerable plane trees sheltered an enraptured mouth organist whose amplified melodies carried plaintively across the ancient sacrificial space itself, a fenced-off expanse of marble that is only rarely opened. But modern life peeked in too, and the jagged corners of the nearby CCTV and China World Trade buildings were visible over the treetops.

As a final stop, the park offered space to contemplate the northern lands on whose edge Beijing lies, and what I had seen there. The Russians, whose shops and export offices spill out from Yabao Road into the streets around the altar, owe their presence here to an ancestral gallop towards the same sun once venerated on this site. Movement eastward over tundra and taiga, through forests and across rivers, ever towards but never reaching that celestial orb, brought steppe Cossacks into contact with a people from similar terrain. Happening to rule over their own vast empire, conquered by moving in the opposite direction, the Manchus in turn brought all of China with them to the confrontation. Observing one another with mirrored wonder, incomprehension, suspicion, admiration and many other emotions over the ensuing centuries, hirsute prospectors, ginseng outlaws, priests, philosophers, revolutionaries, imperial emissaries, converted indigenes, poets, traders, exiles, students, workers, advisors and many others have been brought face to face through the collision of worlds. The affairs of emperors, commissars, presidents and their agents have only ever been part of the story, for everyday contact between peoples so different and yet with so much in common has always been a hallmark of the mirrorlands. Reflecting, I returned through the gate and headed back west.

TIMELINE OF SINO-RUSSIAN EVENTS

1580–Late 1600s	Russian expansion across Siberia.
1613–1917	Rule of Romanov dynasty, Russia.
1632	Foundation of Yakutsk.
1640s–1760s	Chinese expansion into Mongolia and Inner Asia.
1644–1911	Rule of Qing dynasty, China.
1644	Cossacks reach the mouth of the River Amur.
1689	Signing of the Treaty of Nerchinsk.
1727	Signing of the Treaty of Kyakhta.
1858	Signing of the Treaty of Aigun, foundation of Khabarovsk.
1860	Signing of the Treaty of Peking, foundation of Vladivostok.
1890s–1930s	Mass migration of Han Chinese into Manchuria.
1890	Anton Chekhov travels across Siberia to Sakhalin.
1890–1	Future Tsar Nicholas II travels across Siberia to Japan.
1891–1916	Construction of Trans-Siberian Railway.
1897–1903	Construction of China Eastern Railway.

1911	Wuchang Uprising dethrones last Qing Emperor Puyi.
1912	Republic of China founded.
1917	February Revolution dethrones last tsar Nicholas II; October Revolution sees Bolsheviks come to power.
1920–1	Qu Qiubai travels Beijing–Moscow across Manchuria, Siberia.
1920–2	Existence of Far Eastern Republic, capital city at Chita.
1922	USSR founded.
1924	Sergei Tretyakov travels Moscow–Beijing—Japan across Siberia, Manchuria.
1925	Ethel Alec-Tweedie travels Moscow–Beijing across Siberia, Manchuria.
1926	Boris Pilnyak travels Moscow–Beijing across Siberia, Manchuria.
Late 1920s–Early 1930s	Collectivisation of Soviet agriculture under Stalin.
1931	Japanese invasion of Manchuria.
1932–45	Existence of Japanese-backed Manchukuo 'puppet state' under Puyi.
1935	Hu Yuzhi travels Moscow–Beijing across Siberia, Manchuria.
1945–50	Puyi taken prisoner in USSR.
1948	Democratic People's Republic of Korea (North Korea) founded.
1949	People's Republic of China founded.
1950	Signing of the Sino-Soviet Treaty of Friendship, Alliance and Mutual Assistance, Moscow.
1950–3	Korean War.
1953	Soviet 'experts' begin to be dispatched to China.

TIMELINE OF SINO-RUSSIAN EVENTS

1958–62	Great Leap Forward, China.
Early 1960s–Late 1980s	Sino-Soviet Split, Soviet experts withdrawn from China.
1966–76	Great Proletarian Cultural Revolution, China.
1968	Down to the Countryside Movement begins.
1969	Sino-Soviet border conflict over Zhenbao/Damansky Island, Ussuri River.
1974–99	Construction of Baikal–Amur Mainline.
2001	Signing of Treaty of Good-Neighbourliness and Friendly Cooperation between the People's Republic of China and the Russian Federation, Moscow.
2008	Signing of border agreement dividing Heixiazi/Bolshoi Ussuriisky Island between China and Russia, Beijing.

NOTES

PREFACE

1. Lermontov, Mikhail, *A Hero of Our Time*, London: Penguin Classics, 2001.
2. Blok, Alexander, *Скифы* (Scythians) from *Стихотворения. Поэмы. Воспоминания современников* (Poems, verses, memoirs of contemporaries), Moscow: Pravda, 1989, pp. 378–80.

1. MOSCOW: ASIA'S THIRD ROME

1. 'How Chinese Tourists Are Changing the World', *South China Morning Post*, 1 October 2017, http://www.scmp.com/magazines/post-magazine/long-reads/article/2113116/how-chinese-tourists-are-changing-world (last accessed 16 October 2018).
2. 'РСТ: число иностранных туристов в России за два года выросло на 25%' (RST: the number of foreign tourists in Russia has increased by 25 per cent over two years), infox.ru, 4 April 2017, https://www.infox.ru/news/216/lifestyle/travel/173550-rst-cislo-inostrannyh-turistov-v-rossii-za-dva-goda-vyroslo-na-25 (last accessed 16 October 2018).
3. Pilnyak, Boris, *Собрание сочинений т. I: Голый год* (Collected works vol. 1: *The Naked Year*), Moscow: Gosudarstvennoe izdatel'stvo, 1930, p. 55; see also pp. 203–4. The two passages are almost identical.
4. Clark, Katerina, 'Boris Pilniak and Sergei Tretiakov as Soviet Envoys to China and Japan and Forgers of New, Post-Imperial Narratives (1924–1926)', *Cross-Currents: East Asian History and Culture Review*, 28 (2018), pp. 33–4.
5. Historian Elizabeth McGuire notes that up to 10,000 young Chinese travelled to the USSR in the 1920s and '30s. See McGuire, Elizabeth, *Red at Heart: How Chinese Communists Fell in Love with the Russian Revolution*, Oxford: Oxford University Press, 2017, p. 3.
6. Ibid., pp. 39–40.

7. Qu Qiubai (瞿秋白), 饿乡纪程 (Journey to the land of hunger), Xi'an: Taibai wenyi chunabshe, 1995, p. 75.

8. Ibid., pp. 12–13.

9. Yin Fu (殷夫), '我们是年轻的布尔什维克' (We are the young Bolsheviks), in 殷夫选集 (Selected works of Yin Fu), Beijing: Renmin chubanshe, 1958, pp. 107–9.

10. Hu Yuzhi (胡愈之), 莫斯科印象记 (Impressions of Moscow), Changsha: Hunan renmin chubanshe, 1984, p. 87.

11. Wells, Herbert G., *Russia in the Shadows*, New York: George H. Doran, 1921.

12. Alec-Tweedie, Ethel, *An Adventurous Journey: Russia–Siberia–China*, London: Thornton Butterworth, 1929, p. 2.

13. Ibid., p. 4.

14. Ibid., p. 6.

15. Qu op. cit., pp. 76–77.

16. Ibid., pp. 81–2.

17. Hu op. cit., p. 22.

18. Lenin, Vladimir I., *Борьба партий в Китае* (The party struggle in China), published in *Pravda*, 3 May 1913, available at https://lenin-ism.su/works/61-tom-23/2337-borba-partii-v-kitae.html (last accessed 16 October 2018).

19. Guf (Aleksei Sergeevich Dolmatov), 'Кто как играет' (Who is playing and how), track 2 from the album *Город дорог* (City of roads), Moscow: Monolit Records, 2007.

2. MULTI-ETHNIC SIBERIA: THE EAST WITHIN

1. 'Китайцы признали «Аэрофлот» любимой иностранной авиако-мпанией' (The Chinese have named Aeroflot their favourite foreign airline), Lenta.ru, 11 April 2017, https://lenta.ru/news/2017/04/11/aeroflot_chinalove/ (last accessed 16 October 2018).

2. March, G. Patrick, *Eastern Destiny: Russia in Asia and the North Pacific*, Westport: Greenwood Publishing Group, 1996.

3. 'Vladimir Putin: Ethnic Russian Nationalist', *Washington Post*, 19 March 2014, https://www.washingtonpost.com/news/monkey-cage/wp/2014/03/19/vladimir-putin-ethnic-russian-nationalist/?utm_term=.54171b1d405d (last accessed 16 October 2018).

4. 'Ever Wonder Why Vladimir Putin Doesn't Age? We Asked Some Cosmetic Surgeons', *National Post*, 27 April 2017, https://nationalpost.com/news/ever-wonder-why-vladimir-putin-doesnt-age-we-asked-some-cosmetic-surgeons (last accessed 16 October 2018).

5. 'Вспоминая ходя: Китайцы и корейцы старого Якутска' (Remembering the huojia: the Chinese and Koreans of old Yakutsk),

Yakutsk vechernii, 4 August 2017, https://www.yakutskhistory.net/корреспонденции/владимир-попов/китайцы-и-корейцы-якутска/ (last accessed 16 October 2018).

6. Ibid.
7. 'В Якутии ФСБ изъяла у граждан Китая золото и платину на 8 млн рублей' (In Yakutia, the FSB confiscated 8 million roubles-worth of gold and platinum from a Chinese man), RIA Novosti, 9 March 2016, https://ria.ru/incidents/20160309/1387195965.html (last accessed 16 October 2018).
8. 'Мост через Лену могут построить китайцы без проведения конкурса' (The Chinese may build the bridge over the Lena with no tender process), *Vedomosti*, 16 October 2015, https://www.vedomosti.ru/realty/news/2015/10/16/613180-most-cherez-lenu (last accessed 16 October 2018).
9. 'Мост через Лену: японские технологии для общего дела' (Bridge over the Lena: Japanese technology for a common project), News.Ykt.Ru, 17 July 2017, http://news.ykt.ru/article/59622 (last accessed 16 October 2018).

3. SIBERIA'S RAILWAYS: EURASIAN ARTERIES

1. Arnold, Bradley, 'Soviet Views on Mao and Maoism', *Studies in Soviet Thought*, 12 (1972), pp. 77–89.
2. Ward, Christopher, *Brezhnev's Folly: The Building of BAM and Late Soviet Socialism*, Pittsburgh: University of Pittsburgh Press, 2009, p. 80.
3. Etkind, Alexander, *Internal Colonization: Russia's Imperial Experience*, Cambridge: Polity, 2011.
4. While Alexander Solzhenitsyn is much the best-known GULAG writer in the West, Varlam Shalamov provides a more profound and powerful commentary on the institution. See Shalamov, Varlam, *Kolyma Tales*, London: Penguin, 1995.
5. 'Russian Soviet-Era Remembrance Group Memorial Risks Closure', BBC, 30 October 2014, http://www.bbc.com/news/world-europe-29831134 (last accessed 16 October 2018).
6. 'Russian Energy Dispute: Could Gazprom's $400Bn Gas Pipeline to China Be Postponed?', Breaking Energy, 24 March 2015, https://breakingenergy.com/2015/03/24/russian-energy-dispute-could-gazproms-400bn-gas-pipeline-to-china-be-postponed/ (last accessed 16 October 2018).
7. 'China Deepens Oil Ties with Russia in $9 Billion Rosneft Deal', Bloomberg, 9 September 2017, https://www.bloomberg.com/news/articles/2017-09-08/china-s-cefc-buys-stake-in-rosneft-from-glencore-and-qatar (last accessed 16 October 2018).

8. Allan, Pierre and Albert A. Stahel, 'Tribal Guerrilla Warfare against a Colonial Power: Analyzing the War in Afghanistan', *The Journal of Conflict Resolution*, 27, 4 (1983), pp. 590–617.

9. Tretyakov, Sergei, 'Москва–Пекин (Путьфильма)' (Moscow–Beijing (a filmic journey))', *ЛЕФ: Журнал Левого фронта искусств* (LEF: journal of the left front of the arts), 3, 7 (1925), pp. 33–58.

10. Ibid., pp. 34–6.

11. Hu Yuzhi (胡愈之), 莫斯科印象记 (Impressions of Moscow), Changsha: Hunan renmin chubanshe, 1984, 118.

12. Ibid., pp. 21–2.

13. Tretyakov op. cit., pp. 37–40.

14. Qu Qiubai (瞿秋白), 饿乡纪程 (Journey to the land of hunger), Xi'an: Taibai wenyi chunabshe, 1995, pp. 49, 74.

15. Ibid., p. 8.

16. Alec-Tweedie, Ethel, *An Adventurous Journey: Russia–Siberia–China*, London: Thornton Butterworth, 1929, p. 38.

17. Ibid., p. 43.

18. Ibid., pp. 46–7.

19. Forsyth, James, *A History of the Peoples of Siberia: Russia's North Asian Colony, 1581–1990*, Cambridge: Cambridge University Press, 1994, p. 98.

20. Widmer, Eric, *The Russian Ecclesiastical Mission in Peking during the Eighteenth Century*, Cambridge, MA: Harvard University Press, 1976, p. 12.

21. Chekhov, Anton, letter no. 837, 20 June 1890, aboard the steamer *Yermak* on the River Shilka. From *Полное собрание сочинений и писем в 30 т.* (Complete collection of compositions and letters in thirty volumes), vol. 4: letters, January 1890–February 1892, Moscow: Nauka, 1975, pp. 116–19.

22. Ibid., pp. 116–19.

23. Tretyakov op. cit., p. 44.

24. Ibid., p. 45.

25. 'Economics Professor Has Solution for China's Millions of Bachelors: Let Them Share Wives, or Even Marry Each Other', *South China Morning Post*, 22 October 2015, https://www.scmp.com/news/china/society/article/1871096/economics-professor-has-solution-chinas-millions-bachelors-let (last accessed 23 November 2018).

4. INNER MONGOLIA'S LOST RUSSIANS: RUSSIA ON CHINESE TERMS

1. Alec-Tweedie, Ethel, *An Adventurous Journey: Russia–Siberia–China*, London: Thornton Butterworth, 1929, p. 64.

2. Official data reported that Chinese people made a total of 4.44 billion domestic trips in 2016 alone; the industry is growing at around 10 to 15 per cent annually. See 'China's Domestic Tourism Growing Faster than Outbound Traffic in H1 2017', China Travel News, 20 August 2017, https://www.chinatravelnews.com/article/116748 (last accessed 16 October 2018).

3. Pilnyak, Boris, *Письма: В 2 т. Том II: 1923–1937* (Letters in two volumes, vol. 2: 1923–36), Moscow: IMPLI RAN, 2010, pp. 257–8.

4. Tretyakov, Sergei, 'Москва–Пекин (Путьфильма)' (Moscow–Beijing (a filmic journey))', *ЛЕФ: Журнал Левого фронта искусств* (LEF: journal of the left front of the arts), 3, 7 (1925), p. 46.

5. Qu Qiubai (瞿秋白), 饿乡纪程 (Journey to the land of hunger), Xi'an: Taibai wenyi chunabshe, 1995, p. 51.

6. '苏联代印人民币内幕' (Behind the scenes of the Soviet Union's RMB printing), People's Daily Online, 17 August 2006, http://politics.people.com.cn/GB/1026/4711165.html (last accessed 16 October 2018).

7. Zou Yu (邹玉) (ed.), 蒙兀神地 额尔古纳 (E'erguna: holy place of the Mongols), Hohhot: Neimenggu renmin chubanshe, 2010, p. 21.

8. Dong Xianrui (董宪瑞) and Yan Guangqing (闫广庆), 额尔古纳俄罗斯族 (E'erguna's ethnic Russians), Zhuhai: Zhuhai langman zhi cheng xilie chubanshe, 2013, pp. 3–9.

9. Bassin, Mark, *Imperial Visions: Nationalist Imagination and Geographical Expansion in the Russian Far East, 1840–1865*, Cambridge: Cambridge University Press, 1999.

10. Gottschang, Thomas and Diana Lary, *Swallows and Settlers: The Great Migration from North China to Manchuria*, Ann Arbor: University of Michigan Press, 2000, pp. 2–3.

11. Dong and Yan op. cit., pp. 7–8.

5. THE RUSSIAN FAR EAST: AN EMPTYING BREADBASKET

1. Bassin, Mark, *Imperial Visions: Nationalist Imagination and Geographical Expansion in the Russian Far East, 1840–1865*, Cambridge: Cambridge University Press, 1999, p. 176.

2. Chekhov, Anton, letter no. 844, 27 June 1890, in Blagoveshchensk. From *Полное собрание сочинений и писем в 30 т.* (Complete collection of compositions and letters in thirty volumes), vol. 4: letters January 1890–February 1892, Moscow: Nauka, 1975, pp. 126–8.

3. Bassin op. cit., p. 202.

4. Engels, Friedrich, 'Russia's Successes in the Far East', *New-York Daily Tribune*, 18 November 1858, http://marxengels.public-archive.net/en/ME1094en.html#N65 (last accessed 16 October 2018).

5. Bassin op. cit., p. 240.

6. Lattimore, Owen, 'The Gold Tribe, "Fishskin Tatars" of the Lower Sungari', *Memoirs of the American Anthropological Association*, 40 (1933).

7. Dyatlov, Viktor, '"The Blagoveshchensk Utopia": Historical Memory and Historical Responsibility', *Sensus Historiae*, VIII, 3 (2012).

8. Chekhov op. cit., pp. 126–8.

9. Ibid., p. 128.

10. 'Chinese Nationalism Flares Up Ahead of Xi's Visit to Russia', *South China Morning Post*, 20 March 2013, https://www.scmp.com/news/china/article/1195286/chinese-nationalism-flares-ahead-xis-visit-russia (last accessed 16 October 2018).

11. Although officially completed in 2017, cosmodrome construction was dogged by protests amid failures to pay workers. See 'Две тысячи строителей космодрома Восточный уволят' (2,000 construction workers on the Vostochnyi cosmodrome fired), Lenta News, 14 December 2017, https://lenta.ru/news/2017/12/14/ne_jili_bogato/ (last accessed 16 October 2018).

12. 'Meet the People Who Still Live in Russian Ghost Towns', *Russia Beyond*, 5 February 2013, https://www.rbth.com/travel/2013/02/05/life_goes_on_in_russian_ghost_towns_22505.html (last accessed 23 November 2018).

13. Wolff, David, *To the Harbin Station: The Liberal Alternative in Russian Manchuria 1898–1914*, Stanford: Stanford University Press, 1999, p. 102.

14. '«Рубикон» переходит к стыковке' (Rubikon comes into dock), EastRussia.ru, 14 June 2016, https://www.eastrussia.ru/material/rubikon-perekhodit-k-stykovke/ (last accessed 16 October 2018).

15. Chekhov, Anton, letter no. 4402, 13 April 1904, in Yalta. From *Полное собрание сочинений и писем в 30 т.* (Complete collection of compositions and letters in thirty volumes), vol. 12: letters 1904. Moscow: Nauka, 1983.

16. Seabright, Paul (ed.), *The Vanishing Rouble: Barter Networks and Non-monetary Transactions in Post-Soviet Societies*, Cambridge: Cambridge University Press, 2000.

17. Du Halde, Jean-Baptiste, *Description géographique, historique, chronologique, politique, et physique de l'empire de la Chine et de la Tartarie chinoise*, Paris: Le Mercier, 1735.

18. Slezkine, Yuri, *Arctic Mirrors: Russia and the Small Peoples of the North*, Ithaca NY: Cornell University Press, 1994.

19. Turaev, V. A. et al., *История и культура нанайцев: историко-этнографические очерки* (History and culture of the Nanai: historical and ethnographic sketches), St Petersburg: Nauka, 2003.

20. 'Под Хабаровском создают музей на секретной родине Ким Чен

Ира' (Outside Khabarovsk a museum is being built in the secret hometown of Kim Jong Il), Vostokmedia.com, 20 May 2015, http:// www.vostokmedia.com/n238313.html (last accessed 16 October 2018).

21. Ancha, D. A. and N. G. Miz, *Китайская диаспора во Владивостоке: страницы истории* (The Chinese diaspora in Vladivostok: pages of history), Vladivostok: Dal'nauka, 2015, p. 7.

22. Pilnyak, Boris, *Письма: В 2 т. Том II: 1923–1937* (Letters in two volumes, vol. 2: 1923–36), Moscow: IMPLI RAN, 2010, pp. 515–16.

6. THE GREAT NORTHERN WILDERNESS: MANCHURIAN AMUR

1. Kradin, Nikolai, *Харбин—Русская Атлантида: Страницы истории Харбина, бывшего русского города в Китае* (Harbin—Russian Atlantis: pages of history from Harbin, the former Russian city in China). Khabarovsk: Khabarovskaia gorodskaia tipografiia, 2010, p. 14.

2. Tretyakov, Sergei, 'Москва–Пекин (Путьфильма)' (Moscow–Beijing (a filmic journey))', *ЛЕФ: Журнал Левого фронта искусств* (LEF: journal of the left front of the arts), 3, 7 (1925), p. 43.

3. Hu Yuzhi (胡愈之), 莫斯科印象记 (Impressions of Moscow), Changsha: Hunan renmin chubanshe, 1984, p. 83.

4. The Chinese reads: '在一个乡里进行合作化规划的经验'. From: '青年是整个社会力量中最积极最有生气的力量' (The youth are the group where society's strength is most active and vigorous), People's Daily Online, http:// dangshi.people.com.cn/GB/242358/242773/242775/17735071.html (last accessed 26 October 2018).

5. For a description of the recent changes undergone by farms like this, see Meyer, Michael, *In Manchuria: A Village Called Wasteland and the Transformation of Rural China*, London: Bloomsbury, 2015.

6. Hu op. cit., p. 55.

7. On Russia, see Slezkine op. cit.; on China, see Harrell, Stevan (ed.), *Cultural Encounters on China's Ethnic Frontiers*, Seattle, WA: University of Washington Press, 1995.

8. Balmasov, Sergei, *Белоэмигранты на военной службе в Китае* (White emigrants in military service in China), Moscow: Tsentrpoligraf, 2007.

9. Lattimore, Owen, 'The Gold Tribe, "Fishskin Tatars" of the Lower Sungari', *Memoirs of the American Anthropological Association*, 40 (1933).

10. Yang Jisheng (杨继绳), *Tombstone: The Great Chinese Famine, 1958–1962*, London: Allen Lane, 2012.

11. 'Country's Oldest Car Marque to Rise Again, Launch Next Era', *China Daily*, 15 January 2018, http://www.chinadaily.com.cn/a/201801/15/WS5a5c4268a3102c394518f474.html (last accessed 31 October 2018).

7. HARBIN: EURASIAN ATLANTIS

1. Wolff, David, *To the Harbin Station: The Liberal Alternative in Russian Manchuria 1898–1914*, Stanford: Stanford University Press, 1999, p. 15.

2. Fu Tingqi (傅庭起) and Dong Yuqin (董玉琴), 哈尔滨旧影大光 (A grand view of old Harbin), Harbin: Heilongjiang renmin chubanshe, 2005, p. 16.

3. Kradin, Nikolai, *Харбин—Русская Атлантида: Страницы истории Харбина, бывшего русского города в Китае* (Harbin—Russian Atlantis: pages of history from Harbin, the former Russian city in China), Khabarovsk: Khabarovskaia gorodskaia tipografiia, 2010, pp. 19–20.

4. Pilnyak, Boris, *Письма: В 2 т, Том II: 1923–1937* (Letters in two volumes, vol. 2: 1923–36), Moscow: IMPLI RAN, 2010, p. 258.

5. Wolff op. cit., p. 35.

6. Pan Guxi (潘谷西) (ed.), 中国建筑史 (History of Chinese architecture), Beijing: Zhongguo jianzhu gongye chubanshe, 2014, p. 423; Kradin op. cit., pp. 187–204.

7. Wolff op. cit., p. 18.

8. Kradin op. cit., p. 284.

9. Alec-Tweedie, Ethel, *An Adventurous Journey: Russia–Siberia–China*, London: Thornton Butterworth, 1929, p. 66.

10. Kradin op. cit., p. 5.

11. Fu and Dong op. cit., p. 1.

12. Kradin op. cit., p. 18.

13. Ibid., pp. 8, 18.

14. Fu and Dong op. cit., pp. 36, 46, 84.

15. Ibid., p. 90.

16. Ibid., p. 224.

17. Qu Qiubai (瞿秋白), 饿乡纪程 (Journey to the land of hunger), Xi'an: Taibai wenyi chunabshe, 1995, p. 35.

18. Pilnyak op. cit., p. 257.

19. Kradin op. cit., p. 49.

20. Qu op. cit., p. 32.

21. Ibid., p. 43.

22. Tretyakov, Sergei, 'Москва–Пекин (Путьфильма)' (Moscow–Beijing (a filmic journey))', *ЛЕФ: Журнал Левого фронта искусств* (LEF: journal of the left front of the arts), 3, 7 (1925), pp. 48–9.

23. 'История торговой империи «ЧУРИН И Ко»' (History of the 'Churin & Co.' trade empire), Old Vladivostok, http://oldvladivostok.ru/articles/?a=259&s=123 (last accessed 31 October 2018).

24. Wolff op. cit., p. 97.

25. Kradin op. cit., p. 290.
26. Ibid., p. 85.
27. Wolff op. cit., p. 85.
28. Balmasov, Sergei, *Белоэмигранты на военной службе в Китае* (White emigrants in military service in China), Moscow: Tsentrpoligraf, 2007.
29. Kradin op. cit., pp. 292–3.
30. Elliott, Mark, *The Manchu Way: The Eight Banners and Ethnic Identity in Late Imperial China*, Stanford, CA: Stanford University Press, 2001.

8. SOUTHERN MANCHURIA: ISLANDS OF THE IN-BETWEEN

1. Goncharov, Sergei, John Lewis and Xue Litai, *Uncertain Partners: Stalin, Mao, and the Korean War*, Stanford, CA: Stanford University Press 1993, pp. 213, 263.
2. Lankov, Andrei, *Crisis in North Korea: The Failure of De-Stalinization, 1956*, Honolulu, HI: University of Hawai'i Press, 2007.
3. McGuire, Elizabeth, *Red at Heart: How Chinese Communists Fell in Love with the Russian Revolution*, Oxford: Oxford University Press, 2017, pp. 233–47.
4. Galenovich, Iurii, *Великий Мао: Гений и злодейство* (The great Mao: genius and villainy). Moscow: Eksmo, 2012.
5. Park, Hyun-Gwi, *The Displacement of Borders among Russian Koreans in Northeast Asia*, Amsterdam: Amsterdam University Press, 2017.
6. Khan, Valeriy, *Корё сарам: кто мы?* (Koryŏ saram: who are we?), Bishkek: Izdatel'skii Tsentr 'Arkhi', 2009.
7. Fahy, Sandra, *Marching through Suffering: Loss and Survival in North Korea*, New York: Columbia University Press, 2015.
8. 'North Korea Sentences Two US Journalists to 12 Years in Jail', *The Guardian*, 8 June 2009, https://www.theguardian.com/world/2009/jun/08/north-korea-us-journalists (last accessed 31 October 2018).
9. '朝鲜逃兵枪杀4名中国人细节披露' (Details revealed about defecting North Korean soldier who shot four Chinese people dead), *People's Daily*, 6 January 2015, http://world.people.com.cn/n/2015/0106/c157278-26334226.html (last accessed 31 October 2018).
10. '"Like Prisoners of War": North Korean Labour behind Russia 2018 World Cup', *The Observer*, 4 June 2017, https://www.theguardian.com/football/2017/jun/04/like-prisoners-of-war-north-korean-labour-russia-world-cup-st-petersburg-stadium-zenit-arena (last accessed 31 October 2018).
11. Zakharova, Liudmila, 'Economic Cooperation between Russia and North Korea: New Goals and New Approaches', *Journal of Eurasian Studies*, 7, 2 (2016), pp. 151–61.

12. Thanks to Jon Cheng for pointing out the pre-Mao origins of this saying.
13. Matveev, N. P., *Краткий исторический очерк г. Владивостока* (Short historical study of the city of Vladivostok), Vladivostok: Rubezh, 2012, p. 65.
14. Scott, James, *The Art of Not Being Governed: An Anarchist History of Upland Southeast Asia*, New Haven, CT: Yale University Press, 2009.
15. Wolff, David, *To the Harbin Station: The Liberal Alternative in Russian Manchuria 1898–1914*, Stanford: Stanford University Press, 1999, p. 20.
16. Luo Binji (骆宾基), 边陲线上 (On the borderline), Changchun: Jilin renmin chubanshe, 1984 [1937].
17. Qu Qiubai (瞿秋白), 饿乡纪程 (Journey to the land of hunger), Xi'an: Taibai wenyi chunabshe, 1995, pp. 30–2.
18. Tretyakov, Sergei, 'Москва–Пекин (Путьфильма)' (Moscow–Beijing (a filmic journey))', *ЛЕФ: Журнал Левого фронта искусств* (LEF: journal of the left front of the arts), 3, 7 (1925), p. 51.
19. Alec-Tweedie, Ethel, *An Adventurous Journey: Russia–Siberia–China*, London: Thornton Butterworth, 1929, p. 95.
20. Li Lifu (李立夫) (ed.), 末代皇帝溥仪在苏联 (Late Emperor Puyi in the Soviet Union), Tianjin: Tianjin renmin chubanshe, 2011, pp. 136–7.
21. Ibid., p. 5.
22. Ibid., pp. 8–9.
23. 'Геннадий Константинов: Путевые заметки по Китаю' (Gennadii Konstantinov: travel notes from China'), Debri-DV.com, 25 December 2011, http://debri-dv.com/article/4757 (last accessed 31 October 2018); 'Где жил Пу И?' (Where did Puyi live?), MK.ru Khabarovsk, 13 February 2012, http://hab.mk.ru/articles/2012/02/13/671116-gde-zhil-pu-i.html (last accessed 31 October 2018).
24. Levine, Steven, *Anvil of Victory: The Communist Revolution in Manchuria, 1945–1948*, New York: Columbia University Press, 1987.
25. Li op. cit., p. 139.
26. Ibid., pp. 129, 140.
27. Ibid., p. 2.

9. BEIJING: REVOLUTIONARY CITY OF THE STEPPE KHANS

1. 'Здесь вам не Москва: 10 причин перенести столицу в Сибирь' (It's not Moscow here: ten reasons to move the capital to Siberia), NGS.Novosti, 21 August 2017, http://news.ngs.ru/articles/51012651/ (last accessed 31 October 2018).
2. 'Куда переносить столицу России?' (Where should Russia's capital

be moved to?), *Svobodnaia Pressa*, 13 February 2011, https://svpressa.ru/politic/article/38865/ (last accessed 31 October 2018).

3. 'Move Russia's Capital from Moscow to Siberia?', *Voice of America*, 6 May 2012, https://blogs.voanews.com/russia-watch/2012/05/06/move-russias-capital-from-moscow-to-siberia/ (last accessed 31 October 2018).

4. 'Rumor Says China Will Move Capital from Beijing in 2016', *Business Insider*, 15 February 2013, http://www.businessinsider.com/china-to-move-capital-to-xinyang-2013–2 (last accessed 31 October 2018).

5. Wadley, Stephen, 'Altaic Influences on Beijing Dialect: The Manchu Case', *Journal of the American Oriental Society*, 116, 1 (January–March 1996), pp. 99–104.

6. Tretyakov, Sergei, 'Москва–Пекин (Путьфильма)' (Moscow–Beijing (a filmic journey))', *ЛЕФ: Журнал Левого фронта искусств* (LEF: journal of the left front of the arts), 3, 7 (1925), p. 58.

7. Chudodeev, Iurii, *На китайской земле: воспоминания Советских добровольцев 1925–1945* (On Chinese soil: memoirs of Soviet volunteers 1925–45), Moscow: Nauka, 1974.

8. Zou Deyi (邹德侬) (ed.), 中国现代建筑二十讲 (Twenty essays on modern Chinese architecture), Beijing: The Commercial Press, 2015, pp. 148–62.

9. Pan Guxi (潘谷西) (ed.), 中国建筑史 (History of Chinese architecture), Beijing: Zhongguo jianzhu gongye chubanshe, 2014, p. 504.

10. Ibid., p. 434.

11. Ibid., p. 436.

12. '天安门广场的石头，原来出自这里!' (Tiananmen Square's stone originally came from here!), *China Hightech*, 8 July 2016, http://www.china-hightech.com/html/Info/shenghuo/2016/0708/331940.html (last accessed 31 October 2018).

13. Zou op. cit., p. 151.

14. Ibid., p. 152.

15. Heinzig, Dieter, *The Soviet Union and Communist China 1945–1950: The Arduous Road to the Alliance*, Armonk, NY: M. E. Sharpe, 2004.

16. Qu Qiubai (瞿秋白), 饿乡纪程 (Journey to the land of hunger), Xi'an: Taibai wenyi chunabshe, 1995, pp. 12–13.

17. Ibid., p. 14.

18. Alec-Tweedie, Ethel, *An Adventurous Journey: Russia–Siberia–China*, London: Thornton Butterworth, 1929, p. 178.

19. Yin Fu (殷夫), 殷夫选集 (Selected works of Yin Fu), Beijing: Renmin chubanshe, 1958, pp. 97–8.

20. Kaple, Deborah, 'Soviet Advisors in China in the 1950s', in Westad, Odd Arne (ed.), *Brothers in Arms: The Rise and Fall of the Sino-Soviet Alliance, 1945–1963*, Stanford, CA: Stanford University Press, 1998.

21. Salisbury, Harrison, *War between Russia and China*, New York: Norton, 1969.
22. 'Beijing's Underground City', China.org, 15 April 2005, http://www.china.org.cn/english/travel/125961.htm (last accessed 31 October 2018).
23. Widmer, Eric, *The Russian Ecclesiastical Mission in Peking during the Eighteenth Century*, Cambridge, MA: Harvard University Press, 1976, pp. 9–10.
24. Ibid., pp. 14, 20–1.
25. Alec-Tweedie op. cit., p. 169.
26. 'Успенский храм в Пекине' (The Assumption Church in Beijing), Orthodox.cn, November 2009, http://www.orthodox.cn/contemporary/beijing/dormition_ru.htm (last accessed 31 October 2018).
27. Bichurin, Iakinf, *Описание Пекина* (Description of Peking), St Petersburg: A. Smirdin, 1829, p. 69.
28. 'His Holiness Patriarch Kirill: China Came to the Knowledge of Russia through Russian Orthodox Mission', PravMir.ru, 13 May 2013, http://www.pravmir.com/his-holiness-patriarch-kirill-china-came-to-the-knowledge-of-russia-through-russian-orthodox-mission/ (last accessed 31 October 2018).
29. Zhou Fengling (周凤岭), '雅宝路' (Yabao road), track 1 from the album 雅宝路 (*Yabao Road*), Beijing: Modernsky Records, 2012.

ACKNOWLEDGEMENTS

My thanks go mainly to the people I met and spoke to while meandering between their countries on the journey described in this book. Before this, teachers and friends at Wuhan and Xinjiang Universities in China, Far Eastern National University in Vladivostok, and the catchily named St Petersburg State Polytechnic University in Russia introduced me to many of the authors, words and ideas that helped me attain my still-imperfect understanding of their worlds. Longer ago still, James Marson told me to read Mikhail Lermontov's *A Hero of Our Time*, a recommendation that has a lot to answer for. As mentors and advisors of unmatched expertise, wisdom, experience and energy, both Jana Howlett and Caroline Humphrey have inspired me far beyond the academic context in which I had the privilege to learn from them.

Zooming back up to nearer times and Seoul, South Korea, where this project eventually took decisive shape, my thanks go to friends who were encouraging or at least sounded convincingly interested between mouthfuls of IPA or fried chicken, including James Pearson, Jon Cheng, Andray Abrahamian, Dan Tudor, Alek Sigley, Peter Ward and 예지. It came late in the game, but I'm grateful too to Edward Tyerman for tips on Sino-Russian voyagers of a century ago. At Hurst, thanks to Michael Dwyer, Lara Weisweiller-Wu, Farhaana Arefin, Alison Alexanian and Daisy Leitch for making me think this book could actually exist and then ensuring that it did so. The Japan Society for the Promotion of Science allowed me to pay rent and buy soup curry to live as I rounded off the project.

James and Dids, my own mirror-siblings, read some earlier bits of the text and offered ideal tips and encouragement. They and Mum,

ACKNOWLEDGEMENTS

Dave, Sarah and William have always been an anchor during any number of difficult-to-explain Eurasian travels, and their love and understanding give me the confidence to go to places and try to reach new understandings of my own. This book, and a lot of what I do in a roundabout and inarticulable way, is for them.

BIBLIOGRAPHY

Alec-Tweedie, Ethel, *An Adventurous Journey: Russia–Siberia–China*, London: Thornton Butterworth, 1929.

Allan, Pierre and Albert A. Stahel, 'Tribal Guerrilla Warfare against a Colonial Power: Analyzing the War in Afghanistan', *The Journal of Conflict Resolution*, 27, 4 (1983).

Ancha, D. A. and N. G. Miz, *Китайская диаспора во Владивостоке: страницы истории* (The Chinese diaspora in Vladivostok: pages of history), Vladivostok: Dal'nauka, 2015.

Arnold, Bradley, 'Soviet Views on Mao and Maoism', *Studies in Soviet Thought*, 12 (1972).

Balmasov, Sergei, *Белоэмигранты на военной службе в Китае* (White emigrants in military service in China), Moscow: Tsentrpoligraf, 2007.

Bassin, Mark, *Imperial Visions: Nationalist Imagination and Geographical Expansion in the Russian Far East, 1840–1865*, Cambridge: Cambridge University Press, 1999.

Bichurin, Iakinf, *Описание Пекина* (Description of Peking), St. Petersburg: A. Smirdin, 1829.

Blok, Alexander, *Скифы* (Scythians), from *Стихотворения. Поэмы. Воспоминания современников* (Poems, verses, memoirs of contemporaries), Moscow: Pravda, 1989.

Chekhov, Anton, *Полное собрание сочинений и писем в 30 т.* (Complete collection of compositions and letters in thirty volumes), vol. 4: letters January 1890–February 1892, Moscow: Nauka, 1975.

———— *Полное собрание сочинений и писем в 30 т.* (Complete collection of compositions and letters in thirty volumes), vol. 12: letters 1904, Moscow: Nauka, 1983.

Chudodeev, Iurii, *На китайской земле: воспоминания Советских добровольцев 1925–1945* (On Chinese soil: memoirs of Soviet volunteers 1925–45), Moscow: Nauka, 1974.

BIBLIOGRAPHY

Clark, Katerina, 'Boris Pilniak and Sergei Tretiakov as Soviet Envoys to China and Japan and Forgers of New, Post-Imperial Narratives (1924–1926)', *Cross-Currents: East Asian History and Culture Review*, 28 (2018).

Du Halde, Jean-Baptiste, *Description géographique, historique, chronologique, politique, et physique de l'empire de la Chine et de la Tartarie chinoise*, Paris: Le Mercier, 1735.

Elliott, Mark, *The Manchu Way: The Eight Banners and Ethnic Identity in Late Imperial China*, Stanford, CA: Stanford University Press, 2001.

Etkind, Alexander, *Internal Colonization: Russia's Imperial Experience*, Cambridge: Polity, 2011.

Fahy, Sandra, *Marching through Suffering: Loss and Survival in North Korea*, New York: Columbia University Press, 2015.

Forsyth, James, *A History of the Peoples of Siberia: Russia's North Asian Colony, 1581–1990*, Cambridge: Cambridge University Press, 1994.

Fu Tingqi (傅庭起) and Dong Yuqin (董玉琴), 哈尔滨旧影大光 (A grand view of old Harbin), Harbin: Heilongjiang renmin chubanshe, 2005.

Ghosh, Amitav, *The Shadow Lines*, London: Black Swan, 1989.

Goncharov, Sergei, John Lewis and Xue Litai, *Uncertain Partners: Stalin, Mao, and the Korean War*, Stanford, CA: Stanford University Press, 1993.

Gottschang, Thomas and Diana Lary, *Swallows and Settlers: The Great Migration from North China to Manchuria*, Ann Arbor: University of Michigan Press, 2000.

Harrell, Stevan (ed.), *Cultural Encounters on China's Ethnic Frontiers*, Seattle, WA: University of Washington Press, 1995.

Heinzig, Dieter, *The Soviet Union and Communist China 1945–1950: The Arduous Road to the Alliance*, Armonk, NY: M. E. Sharpe, 2004.

Hu Yuzhi (胡愈之), 莫斯科印象记 (Impressions of Moscow), Changsha: Hunan renmin chubanshe, 1984.

Kaple, Deborah, 'Soviet Advisors in China in the 1950s', in Westad, Odd Arne (ed.), *Brothers in Arms: The Rise and Fall of the Sino-Soviet Alliance, 1945–1963*, Stanford, CA: Stanford University Press, 1998.

Khan, Valeriy, *Корё сарам: кто мы?* (Koryŏ saram: who are we?), Bishkek: Izdatel'skii Tsentr 'Arkhi', 2009.

Kradin, Nikolai, *Харбин—Русская Атлантида: Страницы истории Харбина, бывшего русского города в Китае* (Harbin—Russian Atlantis: pages of history from Harbin, the former Russian city in China), Khabarovsk: Khabarovskaia gorodskaia tipografiia, 2010.

Lankov, Andrei, *Crisis in North Korea: The Failure of De-Stalinization, 1956*, Honolulu, HI: University of Hawai'i Press, 2007.

Lattimore, Owen, 'The Gold Tribe, "Fishskin Tatars" of the Lower Sungari', *Memoirs of the American Anthropological Association*, 40 (1933).

Lermontov, Mikhail, *A Hero of Our Time*, London: Penguin Classics, 2001.

BIBLIOGRAPHY

Levine, Steven, *Anvil of Victory: The Communist Revolution in Manchuria, 1945–1948*, New York: Columbia University Press, 1987.

Li Lifu (李立夫) (ed.), 末代皇帝溥仪在苏联 (Late Emperor Puyi in the Soviet Union), Tianjin: Tianjin renmin chubanshe, 2011.

Luo Binji (骆宾基), 边陲线上 (On the borderline), Changchun: Jilin renmin chubanshe, 1984 [1937].

March, G. Patrick, *Eastern Destiny: Russia in Asia and the North Pacific*, Westport: Greenwood Publishing Group, 1996.

Matveev, N. P., *Краткий исторический очерк г. Владивостока* (Short historical study of the city of Vladivostok), Vladivostok: Rubezh, 2012.

McGuire, Elizabeth, *Red at Heart: How Chinese Communists Fell in Love with the Russian Revolution*, Oxford: Oxford University Press, 2017.

Meyer, Michael, *In Manchuria: A Village Called Wasteland and the Transformation of Rural China*, London: Bloomsbury, 2015.

Pan Guxi (潘谷西) (ed.), 中国建筑史 (History of Chinese architecture), Beijing: Zhongguo jianzhu gongye chubanshe, 2014.

Park, Hyun-Gwi, *The Displacement of Borders among Russian Koreans in Northeast Asia*, Amsterdam: Amsterdam University Press, 2017.

Pilnyak, Boris, *Письма: В 2 т. Том II: 1923–1937* (Letters in two volumes, vol. 2: 1923–36), Moscow: IMPLI RAN, 2010.

——— *Собрание сочинений т. I: Голый год* (Collected works vol. 1: *The Naked Year*), Moscow and Leningrad: Gosudarstvennoe izdatel'stvo, 1930.

Qu Qiubai (瞿秋白), 饿乡纪程 (Journey to the land of hunger), Xi'an: Taibai wenyi chunabshe, 1995.

Salisbury, Harrison, *War between Russia and China*, New York: Norton, 1969.

Scott, James, *The Art of Not Being Governed: An Anarchist History of Upland Southeast Asia*, New Haven, CT: Yale University Press, 2009.

Seabright, Paul (ed.), *The Vanishing Rouble: Barter Networks and Non-monetary Transactions in Post-Soviet Societies*, Cambridge: Cambridge University Press, 2000.

Shalamov, Varlaam, *Kolyma Tales*, London: Penguin, 1995.

Slezkine, Yuri, *Arctic Mirrors: Russia and the Small Peoples of the North*, Ithaca, NY: Cornell University Press, 1994.

Tretyakov, Sergei, 'Москва–Пекин (Путьфильма)' (Moscow–Beijing (a filmic journey))', *ЛЕФ: Журнал Левого фронта искусств* (LEF: journal of the left front of the arts), 3, 7 (1925), pp. 33–58.

Wadley, Stephen, 'Altaic Influences on Beijing Dialect: The Manchu Case', *Journal of the American Oriental Society*, 116, 1 (January–March 1996), pp. 99–104.

Ward, Christopher, *Brezhnev's Folly: The Building of BAM and Late Soviet Socialism*, Pittsburgh: University of Pittsburgh Press, 2009.

Wells, Herbert G., *Russia in the Shadows*, New York: George H. Doran, 1921.

BIBLIOGRAPHY

Widmer, Eric, *The Russian Ecclesiastical Mission in Peking during the Eighteenth Century*, Cambridge, MA: Harvard University Press, 1976.

Wolff, David, *To the Harbin Station: The Liberal Alternative in Russian Manchuria 1898–1914*, Stanford: Stanford University Press, 1999.

Yang Jisheng (杨继绳), *Tombstone: The Great Chinese Famine, 1958–1962*, London: Allen Lane, 2012.

Yin Fu (殷夫), 殷夫选集 (Selected works of Yin Fu), Beijing: Renmin chubanshe, 1958.

Zakharova, Liudmila, 'Economic Cooperation between Russia and North Korea: New Goals and New Approaches', *Journal of Eurasian Studies*, 7, 2 (2016).

Zou Deyi (邹德侬) (ed.), 中国现代建筑二十讲 (Twenty essays on modern Chinese architecture), Beijing: The Commercial Press, 2015.

Zou Yu (邹玉) (ed.), 蒙兀神地 额尔古纳 (E'erguna: holy place of the Mongols), Hohhot: Neimenggu renmin chubanshe, 2010.

INDEX

INDEX

INDEX

INDEX

INDEX

INDEX